Lecture Notes in Artificial Intelligence 728

Subseries of Lecture Notes in Computer Science
Edited by J. Siekmann

Lecture Notes in Computer Science
Edited by G. Goos and J. Hartmanis

Advances in Artificial Intelligence

Third Congress of the Italian Association
for Artificial Intelligence, AI*IA '93
Torino, Italy, October 26-28, 1993
Proceedings

Springer-Verlag
Berlin Heidelberg New York
London Paris Tokyo
Hong Kong Barcelona
Budapest

Series Editor

Jörg Siekmann
University of Saarland
German Research Center for Artificial Intelligence (DFKI)
Stuhlsatzenhausweg 3,
D-66123 Saarbrücken, Germany

Volume Editor

Pietro Torasso
Dipartimento di Informatica, Università di Torino
Corso Svizzera 185, I-10149 Torino, Italia

CR Subject Classification (1991): I.2

ISBN 3-540-57292-9 Springer-Verlag Berlin Heidelberg New York
ISBN 0-387-57292-9 Springer-Verlag New York Berlin Heidelberg

Typesetting: Camera ready by author
Printing and binding: Druckhaus Beltz, Hemsbach/Bergstr.
45/3140-543210 - Printed on acid-free paper

Preface

This book contains 22 long papers and 13 short ones which have been selected for the Scientific Track of the Third Congress of the Italian Association for Artificial Intelligence. Long papers are intended to report completed work, whereas short papers are mainly devoted to ongoing research. The Program Committee has strictly enforced the rule that only original and unpublished work can be considered for inclusion in the Scientific Track.

The papers report on significant work carried out in the different subfields of Artificial Intelligence, not only in Italy, but also in other European countries as well as outside Europe. Although the congress is organized by the Italian Association for Artificial Intelligence, it has a truly international character because of the invited speakers (Prof. Tom Mitchell, CMU, USA, Prof. Jean-Paul Barthes, Université de Technologie de Compiegne, France, Dr. Bernhard Nebel, DFKI, Germany), the number of papers presented by foreign authors, and the large number of submissions (roughly 40% of the total) coming from abroad.

The Program Committee had a hard job in evaluating the manuscripts submitted for publications since for most papers three independent reviews have been obtained (in some cases four).

Therefore, we believe that the book is a relevant source of information for understanding which are the currently active areas of research and the new promising directions in the AI field. Even if a single book cannot provide a complete picture of what is going on in AI (for example the areas of Perception and Vision, Qualitative Reasoning and Distributed Artificial Intelligence are somewhat underrepresented with respect the amount of activity carried on in Italy), some directions can be singled out.

Areas such as Automated Reasoning, Knowledge Representation and Natural Language (which have a well-established tradition in Italy) continue to attract significant amount of interest.

Machine Learning has recently attracted a lot of attention (not only among Italian scientists): the area has matured rapidly and a variety of approaches are currently being investigated, ranging from logical approaches (such as in Inductive Logic Programming) to numeric ones (as in genetic algorithms). This variety of approaches is well documented in the papers collected in the book.

Connectionism (or, more generally, subsymbolic approaches) has recently attracted significant interest within the AI community. In the book the application of subsymbolic approaches to perception and vision as well as to quite different problems is documented. Moreover, a increasing attention is being paid to the mechanisms for integrating symbolic and subsymbolic methods.

Inspecting the contents of the book, a growing interest for an explicit representation of time is apparent. The capability of developing an explicit representation of time and the need of performing temporal reasoning in an efficient way is relevant not only in the area of knowledge representation, but also in planning, robotics and reasoning about physical systems.

In achieving the goal of organizing a congress of high scientific level, the contribution and the efforts of many persons have to be acknowledged: beside authors, the Program Committee members and the referees (whose names are listed in the following pages) deserve my gratitude.

The financial support by Consiglio Nazionale delle Ricerche (Comitato Scienze d'Ingegneria e Architettura e Comitato Scienze e Tecnologia dell'Informazione) for partially covering the publication cost of the book is acknowledged.

Torino, July 1993   Piero Torasso
                                     AI*IA '93 Program Chairman

Referees

Albesano
Attardi B.
Badaloni S.
Biagioli C.
Bonatti P.
Brajnik G.
Callari F.
Caselli S.
Chittaro L.
Console L.
Cristiani M.
D'Angelo A.
Donini F.
Ferrari G.
Gaspari M.
Giaretta P.
Lavelli A.
Magnini B.
Mana F.
Miola A.
Omodeo E.
Pirri F.
Pogliano P.
Roberto V.
Sapino M.L.
Semeraro G.
Straccia U.
Temperini M.
Tornielli G.
Vaggi A.
Zanichelli F.

Amati G.
Atzeni P.
Bagnara R.
Bisiani R.
Botta M.
Broggi A.
Caprile B.
Cesta A.
Cialdea Mayer M.
Conte R.
D'Aloisi D.
De Giacomo G.
Fanelli A.M.
Fum D.
Gemello R.
Giordano L.
Lesmo L.
Maier E.
Martini S.
Moretti L.
Pedreschi D.
Pirrone R.
Prodanof I.
Romano G.
Schaerf M.
Serafini L.
Strapparava C.
Terenziani P.
Trautteur G.
Varzi A.

Ardizzone E.
Avesani P.
Bergadano F.
Boldrin L.
Braggiotti A.
Cadoli M.
Carpineto C.
Chella A.
Cocco N.
Crespi B.
D'Andrea V.
Delmonte R.
Federico M.
Furlanello C.
Gerevini A.
Giunchiglia E.
Lombardo V.
Malerba D.
Miceli M.
Nardi D.
Pernici B.
Poggi A.
Ricci F.
Saitta L.
Sebastiani R.
Starita A.
Tecchioli G.
Toppano E.
Traverso P.
Zaccaria R.

Contents

Knowledge Representation

Languages, Architectures and Tools for AI

Machine Learning

Natural Language

Planning and Robotics

Reasoning about Phisical Systems and Artifacts

Proving Formulas through Reduction to Decidable Classes

Mauro Di Manzo
Enrico Giunchiglia
Alessandro Armando
Paolo Pecchiari

Mechanized Reasoning Group
DIST - University of Genoa
Via Opera Pia 11A, 16145 Genoa, Italy
{mauro,enrico,armando,peck}@dist.unige.it

Keywords: interactive theorem proving, decision procedures

Abstract. As it is well known, it is important to enrich the basic deductive machinery of an interactive theorem prover with complex decision procedures. In the GETFOL system we have implemented a hierarchical and modular structure of procedures which can be either invoked individually or jointly with the others. At the top of the hierarchy there is a decision procedure for a set of formulas which can be *reduced* to the class of prenex universal-existential formulas via finitely many application of rewriting rules. In this paper we give a formal account of such a reduction process, arguing that (*i*) it greatly enlarges the set of formulas which can proven through a decision process and (*ii*) in some cases makes the resulting formula easier to prove. We also provide an extensional characterization of a class of formulas which can be reduced and thus decided. The implementation of such reducing procedure in GETFOL is also sketched.

1 Introduction

Much of the work in interactive theorem proving deals with the definition of powerful and effective proof strategies. However, due to the simplicity of the basic inference steps, the design and synthesis of complex proof strategies may turn out to be a boring, hard and even unnatural activity. For example, in GETFOL [1], FOL [2] and LCF [3] it is neither easy nor natural to write a proof strategy for quantifier-free formulas basing on the rules provided by such systems (analogous to the rules for system of classical Natural Deduction as described in [4]).

A way to tackle this problem is to enrich the basic deductive machinery of the interactive theorem prover with complex decision procedures [5, 6, 7]. For example, in the GETFOL system we have implemented a hierarchical and modular structure of procedures which can be either invoked individually or jointly with the others [8, 9, 10]. At the top of the hierarchy there is a decision procedure for a set of formulas which can be *reduced* to the class of prenex universal-existential formulas (UE-formulas)[1] via finitely many application of truthful preserving rewriting rules.

Two are the main advantages of incorporating such a reduction process in an interactive theorem prover. First, supposing a decider for UE-class is already available (as in the GETFOL system), it significantly enlarges the class of formulas which can be proven through a decision process (see theorem 9). Second, in some cases the reduction process makes the resulting formula easier to prove (see example 1). This paper provides both a presentation of the theoretical properties of such a reduction process and a brief discussion of its implementation. While the former should give evidence of effectiveness of the procedures the latter should act as a more precise guideline for the understanding of how it is mechanized.

The procedures described in this paper have been implemented and are currently available inside the GETFOL system [1]. We want to recall that GETFOL provides the user with a set of inference rules which are very close to those of Natural Deduction [4]. In proving a theorem, it is possible to use only decision procedures (*e.g.* if the goal exactly matches the applicability conditions of the decision procedure), or to mix the application of inferences rules and decision procedures (*e.g.* for proving some sub-goals), or to use only inference rules (*e.g.* if decision procedures are not applicable or effective enough).

2 Enlarging the class of solved formulae

Consider the set S of rewriting rules (from now on S-rules) expressing the well-known properties of associativity, commutativity and distributivity of the propositional connectives (S_2-rules) and the distributivity of quantifiers through propositional connectives (S_1-rules). Many formulae not in UE-form can be *reduced* to UE-formulae by finitely many applications of S-rules. The **reduce** procedure implements the notion of reducibility w.r.t. S. However, we want to point out that the notion of reducibility, upon which **reduce** has been built, is not bound to any particular set of rewriting rules. Hence the same methodology we used for building reduce can be used to build new procedures relying on other sets of rewriting rules.

The use of **reduce** greatly enlarges the class of formulae solved by the overall system. Here some examples of S-reducible (to UE-form) formulae follow (If C is a set of rewriting rules then $\mapsto_C$ is the reducibility relation induced by C and $\overset{*}{\mapsto}_C$ is the reflexive and transitive closure of $\mapsto_C$.)

---

[1] UE-formulae are formulae not containing function symbols and such that any universal quantifier does not contain free occurrences of existentially bounded variables in its scope. The UE-class is the set of UE-formulae. Obviously, the class of prenex Universal-Existential formulae not containing function symbol is contained in the UE-class.

Example 1.

(1) $\exists x.\forall y.(P(x,a)\vee R(y))$ $\qquad\qquad \mapsto_{S_1} \exists x.(P(x,a)\vee\forall y.R(y))$

(2) $\exists x.\forall y.\exists z.(P(x,z)\vee P(y,z))$ $\qquad \mapsto_{S_1} \exists x.\forall y.(\exists z_1.P(x,z_1)\vee\exists z_2.P(y,z_2))$
$\qquad\qquad\qquad\qquad\qquad\qquad\quad \mapsto_{S_1} \exists x.(\exists z_1.P(x,z_1)\vee\forall y.\exists z_2.P(y,z_2))$

(3) $\exists x.\forall y.((P(y,a)\vee Q(x))\vee Q(y))$ $\qquad \mapsto_{S_2} \exists x.\forall y.((P(y,a)\vee Q(y))\vee Q(x))$
$\qquad\qquad\qquad\qquad\qquad\qquad\qquad \mapsto_{S_1} \exists x.(\forall y.(P(y,a)\vee Q(y))\vee Q(x))$

(4) $\exists x.\forall y.\exists z.((P(y,z)\wedge Q(x))\wedge Q(z))$ $\mapsto_{S_2} \exists x.\forall y.\exists z.((P(y,z)\wedge Q(z))\wedge Q(x))$
$\qquad\qquad\qquad\qquad\qquad\qquad\qquad\quad \mapsto_{S_1} \exists x.\forall y.(\exists z.(P(y,z)\wedge Q(z))\wedge Q(x))$
$\qquad\qquad\qquad\qquad\qquad\qquad\qquad\quad \mapsto_{S_1} \exists x.(\forall y.\exists z.(P(y,z)\wedge Q(z))\wedge Q(x))$

As the formula (1) in example 1 shows, the idea is to try to reduce the scope of universal quantifiers till they no longer contain free occurrences of existentially bounded variables. Formula (2) shows that in some case it is necessary also to consider the rules for pushing existential quantifiers. Formulas (3) and (4) evidence that in some cases to reduce the scope of an universal quantifier we have (first) to apply rules for a propositional manipulation of the matrix of a quantifier.

2.1 Basic definitions and theorems

This section is devoted to formally state and prove standard properties (*i.e.* noetherianity and confluence [11]) of the rewriting rules which we have informally spoken about. In order to provide a precise account of the rewriting rules used by **reduce** and to discuss their formal properties we introduce some notational conventions and definitions. $\alpha(x)$ denotes a formula in which there is at least one free occurrence of the variable x. $\alpha[x]$ denotes a formula in which there is no free occurrences of x. Q and Q' stand either for $\forall$ or for $\exists$. If $Q=\forall$, then $\circ=\wedge$ and $+=\vee$. If $Q=\exists$, then $\circ=\vee$ and $+=\wedge$.

Definition 1 minimality. A formula β is *minimal w.r.t.* $\langle Q,x\rangle$ if and only if satisfies one of the following clauses:

$\quad(i)\quad$ is a literal in which x occurs free,
$\quad(ii)\quad \beta=Q'y.\gamma(x)$, with γ minimal w.r.t. $\langle Q',y\rangle$,
$\quad(iii)\quad \beta=(\gamma(x)+\delta(x))$ with γ, δ minimal w.r.t. $\langle Q,x\rangle$.

A formula α is *minimal* if and only if each subformula $Qx.\beta$ of α is such that β is minimal w.r.t. $\langle Q,x\rangle$.

Definition 2 normalization. A formula β is *normalized w.r.t.* $\langle Q,x\rangle$ if and only if satisfies one of the following clauses:

$\quad(i)\quad$ is minimal w.r.t. $\langle Q,x\rangle$,

(ii) $\beta = \beta[x]$ (β does not contain free occurrences of x),

(iii) $\beta = (\gamma \circ \delta)$ with γ, δ normalized w.r.t. $\langle Q, x \rangle$,

(iv) $\beta = (\gamma[x] + \delta)$ with δ normalized w.r.t. $\langle Q, x \rangle$ (note that by clause
(i) γ is normalized w.r.t. $\langle Q, x \rangle$).

A formula α is *normalized* if and only if each subformula $Qx.\beta$ of α is such that
β is normalized w.r.t. $\langle Q, x \rangle$.

We also say that $\beta = (\gamma(x) + \delta)$ is a *top normalizable formula w.r.t.* $\langle Q, x \rangle$
if and only if γ and δ are normalized w.r.t. $\langle Q, x \rangle$ and β is not normalized
w.r.t. $\langle Q, x \rangle$.

Given a formula α, β is a *top normalizable formula*[2] if and only if there exists
$\langle Q, x \rangle$ such that:

(i) β is a top normalizable formula w.r.t. $\langle Q, x \rangle$,

(ii) descending α construction tree, $\langle Q, x \rangle$ are the last quantifier symbol
and bound variable that we meet before β.

The rewriting rules used by reduce are listed in table 1. In the following we
will refer to the sets of rules $\{(1) - (8)\}$, $\{(1) - (3)\}$ and $\{(4) - (8)\}$ by S, S_1
and S_2 respectively. Notice that no rule in S is applicable to a minimal formula
and that no rule in S_2 is applicable to a normalized formula. The following two
theorems establish the *noetherianity* and *confluence* of S, S_1 and S_2.

(1)	$Qx.\alpha[x] \longmapsto \alpha$
(2)	$Qx.(\alpha \circ \beta)(x) \longmapsto (Qx.\alpha \circ Qx.\beta)$
(3)	$Qx.(\alpha[x] + \beta(x)) \longmapsto (\alpha[x] + Qx.\beta(x))$
(4)	$(\alpha(x) + \beta[x]) \longmapsto (\beta[x] + \alpha(x))$
(5)	$((\alpha[x] + \beta(x)) + \gamma(x)) \longmapsto (\alpha[x] + (\beta(x) + \gamma(x)))$
(6)	$((\alpha \circ \beta)(x) + \gamma(x)) \longmapsto ((\alpha + \gamma(x)) \circ (\beta + \gamma(x)))$
(7)	$(\alpha(x) + (\beta[x] + \gamma(x))) \longmapsto (\beta[x] + (\alpha(x) + \gamma(x)))$
(8)	$(\alpha(x) + (\beta \circ \gamma)(x)) \longmapsto ((\alpha(x) + \beta) \circ (\alpha(x) + \gamma))$

Restrictions:

- In rules $\{(4) - (8)\}$ the left hand side must be a top normalizable formula.
- In rules $\{(7), (8)\}$ α must be minimal w.r.t. $\langle Q, x \rangle$.

Table 1. The rewriting rules

---

[2] More precisely, we should say *"top normalizable formula occurrence in α"*.

Theorem 3. S, S_1, S_2 *are* noetherian.

Proof. For any formula α, define $\mathcal{F}(\alpha)$ to be the cardinality of the set of proper subformulae in the scope of a quantifier in α. As result of an application of one of the rules in $\{(1) - (3)\}$, $\alpha \mapsto \alpha'$ and $\mathcal{F}(\alpha') < \mathcal{F}(\alpha)$. Hence S_1 is noetherian since $\{(1) - (3)\}$ can be applied only finitely many times to a formula. For any formula α, define $\mathcal{C}(\alpha)$ to be the cardinality of the set of proper subformulae of a top normalizable formula in α. Also note that to any top normalizable formula, one of rule in $\{(4) - (8)\}$ must be applicable. If α' is the formula obtained by applying such a rule then $\mathcal{C}(\alpha') < \mathcal{C}(\alpha)$. Hence also S_2 is noetherian since $\{(4) - (8)\}$ can be applied only finitely many times. S is noetherian since, if we define $\mathcal{G}(\alpha) = (\mathcal{F}(\alpha) + 2 \times \mathcal{C}(\alpha))$ then the application of the rules in S makes $\mathcal{G}$ to decrease.

In defining $\mathcal{G}(\alpha)$, we give a different weight to $\mathcal{C}(\alpha)$ because if we apply rules (6) or (8), $\mathcal{F}(\alpha)$ can increase. With such weights, even for such rules, $\mathcal{G}(\alpha)$ is strictly decreasing.

Theorem 4. S, S_1, S_2 *are* confluent.

Proof. It is sufficient to notice that there are no critical pairs in S, *i.e.* no two (variables disjoint) rewriting rules $(l_1 \mapsto r_1)$, $(l_2 \mapsto r_2)$ such that any (non variable) sub-term of l_1 is unifiable with l_2. Hence, also S_1, S_2 are trivially confluent.

2.2 Formal results about reducibility

We are now ready to discuss the properties of S with respect to the problem of reducing formulae in UE-form. As already said, the UE-reducibility of fairly wide classes of formulae is proved (theorem 9 and corollary 10). Such a result is a consequence of theorem 8 which states that indefinite applications of the rules in S have the effect to reduce the input formula to an equivalent minimal one. An effective way to accomplish such a reduction process is to recursively descend the formula tree and then apply the rewriting rules in a bottom up fashion (see procedure S-normalize in figure 1) exploiting the following facts:

- literals, conjunctions and disjunctions of minimal formulae are minimal,
- a minimal formula occurring in the scope of "Qx" can be rewritten into a normalized formula w.r.t. $\langle Q, x \rangle$ by applying the rules in S_2 (procedure S2-normalize - lemma 7),
- A normalized formula (wrt $\langle Q, x \rangle$) can be turned into minimal form by application of the rules in S_1 (procedure S1-normalize - lemma 5).

The S-normalize procedure, given the S1-normalize and S2-normalize procedures, (whose implementation is omitted for lack of space) has the effect to reduce the input formula **w** in minimal form. Before formally enunciating and proving theorems, the following example justifies the initial claim that in some cases the reduction process makes the formula easier to prove.

```
(DEFLAM S-normalize (w)
 (IF (LITERAL w) w
  (IF (CONJ w)
   (mkand (S-normalize (wff-get-lf w)) (S-normalize (wff-get-rt w)))
   (IF (DISJ w)
    (mkor (S-normalize (wff-get-lf w)) (S-normalize (wff-get-rt w)))
    (IF (QUANTWFF w)
     (S1-normalize
      (S2-normalize
       (mkquantwff (quantof w) (bvarof w) (S-normalize (matrix w)))))
     (ERRMESS "wff not in negative normal form")))))))
```

Fig. 1. The S-normalize routine.

Example 2. Problem 29 from [12].[3] The formula to be proven is:

$$((\exists x.F(x) \wedge \exists x.G(x)) \rightarrow ((\forall x.(F(x) \rightarrow H(x)) \wedge \forall x.(G(x) \rightarrow J(x))) \leftrightarrow$$
$$(\forall x.\forall y.((F(x) \wedge G(y)) \rightarrow (H(x) \wedge J(y))))))$$

Applying **reduce** we get:

$$((\exists x.F(x) \wedge \exists x.G(x)) \rightarrow ((\forall x.(F(x) \rightarrow H(x)) \wedge \forall x.(G(x) \rightarrow J(x))) \leftrightarrow$$
$$((\exists x.G(x) \rightarrow \forall x.(F(x) \rightarrow H(x))) \wedge$$
$$(\exists x.F(x) \rightarrow \forall x.(G(x) \rightarrow J(x))))))$$

which can be proven using only propositional argumentations. For example, mapping each quantified formula into a distinct propositional letter, we obtain

$$((A \wedge B) \rightarrow ((C \wedge D)) \leftrightarrow ((B \rightarrow C)) \wedge (A \rightarrow D))$$

which is a tautology.

The following lemmas are needed to make the proof of theorem 8 easier.

Lemma 5. *If α is normalized w.r.t. $\langle Q, x \rangle$ then $Qx.\alpha \overset{*}{\mapsto}_{S_1} \beta$ with β minimal.*

Such a lemma easily follows from the definitions of formula normalized wrt $\langle Q, x \rangle$ and of minimality.

Lemma 6. *If α is a top normalizable formula w.r.t. $\langle Q, x \rangle$ then $Qx.\alpha \overset{*}{\mapsto}_{S_2} Qx.\alpha'$ with α' normalized w.r.t. $\langle Q, x \rangle$.*

---

[3] To this example it is attributed a difficulty of seven points out of ten. In order to make the example easier to follow, we do not translate the formula in negative normal form and suppose that reduce exploits also the rules for the implication. In any case, such rules can be easily derived from those listed in table 1.

Proof. By induction on the number of subformulae in α ($\mathcal{B}(\alpha)$). (To simplify the presentation we consider the case $Q = \forall$). By definition of top normalizable formula, $\alpha = (\beta(x) \vee \gamma)$, with β, γ normalized w.r.t. $\langle \forall, x \rangle$.

($\mathcal{B}(\alpha) = 3$). $\alpha = (P(x) \vee R[x])$ with $P(x)$ and $R[x]$ (distinguished) literals. By rule (4) $\forall x.(P(x) \vee R[x]) \mapsto \forall x.(R[x] \vee P(x))$.

($\mathcal{B}(\alpha) = m + 1$). By cases:

- β is minimal w.r.t. $\langle \forall, x \rangle$. γ cannot be minimal w.r.t. $\langle \forall, x \rangle$ (otherwise also α is minimal and hence normalized).

  (a) If $\gamma = \gamma[x]$, by applying rule (4) $\forall x.(\beta(x) \vee \gamma[x]) \mapsto \forall x.(\gamma[x] \vee \beta(x))$.

  (b) If $\gamma = (\eta \wedge \mu)(x)$, by applying rule (8) $\forall x.(\beta(x) \vee (\eta \wedge \mu)(x)) \mapsto \forall x.((\beta(x) \vee \eta) \wedge (\beta(x) \vee \mu))$. Since $max\{\mathcal{B}(\beta(x) \vee \eta), \mathcal{B}(\beta(x) \vee \mu)\} < \mathcal{B}(\beta(x) \vee (\eta \wedge \mu))$ then, by inductive hypothesis, both $(\beta(x) \vee \eta)$ and $(\beta(x) \vee \mu)$ can be normalized. Then $((\beta(x) \vee \eta) \wedge (\beta(x) \vee \mu))$ and hence α are normalizable.

  (c) If $\gamma = (\eta[x] \vee \mu(x))$, by applying rule (7) $\forall x.(\beta(x) \vee (\eta[x] \vee \mu(x))) \mapsto \forall x.(\eta[x] \vee (\beta(x) \vee \mu(x)))$. Since $\mathcal{B}(\beta(x) \vee \mu(x)) < \mathcal{B}(\beta(x) \vee (\eta[x] \vee \mu(x)))$ then, by inductive hypothesis, $(\beta(x) \vee \mu(x))$ is normalizable. Then $(\eta[x] \vee (\beta(x) \vee \mu(x)))$ and hence α are normalizable.

  Notice that this includes also the case in which $\beta = Q'y.\gamma$ since $\beta = Q'y.\gamma$ normalized w.r.t. $\langle Q, x \rangle$ means that it is also minimal w.r.t. $\langle Q, x \rangle$.

- Analogously, if $\beta = (\eta \wedge \mu)(x)$ we can apply rule (6). If $\beta = (\eta[x] \vee \mu(x))$ we can apply rule (5). In both cases, the top normalizable formulae in the resulting formula are normalizable for the induction hypothesis.

Lemma 7. *For any minimal formula α and pair $\langle Q, x \rangle$ $Qx.\alpha \overset{*}{\mapsto}_{S_2} Qx.\alpha'$ with α' normalized w.r.t. $\langle Q, x \rangle$.*

Proof. By induction on the number of subformulae in α ($\mathcal{B}(\alpha)$).

($\mathcal{B}(\alpha) = 1$). α is a literal. Then α is normalized w.r.t. $\langle Q, x \rangle$ for any $\langle Q, x \rangle$.

($\mathcal{B}(\alpha) = m + 1$). We know, for the induction hypothesis, that for any minimal formula β such that $\mathcal{B}(\beta) \leq m$, β can be normalized w.r.t. any pair $\langle Q, x \rangle$. By cases:

- $\alpha = (\beta \circ \gamma)$ By inductive hypothesis $Qx.\beta \overset{*}{\mapsto}_{S_2} Qx.\beta'$ and $Qx.\gamma \overset{*}{\mapsto}_{S_2} Qx.\gamma'$ where β', γ' are normalized w.r.t. $\langle Q, x \rangle$. Hence $Qx.(\beta \circ \gamma) \overset{*}{\mapsto}_{S_2} Qx.(\beta' \circ \gamma')$ with $\beta' \circ \gamma'$ normalized w.r.t. $\langle Q, x \rangle$.

- $\alpha = (\beta + \gamma)$. By inductive hypothesis $Qx.\beta \overset{*}{\mapsto}_{S_2} Qx.\beta'$ and $Qx.\gamma \overset{*}{\mapsto}_{S_2} Qx.\gamma'$ where β', γ' are normalized w.r.t. $\langle Q, x \rangle$. Hence $\alpha' = (\beta' + \gamma')$ is either normalized (*e.g.* $\beta' = \beta'[x]$) or a top normalizable formula wrt $\langle Q, x \rangle$. In this last case, $Qx.(\beta' + \gamma')$ can be normalized by lemma 6.

- $\alpha = Q'y.\beta$. Since α is minimal, then it is also normalized wrt any $\langle Q, x \rangle$.

Theorem 8 minimality of S normal form. *If $\alpha \overset{*}{\mapsto}_S \beta$ then β is minimal.*

Proof. By induction.

(α literal). $\alpha \overset{*}{\mapsto}_S \alpha$ and α is minimal.

($\alpha = (\beta \bullet \gamma)$). With $\bullet \in \{\wedge, \vee\}$. For the induction hypothesis, $\beta \overset{*}{\mapsto}_S \beta'$ and $\gamma \overset{*}{\mapsto}_S \gamma'$ with β' and γ' minimal. Hence $\alpha = (\beta \bullet \gamma) \overset{*}{\mapsto}_S (\beta' \bullet \gamma')$ with $(\beta' \bullet \gamma')$ minimal.

($\alpha = Qx.\beta$). For the induction hypothesis, $\beta \overset{*}{\mapsto}_S \beta'$ with β' minimal. By lemma 7 $\beta' \overset{*}{\mapsto}_{S_2} \beta''$ with β'' normalized w.r.t. $\langle Q, x \rangle$. By lemma 5 $Qx.\beta'' \overset{*}{\mapsto}_{S_1} \beta'''$ with β''' minimal. Hence $Qx.\beta \overset{*}{\mapsto}_S \beta'''$ with β''' minimal.

We say that a formula α is S-reducible to UE-form (for short S-reducible) if and only if $\alpha \overset{*}{\mapsto}_S \beta$ and β is a UE-formula. Obviously a UE-formula is S-reducible.

The following theorem, while providing a syntactic characterization of a subset of S-reducible formulae, should give evidence of the fact that the set of S-reducible formulae is fairly wide. Let $\forall \mathbf{x}.\phi$ ($\exists \mathbf{y}.\phi$) stands for $\forall x_1 \ldots x_r.\phi$ ($\exists y_1 \ldots y_s.\phi$) for any $r, s \geq 1$.

Theorem 9. *Let* $\alpha = \forall \mathbf{y}_n \exists \mathbf{x}_n \ldots \forall \mathbf{y}_i \exists \mathbf{x}_i \ldots \forall \mathbf{y}_1 \exists \mathbf{x}_1.\Phi$. *If* Φ *is a quantifier-free formula such that each literal contains no variables in* $\mathbf{y}_k$ *and in* $\mathbf{x}_l$ *with* $k < l$, *or in* $\mathbf{x}_k$ *and in* $\mathbf{x}_l$ *with* $k \neq l$, *then* α *is S-reducible to UE-form.*

Proof. By induction on n.

($n = 1$). $\alpha \overset{*}{\mapsto}_S \alpha'$. Since α is a UE-formula, also α' is.

($n = m + 1$). $\alpha = \forall \mathbf{y}_n \exists \mathbf{x}_n.\beta$ where $\beta = \forall \mathbf{y}_m \exists \mathbf{x}_m \ldots \forall \mathbf{y}_1 \exists \mathbf{x}_1.\Phi$. For the induction hypothesis $\beta \overset{*}{\mapsto}_S \beta'$ with β' in UE-form and (by theorem 8) minimal. From minimality it follows that there are no free occurrences of variables in $\mathbf{x}_n$ in the scope of any quantifier in β'. (In Φ and hence also in β' each literal containing $\mathbf{x}_n$ does not contain other bound variables but those (eventually) in $\mathbf{y}_n$). Since β' is in UE-form also $\forall \mathbf{y}_n \exists \mathbf{x}_n.\beta'$ is in UE-form. Hence, by finitely many applications of the rules in S, α can be rewritten into $\forall \mathbf{y}_n \exists \mathbf{x}_n.\beta'$. Finally $\forall \mathbf{y}_n \exists \mathbf{x}_n.\beta' \overset{*}{\mapsto}_S \alpha'$ with α' in UE-form.

As an immediate consequence we have that the monadic class together with two other classes are S-reducible to UE-form and hence decidable.

Corollary 10. *The classes of*

- *monadic formulae,*
- *formulae in which predicates contains at most one bound variable,*
- *formulae in which each predicates either contains no existentially bound variables or, if it contains one, it is the only bound variable it contains,*

are S-reducible to UE-form.

However there are formulae which are S-reducible and are not in the class specified in theorem 9. The formula $\exists x.\forall y.\exists z.(P(x, z) \vee P(y, z))$ (formula number (2) in example 1) is a proof of this fact. On the other hand, a slight variation of a S-reducible formula may not be S-reducible. For example, the formula

$\exists x.\forall y.\exists z.(P(x,z)\wedge P(y,z))$ turns out not to be $\mathcal{S}$-reducible. So far, we have failed to find a simple syntactic characterization of the class of $\mathcal{S}$-reducible formulae.

3 Conclusions and future work

We have proposed a set of rewriting rules which are noetherian, confluent and greatly enlarge the set of formulas which can be proved by a decision procedure for UE-formulas. Example 1 shows also that in some cases the formula result of the reduction process is easier to prove.

We want to emphasize that in this paper we have studied the reducibility to the UE-class given the set $\mathcal{S}$ of rewriting rules. However, the same methodology applies w.r.t. any other (decidable) class and set of rewriting rules. In the future, we plan to extend the above results to other decidable classes maintaining the same set of rewriting rules.

4 Acknowledgements

A first version of the reduction procedure described in this paper was implemented in FOL [2]. Fausto Giunchiglia, Andrea Parodi, Fulvio Rappa and Richard Weyhrauch have provided useful feedback and/or suggestions. This work has been supported by the Italian National Research Council (CNR), Progetto Finalizzato Sistemi Informatici e Calcolo Parallelo (Special Project on Information Systems and Parallel Computing).

References

1. F. Giunchiglia. The GETFOL Manual - GETFOL version 1. Technical Report 9204-01, DIST - University of Genova, Genoa, Italy, 1992. Forthcoming IRST-Technical Report.
2. R.W. Weyhrauch. Prolegomena to a Theory of Mechanized Formal Reasoning. *Artif. Intell.*, 13(1):133–176, 1980.
3. M.J. Gordon, A.J. Milner, and C.P. Wadsworth. *Edinburgh LCF - A mechanized logic of computation*, volume 78 of *Lecture Notes in Computer Science*. Springer Verlag, 1979.
4. D. Prawitz. *Natural Deduction - A proof theoretical study*. Almquist and Wiksell, Stockholm, 1965.
5. A. Armando and E. Giunchiglia. Embedding Complex Decision Procedures inside an Interactive Theorem Prover. Technical Report 9205-01, DIST, University of Genova, Genova, Italy, 1992.
6. R.S. Boyer and J.S. More. Integrating decision procedures into heuristic theorem provers: A case study of linear arithmetic. *Machine Intelligence*, 11:83–124, 1988.
7. A. Bundy, A. Smaill, and J. Hesketh. Turning eureka steps into calculations in automatic program synthesis. In S.L.H. Clarke, editor, *Proceedings of UK IT 90*, pages 221–6, 1990. Also available from Edinburgh University as DAI Research Paper no. 448.
8. F. Giunchiglia and E. Giunchiglia. Building complex derived inference rules: a decider for the class of prenex universal-existential formulas. In *Proc. 7th European Conference on Artificial Intelligence*, pages 607–609, 1988. Extended version available as DAI Research Paper 359, Dept. of Artificial Intelligence, Edinburgh.
9. F. Giunchiglia, A. Armando, A. Cimatti, E. Giunchiglia P. Pecchiari, L. Serafini, A. Simpson, and P. Traverso. GETFOL Programmer Manual - GETFOL version 1. Technical Report 9107-03, DIST - University of Genova, Genova, Italy, 1991.
10. A. Armando, E. Giunchiglia, and P. Traverso. From Propositional Deciders to First Order Deciders: a Structured Approach to the Decision Problem. In *Proceedings 5th Irish Conference on Artificial Intelligence and Cognitive Science*, Limerick, Ireland, 1992. Springer Verlag. Also IRST-Technical Report 9208-07, IRST, Trento, Italy.
11. G. Huet and D.C. Oppen. Equations and rewrite rules: a survey. In R. Book, editor, *Formal languages: perspectives and open problems*. Academic Press, 1980. Presented at the conference on formal language theory, Santa Barbara, 1979. Available from SRI International as technical report CSL-111.
12. F.J. Pelletier. Seventy-Five Problems for Testing Automatic Theorem Provers. *Journal of Automated Reasoning*, 2:191–216, 1986. See also Errata Corrige in Journal of Automated Reasoning, 4:235–236, 1988.

Building and Executing Proof Strategies in a Formal Metatheory*

Alessandro Armando[1]
Alessandro Cimatti[2]
Luca Viganò[1]

[1] DIST, University of Genoa, Via all'Opera Pia 11A, Genova, Italy
[2] IRST, Povo, 38050 Trento, Italy

Abstract. This paper describes how "safe" proof strategies are represented and executed in the interactive theorem prover GETFOL. A formal metatheory (MT) describes and allows to reason about object level inference. A class of MT terms, called *logic tactics*, is used to represent proof strategies. The semantic attachment facility and the evaluation mechanism of the GETFOL system have been used to provide the procedural interpretation of logic tactics. The execution of logic tactics is then proved to be "safe" under the termination condition. The implementation within the GETFOL system is described and the synthesis of a logic tactic implementing a normalizer in negative normal form is presented as a case study.

1 Introduction

As pointed out in [GMMW77], *interactive theorem proving* [GMW79, CAB+86, Pau89] has been growing up in the continuum existing between *proof checking* [deB70, Wey80] on one side and *automated theorem proving* [Rob65, And81, Bib81] on the other. Interactive theorem provers were built with the goal in mind to overtake the deficiencies of the extreme solutions: proof checkers force the user to lengthy and laborious interactions, while automated theorem provers (relying on uniform and hence inefficient proof strategies) turn out to be ineffective on problems of practical significance.

Like proof checkers, interactive theorem provers provide the user with a set of basic inference rules, but - most important - they provide also the means to define complex proof strategies, which are guaranteed to be safe (i.e. they never build faulty proofs). The correctness of the proof strategies is usually ensured by the adoption of a type checking discipline. The major drawback of the approach is that each proof procedure (even the most sophisticated ones) must ultimately

---

* This work has been partly done as part of the MAIA project developed at IRST. It has been partly supported by the Italian National Research Council (CNR), Progetto Finalizzato Sistemi Informatici e Calcolo Parallelo (Special Project on Information Systems and Parallel Computing). The authors thank the members of the Mechanized Reasoning Group for useful feedback and discussions. Fausto Giunchiglia and Paolo Traverso are specially thanked for their previous work on tactics.

invoke the basic inference rules. In many cases this turns out to be both unnatural and ineffective. Indeed, most of the decision procedures for decidable theories (e.g. the truth table method for propositional calculus) can be hardly rephrased as proof strategies based on the inference rules of the corresponding calculus. Moreover, the performance of the translated proof strategies is much less effective than a direct implementation of the original procedure.

The work presented in this paper is part of a larger project, aiming to enrich the interactive theorem prover **GETFOL**[3] [Giu92] with metatheoretic theorem proving capabilities [GT91a, GT92, GTCP92, GC92a, GA93, GT93] to overcome the problems discussed above. More precisely, (some of) the goals of this project are the formal characterization and the implementation of a framework where tactics of different forms can be defined, reasoned about (e.g. proved correct) in a formal metatheory, used to prove theorems interactively and possibly compiled into system code to improve performances. The ability to perform arbitrary theorem proving rather than simply type checking opens up the possibility to reason about different kinds of tactics, such as normalization and decision procedures.

In this paper we focus on the problem of introducing and executing tactics in **GETFOL**. In section 2 we describe a formal metatheory where tactics can be represented and reasoned about, and we give sufficient criteria identifying a class of "safe" tactics. In section 3 we focus on implementational issues: we show how new tactics can be introduced in the **GETFOL** library of tactics (with the command **NEWTAC**), and how a tactic in the library can be executed to perform the proof strategy it represents (with the command **TACEXEC**). In section 4, as a case study, we show the synthesis and the execution of a proof strategy for converting formulas in negative normal form. In section 5 we draw some conclusions.

2 Representing proof strategies in the Metatheory MT

In this section we present the formal theory MT, used to represent object level inference and proof strategies.[4] Although this work is largely independent of the particular logic chosen, we shall concentrate on a classical Natural Deduction style [Pra65] first order object theory OT, in which inference rules apply to pairs (Γ, A), written $\Gamma \longrightarrow A$ and called *sequents*. A is a formula (the *endformula of the sequent*) and Γ is a finite set of formulas (the *assumptions of the sequent*). For instance, the inference rules performing left $\wedge$-elimination ($\wedge El$) and $\wedge$-introduction ($\wedge I$) are:

$$\frac{\Gamma \longrightarrow w_1 \wedge w_2}{\Gamma \longrightarrow w_1} \wedge El \qquad \frac{\Gamma \longrightarrow w_1 \quad \Delta \longrightarrow w_2}{\Gamma, \Delta \longrightarrow w_1 \wedge w_2} \wedge I$$

The metatheory MT is a first order classical ND calculus [Pra65] with equality, completely separated from OT. MT is formally defined as a triple MT=$\langle \mathcal{ML},$

---

[3] GETFOL is a reimplementation/extension of the FOL system [Wey80]. GETFOL has, with minor variations, all the functionalities of FOL plus extensions, some of which described here, to allow metatheoretic theorem proving.

[4] The formal metatheory MT presented in this paper is, with minor variations, the MT originally defined in [GT91a, GT92, GT93].

$\mathcal{MA}x, \mathcal{MR}\rangle$ where $\mathcal{ML}$, $\mathcal{MA}x$ and $\mathcal{MR}$ are the language, the axioms and the inference rules of MT, respectively.[5]

Expressions in $\mathcal{ML}$ have to be able to refer to the objects of OT. For each object (constant c, parameter a, variable x, term t, sequent s) of OT, $\mathcal{ML}$ contains an individual constant ("c", "a", "x", "t", "s", respectively) called *quotation mark name* of the object of OT. In order to handle sequents, $\mathcal{ML}$ contains three function symbols (the binary constructor $smak$, and the unary selectors $s2w$ and $s2a$), characterized by the following axioms:

$$(\mathcal{A}_{smak}) : smak(\text{``}\Gamma\text{''}, \text{``}w\text{''}) = \text{``}\Gamma \longrightarrow w\text{''}$$
$$(\mathcal{A}_{s2w}) : s2w(\text{``}\Gamma \longrightarrow w\text{''}) = \text{``}w\text{''}$$
$$(\mathcal{A}_{s2a}) : s2a(\text{``}\Gamma \longrightarrow w\text{''}) = \text{``}\Gamma\text{''}$$

$\mathcal{ML}$ also contains predicates for recognizing expressions (e.g. $Conj$, Neg), which are characterized by axioms of the form:

$$(\mathcal{A}_\wedge) : Conj(\text{``}w_1 \wedge w_2\text{''})$$
$$(\mathcal{A}_\neg) : Neg(\text{``}\neg w\text{''})$$

Basically, MT is used to reason about provability in the object theory. Every inference rule of OT is represented in MT by a function symbol. For instance, the rules for $\wedge$-introduction and elimination are represented in MT by the binary function symbol $anditac$ and the unary function symbol $andeltac$, respectively. The results of inference rules are characterized by axioms of the form:

$$(\mathcal{A}_{Res\wedge\mathcal{E}l}) : andeltac(\text{``}\Gamma \longrightarrow w_1 \wedge w_2\text{''}) = \text{``}\Gamma \longrightarrow w_1\text{''}$$
$$(\mathcal{A}_{Res\wedge\mathcal{I}}) : anditac(\text{``}\Gamma \longrightarrow w_1\text{''}, \text{``}\Delta \longrightarrow w_2\text{''}) = \text{``}\Gamma, \Delta \longrightarrow w_1 \wedge w_2\text{''}$$

The unary predicate T expresses the provability (relative to sequents) in OT. The axioms characterizing provability are:

$$(\mathcal{A}_{ass}) : T(\text{``}w \longrightarrow w\text{''})$$
$$(\mathcal{A}_{Ax}) : T(\text{``}s\text{''}) \text{ for each axiom } s \text{ of OT}$$
$$(\mathcal{A}_{\wedge\mathcal{E}l}) : \forall x.(T(x) \wedge Conj(s2w(x)) \supset T(andeltac(x)))$$
$$(\mathcal{A}_{\wedge\mathcal{I}}) : \forall x_1 \forall x_2.(T(x_1) \wedge T(x_2) \supset T(anditac(x_1, x_2)))$$

Axiom $(\mathcal{A}_{\wedge\mathcal{E}l})$ states that if the argument sequent of $andeltac$ is a provable sequent (i.e. $T(x)$), and its endformula is a conjunction (i.e. $Conj(s2w(x))$), then the result of $\wedge$-elimination is a provable sequent (i.e. $T(andeltac(x))$).

The correctness and completeness of MT with respect to the provability in OT have been established in [GT92]. This fact ensures the admissibility of the following rules (*reflection principles*):

$$\frac{\vdash_{OT} s}{\vdash_{MT} T(\text{``}s\text{''})} R_{up} \qquad \frac{\vdash_{MT} T(\text{``}s\text{''})}{\vdash_{OT} s} R_{down}$$

---

[5] For lack of space, we shall consider only some relevant parts of MT; a complete definition can be found in [GT92].

which play a central role in the interplay between object level and meta level reasoning.

The theory presented above describes the provability relation of OT when the preconditions of inference rules are satisfied. However, while trying to prove a theorem, rarely a detailed proof schema is available in advance, and inference rules may be tried without knowing whether they are applicable or not. A proof strategy can behave differently according to the success or failure of its substeps. We thus want to represent in MT the notion of failure in application of inference rules. For this purpose MT contains the individual constant $fail$, which is stated to be different from all quotation mark names. The basic concept of being a failure is then expressed by the predicate $Fail$ defined by $(\mathcal{A}_{Fail})$. $(\mathcal{A}_{notTfail})$ states that failure is not provable. $(\mathcal{A}_{notTFail})$ states that T and $Fail$ are disjoint. Being a proof step (either successful or failing) is expressed by the predicate Tac, defined by the axiom $(\mathcal{A}_{Tac})$.

$$
\begin{array}{l}
(\mathcal{A}_{Fail}) : \forall x.(Fail(x) \leftrightarrow x = fail) \\
(\mathcal{A}_{notTfail}) : \neg T(fail) \\
(\mathcal{A}_{notTFail}) : \forall x.\neg(T(x) \wedge Fail(x)) \\
\quad (\mathcal{A}_{Tac}) : \forall x.(Tac(x) \leftrightarrow (T(x) \vee Fail(x)))
\end{array}
$$

Inference rules deal with failure in the appropriate way: they return a failure when their applicability conditions are not satisfied, and propagate failure, i.e. return $fail$, when failure is provided as argument.

$$
\begin{array}{l}
(\mathcal{A}_{Genfail \wedge \mathcal{E}l}) : \quad andeltac(``s") = fail, \qquad \text{if } ``s" \text{ is not } ``\Gamma \longrightarrow w_1 \wedge w_2" \\
(\mathcal{A}_{Genfail \wedge \mathcal{I}}) : \quad anditac(``s_1", ``s_2") = fail, \text{ if } s_1, s_2 \text{ are not sequents} \\
(\mathcal{A}_{Propfail \wedge \mathcal{E}l}) : \quad andeltac(fail) = fail \\
(\mathcal{A}_{Propfail \wedge \mathcal{I}}) : \quad anditac(fail, ``s") = anditac(``s", fail) = fail
\end{array}
$$

We turn now to the problem of representing proof strategies in MT. Intuitively, proof strategies are represented by terms in MT, called *logic tactics* (this notion was first introduced and formally defined in [GT93]). The basic building blocks for proof strategies are the primitive inference rules of OT. Therefore we call the symbols of MT representing OT inference rules (e.g. *anditac*, *andeltac*, *impitac*) *primitive tactic symbols*. Proof strategies corresponding to the application of a finite number of inference rules can be simply represented by compound terms built out of primitive tactic symbols. However, in MT we want to be able to represent, reason about and execute more complex (e.g. conditional, recursive) proof strategies in a natural and efficient way. This is achieved by including in $\mathcal{ML}$ two hybrid connectives: a conditional term constructor (**trmif** *wff* **then** *term1* **else** *term2*), and an environment term constructor (**let** (*var* = *term*) **in** *terms*). The corresponding rules for introduction and elimination are:

$$
\frac{\Gamma_1, \{A\} \longrightarrow B(t_1) \quad \Gamma_2, \{\neg A\} \longrightarrow B(t_2)}{\Gamma_1, \Gamma_2 \longrightarrow B(\textbf{trmif } A \textbf{ then } t_1 \textbf{ else } t_2)} \; trmifI
$$

$$
\frac{\Gamma_1 \longrightarrow A \quad \Gamma_2 \longrightarrow B(\textbf{trmif } A \textbf{ then } t_1 \textbf{ else } t_2)}{\Gamma_1, \Gamma_2 \longrightarrow B(t_1)} \; trmifE
$$

$$
\frac{\Gamma_1 \longrightarrow \neg A \quad \Gamma_2 \longrightarrow B(\textbf{trmif } A \textbf{ then } t_1 \textbf{ else } t_2)}{\Gamma_1, \Gamma_2 \longrightarrow B(t_2)} \; trmifE_{\neg}
$$

$$\frac{\Gamma \rightarrow P(t_1[t])}{\Gamma \rightarrow P(\text{let } (x = t) \text{ in } t_1[x])} \; letI \qquad \frac{\Gamma \rightarrow P(\text{let } (x = t) \text{ in } t_1[x])}{\Gamma \rightarrow P(t_1[t])} \; letE$$

with the proviso that no capture of free variables occurs during substitution. Given the ability to represent and deal with such control constructs, we are left with the problem of characterizing safe proof strategies. We regard a proof strategy τ as safe, if it is provably equal to *fail* or to a provable sequent. In other words, if $\vdash_{\text{MT}} Tac(\tau)$. In the following we provide the theoretical foundations for the functionalities of **GETFOL** (introduction of new tactics in the library, execution of stored tactics) described in next section. The class of *logic tactics*, defined below[6], is a class of terms of MT representing proof strategies which can be safely executed to prove theorems in OT. More precisely, we define the notion of *logic tactic, with free variables $x_1 \ldots x_n$, depending on a set of function symbols* Φ (formally $LT_\Phi[x_1 \ldots x_n]$). The intuition is that Φ represents the library of already defined tactics; in particular, it is intended to contain all the primitive tactic symbols. Free variables are explicited so that during the interpretation they can not turn out to be "unbound".

Definition 1 logic tactic. Let Φ be a set of function symbols. The set of logic tactics depending on Φ with free variables $x_1 \ldots x_n$ ($LT_\Phi[x_1 \ldots x_n]$) is the smallest set such that:

(i) $x_i \in LT_\Phi[x_1 \ldots x_n]$.

(ii) $fail \in LT_\Phi[x_1 \ldots x_n]$.

(iii) If $lts \in \Phi$, of arity m, and $\tau_i \in LT_\Phi[x_1 \ldots x_n]$ for each $1 \le i \le m$, then $lts(\tau_1 \ldots \tau_m) \in LT_\Phi[x_1 \ldots x_n]$.

(iv) If $A \in wff[x_1 \ldots x_n]$ and $\tau_1, \tau_2 \in LT_\Phi[x_1 \ldots x_n]$, then **trmif** A **then** τ_1 **else** $\tau_2 \in LT_\Phi[x_1 \ldots x_n]$.

(v) If $\tau_1, \tau_2 \in LT_\Phi[x_1 \ldots x_n]$, then **let** $(y = \tau_1)$ **in** $\tau_2 \in LT_\Phi[x_1 \ldots x_n]$.

We call *primitive tactics* the proof strategies obtained from definition 1, by Φ being the set of primitive tactic symbols, and by considering only clauses (i) and (iii).

Notice that logic tactics may be built by means of the basic constructs of a programming language. This allows to represent complex theorem proving strategies. The formal framework allows for reasoning about these constructs with the deductive machinery which is proved to be correct.

One of the implemented functionalities is the introduction in the library of tactics of function symbols corresponding to new proof strategies. However, in order to guarantee that the symbol actually represents a safe proof strategy, its definition must verify certain conditions. The notion of *logic tactic definition* provides sufficient syntactic criteria to be verified when a new tactic symbol has to be added to the library of tactics.

---

[6] The notions of primitive tactic and logic tactic are a modification of the definitions in [GT93].

Definition 2 logic tactic definition. Let Φ be a set of function symbols, and lts a function symbol not in Φ. If $\tau \in LT_{\Phi \cup \{lts\}}[x_1 \ldots x_n]$ then the formula

$$\forall x_1 \ldots x_n . (lts(x_1 \ldots x_n) = \tau[x_1 \ldots x_n])$$

is a logic tactic definition of lts depending on Φ.

Some observations. Φ is intended to represent the state of the library of tactics at the moment of defining a new tactic. Recursive definitions are allowed by definition 2 by the condition that τ is a logic tactic depending on $\Phi \cup \{lts\}$.

We now show that logic tactics describe safe proof strategies. The following theorem states that if a logic tactic symbol is provided provable sequents of OT as arguments, and the evaluation terminates, then the corresponding result is either a provable sequent or a failure.

Theorem 3. *If $\tau \in LT_\Phi[x_1 \ldots x_n]$ and there exists a primitive tactic $\tau^p[x_1 \ldots x_n]$ such that $\vdash_{\mathrm{MT}} \tau[t_1 \ldots t_n] = \tau^p[t_1 \ldots t_n]$, then*

$$\vdash_{\mathrm{MT}} T(t_1) \wedge \ldots \wedge T(t_n) \supset Tac(\tau[t_1 \ldots t_n])$$

The theorem requires the existence of a term corresponding to the result of the interpretation of the tactic in case of termination. This is a rather strong theoretical condition. However, from a practical point of view, theorem 3 is enough. In fact, the execution of the tactic amounts to building the sequent required to guarantee the safeness of the tactic (i.e. we have obtained either *fail* or a provable sequent). Criteria for recognizing the termination of a proof strategy under general applicability conditions have been widely studied in the past [BM79, Wal88]. However, since they require an arbitrary amount of theorem proving, we have preferred not to introduce them within our framework.

In order to prove theorem 3 we prove the following lemma, stating that primitive tactics enjoy the property of representing correct proof strategies. The theorem trivially follows by substitution.

Lemma 4. *Let $\tau^p[x_1 \ldots x_n]$ be a primitive tactic, and let $t_1 \ldots t_n$ be terms. Then it holds:*

$$\vdash_{\mathrm{MT}} T(t_1) \wedge \ldots \wedge T(t_n) \supset Tac(\tau^p[t_1 \ldots t_n])$$

Proof. We proceed by induction on the complexity of $\tau^p[x_1 \ldots x_n]$.
Let us abbreviate the name of the inference rules: e.g. we write $\vee I$ ($\vee E$) for $\vee$-introduction ($\vee$-elimination).
Base. Let $\tau^p[x_1 \ldots x_n]$ be x_i. From $T(x_i) \vdash_{\mathrm{MT}} T(x_i)$, by $\vee I$, we have $T(x_i) \vdash_{\mathrm{MT}} T(x_i) \vee Fail(x_i)$. From axiom $(\mathcal{A}_{Tac})$ and by $\supset I$ we obtain $\vdash_{\mathrm{MT}} T(x_i) \supset Tac(x_i)$.
Step cases. $\tau^p[x_1 \ldots x_n]$ has the form $f(\tau_1^p \ldots \tau_n^p)$, where f is a primitive tactic symbol and $\tau_1^p \ldots \tau_n^p$ are primitive tactics. Here we only show the cases when f is *andeltac* or *anditac*.
$\boxed{f = andeltac}$ We show that $\vdash_{\mathrm{MT}} T(t_1) \wedge \ldots \wedge T(t_n) \supset Tac(andeltac(\tau_1^p[t_1 \ldots t_n]))$.
By induction hypothesis we know that $\vdash_{\mathrm{MT}} T(t_1) \wedge \ldots \wedge T(t_n)) \supset Tac(\tau_1^p[t_1 \ldots t_n])$.
Using propositional rules we obtain $T(t_1), \ldots, T(t_n) \vdash_{\mathrm{MT}} Tac(\tau_1^p[t_1 \ldots t_n])$. From

axiom $(\mathcal{A}_{Tac})$ we obtain (*): $T(t_1), \ldots, T(t_n) \vdash_{\mathrm{MT}} T(\tau_1^p[t_1 \ldots t_n]) \vee Fail(\tau_1^p[t_1 \ldots t_n])$. We reason by cases. We assume first $Fail(\tau_1^p[t_1 \ldots t_n])$, and using axiom $(\mathcal{A}_{Propfail \wedge \mathcal{E}l})$ we obtain $Fail(\tau_1^p[t_1 \ldots t_n]) \vdash_{\mathrm{MT}} Fail(andeltac(\tau_1^p[t_1 \ldots t_n]))$. By $\vee I$ and from $(\mathcal{A}_{Tac})$ we have $Fail(\tau_1^p[t_1 \ldots t_n]) \vdash_{\mathrm{MT}} Tac(andeltac(\tau_1^p[t_1 \ldots t_n]))$. We then assume $T(\tau_1^p[t_1 \ldots t_n])$, and we reason by cases. We first assume $Conj(s2w(\tau_1^p[t_1 \ldots t_n]))$. We have the preconditions of axiom $(\mathcal{A}_{\wedge \mathcal{E}l})$, suitably instantiated, and by $\forall E$ and $\supset I$ we have: $T(t_1), \ldots, T(t_n), T(\tau_1^p[t_1 \ldots t_n])$, $Conj(s2w(\tau_1^p[t_1 \ldots t_n])) \vdash_{\mathrm{MT}} T(andeltac(\tau_1^p[t_1 \ldots t_n]))$, from which $T(t_1), \ldots,$ $T(t_n), T(\tau_1^p[t_1 \ldots t_n]), Conj(s2w(\tau_1^p[t_1 \ldots t_n])) \vdash_{\mathrm{MT}} Tac(andeltac(\tau_1^p[t_1 \ldots t_n]))$. We assume then $\neg Conj(s2w(\tau_1^p[t_1 \ldots t_n]))$. From axiom $(\mathcal{A}_{Genfail \wedge \mathcal{E}l})$, we obtain $T(\tau_1^p[t_1 \ldots t_n]), \neg Conj(s2w(\tau_1^p[t_1 \ldots t_n])) \vdash_{\mathrm{MT}} Fail(andeltac(\tau_1^p[t_1 \ldots t_n]))$. Then we derive $T(\tau_1^p[t_1 \ldots t_n]), \neg Conj(s2w(\tau_1^p[t_1 \ldots t_n])) \vdash_{\mathrm{MT}} Tac(andeltac(\tau_1^p[t_1 \ldots t_n]))$. By $\vee E$ applied to the tautology $Conj(s2w(\tau_1^p[t_1 \ldots t_n])) \vee \neg Conj(s2w(\tau_1^p[t_1 \ldots t_n]))$, we obtain $T(t_1), \ldots, T(t_n), T(\tau_1^p[t_1 \ldots t_n]) \vdash_{\mathrm{MT}} Tac(andeltac(\tau_1^p[t_1 \ldots t_n]))$. A further application of $\vee E$ to (*) yields $T(t_1), \ldots, T(t_n) \vdash_{\mathrm{MT}} Tac(andeltac(\tau_1^p[t_1 \ldots t_n]))$. The thesis follows from propositional rules.

$\boxed{f = anditac}$ We show that $\vdash_{\mathrm{MT}} T(t_1) \wedge \ldots \wedge T(t_n) \supset Tac(anditac(\tau_1^p[t_1 \ldots t_n], \tau_2^p[t_1 \ldots t_n])$. By induction hypothesis we have $\vdash_{\mathrm{MT}} T(t_1) \wedge \ldots \wedge T(t_n) \supset Tac(\tau_1^p[t_1 \ldots t_n])$, and $\vdash_{\mathrm{MT}} T(t_1) \wedge \ldots \wedge T(t_n) \supset Tac(\tau_2^p[t_1 \ldots t_n])$. We assume $T(t_1), \ldots,$ $T(t_n)$, and we reason by cases.

We assume first that the arguments of the object level $\wedge I$ are provable sequents, i.e. $T(\tau_1^p[t_1 \ldots t_n]) \wedge T(\tau_2^p[t_1 \ldots t_n])$. From axiom $(\mathcal{A}_{\wedge \mathcal{I}})$ we derive $T(anditac(\tau_1^p[t_1 \ldots t_n], \tau_2^p[t_1 \ldots t_n]))$. By $\vee I$ and from $(\mathcal{A}_{Tac})$ we obtain (†): $Tac(anditac(\tau_1^p[t_1 \ldots t_n], \tau_2^p[t_1 \ldots t_n]))$.

We assume then that one of the arguments of the object level $\wedge I$ is a failure, i.e. $Fail(\tau_1^p[t_1 \ldots t_n]) \vee Fail(\tau_2^p[t_1 \ldots t_n])$. From $(\mathcal{A}_{Propfail \wedge \mathcal{I}})$ we derive $Fail(anditac(\tau_1^p[t_1 \ldots t_n], \tau_2^p[t_1 \ldots t_n]))$. By $\vee I$ and from $(\mathcal{A}_{Tac})$ we obtain (‡): $Tac(anditac(\tau_1^p[t_1 \ldots t_n], \tau_2^p[t_1 \ldots t_n]))$.

Starting from the inductive hypotheses we derive $(T(\tau_1^p[t_1 \ldots t_n]) \wedge T(\tau_2^p[t_1 \ldots t_n])) \vee (Fail(\tau_1^p[t_1 \ldots t_n]) \vee Fail(\tau_2^p[t_1 \ldots t_n]))$. By applying $\vee E$ to (†) and (‡) and by propositional rules we obtain the thesis.

3 Mechanizing MT and tactical reasoning in GETFOL

GETFOL [Giu92] is an interactive theorem prover for first order logic. The object theory OT and the metatheory MT are mechanized exploiting the ability of GETFOL to reason about different theories (encoded in data structures called *contexts*), each with its own language and axioms.

A problem in the mechanization of MT is that it contains an infinite set of ground axioms; for instance there is a distinct axiom $(\mathcal{A}_{Conj})$ for each sequent of MT whose end-formula is a conjunction. Since the mechanization of OT (namely the data structures representing the linguistic entities of OT, and the code implementing the inference rules) is a finite presentation of the intended model of MT [GT92], ground properties of OT can be proved in MT via model checking. This is done by exploiting the *simulation structure* and the *semantic attachment* facilities, which enable the user to specify a link between symbols of the formal language and the corresponding computational entities. Individual constants in MT are attached to the data structures mechanizing the objects they denote. For instance, the quotation mark name "x" is attached to the data structure representing the individual variable x of OT. Attachment is also performed for predicate and function symbols of MT. For instance, $Conj$ is attached to CONJ, the HGKM[7] function testing if an expression is a conjunction. Primitive tactic symbols of MT (e.g. *andeltac*) are attached to HGKM functions (e.g. andeltac) implementing the inference rules of OT. Given an expression, the *semantic simplifier* checks for the interpretation in the simulation structure, by applying the HGKM functions attached to function and predicate symbols to the data structures attached to individual constants. The contexts mechanizing OT and MT are connected together by reflection commands, which implement the reflection principles defined in section 2.

In order to perform tactical reasoning, the mechanized metatheory MT has been provided with a library of tactics. Our aim is to allow the user to safely augment this library, which initially consists of a collection of primitive tactics, and then to execute stored tactics. Safeness is guaranteed by the theoretical results of section 2. In particular, theorem 3 states that terminating logic tactics enjoy the property of representing a "safe" proof strategy. The great advantage is that being a logic tactic definition is a syntactic property: therefore, verifying if a tactic can be safely added to the system requires a limited amount of computation. The command NEWTAC verifies if the tactic proposed by the user is actually a logic tactic. The syntax of NEWTAC is:

$$\text{NEWTAC } tactic\_name \text{ by } fact$$

NEWTAC tests if the formula stored in *fact* complies to definition 2. Facts are data structures containing (amongst other things) the formulas asserted in the context [GT91b]. If so, then the tactic is recognized to be safe, and it is added to the library. Furthermore, the definitional axiom of the tactic is used to generate a set of rewriting rules, which will be exploited during the execution of the tactic.

Given the library of tactics, the command TACEXEC allows the user to apply a specified strategy in OT. Its syntax is the following:

$$\text{TACEXEC } tactic\_name \ arg_1 \ ... \ arg_n$$

where the *args* identify asserted theorems of OT.

The steps performed by TACEXEC are:

1. *tactic_name* is parsed, and a check is performed to see whether it is contained in the library of tactics. If this is the case, then the data structures associated to $arg_1 ... arg_n$ are retrieved, n distinguished individual constants (say "arg1", ..., "argN") are declared in MT and attached to the retrieved data structures. The execution mechanism described in [GT92] demands a

---

[7] HGKM [GC91] is the implementation language of GETFOL.

further step for removing the preconditions of the form $T(t)$ via repeated applications of R_{up}. **TACEXEC** implicitly tests the provability of the arguments by calling the appropriate parsing routine. This avoids explicit executions of R_{up}.

2. By accessing the library of tactics the defined tactic symbol (say lts) associated to *tactic_name* is retrieved. The ground tactic obtained by applying lts to "arg1", ..., "argN" (i.e. lts("arg1",...,"argN")) is executed by invoking the **GETFOL** evaluator. The **GETFOL** evaluator combines semantic evaluation (based on computation in the simulation structure) with syntactical rewriting (exploiting the set of rewriting rules built when the tactic has been added to the library).

3. If the simplification terminates, then we obtain either the quotation mark name of a sequent or an explicit failure. In the first case, we have theoretical evidence that the sequent is provable in OT; therefore R_{down} can be applied to assert the result of tactic execution as a theorem of OT. Otherwise failure is signalled.

4   A case study: a normalizer in negative normal form

Many theorem proving procedures require the input formula to be in some normal form [Rob65, And81]. To show the power of the machinery set up in the previous section we build and execute a tactic, called **nnftac**, implementing a negative normal form normalizer. Translation in negative normal form is easily achieved by repeated application of the following rewriting rules:

Law	Rewriting Rule	Tactic
Law of double negation	$\neg\neg A \Longrightarrow A$	doublenegtac
De Morgan law	$\neg(A \wedge B) \Longrightarrow (\neg A) \vee (\neg B)$	DMandtac
De Morgan law	$\neg(A \vee B) \Longrightarrow (\neg A) \wedge (\neg B)$	DMortac

The tactics corresponding to such rules can be easily defined as follows (for the lack of space we present only the definition of **doublenegtac**):

```
GETFOL:: axiom doublenegtacdef: forall x. (doublenegtac(x) =
trmif Neg(s2w(x)) and Neg(body(s2w(x)))
then notetac(falseitac(x,mkass(body(s2w(x)))),body(s2w(x)))
else fail );
```

The negative normal form proof strategy **nnftac** is defined by the axiom **nnfdef**:[8]

```
GETFOL:: axiom nnfdef: forall x. (nnftac(x) =
let R = doublenegtac(x) in
 trmif R = fail
 then let R1 = DMandtac(x) in
      trmif R1 = fail
      then let R2 = DMortac(x) in
```

---

[8] We assume that the necessary constants, variables, functions and predicates have already been declared in MT, together with a suitable object theory OT.

```
            trmif R2 = fail
            then trmif Conj(s2w(x))
                 then anditac(nnftac(andeltac(x)),nnftac(andertac(x)))
                 else trmif Disj(s2w(x))
                      then let R3 = nnftac(mkass(lfor(s2w(x)))) in
                           let R4 = nnftac(mkass(rtor(s2w(x)))) in
                             oretac(x,orirtac(R3,s2w(R4)),
                                      oriltac(R4,s2w(R3)))
                      else x
            else nnftac(R2)
        else nnftac(R1)
else nnftac(R) );
```

We invoke **NEWTAC** to see if our tactic is executable, and **GETFOL** answers by stating that **nnftac** has been added to the library, its set of rewriting rules has been built, and it is ready for execution:

```
GETFOL:: NEWTAC nnftac BY nnfdef;
nnftac has been recognized as an executable tactic
```

We can now switch to OT[9], and execute **nnftac** in order to normalize the assumption[10] labelled with 1.

```
GETFOL:: switchcontext OT;
You are now using context: OT

GETFOL:: assume not((not (not A)) or B);
1   not((not (not A)) or B)       (1)

GETFOL:: TACEXEC nnftac FACT:1;

. . . . . . . . . . . . . . . . .
Creating "s"
"s" attached to not((not (not A)) or B)
. . . . . . . . . . . . . . . . .
Syntactic simplification of nnftac("s") gives let R = doublenegtac("s")
 in trmif R = fail then let R1 = DMandtac("s") in trmif R1 = fail then
let R2 = DMortac("s") in trmif R2 = fail then trmif Conj(s2w("s")) then
anditac(nnftac(andeltac("s")),nnftac(andertac("s"))) else
trmif Disj(s2w("s")) then let R3 = nnftac(mkass(lfor(s2w("s")))) in
let R4 = nnftac(mkass(rtor(s2w("s")))) in
oretac("s",orirtac(R3,s2w(R4)), oriltac(R4,s2w(R3))) else "s" else
nnftac(R2) else nnftac(R1) else nnftac(R)
. . . . . . . . . . . . . . . . .
Evaluating doublenegtac("s") gives fail
Binding R to fail
Evaluating R = fail gives TRUE
. . . . . . . . . . . . . . . . .
```

---

[9] Note that the previous commands have been executed in the context MT. The context switch to the object theory is performed by the command **switchcontext**.

[10] When **GETFOL** asserts a proof line, it shows on the screen the label, the wff and the dependencies of the line itself; see [Giu92].

```
Evaluating DMandtac("s") gives fail
Binding R1 to fail
Evaluating R1 = fail gives TRUE
...................
Syntactic simplification of DMortac("s") gives ..........
...................
Evaluating nnftac("s") gives "(not A) and (not B)"
Reflecting down T("s")

2   (not A) and (not B)      (1)
I'm finished executing nnftac
```

It is easy to identify in the trace the steps of the process described in the previous section.

5   Conclusions and future work

In this paper we have presented an extension of the interactive theorem prover GETFOL for performing tactical reasoning. In section 2 we have presented the metatheory MT, that describes provability and proof strategies for the object theory OT, and we have shown the metatheorem which provides the theoretical basis for the implemented functionalities. We have described the mechanization of MT in GETFOL, the command NEWTAC which allows to safely augment the system's library of executable tactics, and the command TACEXEC, which allows the user to execute proof strategies to perform theorem proving at the object level. As a simple, yet significant case study, we have discussed the definition and execution of a negative normal form normalizer, showing the commands NEWTAC and TACEXEC at work.

At the moment we are concentrating on the extension of the library with more complex tactics. Moreover, we plan to add the capability to automatically synthesize the HGKM code implementing the proof strategies represented by a tactic, i.e. the operation of *flattening* (see, for instance, [GC92b]), which projects logical metatheoretic statements into executable code. The extension of MT to take into account the deciders of GETFOL [AG93] is also under study.

References

[AG93]   A. Armando and E. Giunchiglia. Embedding Complex Decision Proce-
           dures inside an Interactive Theorem Prover. *Annals of Artificial Intelli-
           gence and Mathematics*, 8(3–4), 1993. In press.

[And81]   P.B. Andrews. Theorem Proving via General Matings. *Journal of the
           ACM*, 28(2):193–214, 1981.

[Bib81]   W. Bibel. On Matrices with Connections. *Journal of the ACM*, 28(4):633–
           645, 1981.

[BM79]   R.S. Boyer and J.S. Moore. *A Computational Logic*. Academic Press,
           1979. ACM monograph series.

[CAB+86]   R.L. Constable, S.F. Allen, H.M. Bromley, et al. *Implementing Mathe-
           matics with the NuPRL Proof Development System*. Prentice Hall, 1986.

[deB70]   N.G. deBruijn. The mathematical language automath. In *Symposium in Automatic Demonstration, Lecture Notes in Mathematics*, volume Vol. 125, pages 29–61. Springer-Verlag, 1970.

[GA93]   F. Giunchiglia and A. Armando. A Conceptual Architecture for Introspective Systems. Forthcoming IRST-Technical Report, 1993.

[GC91]   F. Giunchiglia and A. Cimatti. HGKM User Manual - HGKM version 2. Technical Report 9107-05, DIST - University of Genova, Genova, Italy, 1991.

[GC92a]   F. Giunchiglia and A. Cimatti. Introspective Metatheoretic Reasoning. Technical Report 9211-21, IRST, Trento, Italy, 1992.

[GC92b]   F. Giunchiglia and A. Cimatti. Introspective Metatheoretic Theorem Proving. Technical Report 9211-22, IRST, Trento, Italy, 1992.

[Giu92]   F. Giunchiglia. The GETFOL Manual - GETFOL version 1. Technical Report 9204-01, DIST - University of Genova, Genoa, Italy, 1992. Forthcoming IRST-Technical Report.

[GMMW77] M.J. Gordon, R. Milner, L. Morris, and C. Wadsworth. A Metalanguage for Interactive Proof in LCF. CSR report series CSR-16-77, Department of Artificial Intelligence, Dept. of Computer Science, University of Edinburgh, 1977.

[GMW79]   M.J. Gordon, A.J. Milner, and C.P. Wadsworth. *Edinburgh LCF - A mechanized logic of computation*, volume 78 of *Lecture Notes in Computer Science*. Springer Verlag, 1979.

[GT91a]   F. Giunchiglia and P. Traverso. Reflective reasoning with and between a declarative metatheory and the implementation code. In *Proc. of the 12th International Joint Conference on Artificial Intelligence*, pages 111–117, Sydney, 1991. Also IRST-Technical Report 9012-03, IRST, Trento, Italy.

[GT91b]   F. Giunchiglia and P. Traverso. GETFOL User Manual - GETFOL version 1. Manual 9109-09, IRST, Trento, Italy, 1991. Also MRG-DIST Technical Report 9107-01, DIST, University of Genova.

[GT92]   F. Giunchiglia and P. Traverso. A Metatheory of a Mechanized Object Theory. Technical Report 9211-24, IRST, Trento, Italy, 1992.

[GT93]   F. Giunchiglia and P. Traverso. Program tactics and logic tactics. Technical Report 9301-01, IRST, Trento, Italy, 1993.

[GTCP92]   F. Giunchiglia, P. Traverso, A. Cimatti, and P. Pecchiari. A System for Multi-Level Reasoning. In A. Yonozawa and B.C. Smith, editors, *Proc. IMSA '92 International Workshop on Reflection and Meta-level Architecture*, pages 190–195, Tokyo, 1992. Also IRST-Technical Report 9211-18, IRST, Trento, Italy.

[MW80]   Z. Manna and R. Waldinger. A deductive approach to program synthesis. *ACM Transactions on Programming Languages and Systems*, 2:90–121, 1980.

[Pau89]   L. Paulson. The Foundation of a Generic Theorem Prover. *Journal of Automated Reasoning*, 5:363–396, 1989.

[Pra65]   D. Prawitz. *Natural Deduction - A proof theoretical study*. Almquist and Wiksell, Stockholm, 1965.

[Rob65]   A. Robinson. A Machine oriented Logic Based on the resolution principle. *Journal of the ACM*, 12:23–41, 1965.

[Wal88]   C. Walther. Argument-Bounded Algorithms as a Basis for Automated Termination Proofs. In *Proc. of the 9th Conference on Automated Deduction*, 1988.

[Wey80]   R.W. Weyhrauch. Prolegomena to a Theory of Mechanized Formal Reasoning. *Artif. Intell.*, 13(1):133–176, 1980.

Computing 3-valued Stable Models by using the ATMS

Evelina Lamma[1] and Paola Mello[2]

[1] Dipartimento di Matematica e Informatica
Università di Udine, Via Zanon 6, 33100 Udine, Italy
lamma@udmi5400.cineca.it
[2] Dipartimento di Elettronica, Informatica e Sistemistica
Università di Bologna, Viale Risorgimento 2, 40136 Bologna, Italy
paola@deis33.cineca.it

Abstract. In this paper, we present a (sound and complete) procedure for computing the maximal 3-valued stable models (preferred extensions) of propositional logic programs with negation as failure. This procedure uses the Assumption-based Truth Maintenance System (ATMS) data structures and mechanisms, and is grounded on the concept of acceptability of a (negative) hypothesis.

1 Introduction

Recently the stable model semantics (see [9]) has been introduced for modelling the intended meaning of normal logic programs (i.e., logic programs possibly containing negation as failure in the body of clauses [14]). Stable model semantics is closely related to autoepistemic and default approaches to non-monotonic reasoning. However, the stable semantics has also some important drawbacks. First of all, it is defined only for a restricted class of normal logic programs, and, secondly, it does not always seem to lead the expected semantics. Thus, alternative semantics have been provided for normal logic programs. Among others, we mention: the *well-founded semantics* [23], the *3-valued stable model semantics* [18], and the *preferential semantics* [6]. In particular, in [18] 3-valued stable model semantics is introduced to overcome the drawbacks of the 2-valued one. Differently from stable models, each logic program has at least one 3-valued stable model. The 3-valued stable model semantics also naturally corresponds to suitable extensions of non-monotonic formalisms in Artificial Intelligence such as McCarthy's circumscription, Reiter's closed world assumption, Moore's autoepistemic logic and Reiter's default logic (see [18] for details). Moreover, 3-valued stable semantics subsumes other semantics for normal logic programs introduced in the literature. As respectively shown in [18] and [2], the least 3-valued stable model of a program P corresponds to the well-founded model of P and the maximal 3-valued stable models are equivalent to preferred extensions (introduced in [6]).

In the meanwhile, several papers have extended the Assumption-based Truth Maintenance System (ATMS, [4]) with non-monotonic justifications [5,10] and shown its relationship with the (total) stable model semantics and autoepistemic logic (see [8,16,19]). In particular, in [8], an algorithm is described which computes the stable models of propositional normal logic programs using the ATMS. However, the procedure defined in [8] maintains all the drawbacks of the (2-valued) stable semantics.

In this paper, we present a procedure (subsuming that presented in [8]) based on the ATMS data structures which is sound and complete with respect to the set of maximal 3-valued stable models of a normal logic program. This allows us to correctly deal with credulous reasoning in a logic programming setting. Maximalism (or credulism) tries to conclude as much as possible, and it is modeled through the maximal 3-valued stable models (i.e., preferred extensions). The procedure here presented is grounded on the concept of acceptability of a (negative) hypothesis defined in [6]. No significant extension is needed to the standard ATMS, provided that negative literals are treated as ATMS assumptions, and appropriate constraints are introduced as in [7,8]. With respect to the basic ATMS, we now maintain in node labels also the (minimal) nogood environments, and record in a new label (called *complement label*) the conditions making each negative literal an *acceptable* hypothesis.

It has already been argued that the ATMS is an appropriate reasoning tool for dealing with non-monotonic justifications [5,10]. This paper further strengthens this relationship. Thanks to the direct correspondence established in [18] between the 3-valued stable model semantics for logic programs and non-monotonic formalisms, the ATMS, when associated with the procedure defined in this paper, can be considered as a correct inference engine for these different formalisms of non-monotonic reasoning.

2   3-valued Stable Models of Logic Programs

We will refer to the basic concepts and terminology of standard logic programming ([14]). Then, a *normal logic program* P is a set of clauses of the form $A \leftarrow L_1, \ldots, L_n, (n \geq 0)$, where A is an atom and $L_1, \ldots, L_n$ are literals. Without loss of generality, we consider only (possibly infinite) propositional programs, thus assuming that a program P has already been instantiated.

Let P be a program and HB the Herbrand Base associated with P. A *3-valued interpretation* I of P is any pair, $\langle I^+; I^- \rangle$, where I^+ and I^- are disjoint subsets of the Herbrand base HB. I^+ contains all the ground atoms *true* in I, I^- all the ground atoms *false* in I. Any atom occurring neither in I^+ nor in I^- is *unknown* or undefined in I. An interpretation I is *total* iff $I^+ \cup I^- = HB$.

In [18], Przymusinski extended the stable model semantics to *3-valued stable models* which is defined for any normal logic program. The major drawback of 3-valued stable model semantics is that its original definition (see [18]) is not intuitive and rather complex. In the following, instead of presenting the original definition ([18]) based on a syntactic transformation, we take advantage from the notion of *acceptability* introduced by Dung (see [6]) – more suitable for the ATMS - and the equivalence results between Dung's and Przymusinski's semantics reported in [2].

Dung has studied the treatment of negation as hypothesis in logic programming, which was first introduced in [7] in the framework of abductive reasoning. The main idea of this approach is to look at negative literals *not h* as abductive hypotheses *not_h*, add constraints of the form $\leftarrow h, not\_h$, and give the semantics of a normal logic program P through the notions of *extension* of P and *acceptability*. Extensions (called *scenaria* in [6]) are obtained by augmenting P with a set of abductive hypotheses $H \subseteq not\_H B$ such that the first order theory $P \cup H$ is consistent (notice that $not\_H B = \{not\_h \mid h \in H B\}$).

Given a scenario $P \cup H$, a hypothesis *not_h* is acceptable with respect to $P \cup H$ if and only if there is "no evidence to the contrary", that is there is no way to derive h in $P \cup H$. More formally:

Definition 1. *(Acceptability of a Hypothesis w.r.t. a Scenario)*
A hypothesis *not_h* is acceptable with respect to a scenario $P \cup H$ if and only if:
$\forall E \subseteq not\_H B$ such that $P \cup E \vdash h$, $Der(P, H) \cup E$ is inconsistent.
$Der(P, H)$ stands for the set of atoms derivable from P and H:
$Der(P, H) = \{h \in H B \mid P \cup H \vdash h\}$. $\qquad\qquad \square$

Among the scenaria of a normal logic program P, it is possible to identify the *complete scenaria*. Complete scenaria are scenaria where all the acceptable hypotheses are accepted. In his paper, Dung models normal logic programs through maximal complete scenaria (called *preferred extensions*). In a recent paper [2], complete scenaria and 3-valued stable models have been proved equivalent. This equivalence is formally established by the following proposition.

Proposition 2. *(Equivalence of 3-valued Stable Models and Complete Scenaria)*
Let P be a normal logic program. Then, $M = \langle M^+; M^- \rangle$ is a 3-valued stable model of P iff $P \cup not\_M^-$ is a complete scenario of P. $\qquad \square$

3 The ATMS

3.1 Preliminaries

The ATMS [4] records inferences performed by an associated problem-solver in terms of dependencies among atomic propositions. In particular, given a set of atoms N, the ATMS distinguishes among them a subset S of atoms called *assumptions*. Inferences are transmitted from the problem-solver by means of *justifications* which are propositional definite clauses. Among justifications, integrity constraints (only denials, in practice) are expressed by clauses with head *false*. When transmitting S and a set of justifications J to the ATMS, it computes: (*i*) All the minimal sets of assumptions E such that $J \cup E$ is inconsistent (i.e., $J \cup E \vdash false$). These sets are called *nogoods*; (*ii*) For each atom $n \in N$, all the minimal, consistent sets of assumptions E such that $J \cup E \vdash n$. E is called an *environment* of n.

Every atomic proposition $n \in N$ is represented by a *node* of the form $\langle n, L, J_n \rangle$, where L is the set of environments of n (called *label*), and J_n the set of justifications having n as consequence. Given the set of justifications J, the set of assumptions S and an environment E, the context characterised by E (denoted as $ctx^{J,S}(E)$) is the set of atoms $\{A \in N \mid J \cup E \vdash A\}$. In the following, given the set of assumptions S and the set of justifications J, we will indicate the label of n as $lab^{J,S}(n)$, and the set of nogood environments as $nogood^{J,S}$.

3.2 ATMS and Complete Scenaria

In this section, we re-interpret the definition of 3-valued stable model given in section 2 in terms of ATMS data structures. First, we map a propositional normal logic program P in the ATMS representation, proceeding as in [7,8]. In particular, starting from P, we add to the ATMS the set of justifications J constituted by:

- The set of definite clauses, P^*, obtained by replacing each negative literal *not q* in some clause of P with a new predicate symbol *not_q*;
- The set of constraints $false \leftarrow q, not\_q$ for each predicate symbol q occurring (positively or negatively) in P. In the following, we will represents constraints simply as denials.

Moreover, we consider a set of assumptions S composed by all the atoms *not_q* such that q occurs (positively or negatively) in P.

Example 1. Consider the following program P:

$$p \leftarrow not\ q \qquad q \leftarrow not\ r$$

The corresponding set of ATMS justifications is:

$$p \leftarrow not\_q \qquad q \leftarrow not\_r$$
$$\leftarrow q, not\_q \qquad \leftarrow r, not\_r$$
$$\leftarrow p, not\_p$$

and the assumptions are $\{not\_q, not\_r, not\_p\}$. Thus, we obtain the following ATMS representation where, for the sake of simplicity, justifications are omitted:

$$\langle p, \{\{not\_q\}\}\rangle \qquad\qquad \langle not\_p, \{\{not\_p\}\}\rangle$$
$$\langle q, \{\{not\_r\}\}\rangle \qquad\qquad \langle not\_q, \{\{not\_q\}\}\rangle$$
$$\langle r, \{\}\rangle \qquad\qquad \langle not\_r, \{\{not\_r\}\}\rangle$$
$$\langle false, \{\{not\_q, not\_r\}, \{not\_q, not\_p\}\}\rangle$$

$\square$

We relate the 3-valued stable models of a program P with the environments and nogoods of the corresponding ATMS representation. To this purpose, notice that since negative hypotheses have been mapped into ATMS assumptions, each scenario $P \cup H$ corresponds to a consistent environment H in the ATMS domain, and $Der(P, H)$ corresponds to $ctx^{J,S}(H)$. The acceptability condition (see definition 1) of a hypothesis with respect to a scenario can be restated in terms of acceptability of an assumption with respect to a consistent environment as follows:

Definition 3. *(Acceptability of an Assumption w.r.t. an Environment)*
Let H be a consistent environment. The assumption not_h is acceptable with respect to H if and only if:

(*) $\forall E \in lab^{J,S}(h)$ ($\exists not\_a \in E$ such that $a \in ctx^{J,S}(H)$).

(Note: a is the complement of not_a)   □

Notice that in the definition of acceptability of a hypothesis (definition 1) also evidences which can generate inconsistency are considered, while the standard ATMS deletes inconsistent environments from node labels.

Example 2. Consider the following program P:

$p \leftarrow not\ p$

and its ATMS representation:

$\langle p, \{\} \rangle$
$\langle not\_p, \{\} \rangle$
$\langle false, \{\{not\_p\}\} \rangle$

where the nogood environment $\{not\_p\}$ has been deleted from node p. The assumption not_p is acceptable w.r.t. the environment $\{\}$, whereas the hypothesis not_p is not acceptable w.r.t. the scenario $P \cup \{\}$.   □

In order to guarantee the equivalence between the hypotheses acceptable w.r.t. a scenario (definition 1) and the assumptions acceptable w.r.t. the corresponding environment (definition 3), we need to maintain also (minimal) nogood environments in the ATMS representation.

Thus, from now on, we suppose that $lab^{J,S}(n)$ records minimal (consistent and inconsistent) environments for node n. This is the only modification in ATMS behaviour that we have to impose in order to guarantee the one-to-one correspondence between definition 1 and 3.

Proposition 4. *(Acceptability of Hypotheses and Assumptions)*
Given the scenario $P \cup H$, the hypothesis not_h is acceptable with respect to $P \cup H$ if and only if the assumption not_h is acceptable with respect to the consistent environment H.
Proof: *See [13].*   □

In the following, any environment which contains all its acceptable hypotheses is called a *stable environment*. Stable environments are the ATMS counterpart of complete scenaria. The definition directly descends from that of acceptability for an assumption (definition 3).

Definition 5. *(Stable Environment)*
An environment H is a stable environment of P iff:
(i) $\forall E \in nogood^{J,S}$ $E \not\subseteq H$;
(ii) $\forall not\_h \in S$
$not\_h \in H \iff \forall E \in lab^{J,S}(h)$ $(\exists not\_a \in E$ such that $a \in ctx^{J,S}(H))$.   □

The first requirement (i) simply corresponds to identify consistent environments. Condition (ii) corresponds to consider environments which are composed by all the acceptable assumptions.

The following proposition formally establishes the correspondence between stable environments and complete scenaria (and therefore 3-valued stable models).

Proposition 6. *(Equivalence of Stable Environments and Complete Scenaria)*
Let P be a normal logic program, S the associated set of assumptions and $E \subseteq S$. E is a stable environment of P iff $P \cup E$ is a complete scenario of P.
Proof: *Straightforward from proposition 4.*   □

When defining complete scenaria and stable environments, the main difference is that definition 5, based on ATMS, considers only environments, and then evidences, which are minimal. This possibly reduces the complexity in determining stable environments with respect to determining complete scenaria, since a smaller number of evidences have to be considered.

Given a stable environment, we can directly obtain the corresponding 3-valued stable model. In particular, a stable environment H corresponds to the 3-valued stable model $\langle M^+; M^- \rangle$ where:
$$M^- = \{a \in HB \mid not\_a \in H\}$$
$$M^+ = \{a \in HB \mid a \in ctx^{J,S}(H)\}$$
As a corollary, we also have that maximal stable environments correspond to maximal complete scenaria (called preferred extensions in [6]), and thus to maximal 3-valued stable models.

4 Computing Maximal Stable Environments

In this section, we present an algorithm (based on definitions 3 and 5) for computing the maximal stable environments of a normal logic program P from the environments and nogoods of the ATMS representation of P.

In [8], Eshghi identifies stable models by finding sets of assumptions, τ, which for sure do not belong to any stable model of the program. As in [8] for stable models, here we identify a (maximal) stable environment by finding a set of assumptions τ such that $S \setminus \tau$ is a stable environment. The main difference is that the requirement here checked to state whether an environment is stable is more complex than the one embedded in the original algorithm for computing stable models.

In order that the remaining set of assumptions $S \setminus \tau$ satisfies the (i) requirement of definition 5, no nogood must be a subset of $S \setminus \tau$. This can be accomplished by choosing one assumption from each nogood and including it in τ. However, if we remove from S an assumption not_h, we could violate requirement (ii) of definition 5. Therefore, we can drop an assumption from S only if this requirement is not satisfied.

Since now we are interested in determining whether an assumption is *not acceptable* (i.e., it can be safely removed from S and inserted in τ), we restate the stability condition for an environment H (requirement (ii), definition 5) as follows:

$$\forall not\_h \in S \ (not\_h \notin H \ \Leftrightarrow \ \exists E \in lab^{J,S}(h): \ \forall not\_a \in E \ a \notin ctx^{J,S}(H))$$

It is straightforward to show that with this (equivalent) condition, we identify the complement set $\tau = S \setminus H$ of a stable environment H (according to definition 5).

Determining that an assumption is not acceptable with respect to an environment H requires to compute the context characterised by H. Since computing the context is a costly operation (as discussed in [4]), we replace this operation with a simpler one, involving only subset tests. We say that an assumption not_h is not acceptable with respect to the environment H if and only if:

$$\exists E \in lab^{J,S}(h): \ \forall not\_a \in E \ (\forall E' \in lab^{J,S}(a) \ E' \nsubseteq H)$$

Finally, to better check this condition and avoid the repetition of computations, for each assumption $not\_h \in S$ we maintain a *complement label*.

Definition 7. *(Complement Label)*
Let us consider $not\_h \in S$, and let $lab^{J,S}(h) = \{E_1, \ldots, E_n\}$. The complement label of not_h, $c\_lab^{J,S}(not\_h)$, has the following structure:

$$c\_lab^{J,S}(not\_h) = \{s\_lab_1, \ldots, s\_lab_n\}$$

where each element s_lab_i (called *supporting label*) is determined starting from the structure of the i-th environment of h.
In more detail, if $E_i = \{not\_c_{i,1}, \ldots, not\_c_{i,m_i}\}$, then the i-th supporting label is defined as:

$$s\_lab_i = \bigcup_{(j=1,\ldots,m_i)} lab^{J,S}(c_{i,j})$$

$\square$

Thus, the complement label of not_h is the minimised collection of all the supporting labels of not_h. In practice, $c\_lab^{J,S}(not\_h)$ has as many elements (the supporting labels s_lab_i) as the number of (minimal) evidences for h. A supporting label of not_h records minimal environments, each one supporting the positive counterpart a of a negative atom not_a occurring in some evidence for h. If each supporting label of the assumption not_h contains an environment E which is a subset of H, then not_h is acceptable with respect to H. The following proposition formally establishes this correspondence between acceptability (and thus the stability condition of an environment) and complement labels.

Proposition 8. *(Acceptability and Complement Labels)*
Let not_h be an assumption and H a consistent environment. not_h is acceptable w.r.t. H if and only if $\forall SL \in c\_lab^{J,S}(not\_h) \ \exists E \in SL$ such that $E \subseteq H$.
Proof: *Straightforward from definition 7.* $\square$

Example 3. Consider the program P of example 1:

$$p \leftarrow not\ q \qquad q \leftarrow not\ r$$

and its ATMS representation. The complement labels of its assumptions are:

$\langle not\_p, \{\{\{not\_r\}\}\}\rangle$
$\langle not\_q, \{\{\}\}\rangle$
$\langle not\_r, \{\}\rangle$

$\square$

To compute stable environments, we are interested in efficiently determining whether an assumption not_h can be inserted in τ. Building the set τ, we have that $not\_h \in \tau$ if and only if there exists at least one supporting label of not_h such that all its elements E' are not subsets of H ($E' \not\subseteq H$). In other words, each E' must contain at least one element of τ. This guarantees that there exists some evidence $E \in lab^{J,S}(h)$ which is not inconsistent with $ctx^{J,S}(H)$, and therefore not_h is not acceptable w.r.t. H.

Example 4. Let us consider the program P of example 3 and its ATMS data structures. The assumption not_q does not belong to any stable environment, since its single supporting label is empty. The assumption not_r, instead, belongs to each stable environment. In fact, there is no supporting label for not_r. Also the assumption not_p has to belong to each stable environment of P. In fact, its single supporting label is $\{\{not\_r\}\}$ and not_r cannot belong to τ, since it belongs to each stable environment. $\square$

The (iterative) algorithm for computing maximal stable environments is structured into the following steps:

1. First build the set $\mathcal{T}_{basic} = \{\}$ and the set $\mathcal{T} = \{\tau_1, \ldots, \tau_n\}$ which is the minimised collection of the environment τ_i built by choosing one assumption from each nogood set (this guarantees that the set $S \setminus \tau_i$ we are trying to build is consistent and maximal);
2. For each element $\tau_i \in \mathcal{T}$:
   2.1. For each assumption $not\_h \in \tau_i$, update the complement labels of all the ATMS assumptions, $\{not\_h'\}$, by removing all the environments in some supporting label of not_h' which include the chosen element not_h;
   2.2 If $\tau_i = \{not\_h_1, \ldots, not\_h_k\}$ is such that at least one supporting label of not_h_j is empty (for $j = 1, \ldots, k$) then τ_i is a *candidate* set;
   2.3 The candidate set possibly determined at step 2.2 has to be enlarged by adding all the assumptions not_a, not yet included in τ_i, having at least one supporting label empty. The resulting set is called *basic*. Let $\tau_{basic} = \tau_i \cup \{not\_a | \exists SL \in c\_lab^{J,S}(not\_a) \wedge SL = \{\}\}$. If $\tau_{basic} \neq \tau_i$, repeat step 2.1.
   2.4 The basic set possibly determined at step 2.3 is inserted in the set $\mathcal{T}_{basic}$.
3. Finally, the set $\mathcal{T}_{basic}$ is minimised.

This algorithm is able to compute the maximal 3-valued stable models of a program. More precisely, if $\tau \in \mathcal{T}_{basic}$, then the set $S \setminus \tau$ is a maximal stable environment (and "viceversa"), as stated by the following result of soundness and completeness with respect to preferential semantics.

Theorem 9. *(Soundness and Completeness w.r.t. Preferential Semantics)*
Let P be a normal logic program, S the associated set of assumptions and $E \subseteq S$. E is a maximal stable environment of P iff $\tau = S \setminus E$ belongs to $\mathcal{T}_{basic}$.
Proof: *See [13].* □

If one consider candidate sets which are not basic, soundness with maximal 3-valued stable semantics could be lost.

Example 5. Let us consider the following program P:

$$p \leftarrow not\ p$$
$$r \leftarrow not\ p$$

whose ATMS representation is (assumptions are omitted):

$\langle p, \{\{not\_p\}\}\rangle$
$\langle r, \{\{not\_p\}\}\rangle$
$\langle false, \{\{not\_p\}\}\rangle$

The complement labels are:

$\langle not\_p, \{\{\{not\_p\}\}\}\rangle$
$\langle not\_r, \{\{\{not\_p\}\}\}\rangle$

The set $\tau = \{not\_p\}$ is the only one you can build from the nogood set. It is a candidate set for P, but does not correspond to any stable environment of P. In fact, the set $\langle \{\}; \{r\}\rangle$ is not a maximal 3-valued stable model of P. However, choosing $\tau = \{not\_p\}$ makes empty the single supporting label of not_r. Adding not_r to τ produces the basic set $\tau = \{not\_p, not\_r\}$, which corresponds to the single 3-valued stable model of P. □

Among maximal 3-valued stable models, the algorithm also computes stable models [9] (if they exist), being (2-valued) stable models total models and therefore also maximal 3-valued stable models (see [2]). Therefore, the algorithm here presented subsumes the one presented in [8], but it is of course more complex.

5   Related Work

A lot of work has been devoted in defining procedures for computing (implicitly or explicitly) stable models of normal logic programs. Some works directly define top-down or bottom-up procedures and "ad hoc" data structures for computing them, while other ones derive stable models from TMS or ATMS structures, thus establishing a link between negation in logic programming and Artificial Intelligence mechanisms.

Works presented in [7,6,16,20,22,21,15], just to mention some related works, classify in the first approach.

In [16] an algorithm is presented able to compute (total, 2-valued) stable models of a normal logic program by using a label propagation algorithm and specific tree data structures. The authors advocate the use of this algorithm as an alternative to the TMS approach.

In [20], a constructive (bottom-up) definition for stable models is given, with the introduction of a procedure, called *backtracking fixpoint*, that non-deterministically constructs a stable model if such a model exists.

In [7,6] a top-down abductive procedure is presented for dealing with negation as failure in logic programming. This procedure, however, is not sound with respect to the stable model semantics, while it is sound (but not complete) with respect to preferential semantics. In [22], on the other hand, the authors presents a query-based procedure which deals correctly with the stable model semantics, but still not complete with respect to preferential semantics.

Finally, in [21] a bottom-up procedure (dual to the one in [22]) is presented for dealing with normal logic programs possibly containing abducible predicates and integrity constraints. This procedure computes generalised stable models [11] for an abductive framework, and is grounded on the procedure for computing stable models defined by Saccà and Zaniolo [20].

Differently from the papers mentioned above where only total stable models are considered, in [15] top-down derivation procedures are defined for 3-valued semantics. In particular, the authors present two procedures that given a normal logic program P and a literal L respectively succeed if L is in the well-founded or in some 3-valued stable model of P.

Works in [1,5,8,10,12,19] follow the second approach, deriving stable models from TMS or ATMS data structures.

In [8,10,19] particular sets of assumptions (respectively called extension bases, stable generators and stable bases) are determined by using suitable algorithms, based on ATMS data structures. A one-to-one correspondence is then established between these sets of assumptions and stable models.

In [5], the ATMS data structures are extended to deal with non-monotonic justifications. While in [10] an extension base is constructed in order to prove that there is one, in [5] the author only checks for conditions that could block the construction of such an extension.

The use of TMS within the Eshghi-Kowalski's abductive procedure has been considered in [12]. In that work, in particular, a TMS is used as cache for recording the abductive hypotheses which are generated by a revised version of the backward abductive procedure defined in [7].

In [1], instead, the abductive procedure defined in [7] is restated directly in terms of ATMS data structures.

The work presented in this paper follows the second approach since it directly uses the ATMS data structures for computing stable semantics, and extends the one presented in [8]. The main novelty with respect to all the works mentioned above and following the second approach, is that we relax the totality requirement, too strong in some cases, and are able to deal with *3-valued* stable models. The definition of stable environment generalises that of stable generator introduced in [8]. It is straightforward to prove that if a set of assumptions H is a stable generator, then it is also a stable environment, while the converse does not hold in general. Moreover, our procedure – even if more computationally expensive – is (sound and) complete with respect to preferential semantics.

Conclusions and Future Work

We presented a (sound and complete) method for computing the maximal 3-valued stable models of propositional normal logic programs.

The method directly extends the one presented in [8] using the ATMS, and is grounded on the concept of acceptability of a (negative) hypothesis. The algorithm has been implemented in Common LISP on a SUN SparcStation2.

The use of the ATMS is not completely satisfactory from the computational cost point of view, too high to be used in real applications (see [17] for a complexity analysis of the generation of ATMS node labels). However, the procedure discussed in the paper allow us to obtain completeness result with respect to 3-valued stable model semantics, and can be easily extended to also deal with abductive reasoning. An issue recently faced in the literature (see for example [3]) is how to extend the 3-valued stable semantics with abduction, in the style of what have been done for the 2-valued semantics by Kakas and Mancarella ([11]). It is often the case, in fact, that *abductive* logic programs with both negation by default and explicit negation are used to build Artificial Intelligence applications. Proof procedures for the resulting semantics have to be defined. In the future, we intend to investigate whether the procedure here presented can be applied to this case as well.

Acknowledgements:
We thank Ken Satoh for useful suggestions and remarks, and Are Sorli who took care of the implementation in Common LISP. This work has been partially supported by C.N.R. PFI "Sistemi Informatici e Calcolo Parallelo" under grant n. 9201606.PF69.

References

1. A. Brogi, E. Lamma, and P. Mello. ATMS for Implementing Logic Programming. In B. Neumann, editor, *Proceedings 10th European Conference on Artificial Intelligence*, pages 114-118. John Wiley and Sons, 1992.
2. A. Brogi, E. Lamma, P. Mancarella, and P. Mello. Normal Logic Programs as Open Positive Programs. In *Proceedings Joint International Conference and Symposium on Logic Programming JICSLP92*, pages 783-797. Washington (USA), November 1992, The MIT Press.
3. A. Brogi, E. Lamma, P. Mancarella, and P. Mello. Semantics for Abductive Logic Programs. In *Proceedings ICLP93 Workshop on Abductive Reasoning*. Budapest (H), 24-25 June 1993.
4. J. de Kleer. An Assumption-based TMS. *Artificial Intelligence*, 28: 127-162,1986.

5. O. Dressler. Problem Solving with the NM-ATMS. In Y. , editor, *Proceedings 9th European Conference on Artificial Intelligence*, pages 253-258. Pitman Publishing, 1988.

6. P. M. Dung. Negation as Hypothesis: An Abductive Foundation for Logic Programming. In K. Furukawa, editor, *Proceedings 8th International Conference on Logic Programming*. The MIT Press, 1991.

7. K. Eshghi and R.A. Kowalski. Abduction compared with negation by failure. In G. Levi and M. Martelli, editors, *Proceedings 6th International Conference on Logic Programming*, page 234-254. The MIT Press, 1989.

8. K. Eshghi. Computing Stable Models by Using the ATMS. In *Proc. AAAI90*, pages 272-277. AAAI, 1990.

9. M. Gelfond and V. Lifschitz. The Stable Models Semantics for Logic Programs. In R. A. Kowalski and K. A. Bowen, editors, *Proc. Fifth International Conference on Logic Programming*, pages 1070-1080. The MIT Press, 1988.

10. U. Junker. A Correct Non-Monotonic ATMS. *Proc. IJCAI89*, Morgan Kaufman 1989.

11. A.C. Kakas and P. Mancarella. Generalized stable models: a semantics for abduction. In L. Carlucci Aiello, editor, *Proceedings of 9th European Conference on Artificial Intelligence*, pages 385-391. Pitman, 1990.

12. A.C. Kakas and P. Mancarella. On the Relation between Truth Maintenance and Abduction. In *Proc. PRICAI,1991*.

13. E. Lamma, and P. Mello. Computing 3-valued Stable Models by using the ATMS. *DEIS Tecnical Report*. University of Bologna (I), June 1993.

14. J.W. Lloyd. *Foundations of logic programming*. Springer-Verlag, second edition, 1987.

15. L.M. Pereira, J.N. Aparicio, J.J. Alferes. Derivation Procedures for Extended Stable Models. *Proc. IJCAI91*, pages 863-868. Morgan Kaufman 1991.

16. S.G. Pimentel, and J.L. Cuadrado. A Truth Maintenance System Based on Stable Models. In E.W. Lusk, and R.A. Overbeek, editors, *Proc. NACLP89*, pages 274-288. The MIT Press, 1989.

17. G.M. Provan. The Computational Complexity of Multiple-context Truth Maintenance Systems. In L. Carlucci Aiello, editor, *Proceedings of 9th European Conference on Artificial Intelligence*, pages 522-527. Pitman, 1990.

18. T.C. Przymusinski. Extended Stable Semantics for Normal and Disjunctive Programs. In D.H.D. Warren and P. Szeredi, editors, *Proc. 7th International Conference on Logic Programming*, page 459-477. The MIT Press, 1990.

19. W.L. Rodi and S.G. Pimentel. A Nonmonotonic Assumption-based TMS Using Stable Bases. In *Proc. KR91*, pages 485-495, 1991.

20. Saccà, D., and Zaniolo, C., "Stable models and non determinism in logic programs with negation", In *Proc. PODS'90*, 1990.

21. K. Satoh, and N. Iwayama. Computing Abduction Using the TMS. in *Proceedings 8th International Conference on Logic Programming ICLP91*, pages 505-518. Paris (F). June 1991. The MIT Press.

22. K. Satoh, and N. Iwayama. A Query Evaluation Method for Abductive Logic Programming. *Proceedings Joint International Conference and Symposium on Logic Programming JICSLP92*, pages 671-685. Washington (USA), November 1992, The MIT Press.

23. A. Van Gelder, K.A. Ross, and J.S. Schlipf. The Well-Founded Semantics for General Logic Programs. In *Journal of the ACM*, Vol. 38, No. 3, pages 620-650. ACM, 1991.

Abstract properties for the choice provability relation in nonmonotonic logics

Grigoris Antoniou

University of Osnabrück
Dept. of Mathematics and Computer Science
Albrechtstrasse 28, D-4500 Osnabrück, Germany
e-mail: ga@informatik.uni-osnabrueck.de

Abstract. We analyze the relationship between choice provability (derivability in at least one extension) of nonmonotonic logics, and the abstract properties of nonmonotonic inference relations proposed in the literature. We show that choice provability in default, autoepistemic and even cumulative default logic does not satisfy most of these properties. This is not accidental, but lies at the heart of choice provability, as far as formula-manipulating logics are concerned: Any such logic respecting some natural conditions has a noncumulative choice provability relation. In contrast to this result, we show that choice provability in the logic L1 recently introduced by Brewka is cumulative. This is possible because L1 manipulates defaults and not formulas.

1 Motivation

The semantics of several main nonmonotonic logics like default [7] or autoepistemic logic [5,6] is grounded on the notion of *extension* describing 'views of the world' that are possible w.r.t. the given knowledge. On the other side, inference relations must be defined for such nonmonotonic logics, as usual in logical formalisms. There are two principal possibilities to define such a relation. According to the *skeptical approach* (*skeptical provability*), a formula follows from the given (nonmonotonic) theory if it is contained in every extension of the theory. In the *credulous approach* (*choice provability*), a formula is inferred from a theory if it is member of at least one extension of the theory.

In this paper we shall consider abstract properties of the credulous approach. [3] is a very important work collecting some properties every nonmonotonic inference relation should fulfill, and discusses the semantics of such relations. The relationship to skeptical inference relations of concrete logics was thoroughly investigated, and it turned out that default logic does not satisfy the important property of *cumulativity*; this led to the development of cumulative versions of default logic [1,2].

Few attention has been paid until now to the relationship between the choice inference relation (according to the credulous approach) and the general properties. There is only partial knowledge about some properties that are not fulfilled by some concrete knowledge, and a feeling that choice provability is usually unsatisfactory from a logical point of view. In the present paper, we want to complete this picture by giving some formal results.

First we shall give an overview over properties that are or are not fulfilled by the credulous approach in default and in autoepistemic logic. Not very surprisingly, most results will be negative.

Then we turn our attention to cumulativity. First we show with a very simple example that choice provability in Brewka's Cumulative Default Logic is *not* cumulative (This must have been known to Brewka, so he uses a modified definition of choice cumulativity which is satisfied; see [1] for details). This result raises the question whether logics like CDL are not appropriate, and we should look for other versions of default logics. We give a negative answer by showing that the problem is a fundamental one: Choice provability and cumulativity are incompatible regarding *logics that manipulate formulas*. More precisely, we show that any nonmonotonic inference relation $\mid\sim$ is not cumulative if:

> *there exist a theory T and a formula φ satisfying some nontriviality conditions (see chapter 3 for details) such that* $T \mid\sim \varphi$ *and* $T \mid\sim \neg\varphi$.

In contrast to this result, we show in chapter 3 that Brewka's logic L1 [2] is cumulative in the credulous approach. This does not contradict the result sketched above because *L1 is actually manipulating defaults* instead of formulas.

Throughout the rest of the paper we assume that the reader is familiar with the basic concepts of default logic and autoepistemic logic.

2 Abstract properties for choice provability in default and autoepistemic logic: An overview

Definition (Abstract properties)

1.	Right weakening	$\models (\varphi \rightarrow \psi)$ and $\chi \mid\sim \varphi$ implies $\chi \mid\sim \psi$
2.	Reflexivity	$\varphi \mid\sim \varphi$
3.	Right And	$\varphi \mid\sim \psi$ and $\varphi \mid\sim \chi$ implies $\varphi \mid\sim (\psi \wedge \chi)$
4.	Or	$\varphi \mid\sim \chi$ and $\psi \mid\sim \chi$ implies $(\varphi \vee \psi) \mid\sim \chi$
5.	Left logical equivalence	$\models (\varphi \leftrightarrow \psi)$ and $\psi \mid\sim \chi$ implies $\varphi \mid\sim \chi$
6.	Cautious Monotonicity	$\varphi \mid\sim \psi$ and $\varphi \mid\sim \chi$ implies $(\varphi \wedge \psi) \mid\sim \chi$
7.	Cumulativity	If $\varphi \mid\sim \psi$, then $\varphi \mid\sim \chi$ and $(\varphi \wedge \psi) \mid\sim \chi$ are equivalent
8.	Rationality	$\varphi \mid\sim \chi$ and not $\varphi \mid\sim \neg\psi$ implies $(\varphi \wedge \psi) \mid\sim \chi$

> **Theorem** *The relationship between choice provability in default and autoepistemic logic and the abstract properties is given by Figure 1.*

Proof Right Weakening and Reflexivity are fulfilled because extensions are defined as deductively closed sets including the premises. Left Logical Equivalence holds for both logics because the definition of extensions refers to the semantics and not to the syntax of the premises. The results for Right And, Cautious Monotonicity and Cumulativity is easily shown using the Nixon diamond.

Property	Default logic	Autoepistemic logic
Right weakening	yes	yes
Reflexivity	yes	yes
Right And	no	no
Or	no	no
Left logical equivalence	yes	yes
Cautious Monotonicity	no	no
Cumulativity	no	no
Rationality	no	no

Figure 1

Here is a counterexample for choice provability in default logic satisfying Or: Consider the default theory {emu:flies/flies, ostrich:flies/flies}. Then emu |~ flies, ostrich |~ flies, but not emu∨ostrich |~ flies.

A counterexample for AE logic and Or: Let T = {Lp→r, Lq→r}. Then T∪{p} |~ r, T∪{q} |~ r, but not T∪{p∨q} |~ r. Finally, a counterexample for Rationality in default logic is the default φ:¬ψ/χ, in AE-logic the rule (φ∧¬Lψ→χ). ∎

Cumulative Default Logic [1] was developed by Brewka in order to overcome the lack of default logic to fulfill cumulativity [4]. The idea of the new logic is to keep the justifications used to infer a formula. Thus the logic treats assertions of the form <φ,J>, where φ is a formula and J a set of formulas, the justifications for φ. CDL can be shown to be cumulative in the skeptical sense. Unfortunately, it is *not* cumulative in the credulous approach, as shown by the following simple example.

Consider the assertional default theory with truths <rep,∅> and <qua,∅>, and defaults rep:¬pac/¬pac and qua:pac/pac. It has two extensions, one containing <pac,{pac}> and one containing <¬pac,{¬pac}>. But if we add <pac,{pac}> to the truths, then the first default becomes inapplicable, so <¬pac,{¬pac}> is no more choice deducible.

This example also shows that CDL choice provability does not satisfy Right And and Cautious Monotonicity. It neither satisfies Or and Rationality (use an adapted version of the counterexample for default logic).

Corollary *CDL choice provability does not satisfy* Right And, Cautious Monotonicity, Or *and* Rationality.

So, if CDL fails to provide cumulative choice provability, we may ask whether this logic is the right one (in this aspect; it is known that CDL has representational drawbacks that have led to the development of further variants of default logic). The following result gives a negative answer.

Definition (NM weak provability relation) $|\sim$ is called a NM weak provability relation iff

(1) For all formulas φ, ψ and sets of formulas M

$$M \cup \{\varphi\} \mid\sim \psi \text{ implies } M \cup \{\varphi\} \mid\sim \varphi \wedge \psi.$$

(2) For all formulas φ, ψ and sets of formulas M

$$M \mid\sim \varphi \text{ and } \varphi \models \psi \text{ implies } M \mid\sim \psi.$$

(3) There exist a formula φ and a set of formulas M such that

    a) $M \mid\sim \varphi$

    b) $M \mid\sim \neg\varphi$

    c) Not $M \cup \{\varphi\} \mid\sim \psi$ for all formulas ψ.

(1) states the premises are included in each extension; (2) means that extensions are deductively closed. (3) expresses that there are extensions including inconsistent information (choice!) in a nontrivial situation; it is essentially an adaption of the Nixon diamond in a general setting. The following observation shows that our definition covers some well-known logics (use the Nixon example!).

> **Lemma** *Choice provability in default logic and autoepistemic logic are NM weak provability relations.*

> **Theorem** *NM weak provability relations are not cumulative.*

Proof Let M and φ be as in (3) in the definition above. So, $M \mid\sim \varphi$ and $M \mid\sim \neg\varphi$. Suppose that $|\sim$ is cumulative. Then, we have also $M \cup \{\varphi\} \mid\sim \neg\varphi$. By (1) we obtain $M \cup \{\varphi\} \mid\sim \varphi \wedge \neg\varphi$, and by (2) $M \cup \{\varphi\} \mid\sim \psi$ for all formulas ψ. This contradicts (3) c). ∎

3 A default logic variant with cumulative choice provability

The argument of the previous section indicates that the choice provability relation of nonmonotonic logics *treating formulas* cannot be expected to be cumulative. Then we could ask what happens if the logic manipulates other syntactic objects. In this section we introduce the nonmonotonic logic L1 from [2] that manipulates defaults. It will turn out to be cumulative in the credulous approach (also in the skeptical; see [2]).

Definition (Rule system R_{L1})

R_{L1} consists of the following rules manipulating defaults:

R0 $\Rightarrow$ true:true/true

R1   true:φ/ψ, $\psi \models \chi \Rightarrow$ true:φ/χ

R2   true:φ_1/ψ_1, true:$\varphi_2/\psi_2 \Rightarrow$ true:$\varphi_1 \wedge \varphi_2/\psi_1 \wedge \psi_2$

R3   true:φ/ψ, $\psi:\rho/\sigma \Rightarrow$ true:$\varphi \wedge \rho/\sigma$

R4 $\varphi_1:\psi_1/\chi$, $\varphi_1 \leftrightarrow \varphi_2$, $\psi_1 \leftrightarrow \psi_2 \Rightarrow \varphi_2:\psi_2/\chi$

R5   true:φ/χ, true:$\psi/\chi \Rightarrow$ true:$\varphi \vee \psi/\chi$

R6 $\varphi_1:\psi_1/\chi_1$, $\varphi_2:\psi_2/\chi_2 \Rightarrow \varphi_1 \vee \varphi_2:\psi_1 \wedge \psi_2/\chi_1 \vee \chi_2$

In the logic L1, truths in form of formulas φ are represented as defaults true:φ/φ. Additionally, a theory may contain arbitrary defaults (for convenience and representational reasons only one justification is admitted).

Definition (L1-extension)
Let T be a default theory, C its closure under the rules in R_{L1}. E is an *extension* of T iff is a maximal subset of C such that

- All defaults of E are prerequisite-free.

- $\{d \in C \mid d = \text{true:true/}\varphi\} \subseteq E$

- Just(E)$\cup$Cons(E) is consistent (Just and Cons are the set of justifications and consequents respectively).

Example
Consider the tweety example: Theory T consists of defaults {true:true/peng, true:true/bird, bird:flies/flies}. Application of R3 to the second and third default and subsequent simplification via R4 yields true:flies/flies. This default is contained in the single extension of T. Addition of

true:true/(peng $\rightarrow \neg$flies)

leads using R2 and R1 to true:true/$\neg$flies. This default must be in any extension by definition, therefore the third default becomes inapplicable.

Example
Let us now consider the default theory for the Nixon diamond: T={true:true/rep, true:true/qua, rep:$\neg$pac/$\neg$pac, qua:pac/pac}. Application of R3 and R4 to defaults 1 and 3 in T yields

5.   true:$\neg$pac/$\neg$pac.

In the same way, application of R3 and R4 to defaults 2 and 4 in T yields

6.   true:pac/pac.

There are thus two extensions, one containing 5 and one containing 6. If we add 5 to the theory T, then there is still one extension containing 6 (since consistency with the consequents and justifications of the original theory is not required!). Contrary to the logics discussed so far, the Nixon diamond does not violate cumulativity of choice provability. This observation leads to the question whether the credulous approach of L1 is cumulative. This is indeed the case.

Theorem *The choice provability relation of L1 is cumulative.*

Proof Let true:φ/ψ be in an extension of a theory T. We have to show that adding it to T does not destroy old extensions and does not create new ones. This is quite trivial: true:φ/ψ is by definition of extensions an element of C, the closure of T under R_{L1}. This closure obviously remains the same if we add the default to T. The rest of the extension definition does not depend on T, but only on C. ∎

Actually, [2] introduces a general framework for the expression of various variants of default logic, and L1 is one of them. For all logics in this framework, the choice provability relation is cumulative.

4 Conclusion

In this paper we presented some results concerning abstract properties of the choice provability relation in nonmonotonic logics. Most of the results had a negative character. In particular, we proved that cumulativity cannot be expected to hold for choice provability in any sensible nonmonotonic logic that manipulates formulas.

The only positive result in this paper concerned logic L1: Its choice provability relation is cumulative. This does not contradict the negative results stated above, since L1 manipulates defaults instead of formulas. As this logic and its variants (see [2]) seem to solve also some known representational problems, it seems to be a good choice for the formalization of nonmonotonic reasoning. In any case, our results indicate that it may be better to switch attention from formula manipulating default logics to logics working on defaults.

Literature

1. Brewka, G.: Cumulative Default Logic - In Defence of Nonmonotonic Inference Relations. Artificial Intelligence 50, 1991

2. Brewka, G.: A Framework for Cumulative Default Logics. Technical Report TR-92-042, International Computer Science Institute, Berkley 1992

3. Kraus, S., Lehmann, D. and Magidor, M.: Nonmonotonic Reasoning, Preferential Models and Cumulative Logics. Artificial Intelligence 44, 167-207 (1990)

4. Makinson, D.: General Theory of Cumulative Inference. In Proc. 2nd International Workshop on Nonmonotonic Reasoning, LNCS 346, Springer 1989

5. Moore, R.C.: Possible-world semantics for autoepistemic logic. In *Proc. Non-monotonic Reasoning Workshop*, New Paltz 1984

6. Moore, R.C.: Semantical Considerations on Nonmonotonic Logic. Artificial Intelligence 25, 1985

7. Reiter, R.: A Logic for Default Reasoning. Artificial Intelligence 13, 1980

Characterizing Prime Implicants as Projective Spaces[*]

Fiora Pirri

Dipartimento di Informatica e Sistemistica

Universita' di Roma 'LaSapienza'

via Salaria 113, 00198 Roma

pirri@assi.ing.uniroma1.it

Clara Pizzuti

CRAI

Localita' S.Stefano

87036 Rende (CS)

clara@crai.it

Abstract

A new formalization of prime implicants through projective spaces is given. A formula is associated with a matrix over the set $\{0,1\}$. Every maximal set of linearly independent rows of such a matrix generates a vector space $\mathbf{V}$. We show that particular projective subspaces associated with the vector subspaces of $\mathbf{V}$ correspond to the prime implicants of the formula. This characterization enables the generation of prime implicants as solution set of a system of linear equations with constrains. Such a system is showed to be equivalent to an integer programming problem.

1 Introduction

The fundamental interest of *prime implicants* of a formula originally rose from the problem of reducing a formula to its simplest equivalent. In fact, in [5], Quine proved that any shortest normal equivalent of a formula ϕ in disjunctive normal form is a disjunction of its prime implicants. Such a minimization problem was relevant to a number of applications in electrical engineering, for example to reduce the number of components needed to realize a switching circuit. More recently it has been explored in diagnostic reasoning, in automated theorem proving and, more generally, in causal and hypothetical reasoning.

In this paper we present a novel approach to compute prime implicants of a formula ϕ in conjunctive normal form. We investigate the properties of prime implicants in a new perspective, i.e. we transform this problem in the equivalent one, in a geometric space, of finding projective spaces with some

[*]This work has been partially supported by "Progetto Finalizzato Sistemi informatici e Calcolo Parallelo" of C.N.R.

peculiar properties. This formalization leads us to the representation of the problem as a system of linear equations with constrains. In order to find the solution set of such system, an equivalent minimization problem, where the objective to minimize has a particular form, is solved. Both subsuming and inconsistency tests consist in just a constraint the problem must satisfy. Our method, therefore, avoids some of the disadvantages of other approaches such as dependency on clause ordering and subsuming test.

The paper is organized as follows: in Section 2 the representation of formulae by means of matrices, the concept of maximal implicant and the characterization of the prime implicants of a formula through the projective spaces are introduced, in Section 3, a method to find prime implicants is given, in Section 4, finally, some implementation issues and related works are presented.

2 Geometric Characterization of Prime Implicants

We assume a standard propositional language $\mathcal{L}$ with an enumerable set of *propositional letters*, denoted by both lowercase and uppercase letters and a set of logical connectives $(\wedge, \vee, \neg)$. The formulae, denoted by greek letters, are built using only these letters and connectives. CNF denotes a *conjunctive normal form*. The elements of a CNF are called *clauses*. An *implicant* of a formula ψ of $\mathcal{L}$ is a fundamental conjunction C such that $C \models \psi$, where $\models$ is logical entailment. C is called *prime implicant* if, given a fundamental conjunction C' such that $C' \models \psi$ and $C \models C'$, then $C' \models C$. For more precise definitions see [3]. Throughout the paper we assume formulae in conjunctive normal form, since as noted in [2], this is the syntactic form most often employed in automated theorem proving. Nevertheless, the same notions and results are applicable to disjunctive normal form by duality. In the following we assume known the concepts of matrix, vector space and projective space. For the formal definitions see [6]. Given a conjunction ϕ of clauses, let S be the set of literals occurring in it, where if $L \in \phi$ and $\neg L \in \phi$, we consider them as different literals without renaming them. ϕ can be represented with an $m \times n$ matrix over the set $\{0, 1\}$ in the following way.

Definition 1 *Let ϕ be given and let S be the literals occurring in it, a matrix A_ϕ with m rows and n columns whose components a_{ij} assume values in the set $\{0, 1\}$, is built as follows: 1) $a_{ij} = 1$ if the literal L_i occurs in the $j - th$ clause; 2) $a_{ij} = 0$ if the literal L_i does not occur in the $j - th$ clause.*

Note that a column of the matrix represents a clause whereas a row represents the presence of a literal in the clause. Every literal L_i is associated with the corresponding row $(a_{ij})_{j=1,...,n}$. In the sequel we denote an $m \times n$ matrix A, also as $< l_1 \ldots l_m >$, where l_i is the i-th row of A, thus every row l_i corresponds to a literal L_i. Given a matrix A of rank h, a *reduced matrix* of A of rank h, is a matrix A' built from A by deleting all the l_i of A which are linear combination of the others l_j. Reduced matrices provide a geometric characterization of some of the implicants of a formula, which will be called *maximal implicants*. In [4] we show that if A_ϕ is the matrix of a CNF ϕ, with rank h, the reduced matrix $A' = < l_1 \ldots l_r >$ of A_ϕ, of rank $r \leq h$, is associated with a *maximal* implicant if: 1) $< l_1 \ldots l_r >$ are linearly independent; 2) the set of literals associated with $< l_1 \ldots l_r >$ is consistent; 3) $< l_1 \ldots l_r >$ form a basis of a vector space $\mathbf{V}$.

Because of the representation of ϕ as a matrix, any formula ψ' such that $\psi \models \psi'$ is a prime implicant if it satisfies the two following conditions: 1) the row vector $\mathcal{V}$ obtained by summing up the row vectors $< l'_1, \ldots, l'_k >$ associated with ψ' can not have a null component; 2) the sum is minimal, i.e. if $\mathcal{V}$ is deprived of a row then it has a null component. This consideration immediately leads to the intuition that the concept of projective space is strictly connected with that of prime implicant. The role played by the unit point is analogous to the vector $\mathcal{V}$ just considered.

In fact, since every maximal implicant ψ of ϕ determines a vector space $\mathbf{V}$ and, consequently, a projective space $\mathbf{P}(\mathbf{V})$, we consider those projective subspaces of $\mathbf{P^{r-1}}(\mathbf{V})$ not contained in any coordinate hyperplane (those hyperplanes having the i-th homogeneous coordinate equal to zero) and having maximal codimension, i.e. there does not exist a subspace with greater codimension and contained in no coordinate hyperplane. The prime implicants of ϕ coincide with such subspaces and, thus, they are: 1) points of $\mathbf{P^{r-1}}(\mathbf{V})$, if they are generated by a single vector, 2) hyperplanes of codimension $r - 2$, i.e. lines, if they are generated by two points, 3) hyperplanes of codimension $r - 3$, i.e. planes, if they are generated by three points, and so on.

Definition 2 *Let* $< l_1, \ldots, l_r >$ *be a basis of* $\mathbf{V}$ *associated with a maximal implicant* ψ. *A projective subspace* $\mathbf{P}(\mathbf{W})$ *associated with a vector subspace* W *of* $\mathbf{V}$, *having* $l'_1, \ldots, l'_k$ *as basis, is said: i) P-implicant if its unit point* $P[x_1, \ldots, x_n] = P(l'_1 + \ldots + l'_k)$ *is such that* $x_i \neq 0 \; \forall i, i = 1, \ldots, n$; *ii) Prime if it does not contain a projective subspace whose unit point satisfies property i).*

Theorem 1 *Given* ϕ *and a maximal implicant* ψ *of* ϕ, *a prime implicant* ψ' *of* ϕ *such that* $\psi \models \psi'$, *generates a vector space whose projective space is a prime P-implicant.*

In the next section we give a method to obtain the prime P-implicant projective spaces.

3 A Method for Finding Prime Implicants

The representation of the original problem, i.e. finding the prime implicants of a formula ϕ in a projective space, allows us to characterize it as a linear programming problem. In fact, we shoh that the prime implicants of ϕ are generable as solutions of a system of linear equations with constraints. Let a conjunction of clauses ϕ, the associated matrix A_ϕ and a maximal implicant ψ, be given. Let $l_1, \ldots, l_r$ be the basis of the vector space $\mathbf{V}$ they generate.

Every row vector l_i can be written as a linear combination of the canonical basis $e_1, \ldots, e_n$ (1) $l_i = a_{i1}e_1 + \ldots + a_{in}e_n$ with numbers $a_{ij} \in \{0,1\}$. For instance, if $l_i = (1\ 0\ 1\ 1)$ then $l_i = 1e_1 + 0e_2 + 1e_3 + 1e_4$.

Let $\mathbf{W}$ be a subspace of the vector space $\mathbf{V}$ generated by A_ψ, $l'_1, \ldots, l'_k$ a basis of $\mathbf{W}$ and $\mathbf{P(W)}$ the projective subspace associated with $\mathbf{W}$ having projective basis $m_0, \ldots, m_k$. Let the dimension of $\mathbf{W}$ be k and, thus, the dimension of $\mathbf{P(W)}$ be k-1. The unit point of $\mathbf{P(W)}$, $m_0 = P(l'_1 + \ldots + l'_k)$ can be written as linear combination of the basis $l_1, \ldots, l_r$ with numbers belonging to $\{0,1\}$ (2) $m_0 = x_1 l_1 + \ldots + x_r l_r$, where $x_i = 1$ if $l_i = l'_j$ for some j and $x_i = 0$ otherwise. By substituting (1) in (2) we get: $m_0 = x_1(a_{11}e_1 + \ldots + a_{1n}e_n) + x_2(a_{21}e_1 + \ldots + a_{2n}e_n) + \ldots + x_r(a_{r1}e_1 + \ldots + a_{rn}e_n)$. If we now distribute the multiplication with respect to the addition and put together the e_i, we obtain $m_0 = (x_1a_{11} + x_2a_{21} + \ldots + x_ra_{r1})e_1 + \ldots + (x_1a_{1n} + x_2a_{2n} + \ldots + x_ra_{rn})e_n = \sum_{i=1}^r x_i a_{i1} e_1 + \ldots + \sum_{i=1}^r x_i a_{in} e_n$. If we now put $\lambda_j = \sum_{i=1}^r x_i a_{ij}$ we have $m_0 = \lambda_1 e_1 + \ldots + \lambda_n e_n$. Let us now consider the following system of linear equations

$$(3) \begin{cases} x_1 a_{11} + x_2 a_{21} + \ldots + x_r a_{r1} = \lambda_1 \\ x_1 a_{12} + x_2 a_{22} + \ldots + x_r a_{r2} = \lambda_2 \\ \quad \ldots \\ x_1 a_{1n} + x_2 a_{2n} + \ldots + x_r a_{rn} = \lambda_n \end{cases}$$

It is constituted by n equations and $r + n$ variables and thus it has ∞^r solutions. In [4] we show that it is possible to obtain a unique solution corresponding to a prime implicant contained in the maximal implicant considered, by imposing suitable constraints on the $r + n$ variables. In particular, we prove that a prime P-implicant projective space $\mathbf{P(W)}$ of dimension k-1 is the set of points solutions of the system of linear equations (3) which satisfies the constraint

$$(C2) \quad k \leq \sum_{i=1}^n \lambda_i \leq nk - (k-1)k$$

for $1 \leq k \leq n$ fixed. Let $Sol(\psi^{(3)})$ denotes the set of solutions of such system satisfying the constraint $(C2)$. Every element of $Sol(\psi^{(3)})$ is a vector of the form $\{x_{i_1} \ldots x_{i_k} x_{i_{k+1}} \ldots x_{i_r}\}$ such that $x_{i_1} = \ldots = x_{i_k} = 1$, $x_{i_{k+1}} = \ldots = x_{i_r} = 0$. The role of each x_{i_j} is to determine the row to choose in the maximal implicant. A matrix $A_{\psi'} = < l_{i_1} \ldots l_{i_k} >$, where each l_{i_j} corresponds to an $x_{i_j} = 1$ is called *solution matrix* of $Sol(\psi^{(3)})$. In [4] we proved *completeness* and *soundness* results of our method. In particular, we showed that if ψ' is a prime implicant of a propositional formula ϕ then there exists a solution matrix $A_{\psi'} = < l_{i_1} \ldots l_{i_k} >$ of $Sol(\psi^{(3)})$. Viceversa, every solution matrix $A_{\psi'} = < l_{i_1} \ldots l_{i_k} >$ of $Sol(\psi^{(3)})$ is associated with a prime implicant ψ' of a propositional formula ϕ, if k is the least k, satisfying C2, for which $x_{i_1} = \ldots = x_{i_k} = 1$.

4 Implementation and Related Works

In order to obtain all the prime implicants of a formula we have to search for all the associated maximal implicants and, then, for every one of them, pick the prime implicants it contains. Such an approach, however, is inefficient since the number of maximal implicants can be high and the same prime implicant, being contained in several maximal implicants, could be regenerated many times. In [4] we showed that the set of solutions of each system of linear equations (3) built from a particular maximal implicant is contained in the set of solutions of the system of linear equations obtained by using all the row vectors of the matrix. Let us call such a system the *complete* system. The complete system differs from system (3) just in the number of elements of every row and the set of its solutions contains the union of the sets of solutions of all the possible systems (3) plus those solutions corresponding with contradictory implicants because of the presence of inconsistent literals, which can not appear in equations of form (3) by definition of maximal implicant. We proved that, if from the set of solutions of the complete system we discard those containing inconsistent literals, the two sets of solutions will coincide. To this end it is sufficient to add to the complete system constraints of the form $x_{j_s} + x_{l_s} = 1$, where x_{j_s} corresponds to a literal L and x_{l_s} to its negation $\neg L$, if L is a literal appearing both positive and negative in the formula ϕ. Furthermore, a sound and complete algorithm for finding all the prime implicants of a formula was defined. The algorithm incrementally generates the prime implicants constituted by a single literal, by two literals, and so on by t literals by solving at each step the complete system of linear equations with constraints. This task is accomplished by transforming the complete system in a problem of *Integer Programming* [1] where the objective to minimize has a particular form. We showed that the algorithm is sound and complete. The algorithm has been implemented by using the *LINDO (Linear INteractive and Discrete Optimizer)* computer program, an interactive linear, quadratic and integer programming system developed by Schrage.

Numerous algorithms [5,7,2,8] for computing prime implicants of formulae in both conjunctive and disjunctive normal form have been proposed in the literature. One of the oldest is due to Quine [5] known as the *consensus method*. In [7] a *depth-first search* through a *semantic tree* is done and the concept of *frequency ordering* on literals occurring in the formula is introduced. In [2] a method, called *Matrix Method*, performs a *breath-first search* through a matrix of clauses ordered with respect to a function on the cardinality of the set of literals already considered and their complements. In [8] a formula is represented by means of a matrix where the rows are labeled with the variables of the formula and the columns with the number of its subformulae. Prime implicants are found by generating all the paths through the matrix.

Our method uses the same data structure as [8] to represent a formula, i.e. an $m \times n$ matrix but in a completely different perspective. In fact, the established correspondence between prime implicants and projective spaces with particular characteristics leaded us to the representation of the problem as a system of linear equations with constrains. The resolution of such a system can be done by exploiting already known and efficient techniques from mathematical programming. In fact in [4], we showed that the system can be transformed in an equivalent optimization problem whose solution set coincides with the solution set of the original system. Such an approach is completely new and provides a method which avoids some of the disadvantages owned by the outlined approaches. In fact, 1) it does not depend on finding the best clause ordering like [7,2], in order to avoid generation of implicants which are not prime or to reduce the search space; 2) both subsuming and inconsistency tests consist in just augmenting the set of constraints.

5 Conclusions

We proposed a novel approach to characterize prime implicants of a formula ϕ through a geometrical method, in particular we represented ϕ by means of a matrix over the set $\{0,1\}$ and we showed that prime implicants of ϕ determine projective spaces satisfying special constraints. In order to obtain them it is sufficient to find the solutions of a system of linear equations with constraints. Such an approach is completely new in the literature and created a link among logical, geometric and mathematical programming concepts.

6 Acknowledgment

We wish to thank Luigia Carlucci Aiello, Margherita D'Aprile and Manlio Gaudioso.

References

[1] Dantzig G., *Linear Programming and Extensions*, Princeton University Press, Princeton, New Jersey, 1963.

[2] Jackson, P. and Pais, J., "Computing Prime Implicants", *Proc. International Conference on Automated Deduction*, Lecture Notes on Artificial Intelligence 449, pp. 543-557, 1990.

[3] Mendelson, E., *Introduction to Mathematical Logic*,Van Nostrand, Princeton, 1964.

[4] Pirri, F. and Pizzuti, C., *A geometric method to compute prime implicants*, DIS, Technical Report, 1992, Università di Roma "La Sapienza".

[5] Quine, W. V. O., "The problem of simplifying truth functions", *American Math. Monthly*, 59 (1952), 521-531.

[6] Sernesi, E., *Geometria1*, Boringhieri, 1989.

[7] Slagle, J. R., Chang, C. L. and Lee, R. C. T., "A New algorithm for generating prime implicants", *IEEE Trans. on Comp.*, **19**(4) (1970), 304-310.

[8] Socher, R., "Optimizing the clausal normal form transformation", *Journal of Automated Reasoning*, 7 (1991), 325-336.

EFH-Soar: Modeling Education in Highly Interactive Microworlds *

Cristina Conati

Intelligent Systems Program, University of Pittsburgh
Pittsburgh, PA, 15260, USA

Jill Fain Lehman

School of Computer Science, Carnegie Mellon University
Pittsburgh, PA 15213-3890 USA

Abstract

The goal of our work is to produce a process model account of education in microworlds based on Soar, a theory of cognition and learning. In
the context of a microworld that supports the exploration of qualitative
electrostatics, we present operational models of both skilled and student
interaction. In addition, we describe an episodic memory mechanism encoded in the student model that gives insight into the processes involved
in learning from incorrect behavior.

1 Introduction

In the field of computer-aided instruction, highly interactive microworlds have
gained importance as educational tools aimed at supporting learning by exploration[7]. In contrast to more traditional educational strategies that "teach" the
target knowledge to the student, learning by exploration focuses on stimulating
the student's initiative in gaining knowledge about the domain[10, 11]. Highly
interactive microworlds provide simulations that allow the student to experience the nature of some subject-matter domain through active exploration of the
model's laws and behaviors.

Claims for the efficacy of interactive education have naturally led to studies
evaluating those claims (for example, [3, 4, 5, 13]). For the most part, the format
of such studies have fallen into the standard psychological experimental paradigm:
a treatment group is exposed to an alternative instructional method (for example,

*This research was sponsored by the Markle Foundation. The views and conclusions con-
tained in this document are those of the authors and should not be interpreted as representing
official policies, either expressed or implied, of the Markle Foundation.

computer-aided drill) while a control group is taught under normal classroom conditions. Performance of the two groups on a post-test measure of learning and transfer is then compared for evidence of a treatment effect. Because this method of evaluation examines only aggregate behavior and does not model the learning process itself, the results are usually difficult to interpret. When a treatment effect is found, it is unclear which aspects of the instructional method were responsible for the effect, i.e., which aspects enabled the superior learning or transfer. Similarly, when treatment effects are absent, it is unclear which aspects are at fault.

In contrast, we adopt a theory-based, cognitive approach to studying the question of instructional efficacy, believing that to evaluate a method of education we must understand the nature of the learning process itself. In essence, we propose to understand student learning behavior in highly interactive environments in terms of Soar, a specific theory of human cognition.

This paper describes the first stage of the EFH-Soar project, consisting of the formalization of the knowledge necessary to interact with a highly interactive environment within a model of a skilled player. Preliminary results obtained from the implementation of a student model are also presented.

2 The Subject-matter Domain

Our subject-matter domain is simple discrete electrostatics (hereafter, simply electrostatics). It consists of the electrostatics of discrete charged particles, all having the same mass. The relevant quantitative knowledge, linear attraction/repulsion of forces, Coulomb's Law and F = ma, is generally covered in about eight weeks of instruction in an elementary physics course.

Our interactive microworld is Electric Field Hockey (hereafter, simply Hockey) [2]. With respect to electrostatics, Hockey involves determining the trajectory of a unit-charge particle (the puck) from a given initial position, around a given set of obstacles, to a fixed final position (the net), by placing a number of additional unit-charge particles (Figure 1). The motion of the puck along its path is shown during the drawing of the trajectory. In addition, the puck's velocity is recorded statically by the spacing of the dots that represent the path followed.

The student has a limited number of options in controlling exploration in Hockey: specifically, the dot representation of velocity can be replaced with a vector representation of acceleration, and any of seven levels of increasingly difficult play may be chosen. Increasing difficulty is achieved by varying the initial state of play along four dimensions: the number and configuration of obstacles, the starting position of the puck with respect to the boundaries of the playing field and the obstacles, the existence of additional, unmoveable charged particles in the field, and the number of charged particles available to the player to maneuver the puck into the net.

As a basis for building the operational models we are interested in, a nearly complete video record of two students' education in the domain has been collected, culminating in sessions in which the students interact with Hockey as a class assignment. The purpose of the curriculum was to teach students a purely

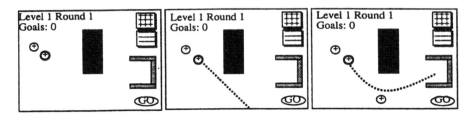

Figure 1: Electric Field Hockey: an example of interaction at Level 1.

qualitative model of electrical and magnetic phenomena as a theoretical basis for later, standard quantitative material [12]. In the course, students worked in groups of two through a notebook of desk-top experiments to be performed and questions to be answered. Our video record is of one such team. To date, we have concentrated on studying the video related to the performance of one of the two students (hereafter, Student 2) in her interaction with Hockey.

3 The Soar Cognitive Architecture

Soar [6, 8] belongs to a family of cognitive theories that share important features both in terms of psychological mechanisms and methods of use (see, e.g., [1, 9, 14]). These theories characterize human cognition as goal-directed problem solving.

As a particular member of this family, Soar can be described as a system that formulates tasks in terms of problem spaces, operators, and states. Problem solving proceeds in a sequence of *decision cycles*. Each decision cycle accumulates knowledge from a long-term, production-based *recognition memory* by allowing all the productions whose conditions match working memory elements in the current state to fire in parallel. The knowledge that is added to the state represents preferences concerning the next step to take. Once quiescence is reached (no more productions fire) a fixed *decision procedure* examines those preferences in order to choose a new problem space, operator, or state. If there is enough knowledge in long term memory to make the decision procedure's choice unequivocal, the preferred next step is taken and the next decision cycle entered.

If, on the other hand, Soar does not know how to proceed in a problem space because there is not enough knowledge to suggest a next step, or there is conflicting knowledge suggesting more than one step, an *impasse* has occurred. In response to an impasse, Soar creates a subgoal and a new problem space in which to acquire the missing knowledge (an impasse within the new space will have the same effect, i.e. Soar creates its own goal-subgoal hierarchy automatically as a result of being unable to proceed). Once an impasse has been resolved by problem solving in the subspace, the Soar learning mechanism (*chunking*) captures the result of problem solving in new productions. Chunking acts as knowledge compilation device and is automatic rather than deliberate, being invoked whenever an impasse is resolved. It has been used successfully to characterize learning in many tasks and domains, although it has not been previously applied to the types of educational environments that are the focus of EFH-Soar.

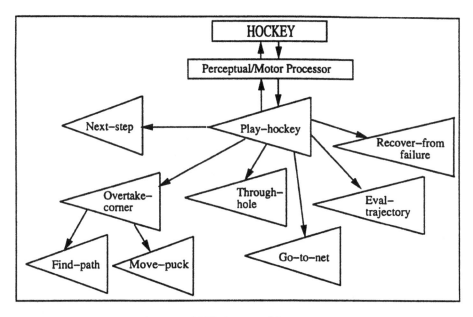

Figure 2: EFH-Soar problem spaces.

Figure 2 shows a portion of the problem spaces and operators that make up the current model. The model possesses the basic functionality for interacting with Hockey as a piece of external software, for re-encoding Hockey's spatial representation in symbolic terms, for reasoning about the placement of charges to create a trajectory that manuevers around or through an obstacle, for interpreting and evaluating a trajectory in terms of the forces that determine it, and for modifying the position of previously placed charges on the basis of the resulting trajectory.

We view the model in Figure 2 as a highly skilled Hockey player. At the lowest three levels of the game, it has the knowledge to play perfectly given the limits of its perceptual representation.[1] Constructing the system as a highly skilled player helps us understand what is necessary to have Soar play Hockey and provides a knowledge-level description of the student who has acquired the subject-matter domain. Thus, much of this system will form the basis of the student models. Indeed, our preliminary analysis of Student 2's behavior shows that the skilled model is a good fit at Level 1 of the game. At Level 3, however, the skilled

---

[1] Like humans, the model uses a symbolic spatial representation which has a grain size much larger than the actual number of unique locations in the field represented inside Hockey. In other words, neither we nor the model can guide the mouse to place a charge at a particular pixel location. Thus, EFH-Soar's intended location corresponds to a region inside the microworld. As a result, positioning of a charge can be correct at the higher level of granularity but slightly off at the lower level.

model performs correctly, while Student 2 does not. The discrepancy allows us to pinpoint both places where a model of Student 2 must differ from the skilled model and instances in Student 2's behavior where learning may occur.

4 EFH-Soar: The Skilled Model

The problem space description shown in Figure 2 gives a static view of the system at one level of detail. In this section we expand this view to include EFH-Soar's main knowledge structures and dynamic behavior.

4.1 Spatial Cognition and Representation

The essential feedback from Hockey takes the form of continuous trajectories of the puck as it moves under the influence of the fixed charges. How does the student perceive this continuous curve, such that it can be reasoned about by the symbolic processes that make up the student's knowledge? An analogous problem exists for output: how does the student's symbolic reasoning result in the placement of a charge in a continuous field? Both of these problems are simply specific (somewhat specialized) instances of the general, deep issue of moving between the continuous and quantitative on the one hand and the symbolic on the other.

In working with Hockey, we have developed a strong hypothesis about the human cognitive representation of the spatial world and how it relates to perception. Its most important property is that it is a highly approximate, qualitative representation that depends on continuous re-perception of the actual external world (the source of high-quality knowledge) to update and correct the low-quality internal representation. Thus, although the internal representation that cognition works with is approximate, it does not degrade. This hypothesis is coupled with many additional (unimplemented) mechanisms for how the symbol representation increases its discrimination, how perception maps the symbolic representation into the spatial world, and so on. EFH-Soar contains an initial realization of the hypothesis that extends prior work in this area [15].

Hockey is implemented in an object-oriented programming language developed at the Center for Design of Educational Computing at Carnegie Mellon University [2, 12]. For each object on the screen, Hockey encodes the coordinates of its position and its type. The objects are the puck, obstacles, net, charges placed on the screen, two boxes containing the available charges, and control buttons. In addition, the trajectory that displays the motion of the puck consists of points placed at equal time intervals, so that their spacing reflects the puck's speed. The program encodes up to 200 pairs of x-y coordinates in a trajectory.

The Perceptual-Motor Processor (PMP, see Figure 2) accomplishes the translation between Hockey's quantitative representation of the screen and the qualitative internal representation that is EFH-Soar's knowledge of the external world. This internal representation is EFH-Soar's *spatial model*. It encodes relative positions among objects whose descriptions vary in level of detail as a function of focus of attention. Specifically, the spatial model consists of:

- A structure, called the *spatial mapping*, with the following attributes:

  - *linear scale*: the scaling factor that filters all distances returned by the visual processor to be within the range of the system's internal resolution. The scaling value in the current model is 10.

  - *angular resolution*: the level of resolution for direction available in the internal representation. Currently the system descriminates 32 angles.[2]

  - *center of focus*: encodes the object that is the center of the focused area.

  - *focused objects*: a list of other objects in the focused area.

- The list of objects present on the screen. The objects explicitly represented in the spatial model are those encoded by the Hockey program plus the corners of the net and obstacles. If an object is not in focus, the only information explicitly available to the system is the object's type. If a shift of attention brings it into the focused area, its other attributes are added to the spatial model.

- Descriptions of the relative positions of objects within the focused area. These descriptions are encoded in two different ways: *spatial relations* define relative position in terms of the attributes left, right, below and above; *displacements* define relative position in terms of the distance and the relative direction between two objects.

The system performs visual operations by issuing visual commands to the PMP. Visual commands are used to perceive new situations and to perform shifts of attention to different areas of the screen.

4.2   An Example of Problem-solving Behavior

The problem spaces in Figure 2 organize the knowledge EFH has to play Hockey. We consider a portion of that knowledge in tracing the system's behavior through the example in Figure 3. For convenience to the reader, the area in focus is circled in each picture, and focused objects appear in boldface in the state representation.

The first operation EFH-Soar performs in playing a new game is to perform a visual operation to acquire the spatial model of the current screen, with the puck as the center of focus (Figure 3a). Once the spatial model has been established, the system uses the *Next-step* problem space to propose a subtask for sending the puck into the net. The system, like our students, chooses subtasks by working its way left to right across the screen. Four subtasks are currently defined. *Overtake-corner* is used when the puck must clear a simple obstacle before reaching the net. *Through-hole* is used when the puck must go through an opening between

---

[2] The numbers in the spatial model have been established empirically by observing the system in interaction with Hockey. We believe that, in theory, a fixed resolution size is wrong and should be replaced with a mechanism for varying resolution depending on the grain size of the spatial reasoning performed. Modeling this variability is one of the project's future goals.

53

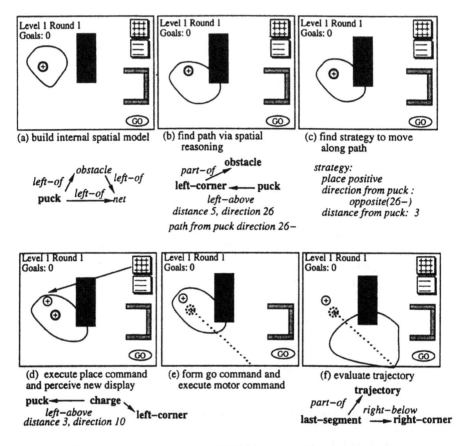

Figure 3: An example of EFH-Soar's problem-solving loop.

complex obstacles (see Figure 4). *Go-to-net* is used when no obstacle remains between the puck and the net. *Recover-from-failure* is used after an action fails to achieve the goal of the subtask.

The problem spaces that implement the first three subtasks have a common structure. They map the current spatial model into a motor action that performs the current subtask. Defining this motor action consists of two main phases:

- The spatial reasoning phase defines the trajectory that the puck must follow to accomplish the current subtask. Spatial reasoning is performed by operators in and subspaces of the *Find-path* problem space. To clear the obstacle in Figure 3, for example, the system defines a path to clear one of the obstacle's left corners by first performing a shift of focus to bring the obstacle into the focused area. Then, to decide which way to clear the obstacle, it brings into focus the obstacle's two left corners. Analyzing the direction between the puck and each of the two corners, the system chooses which corner to use to clear the obstacle, selecting the one that defines the smallest angle. The final path is defined as the direction between the puck and the chosen corner, slightly decremented to allow the puck to clear the edge (Figure 3b).

- The domain reasoning phase uses the *Move-puck* problem space to find a strategy that moves the puck along the desired path via game actions. It is in this space that the system decides whether to use an attractive or a repellent force, how many charges to place, and where to place them. Since we assume that everyone can perform the spatial reasoning to define a path for the puck to follow, it is in the Move-puck space that we expect to find the differences between a skilled and novice player. Only a person with the necessary physics and game knowledge can take into consideration all the factors relevant to arriving at a good move. In the skilled model, the rules in the *Move-puck* space encode knowledge about repulsion and attraction, superposition, and the effect of distance. In the example in Figure 3, these rules suggest both the strategy of placing a repelling charge close to the puck to move it along the desired path (Figure 3c) and a corresponding motor action.

Every motor action proposed by a subtask is translated by the PMP into a Hockey command using the linear-scale and angular resolution contained in the spatial mapping. Once the action has been performed, the PMP perceives the new screen and modifies EFH-Soar's spatial model. As a default, the result of an action becomes the center of focus and all the objects previously focused on remain so (Figure 3d).

The system is now ready to click on the GO button, displaying the trajectory of the puck subject to the electrostatic force created by the placed charge (Figure 3e). The PMP encodes a qualitative representation of the trajectory in the spatial model which the system then focuses on using the *Evaluate-trajectory* problem space. The trajectory is evaluated in terms of the subparts defined by the positions of the objects relevant to the current subtask. In our example (Figure 3f), since the last portion of the trajectory overtook the chosen corner, the performed action is recognized as successful.

Having achieved the subgoal, the system again uses the *Next-step* problem space to define the next subtask to accomplish. Since there are no other obstacles between the puck and the net in our example, EFH-Soar chooses to try sending the puck directly into the net and the *Go-to-net* subtask is proposed. By repeating the phases of finding a path to accomplish the current subtask and a corresponding strategy to achieve the path, the skilled model eventually sends the puck into the net.

5 EFH-Soar: The Student Model

Given the skilled model described above, we have begun to build a student model for one of our two videotaped subjects. At Level 1, Student 2's behavior matches that of the skilled model.

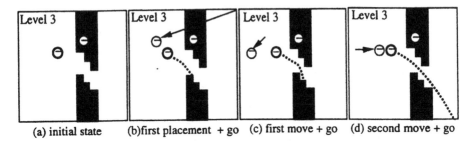

| (a) initial state | (b)first placement + go | (c) first move + go | (d) second move + go |

Figure 4: An example of learning from incorrect behavior.

The performances of the skilled model and the student begin to diverge at Level 3, when Student 2 faces the situation shown in Figure 4a. Her first action is the placement of a repelling charge that is inadequate to overcome the effects of the charge glued to the obstacle (Figure 4b). Her next move (Figure 4c) seems to be an attempt to compensate for the direction of the force produced by the glued charge but is still too far away to produce the desired outcome. Finally, in (Figure 4d), the forces combine correctly to achieve her subgoal of pushing the puck through the hole. When she faces an analogous situation at Level 4 of the game, Student 2 does not repeat this series of actions. Instead, she places the initial repelling charge directly at the position analogous to the one in Figure 4d. This episode is an example of learning from previous error. Although the capability to gain experience from past failures is a basic component of human learning, it tends to be problematic for machine learning systems that, like Soar, learn while doing. The difficulty is not so much in noticing, post hoc, that a choice was wrong, as it is in unlearning what was learned on the way to making that choice. In the remainder of this section we outline a general mechanism we have developed to allow EFH-Soar to model learning from incorrect behavior.

5.1 Learning from Incorrect Behavior

To model the student's initial incorrect behavior (Figure 4b), we eliminate from the skilled model the knowledge that takes into consideration the influence of close charges when computing a new placement. We call this modified model EFH2. The first time EFH2 faces the situation in Figure 4a, the model, like the student, ignores the effects of the glued particle, placing a charge aligned with a path through the opening. It chooses to place the charge at a distance from the puck that was adequate to achieve its goals at Level 1. EFH2 then clicks on the GO button and evaluates the resulting trajectory. Since it detects a failure, problem solving continues in the *Recover-from-failure* space where an action that adjusts the direction of the placed charge is selected (Figure 4c). Another GO reveals the second failure, and the *Recover-from-failure* space proposes an action that brings the charge closer to the puck (Figure 4d), allowing the puck to move through the opening. Chunks are built throughout the problem solving episode just described. When faced with a situation similar to Figure 4a in the future, these chunks will be triggered and EFH2, unlike Student 2, will repeat the sequence of proposing the first wrong placement, evaluating it, performing the direction adjustment, evaluating the second failure, and proposing the final, correct movement.

5.2 Overcoming Incorrect Behavior Through Assimilation and Recall

Our preliminary solution to this problem lies in giving EFH2 a simple episodic memory that is created and used by processes that allow the system to reconstruct past problem solving in order to avoid repeating mistakes. *Assimilation, recognition*, and *recall* are the three processes that must be coordinated. Although the details of the implementation are beyond the scope of this paper, it is critical to note that these mechanisms do not substitute for or supplant chunking; rather, they arise from chunking over additional types of problem solving in the model, as described below.

EFH's simple episodic memory is built up through the process of assimilation. Specifically, when a subtask proposes an action, the system uses an impasse into an *Assimilate* problem space to notice the features of the current situation. A situation is defined by the objects in focus, the current subgoal and the proposed action. The *recognition chunks* that result from the resolution of an Assimilation impasse will recognize the current situation as one that has been seen before, if it is encountered again in future problem solving. Assimilation is also performed after the evaluation of each action. In this case the situation comprises the outcome of the action (success or failure).

How do recognition chunks allow EFH2 to modify its behavior and learn to overcome its previous incorrect actions? The second time the system is in the state in Figure 4a, the chunk that proposes the first placement will fire, allowing the recognition chunks to detect the state and the proposed action as a situation it has seen before. This recognition causes an impasse into the *Recall* problem space where the system tries to avoid performing an unsuccessful move by recalling, *before* it acts, what the outcome of the action will be. In order to recall what happened the last time the proposed action was performed in the same state, the system must "imagine" the result of the action. Imagining means simply that a new charge and its spatial attributes are added to the spatial model without actually being present on the Hockey screen. If we annotate this state with "success" and a recognition chunk fires, we know that the placement was successful in the past. If no recognition chunk fires, we can annotate the state with different failure types; the failure type that triggers a recognition chunk represents the previous outcome of the current action in the current situation.

Once a failure has been recalled, EFH2 must reconstruct its prior problem solving to find the actions that led to success. To accomplish this, the system uses the *Recover-from-failure* space to reason about the imagined state, triggering the chunks that suggest the movement of the charge in Figure 4c. The recall/recognition process continues by imagining the movement of the charged particle, recalling the second failure, recalling the adjustment of the distance and the resulting success. Since the sequence of actions eventually leads to a success, the system resolves the impasse into the Recall space by substituting for the proposed (but unperformed) place action a new action that places the charge in the final position in Figure 4d. As the impasse resolves, chunking creates a new piece of knowledge that maps the original situation (Figure 4a) directly into this new action. Thus, the second time the model encounters the situation in 4a it must recall its prior mistakes to overcome its initial incorrect learning; but the third time it encounters 4a, it behaves skillfully, acting appropriately without problem solving.

6 Conclusions and Future work

The goal of the work presented here is to produce a process model account of education in microworlds. The skilled model helps us to understand what is necessary to have Soar play Hockey and gives a knowledge-level description of the student who has acquired the subject-matter domain. Future work will be directed at developing a model of the processes involved in the transition from naive to skilled player. This model should make clear what (if any) improvement in physics knowledge occurs during the transition. Our observation of student players indicates that it may be possible for a student to become skilled by solving problems in game terms, i.e. without significantly improving her physics knowledge. For this reason, the distinction between physics knowledge and game knowledge is fundamental to predicting the educational effectiveness of the microworld. It is part of our future work to formalize this distinction in EFH-Soar.

A first result in the development of a student model has been the realization of a mechanism for learning from incorrect behavior. Yet, the processes of assimilation, recognition, and recall discussed in the previous section are problematic because they are capable of reconstructing chains of memories of arbitrary length and involving the imagination of an arbitrary number of changes to the spatial model. This flaw in the mechanism is the result of two simplifying assumptions: first, that assimilation captures all and only the necessary details of the situation and second, that assimilation, recognition, and recall are automatic and unmediated by other processes.

The modified form of the mechanism we envision relaxes these assumptions. In it, each episodic memory is constructed by a potentially inaccurate assimilation process that can be automatic or mediated by further problem solving. If assimilation is no longer guaranteed to capture the complete and correct details of the situation, overspecific episodes may result in the breakdown of the recognition and recall processes. This should constrain the recall capabilities of the system with respect to both the length of the problem solving sequence and to the relevance of the performed actions.

References

[1] Anderson, J. R., *Rules of the Mind*, 1993, Lawrence Erlbaum Associates, Hillsdale, New Jersey.

[2] Chabay, R. and Sherwood, B., *The Electricity Project and the cT Programming Language*, 1989, Center for Design of Educational Computing, Carnegie Mellon University, Technical Report No. 89-10.

[3] Clements, D. H., *Effects of Logo and CAI environments on cognition and creativity*, 1986, Journal of Educational Psychology, 78, 309-318

[4] Clements, D. H., *Metacomponential development in a Logo programming environment*, 1990, Journal of Educational Psychology, 82, 141-149.

[5] Klahr, D. and Carver, S. M., *Cognitive objectives in a Logo debugging curriculum: instruction, learning, and transfer*, 1988, Cognitive Psychology, 20, 362-404.

[6] Laird, J. E., Newell, A., and Rosenbloom, P. S., *Soar: An architecture for general intelligence*, 1987, Artificial Intelligence, 33, 1-64.

[7] Lawler, R., *Designing computer based microworlds*, 1987, New Horizons in Educational Technology, Yazdani, M., (eds), Ablex Publishing, Norwood, NJ,

[8] Newell, A., *Unified Theories of Cognition*, 1990 Harvard University Press, Cambridge, Massachusetts.

[9] Polson, P. G. and Kieras, D. E., A quantitative model of the learning and performance of text editing knowledge, 1985, in CHI '85 Proceedings.

[10] Schank, R., C., and Farrel, R. *Creativity in education: a standard for computer-based teaching*, 1988, Machine-Mediated Learning, 2, 175-194.

[11] Schaube, L., Glaser, R., Raghavan, K., and Reiner, M., *Causal models and experimentation strategies in scientific reasoning*, 1991, The Journal of the Learning Sciences, 2, 201-138

[12] Sherwood, B. and Chabay, R., *Electrical Interactions and the Atomic Structure of Matter: Adding Qualitative Reasoning to a Calculus-Based Electricity and Magnetism Course*, 1991, Proceedings of the NATO Advanced Research Workshop on Learning Electricity or Electronics with Advanced Educational Technology, Springer-Verlag, Berlin, Germany.

[13] Simon, T., *Claims for Logo; what should we believe and why?*, 1987, Computers, Cognition, and Development. Rutkowska, J. C. and Crook, C. (eds), Wiley and Sons.

[14] VanLehn, K., *Mind Bugs: The Origins of Procedural Misconceptions*, MIT Press, Cambridge, Massachusetts.

[15] Ward, B., ET-Soar: *Toward an ITS for Theory-based Representations*, Ph.D. dissertation, 1991, School of Computer Science, Carnegie Mellon University.

Foundations for Interaction: The Dependence Theory[1]

Cristiano Castelfranchi, Amedeo Cesta, Rosaria Conte, Maria Miceli

IP-CNR
National Research Council
Viale Marx 15, I-00137 Rome, Italy
pscs@irmkant.bitnet

Abstract. The problem of the interaction among intelligent and autonomous agents is in search of a theoretical foundation. In this paper we claim that this foundation of distributed activity, and in particular the treatment of some basic aspects of a model of sociality (the notion of common world, the reasons for having and pursuing social goals, and the functions of social behavior) presupposes and requires a theory of interdependence among the interacting systems.

1. The Challenge of Interaction, the Search for Foundations, and a Theory of Interdependence

Artificial Intelligence is currently accepting the challenge of dealing with the problems of interaction [BOB91]. It is no longer the case of designing an isolated Agent in a stable and predictable world, time- as well as context-independent. An agent should employ its limited cognitive capabilities to act in a changing and context-dependent world. In particular, it should deal with other agents, in a common world. Interestingly enough, the existence of other agents is on one hand a new source of uncertainty about the world; on the other hand, through sociality, it can turn into an answer to the limits of each individual agent.

The problem of the interaction among intelligent and autonomous agents is in search of a theoretical foundation [GAS91, HEW91]. Our claim is that this foundation of distributed activity, and in particular the treatment of some basic aspects of a model of sociality we are going to address, presupposes and requires a theory of interdependence among the interacting systems.

The notion of "common world". In our opinion, the very notion of *common world* cannot be defined outside such a basic theoretical perspective. In fact, when can one say that system x and system y are in a common world? We assume that x and y share a common world if the effects of y's actions *interfere* with the future of x's goals, and vice versa. That is, x's success or failure in achieving its goals should depend on y's behavior (besides x's own actions and the state of affairs). In order for x to achieve some goal of its own, y should do a certain action (including that of refraining from doing something). This is exactly the *dependence* relation, which we think of as the rational as well as evolutionary grounds of sociality.

The presupposed sociality. At present, the problem of social interdependence is solved by postulating the existence of common goals among the interacting systems, their mutual knowledge of their relations with each other, and of each other's mental states. In fact, AI distributed studies often presuppose a common task, a pre-established cooperativeness, a collective intelligence and capability for problem solving.

---

[1] This work has been partially supported by CNR under "Progetto Finalizzato Sistemi Informatici e Calcolo Parallelo", Grant n.104385/69/9107197 to IP-CNR. The authors participate in the "Project for the Simulation of Social Behavior" at IP-CNR and are listed in alphabetical order.

Conversely, there is little interest in a bottom-up approach, where intelligent autonomous agents, endowed with cognitive capabilities and endogenous goals, are placed in a common world (as defined above), and let interact.

Such a pre-established cooperativeness is a limitative and questionable solution to the problem of social interdependence. Sociality is in fact presupposed while it should be accounted for. Why should an autonomous agent enter into social interactions? Why should it agree to do something for another? How does it succeed in making other autonomous agents do something in its own interest? How does it happen that different agents come to share some of their goals?

If such questions are not addressed and no attempt is made at answering them, the problem of interaction turns into a simple matter of *coordination* of the agents' activities. Since in fact benevolence among the agents is given for granted and their goals are supposed to be common, nothing is to be explored other than the coordination of their acts.

On the contrary, a bottom-up approach to social interaction, which should address the abovementioned basic questions of sociality, in our view represents the only way to discover the agents' needs for sociality, be it cooperative or competitive, without presupposing them. In this perspective, dependence relations among agents in a common world would appear as the ground relations upon which the construction of sociality is based.

Advantages of interdependence and functions of sociality. Unlike Huberman and colleagues [CLE91], we do not assume that the greatest advantage of (cooperative) sociality is to speed up the search for solutions to common problems, or to find better solutions to them, but rather to *multiply individual "powers"*: any agent, while remaining limited in its capabilities, skills and resources, finds the number of goals it can pursue and achieve increased by virtue of its "use" of others' skills and resources. In one sense, any agent's limits of power, and its differences from others in the kind of power it is endowed with, turn into an advantage: although not omnipotent, the agent is allowed to overcome its computational, cognitive, and practical limits through "sociality". If this is true, a theory of distributed action and interaction requires to be grounded upon a theory of interdependence, aimed at exploring how each agent's limited capabilities concur to produce a network of social relations which even pre-exists the agents' behaviors, as well as their knowledge of the objective relations established.

This paper aims exactly at showing how a model of social dependence can be a key to understanding and explaining the basic ingredients of social behavior.

2. For an Explicit Theory of Social Dependence

Our search for the foundations of social interaction is grounded on few basic concepts all aiming at characterizing the agents' interdependence that rule human relationships in a social context. In the following, x and y denote agents with $x \neq y$ always implicitly stated; a denotes an action, and p a formula representing a state of the world.

An important concept is that of social dependence whose basic definition of social dependence is as follows [CAS92]:

$$(S\text{-}DEP \; x \; y \; a \; p) \quad =def \; (GOAL \; x \; p) \wedge \neg \, (CANDO \; x \; a) \wedge \; (CANDO \; y \; a)$$
$$\wedge \, ((DONE\text{-}BY \; y \; a) \supset EVENTUALLY \; p)$$

that is: x depends on y with regard to an act useful for realizing a state p when p is a goal of x's and x is unable to realize p while y is able to do so.

It should be stressed that, unlike what most DAI work seems to take for granted, social dependence is *not fundamentally mental*. It is an *objective* relationship, in that it holds *independently* of the agents' awareness of it. However, many relevant consequences may derive from x's and y's (either unilaterally or mutually) becoming aware of it: to mention just the most salient ones, x may try to *influence* y to pursue p, while y may choose whether to adopt x's goal or not.

Patterns of dependence relationships. Dependence relations may be compound in various ways generating different structures underlying the social context. Such structures are extensively investigated in [CAS92] where we distinguish cases either of *OR-Dependence*, a disjunctive compositions of dependence relations, and *AND-dependence*, cases in which there is a conjunction of dependence relations. To give a flavor of those distinctions we just detail the case of a reciprocal dependence between two agents *(bilateral dependence)*.
There are two possible kinds of bilateral dependence:
* *Mutual dependence*, which occurs when x and y depend on each other for realizing a *common goal* p, which can be achieved by means of a plan including at least two *different* acts such that x depends on y's doing a_1, and y depends on x's doing a_2:

    $(S\text{-}DEP\ x\ y\ a_1\ p) \wedge (S\text{-}DEP\ y\ x\ a_2\ p)$

    As observed in a previous work [CON91], *cooperation* is a function of mutual dependence: there is no cooperation in the strict sense without mutual dependence;
* *Reciprocal dependence*, which occurs when x and y depend on each other for realizing different goals, that is, when x depends on y for realizing x's goal that p_1, while y depends on x for realizing y's goal that p_2:

    $(S\text{-}DEP\ x\ y\ a_1\ p_1) \wedge (S\text{-}DEP\ y\ x\ a_2\ p_2)$

    Reciprocal dependence is to *social exchange* what mutual dependence is to cooperation.

From Dependence to the goal of influencing. The structure of interdependence among agents justifies the interactions among agents and in general biases the behavior of each agent towards the others. Among the social goals predictable from a dependence relationship, a crucial role is played by the *goal of influencing*. According to a simplified version of our definition of x's *goal of influencing* y, *INFL-GOAL*, we mean x's goal that y *has* a certain goal p:

$(INFL\text{-}GOAL\ x\ y\ p) =def (GOAL\ x\ (GOAL\ y\ p))$

Now, if x believes he is dependent on y relative to a, then he will have the goal that y performs a. But given the postulate on rational agenthood, according to which, in order to perform an action, an agent must want that action, *(GOAL x (DONE-BY y a))* is actually equivalent to *(GOAL x (GOAL y (DONE-BY y a)))*. Then x's dependence on y, when assumed, will also imply x's goal that y *has the goal to do a*. Now, being *(GOAL x (GOAL y (DONE-BY y a)))* nothing but a goal of influencing y relative to the goal that *(DONE-BY y a)*, x's dependence on y relative to a certain a useful for p will imply, when assumed, x's goal of influencing y to perform a:

$(BEL\ x\ (S\text{-}DEP\ x\ y\ a\ p)) \supset (INFL\text{-}GOAL\ x\ y\ (DONE\text{-}BY\ y\ a))$

So, if an agent assumes to be dependent on another relative to some goal, he will have the goal of influencing the other to perform the (set of) action(s) that allows him to achieve his goal. And, on the grounds of a given assumed *structure of its social dependence*, a structure is derivable of possible goals and actions of influencing.

3. Dependence as a Requirement for Collective Activities

That of coordination is a matter of major concern in DAI research. Almost by definition sociality is identified with coordination. In the current research about group formation and, in general, about collective activities, the *social agent* is a group whose members might be either social or individual agents. Two issues are therefore ignored or misunderstood: on one hand, the aforesaid *social individual agent* with his own interests in social interaction not necessarily oriented to improve coordination; on the other, the question of the formation of groups and collective entities.

The Joint Persistent Goal View of Collective Agents. The current debate has often been plagued with the strictures of a philosophical dispute around reductionism/non reductionism (see [RAO92]). The question of the formation of collective entities has become a matter of whether collective goals can or cannot be derived from the individual goals of their members. In particular, Cohen and Levesque ([COH90, LEV90]) support a *reductionist* view of collective entities, i.e. that which is derived from and based upon the individual agents' goals. Their view is based upon the notion of *joint persistent goals*: "A team of agents have a joint persistent goal relative to q to achieve p (a belief from which, intuitively, the goal originates) just in case: (1) they mutually believe that p is currently false; (2) they mutually know they all want p to eventually be true; (3) it is true (and mutually knowledge) that until they come to believe either that p is true, that p will never be true, or that q is false, they will continue to mutually believe that they each have p as a *weak achievement goal* relative to q and *with respect to the team*.", where a weak achievement goal with respect to a team has been defined as " a goal that the status of p be mutually believed by all the team members". Now, it is possible to show that this notion is not sufficient to account for a teamwork.

Let us consider Prof. Montaigner, of the Institute Pasteur in France, and Prof. Gallo in the US both have the final goal p "vaccine anti-AIDS be found out" relative to the belief q that "if vaccine is discovered, AIDS is wiped out". They share all three mental attitudes described above ((1), (2) and (3)), but no-one would stretch oneself up to saying that Prof. Gallo and Prof.Montaigner form a team. Indeed, given their parallel goals, they might come to strongly compete with each other. What else is needed for them to form a teamwork?

A Dependence-based notion of collective goals. According to our analysis, a *group of agents form a collective entity when all agents share a common goal or interest, each is required to do its share to achieve the common goal by the group itself or by a subcomponent, and adopts such request.* (To be noted, the notion of collective will is more complex: it also includes that of a normative will, that is, an entitled authority which assigns tasks to the group's members [CON93]. In addition a more analytical treatment of various kinds of group and team would be required. However, we cannot examine these aspects here.)

Our definition of collective agent can be expressed as follows, keeping in one's mind that by $(GOAL\ x\ p)$ it is here meant what [COH90] define as an achievement goal, that is x's goal that p will be eventually true and x's belief that it is not currently true:

$(COLL\text{-}AG\ x_i) = def$

$$\exists p(\wedge_{l=1,n}\ [(C\text{-}GOAL\ x_i\ p)$$
$$\wedge\ (\vee_{i=1,n}\ ((z=x_i)\wedge(BEL\ z\ (\wedge_{i=1,n}\ (DONE\ a_i)\ \supset\ EVENTUALLY\ p)))))$$
$$\wedge\ (C\text{-}GOAL\ x_i\ (BENEVOLENT\ x_i\ z\ p\ )))])$$

a common goal $(C\text{-}GOAL)$ being defined (cf. [CON91]) as *two or more agents having one and the same goal and being mutually dependent to achieve it.* Specializing the definition to the case of two agents we can say:

$(C\text{-}GOAL\ x\ y\ a_x\ a_y\ p) = def$
$$(GOAL\ x\ p) \wedge (GOAL\ y\ p) \wedge (S\text{-}DEP\ x\ y\ a_y\ p) \wedge (S\text{-}DEP\ y\ x\ a_x\ p)$$

The present notion of a collective agent ultimately relies upon the objective structure of interdependence among individual agents. This view allows us to rule out the example of scientific competition examined above: the two scholars do not depend on each other, and therefore they do not need to participate in a teamwork.

4. Dependence Relations and Agent Architecture

A crucial problem to be clarified concerns how this kind of analysis of social interaction can be actually used to improve the performance of intelligent systems. Our claim here is that as long as applications in which both human beings and machines interact in the same environment are going to be developed, the issue of cognitive plausibility of the intelligent machines at the interaction level will be more and more important.

To experiment this issue we have set up a simplified scenario aimed at showing the possible insertion of knowledge about dependence relations in an agent architecture in order for an artificial autonomous agent to achieve a cognitively plausible behavior. In particular we focalize on the process of planning a particular aspect of the agent's behavior, which strongly depends on the abovementioned relations: planning to act on other agents to obtain they perform some needed action he is not able to perform. Two aspects are critical in such a planning:

- the need to produce a social sub-plan by using well-founded heuristics that analyze the agent's social knowledge (i.e. his knowledge about others). Agent x should come to know not only which other agents he depends on and for what, but also some other relevant information about the others' mental states, including their goals as well as their beliefs about x's goals, about their own duties and roles, and about their own dependence relations;
- the need to avoid producing a plan which is in conflict with other general (or personal) goals of the agent .

Agent Architecture and Theory of Dependence. The agent we are currently implementing has a behavior strongly goal driven. It is named *CogAgent* to stress our attempt to endow it with the basic cognitive tools we have described so far. The agent's architecture has two main components: a propositional knowledge representation service, named KRAM [DAL93], developed within our group, and a blackboard style planning service. The planning component is given as input a number of goals *CogAgent* wants to achieve, and works to produce a plan for *CogAgent*. A number of specialists contribute to the creation of the plan that guides the agent's behavior: a *memory based planner* builds up initial plans for achieving the goals; a *resource analysis and allocation module*, once built a plan, is called into play for identifying any problem for the future action execution. In particular, for each plan action, this module tests whether: it is included in the action repertoire, and all resources implied by the action execution are accessible to the agent. After the resource analysis has identified the need for other resources, two specialists are called into play:

- A *social knowledge specialist* responsible for searching social resources, that is any other agent in the common world who might give x some help to get the work done.
- A *social goals conflict analyzer* responsible for scrutinizing social plans provided by other modules, in particular by the previous specialist, in order to check for negative interactions between such a plan and other goals (this module performs a task similar to conflict analysis in classical planning).

Although a lot of work remains to be done, we have been able to describe at least dependence-based criteria for searching agent "useful" to a particular problem solving context. We are also able to sketch the basic plans for obtaining others cooperation according to the context that *CogAgent* is considering (for lack of space we are not able to further describe this part of our work, see [CST93, MIC93] for details).

5. Conclusions

In this work we have attempted to argue in favor of the founding role of a notion of dependence for an explanatory model of sociality, of its arising, its advantages, the notion of common world, and that of collective agent. A sketch has been made of the basic components of a theory of dependence relations. A possible use of the various dependencies among agents has been suggested as "objective" knowledge of cooperation support systems. Finally, the possible insertion of knowledge about dependence relations in a cognitive agent's reasoning and planning modules has been briefly examined. A problem-driven approach to social interaction is typical of this perspective. Here sociality is neither given for granted nor traced back to varying degrees of overlapping among the agents' mental attitudes. On the contrary, the problem of why and under what conditions social interaction occurs is directly justified by the agents' problem solving: others are considered when help for some of the agent's problems is needed.

References

[BOB91] Bobrow, Dimensions for Interaction, *AI Magazine*, Fall 1991.
[CAS92] Castelfranchi, C., Miceli, M., Cesta, A., Dependence Relations among Autonomous Agents, in E.Werner, Y.Demazeau (Eds), *Decentralized A.I. - 3*, Elsevier, 1992.
[CLE91] Clearwater, S.H., Huberman, B.A., Hogg, T., Cooperative Solution of Constraint Satisfaction Problems, *Science*, Vol.254, pp.1181-1183, 1991.
[COH90] Cohen, P.R., Levesque, H.J., Intention Is Choice with Commitment, *Artificial Intelligence*, 42: 213-261, 1990.
[CON91] Conte, R., Miceli, M., Castelfranchi, C., Limits and levels of cooperation: Disentangling various types of prosocial interaction, in Y. Demazeau, J.P. Muller (Eds.), *Decentralized A.I.-2* , 1991.
[CON93] Conte, R., Castelfranchi, C., Norms as Mental Objects. From Normative Beliefs to Normative Goals, *Proc. of MAAMAW '93*, Neuchatel, Switzerland, 1993.
[CST93] Cesta, A., Miceli, M., In Search of Help: Strategic Social Knowledge and Plans, *Proc. of the 12th International Workshop on Distributed AI*, Hidden Valley, PA, 1993.
[DAL93] D'Aloisi, D., Castelfranchi, C., Propositional and Terminological Knowledge Representations, *Journal of Experimental and Theoretical Artificial Intelligence*, 5 (3), 1993.
[GAS91] Gasser, L., Social Conceptions of Knowledge and Action: DAI Foundations and Open Systems Semantics, *Artificial Intelligence*, 47, 1991,pp.107-138.
[HEW91] Hewitt, C., Open Information Systems Semantics for Distributed Artificial Intelligence, *Artificial Intelligence*, 47, 1991, pp.79-106.
[LEV90] Levesque, H.J., Cohen, P.R., Nunez, J., On Acting Together, *Proc. AAAI-90*, Washington, DC, 1990.
[MIC93] Miceli, M., Cesta, A., Strategic Social Planning: Looking for Willingness in Multi-Agent Domains, *Proc. of the Annual Meeting of the Cognitive Science Society*, Boulder, CO, 1993.
[RAO92] Rao, A.S., Georgeff, M.P., Sonenberg, E.A., Social Plans: A Preliminary Report, in E.Werner, Y.Demazeau (Eds), *Decentralized A.I. - 3* , 1992.

Letter Spirit:
An Architecture for Creativity in a
Microdomain

Gary McGraw and Douglas Hofstadter

Istituto per la Ricerca Scientifica e Tecnologica
Loc. Pantè di Povo, I38100 Trento, Italia

Center for Research on Concepts and Cognition, Indiana University
510 North Fess Street, Bloomington, Indiana 47408, USA

gem@cogsci.indiana.edu   dughof@cogsci.indiana.edu

Abstract. The Letter Spirit project explores the creative act of artistic letter-design. The aim is to model how the 26 lowercase letters of the roman alphabet can be rendered in many different but internally coherent styles. Viewed from a distance, the behavior of the program can be seen to result from the interaction of four emergent agents working together to form a coherent style and to design a complete alphabet: the Imaginer (which plays with the concepts behind letterforms), the Drafter (which converts ideas for letterforms into graphical realizations), the Examiner (which combines bottom-up and top-down processing to perceive and categorize letterforms), and the Adjudicator (which perceives and dynamically builds a representation of the evolving style). Creating a gridfont is an iterative process of guesswork and evaluation carried out by the four agents. This process is the "central feedback loop of creativity". Implementation of Letter Spirit is just beginning. This paper outlines our goals and plans for the project.

1 The Motivation of Letter Spirit

The Letter Spirit project is an attempt to model central aspects of human high-level perception and creativity on a computer, focusing on the creative act of artistic letter-design. Implementation of Letter Spirit is just beginning. This paper outlines our goals and plans for the project. The aim is to model the process of rendering the 26 lowercase letters of the roman alphabet in many different, internally coherent styles. Two important and orthogonal aspects of letterforms are basic to the project: the *categorical sameness* possessed by instances of a single letter in various styles (*e.g.*, the letter 'a' in Baskerville, Palatino, and Helvetica) and the *stylistic sameness* possessed by instances of various letters in a single style (*e.g.*, the letters 'a', 'b', and 'c' in Baskerville). Figure 1 illustrates the relationship of these two ideas. Starting with one or more seed letters representing the beginnings of a style, the program will attempt to create the rest of the alphabet in such a way that all 26 letters share the same style, or *spirit*.

Letters in the domain are formed exclusively from straight segments on a 3 × 7 grid (see Figure 2) in order to make decisions smaller in number and more discrete. This restriction allows much of low-level vision to be bypassed and forces concentration on higher-level cognitive processing, particularly the abstract and context-dependent character of concepts.

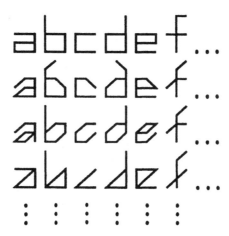

Fig. 1. Items in any column have *letter* in common. Items in any row have *spirit* in common. (Also see Fig. 3.)

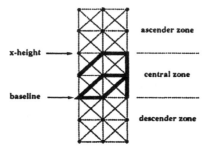

Fig. 2. The Letter Spirit grid, with one of the many possible sets of quanta instantiating an 'a' turned on.

While at first glance, the Letter Spirit domain might be shrugged off as a "toy domain", this would grossly underestimate its subtlety. In spite of, or rather *because* of, the reduction to the grid, the Letter Spirit challenge is, in terms of cognitive-science issues, extremely rich. The cognitive issues are magnified, not reduced, by the act of simplifying the domain. All that has been thrown out is the need for expertise. One need not be a professional typeface designer or lifelong student of letterforms to appreciate the consistency of a well-designed gridfont.

Even a novice can design a passable gridfont, though creating a sophisticated one is very difficult.

2 Letters as Concepts

In order to better distinguish the *concept* of a letter from various geometric shapes that may instantiate it, we introduce some terminology. We distinguish three conceptual levels, running from abstract to nearly concrete as they move toward the actual geometric letterform. The term *letter-concept* refers to the most abstract idea for drawing a letter without reference to style. This level is comprised of a set of *letter-conceptualizations*. A typical letter-conceptualization would be the notion that a 'b' consists of two "roles" — a *post* on the left side attached in two places to an open *bowl* on the right side, sitting on the baseline. A rival conceptualization for the same letter also consists of two roles — a *post* on the left side attached in one place to a closed *loop* on the right side, sitting on the baseline. These conceptualizations, possibly augmented by others, constitute the *letter-concept* of 'b'. Once a specific letter-conceptualization has been chosen, notions of style give rise to a more specific and detailed letter-conceptualization that partially specifies *how each role should be realized* (of course this conceptualization still could be realized in infinitely many ways). This is called a *letter-plan*. A letter-plan is present in a designer's mind before any marks are put on paper. The actual shape drawn on paper is a *letterform*. Letter Spirit is concerned with all these levels: play with letter-conceptualizations, creation of letter-plans, and the design of letterforms based on letter-plans.

A vivid example of the shape/concept distinction involves lowercase 'x'. For most US-educated adults, the only conceptualization for 'x' consists of a forward slash and a backward slash of the same size that cross somewhere near the middle. English children, by contrast, are taught to draw a lowercase cursive 'x' as a pair of small crescents facing away from each other but "kissing" in the middle. If we look at a printed 'x' in this way, we are suddenly struck by this new conceptualization. The shape on our retina is the same, but what is constructed in our mind's eye is very different.

The conceptual pieces into which a letter is broken in the mind's eye are its *roles*. For example, the two crossing slashes in an imagined 'x' are roles. So also are their four tips, and the crossing-point in the middle. Each role has a different degree of *importance* to the letter — the degree to which its presence or absence matters. Of course, different shapes instantiate a given role more strongly or more weakly than others. In other words, roles are also concepts with somewhat nebulous boundaries, just as *wholes* (complete letters) are. The difference is, membership in a role is easier to characterize than in a whole, so that reducing wholes to collections of interacting roles is a step forward in simplification.

The internal structure of a category is represented as a collection of interacting roles. Category membership at the whole-letter level is partially determined by category membership at the lower level of roles. In addition, *stylistic* appropriateness of a shape is judged in terms of *how roles are filled* — in other words, *how norms are violated*. Any such violation is a stylistic hallmark that must be propagated (via analogy) to other letters.

3   A Sketch of the Architecture

Letter Spirit is motivated by the belief that creativity is an automatic outcome of the existence of flexible and context-sensitive concepts. Its architecture is based on the principles of emergent computation, wherein complex high-level behavior emerges as a statistical consequence of the bottom-up cooperation of many small computational actions influenced by many dynamically changing top-down conceptual pressures. Micro-agents known as "codelets" build and destroy perceptual structures in a nondeterministic parallel manner, guided throughout by letter-concepts[1].

The Letter Spirit program will contain four dynamic memories, each concerned with different levels of concreteness and abstraction of shapes (and concepts pertaining to shapes). These memories are:

- the **Scratchpad**, which is *a virtual piece of paper* on which all the letters of a font are drawn and modified; as such it is more a type of external memory than an aspect of mental activity;

- the **Visual Focus**, which is *the site where perception of a given letterform occurs*; in it, perceptual structures are built up and converge to stable categorical and stylistic interpretations;

- the **Thematic Focus**, which is the program's *dynamically changing set of ideas about the stylistic essence of the gridfont under way*; in it are recorded stylistic observations of all sorts concerning letters already designed, and if and when some of these observations are perceived as falling into patterns, those patterns can be taken as determinant of the style, meaning they can be elevated to the status of explicit *themes* — ideas that play an active role in guiding further design decisions, in the sense of serving as "pressures" on the construction of further letters;

- the **Conceptual Memory**, which is the program's *locus of permanent knowledge and understanding of its domain*, and which, for each concept, has three facets: (1) a set of *category-membership criteria*, which specify the recognition requirements for instances of the concept in terms of more primitive concepts; (2) a set of *explicit norms*, which encode aspects of the concept's "core"; and (3) an *associative halo*, consisting of links having time-varying lengths connecting the concept with related concepts, thus giving a sense of where the concept is located in "conceptual space" by saying what it most resembles.

Viewed from a distance, the behavior of the program can be thought of as resulting from the interaction of just four large-scale emergent agents working together to form a coherent style and to design a complete alphabet. These four conceptually separable types of large-scale activities emerge from the many small actions of codelets:

1. the high-level conceptual activity of *devising a new letter-plan* (*i.e.*, either an idea for an as-yet undesigned letter or a possibility for improving an already-designed letter);

---

[1] See [Mitchell, 1993] for more about codelets, pressures, and emergent computation.

2. the intermediary activity of *translating a new letter-plan into a concrete shape* on the Scratchpad;

3. the relatively concrete perceptual activity of *examining a newly-drawn shape and categorizing it* (*i.e.*, deciding which letter of the alphabet it is, and how unambiguously so);

4. the more abstract perceptual activity of *recognizing the stylistic attributes of a newly-drawn letter, and judging them* (*i.e.*, finding "exportable" ways of describing how a given letterform violates norms, and deciding how well the letter's attributes fit with those of other letters in the developing gridfont).

It is convenient to speak as if these emergent activities were carried out by four explicit and cleanly separable modules, together comprising the totality of the program. (These agents could be likened to the agents referred to in [Minsky, 1985].) We call these hypothetical agents the *Imaginer*, the *Drafter*, the *Examiner*, and the *Adjudicator*. It must be borne in mind that these modules are in some sense convenient descriptive fictions, in that each is simply an emergent by-product of the actions of many codelets, and their activities are so intertwined that they cannot be disentangled in a clean way.

The interaction of these four agents, whereby ideas are suggested, critiqued, revised, possibly abandoned and regenerated, and so on, jibes with our intuitive sense of what human creativity really is. It seems to us fair to say that this kind of emergent, unpredictable processing constitutes a program's *making its own decisions*. This continuous process of suggestion and revision makes up the "central feedback loop of creativity". The full realization of the Letter Spirit program will, we believe, shed significant light on the mechanisms of human creativity.

References

[Hofstadter, 1985] Hofstadter, D. (1985). *Metamagical Themas: Questing for the Essence of Mind and Pattern.* Basic Books, New York. ·See especially Chapters 10, 12, 13, 23, 24, and 26.

[Hofstadter, 1987] Hofstadter, D. (1987). Introduction to the letter spirit project and to the idea of "gridfonts". Technical Report 17, Center for Research on Concepts and Cognition, 510 N. Fess, Bloomington, IN, 47408.

[Hofstadter and McGraw, 1993] Hofstadter, D. and McGraw, G. (1993). Letter spirit: An emergent model of the perception and creation of alphabetic style. Technical Report 68, Center for Research on Concepts and Cognition, 510 N. Fess, Bloomington, IN 47405.

[Minsky, 1985] Minsky, M. (1985). *The Society of Mind.* Simon and Schuster, New York.

[Mitchell, 1990] Mitchell, M. (1990). *Copycat: A Computer Model of High-level Perception and Conceptual Slippage in Analogy Making.* PhD thesis, University of Michigan, Ann Arbor, Michigan.

[Mitchell, 1993] Mitchell, M. (1993). *Analogy-making as Perception.* MIT Press/Bradford Books, Cambridge, MA.

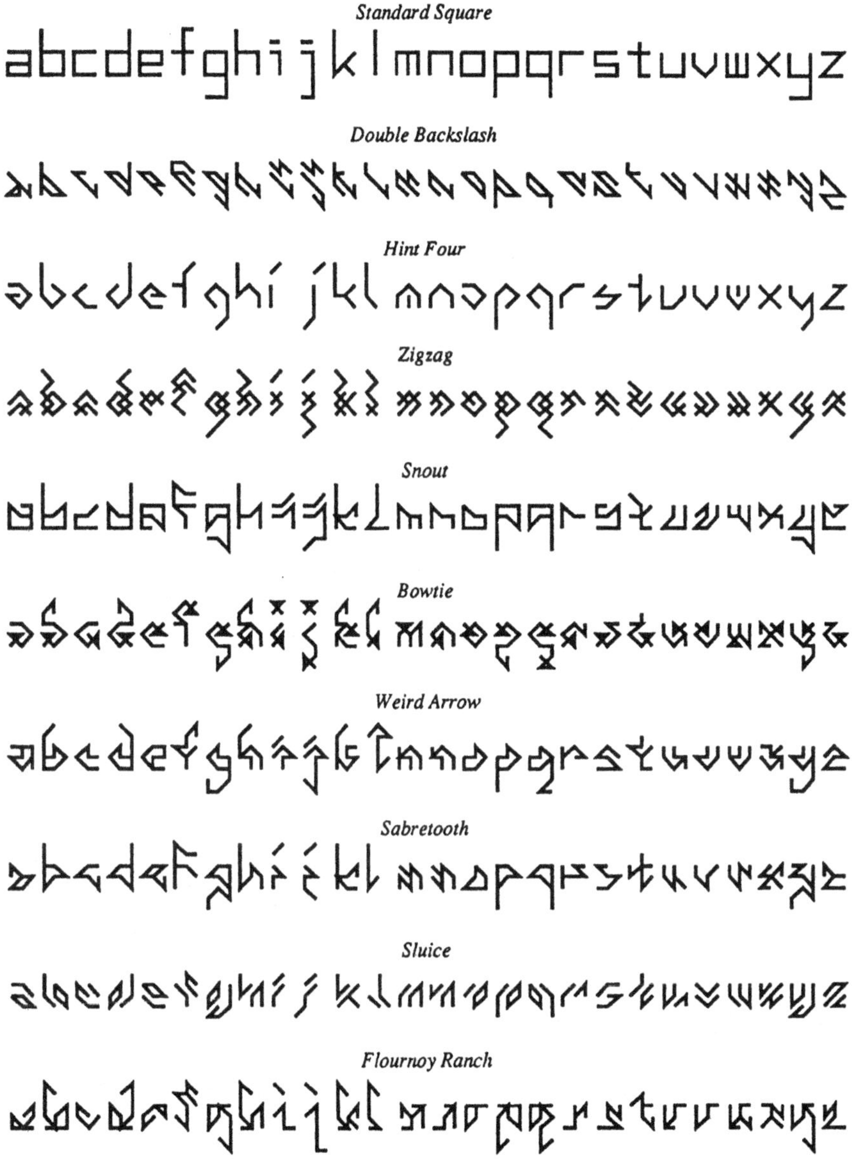

Standard Square

abcdefghijklmnopqrstuvwxyz

Double Backslash

Hint Four

Zigzag

Snout

Bowtie

Weird Arrow

Sabretooth

Sluice

Flournoy Ranch

Fig. 3. This figure, like Fig. 1, can be thought of as illustrating both the vertical problem (categorical sameness) and the horizontal problem (stylistic sameness) for which Letter Spirit is named. All of these gridfonts were designed by people.

New Systems for Extracting 3-D Shape Information from Images

E. Ardizzone, A. Chella, R. Pirrone

DIE - Department of Electrical Engineering - University of Palermo
Viale delle Scienze, 90128 Palermo Italy
E-mail: ardizzone@vlsipa.cres.it tel. +39.91.6566255

Abstract. Neural architectures may offer an adequate way to deal with early vision since they are able to learn shape features or classify unknown shapes, generalising the features of a few meaningful examples, with a low computational cost after the training phase. Two different neural approaches are proposed by the authors: the first one consists of a cascaded architecture made up by a first stage named BWE (Boundary Webs Extractor) which is aimed to extract a brightness gradient map from the image, followed by a backpropagation network that estimates the geometric parameters of the object parts present in the perceived scene. The second approach is based on the extraction of the boundary webs map from the image and its comparison with boundary webs maps exhaustively generated from synthetic superquadrics. A purposely defined error figure has been used to find the best match between the two kinds of maps. A functional comparison between the two systems is described and the quite satisfactory experimental results are presented.

1. Introduction

Tridimensional visual perception is generally modelled as a multi-stage process of information and knowledge processing, starting with the extraction of some features from 2-D images, subsequently used for the construction of an intermediate representation of the scene, for example a volumetric one. Shape from shading algorithms are largely used for the feature extraction [10,12].

The framework followed by the authors for the analysis and description of 3-D scenes, inspired by the Pentland's approach [13], is based on the direct extraction of simple 3-D geometric primitives from the scene. The objects' shapes may be therefore described as combinations of these recognised parts, that really act as "building blocks". This geometric description of 3-D parts is the starting point for the conceptual description of the scene, as pointed out in [1].

The 3-D geometric primitives must be simple and versatile; good candidates are the superquadrics [6]. Superquadrics are geometric forms derived from quadric surfaces by rising the trigonometric functions to two real exponents, called shape factors. Modifying shape factors causes a local surface deformation that can result in squared as well as pinched or rounded shapes (fig. 1). In this way, the simple modification of a few parameters allows for a number of different shapes. Global deformations can also be defined, to take into account stretched, twisted and bent shapes [1, 15]. Thus Boolean combinations and deformations of superquadrics are able to represent with surprising realism scenes and objects of the real world, that can therefore be described, in an extremely compact way, by the list of their parameters.

Quite obviously, the main difficulty in the proposed approach to the scene analysis and description is in the extraction of (pure or deformed) superquadric parameters from 2-D images of the observed scene. Classical shape from shading approaches, based on local surface analysis, suffer of the impossibility of deriving functional and structural relations among objects in the scene, unless heavy, global assumptions (e.g. about surface regularity and object isotropy) are made.

Neural networks may be an appropriate way to face problems of this class [11], owing to their ability to obtain adequate solutions in a non analytic form for all the elements of the domain of interest, after a training process involving a small set of meaningful examples belonging to the same domain. In the case under study, a neural network can not only learn how to estimate the geometric parameters from examples presented during the training phase, but also be capable of generalisation in the assessment of a novel input not at all presented during the learning phase.

Moreover, an approach based on neural networks can overcome some limitations of the classical shape from shading algorithms. For example, the way of operation, which may be regarded as a non-linear regression operation [9], makes the behaviour of such architectures robust with respect to noise and to changes of illumination or of other environmental conditions. Moreover, after the network training, the operation is very fast and does not present the heavy computational load typical of classic algorithms. The intrinsic parallelism of neural architectures makes them well suited for implementations in parallel hardware [2].

Following the idea above mentioned, the authors have developed two different neural-based approaches to the direct extraction of 3-D shape characteristics from 2-D pictorial images. The functional description and the comparison of these two architectures are the object of the present work.

The first system is made up by the cascade of the *BWE* (Boundary Webs Extractor), which derives a brightness gradient map of the surfaces present in the scene, with a backpropagation network that estimates the shape parameters of the superquadrics best fitting these surfaces.

The second system makes minimum the error between the boundary webs map extracted by the BWE and the analytic maps exhaustively generated, starting from synthetic superquadrics, by another stage said *SPS* (Superquadric Parameters Searcher).

In the following sections, after some short notes on superquadrics and backpropagation architectures (Sect. 2), a functional description of the two architectures is presented (Sect. 3). Lastly, some experimental results and a comparison between the two systems are reported (Sect. 4).

2. Theoretical Remarks

2.1 Superquadrics

Superquadrics are geometric shapes derived from the quadrics' parametric equation rising the trigonometric functions to two real exponents [6]. The inside/outside function of the superquadric in implicit form is:

$$F(x,y,z) = \left[\left(\frac{x}{a_1}\right)^{2/\varepsilon_2} + \left(\frac{y}{a_2}\right)^{2/\varepsilon_2}\right]^{\varepsilon_2/\varepsilon_1} + \left(\frac{z}{a_3}\right)^{2/\varepsilon_1} \qquad (1)$$

where the a-parameters are the superquadric semiaxes' lengths and the exponents ε_1 and ε_2, said form factors, are responsible of the shape's aspect. The inside/outside function assumes the value 1 when the point (x,y,z) is belonging to the superquadric's boundary, a value less than 1 when the point is at the inside and a value greater than 1 when the point is at the outside of the superquadric.

Form factors less than 1 cause the superquadric exhibit a squared aspect, while values close to 1 make the shape rounded. Greater values generate a cusp-like aspect. Fig. 1 shows several shapes obtained from the same superquadric by only changing the form factors.

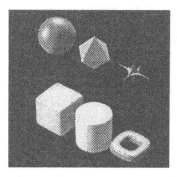

Fig. 1: Some superquadric examples: values of form factors near to 0 correspond to squared shapes, while increasing the factor value to 1 and then approaching 2 it is possible to obtain rounded and pinched shapes.

The previous equation is the parametric equation in canonical form of a superellipsoid. It is characterised by 5 parameters, 3 lengths of semiaxes and 2 form parameters. In order to completely describe a superquadric placed in a generic position, 3 orientation parameters and 3 centre coordinates must also be taken into consideration.

As already mentioned, it is possible to deform a superquadric surface in several ways. This characteristic makes the superquadrics very suited primitives for a geometric modelling system because they can easily approximate the shapes of the real world objects.

To face the problems of object 3-D reconstruction and recognition, a Constructive Solid Geometry (CSG) modelling system has been realised [1], having superquadrics as primitives. Each shape in the system may be described by means of simple Boolean operations among (pure or deformed) superquadrics. This represents the *geometric* level of the representation, in the framework of computational vision adopted by the authors, intermediate between the *sensor* level and the *conceptual* level at which the symbolic knowledge and most inference activities are located.

The geometric level consists of an analog representation of the perceived scene, allowing to specify the entities and the relations of a geometric nature that define the domain of the symbolic representation. The scene is represented by a set of superquadric parameters. At the conceptual level, knowledge is represented in terms of a symbolic formalism with compositional structure. This level includes a component for the structured definition of concepts, and a set of individual constants denoting the objects in the scene (respectively, a terminological component and an assertional component).

In a sense, the geometric level plays the role of a mental model, i. e. of an analog representation internal to the domain, which can be important to carry out some types of inferences. Adequate mapping mechanisms regulate the transitions between the two levels [14].

2.2 Backpropagation architectures

A backpropagation network is a multilayer architecture, with each layer consisting of several elementary units. All the units of a layer receive their input from the lower layers and send their output to the above layers. On a same layer, normally the units are not connected each to others. Connections between units can be more or less strong. This is obtained making use of adaptable weights that can be adjusted during the training phase.

The total input to each unit is made up by the sum of inputs from the other units, each weighted by the connection strength. The total input is processed and the unit, if activated, computes the output using its transfer function (typically, a sigmoid function).

In [14] it is shown that the backpropagation algorithm performs a gradient descent with respect to the Total Sum of Squared root error function (*TSS*):

$$TSS = \sum_p PSS_p = \sum_p \sum_j \left(t_{pj} - o_{pj} \right)^2$$

where t_{pj} and o_{pj} are respectively the target output and the actual output of the j-th output unit of the network. The *TSS* is the squared sum of the differences between the actual output pattern and the target pattern, summed for all patterns in the training set, and it represents a measure of how much the network has learned of the training set.

Another measure is the Pattern Sum of Squared error (*PSS*) [14]:

$$PSS_p = \sum_j \left(t_{pj} - o_{pj} \right)^2$$

that is the squared sum of the differences between the actual output pattern and the target pattern when a single input pattern is presented to the network. It is used to test the operation of the network when the input pattern is not belonging to the training set.

Well known problems of the backpropagation architecture are the choice of the internal parameters, like the learning rate and the momentum, the choice of the number of hidden units and with respect to the complexity of the problem and the number of learning epochs. These critical questions are generally solved by trial and error processes [9].

3. Description of the proposed architectures
3.1 The BWE+Backprop architecture

The first architecture is based on the cascade of the BWE (Boundary Webs Extractor) stage and a backpropagation network. A simplified version of this architecture has been already presented in [5].

The BWE is a neural architecture derived from Grossberg's Boundary Contour System (BCS), which is a mathematical model of physiological low-level visual processes, like contour extraction, texture grouping, shape from shading, etc. [8].

Several competitive-cooperative processes between units make up the basic operations of this model. The general output function of the unit i is:

$$\frac{d}{dt}x_i = -Ax_i + (B - x_i)I_i - x_i \sum_{k \neq i} I_k$$

where A is the spontaneous decay rate, B is the maximum activity level and the term $\sum_{k \neq i} I_k$ is the total input from the other units to unit i.

Each unit of the model is sensitive to a brightness gradient in a small window of the image; units in the same position locally compete in order to find the most probable direction of the brightness gradient. After this competition stage, an on-centre off-surround filtering is performed in order to ensure end-cut and allow the system to correctly operate near contours, where the gradient sharply changes. The last stage performs the cooperation process among the aligned units, in order to preserve smooth variations of the brightness gradient. This stage is modulated by the previous stage: near to the contours the end-cut process is prevalent with respect to the cooperation process, while this one is prevalent far from contours.

The BWE is not an adaptive model and it does not learn from examples. On the contrary, the internal parameters are fixed from the outside. The units of the BWE are sensitive to the brightness variations due to surface shading: the BWE traces contour lines not only for the more sharp brightness variations corresponding to the external contours of the object, but also for the less sharp brightness variations due to the shading. These contours lines are called *boundary webs* and allow to determine the shape information deriving from the image shading.

The BWE filtering allows for a substantial data compression without loss of information about the shapes of the objects: its operation is invariant with the direction of illumination and shows a robust behaviour with respect to the noise. More details about a neural implementation of BWE can be found in [4].

The second block of the proposed architecture executes an estimate of the form parameters of the superquadrics best fitting the objects in the scene. The block is made up by a feed forward architecture implementing the backpropagation learning algorithm.

In summary, the architecture operates in the following way. The input to the BWE is a 512x512x8 grey-level image; the output is a 32x32 map of boundary webs. Each BWE output unit is characterised by the vector *[a , s]*, where *a* is a local medium measure of the orientation of the boundary contour and *s* is the strength of the unit activation.

The output of the BWE stage makes up the input to the backpropagation neural network. In detail, a 10x10 window of the boundary webs map is presented to the input of the backpropagation architecture. The backpropagation input layer is therefore composed by 10x10x2 units, while the output layer is made up by 2 units, one for each form parameter.

3.2 The BWE+SPS Architecture

The second system proposed in this paper is a hybrid two-stage architecture. The first stage is again a BWE block, while the second one is a (not neural) block called *SPS* (Superquadric Parameters Searcher). This stage implements an algorithm of exhaustive search of parameters of the superquadric whose boundary webs map best fits the object's boundary webs map. Fig. 2 shows a functional scheme of the proposed architecture.

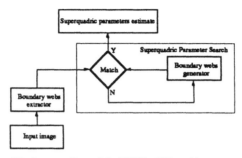

Fig.2: an outline of the BWE+SPS architecture.

The SPS stage is based on an original model of shape from shading. In particular (see also fig. 2), the boundary webs generator is able to exhaustively generate the boundary webs' map of a superquadric, starting from its geometric parameters. This map is analytically generated by sweeping the range of the possible geometric parameters. It is compared with the boundary webs' map extracted from the image by means of an original, purposely defined error measure. When the match is satisfactory, the geometric parameters responsible of the generated boundary webs' map are taken as estimates of the actual superquadric parameters. Analytical details follow.

The SPS generates the boundary webs' map W_g of a superquadric starting from its geometric parameters and compares the generated map with the actual boundary webs' map, furnishing as result the error measure of the match.

The superquadrics taken into consideration are superellipsoids centred at the origin of the reference system, with the x-axis pointing towards the viewer. The light source is at infinite. This condition allows to represent the light spring through a components' cursor l, m, n. If the surface is considered perfectly lambertian, at each point the reflected light is proportional to the cosine of the angle between the light cursor and the normal to the surface, oriented towards the outside of the surface.

To generate the analytic boundary webs' map, superquadrics are sampled according to the points of a grid parallel to the yz-plane. In this way, the sampled points correspond to the points of the boundary webs' map coming from the BWE.

The superquadric equation (1) may be solved for x only on a restricted domain, conveniently defined from the validity range $\{y>0, z>0\}$. This restriction doesn't prevent to calculate the x values also for the grid points falling into the other quadrants, since the superquadrics have an octantal symmetry. Solving the inside/outside function for x gives:

$$x = a_1 \left\{ \left[1 - \left(\frac{z}{a_3} \right)^{2/\varepsilon_1} \right]^{\varepsilon_1/\varepsilon_2} - \left(\frac{y}{a_2} \right)^{2/\varepsilon_2} \right\}^{\varepsilon_2/2} \tag{2}$$

Starting from the equation (2) it is possible to calculate the normal vector to the surface by the following:

$$n_x = \left(\frac{x^2}{a_1 s_1}\right) \cdot \left(\frac{s_1}{s_2}\right)^{\varepsilon_1/2} \cdot \left(\frac{s_2}{x^2}\right)^{\varepsilon_2/2} \tag{3a}$$

$$n_y = \left(\frac{y^2}{a_2 s_1}\right) \cdot \left(\frac{s_1}{s_2}\right)^{\varepsilon_1/2} \cdot \left(\frac{s_2}{y^2}\right)^{\varepsilon_2/2} \tag{3b}$$

$$n_z = \left(\frac{z^2}{a_3 s_1}\right) \cdot \left(\frac{s_1}{s_2}\right)^{\varepsilon_1/2} \tag{3c}$$

with s1 and s2 given by :

$$s_1 = x^2 + y^2 + z^2 \qquad s_2 = x^2 + y^2 \tag{4}$$

When the vector (3) is normalised, its components coincide with the cosine directors of the direction it individuates. Deriving this expression along the three directions gives the three components of the brightness gradient:

$$g_x = \frac{\partial}{\partial_x} \left(n_x \cdot l + n_y \cdot m + n_z \cdot n\right) \tag{5a}$$

$$g_y = \frac{\partial}{\partial_y} \left(n_x \cdot l + n_y \cdot m + n_z \cdot n\right) \tag{5b}$$

$$g_z = \frac{\partial}{\partial_z} \left(n_x \cdot l + n_y \cdot m + n_z \cdot n\right) \tag{5c}$$

The generated boundary webs' map W_g is obtained by projecting on the yz-plane the vector product between the gradient vector (5) and the normal vector (3) at each point:

$$W_g = (g \times n)_{yx} \tag{6}$$

After the projection, a boundary webs' map of elements tangent to the constant brightness curve is obtained.

To compare the generated boundary webs' map W_g with the extracted boundary webs' map W_e , several error functions have been tested to take into account both the angle (phase) difference and the module difference of the boundary web vectors at the corresponding points of the two images. The most satisfactory results have been obtained by considering the product of the absolute values of the differences between modules and angles of the corresponding boundary webs.

More in detail, let $w_g[i, j]$, $\varphi_g[i,j]$ be respectively the module and the phase of the generated boundary web vector at position (i,j) and $w_e[i,j]$, $\varphi_e[i,j]$ be respectively the module and the phase of the extracted boundary web vector. The error function can be defined as:

$$E = \sum_i \sum_j \left|w_e[i,j] - w_g[i,j]\right| \cdot \left|\varphi_e[i,j] - \varphi_g[i,j]\right| \tag{7}$$

where the sums are extended to all the boundary webs of the image. It should be pointed out that this error function is not a metric in the error space because the error value may be null at each point even for vectors with the same phase and different modules, but this problem has revealed itself of scarce relevance in practical applications.

4. Experimental results

4.1 The BWE+Backprop architecture

Several experiments have been accomplished on this system, particularly aimed to determine the right setting of learning parameters and the most adequate topology of the backpropagation network. However, even the BWE's set-up required an accurate analysis of the original BCS model and a patient experimental activity to correctly tune some important constants of the activation functions, in order to obtain a reliable boundary detection.

As regards to the backpropagation architecture, a training set and a test set were built up in order to find a good choice of the internal parameters of the network, such as the number of hidden units, the learning rate, the momentum, and the number of learning epochs. Both the training set and the test set were built up using several synthesised images representing shaded superquadrics of various forms and from several points of view. The superquadrics were generated in a Cartesian reference system with the origin at the screen centre and the x-axis pointing to the outside. The superquadrics were centred in [0,0,0], their normalised sides along x,y,z were respectively 0.5, 1 and 0.7, the latitude of the point of view was fixed at 60° while the longitude ranged in [0°–300°]; both of the form factors to be recovered were in the range [0.2 – 2].

The training set was built up by selecting, for each superquadric image, 6 regions of the corresponding boundary webs map: two of these regions roughly cover the centre of the image, while the other ones cover the corners; in fact the corners are generally characterised by a strong brightness gradient, corresponding to a sharp change of the curvature. On the contrary, the centre of the image is characterised by a smooth change of curvature. The training set size was therefore made up by 1700 elements.

The test set was assembled by selecting, for each superquadric image, a random window of the boundary contour map, summing up to 300 elements not belonging to the training set.

The TSS was used as a measure of the performance of the network. Early simulations were carried out with a smaller training set, in order to find a preliminary value of the learning rate and the momentum value. According to [14], the best results have been found by using the learning rate value of 0.2 and the momentum value of 0.9.

Further simulations have been executed by using the whole training set to find the best number of hidden units and of learning epochs. Fig. 3 shows the TSS measure for the training set vs. the number of learning epochs when the number of hidden units varies in the range 1–10. According to the theory, the network performance improves (i.e. the network better learns the training set) increasing the training time and the number of hidden units.

Fig. 4 shows the performance of the architectures with 1, 2, 3 and 10 hidden units with respect to the test set. It should be noted in this case the well-known overlearning problem: when the number of hidden units and the learning time of the network increase, the network improves its performance with respect to the training set, but it is less able to generalise, i.e. to correctly operate on patterns not presented during the learning phase. The same problem arises if the number of hidden units is increased.

On the basis of the above considerations, the architecture with 2 hidden units trained with 800 learning epochs has been adopted. In fig 3 and 4, the training and test behaviours of the chosen architecture are shown as bold lines. It should be noted that the minimum TSS of the test set is reached at about 800 learning epochs.

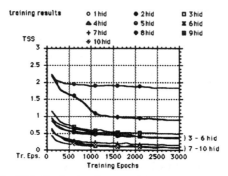

Fig.3: The TSS distribution for the training set over 3000 epochs, with hidden units ranging from 0 to 10.

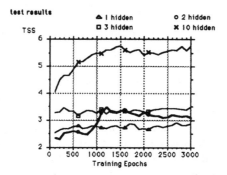

Fig.4: The TSS distribution for the test set over 3000 epochs, with 1, 2, 3 and 10 hidden units.

The analysis of test results also shows that the PSS error is distributed along the training set: the network better operates when both the form factors are round 1, while a sufficient learning level is achieved for very low ε_2 values and the worst learning is obtained when ε_2 reaches values more greater than 1. This is due to the fact that the BWE better operates when the superquadric shape is smooth. If the surface presents cusp points, the BWE is less able to follow the sharp brightness gradient, allowing for some degradation of the performance of the whole architecture.

4.2 The BWE+SPS architecture

To test the system, 75 different superquadrics images in canonical position have been used. The form factors are uniformly sampled in the range [0.2 - 1.8]; the semiaxes' values have been chosen invariably equal to 1. The view point has been placed along the superquadric axis pointing out of the screen, thus hiding the size of the axis itself (it is projected as a point onto the image plane). Superquadric images are 256x256x8 grey-level pictures, while the boundary webs' maps, both the ones extracted by the BWE and the ones generated by the boundary webs generator, are made up by 32x32 elements.

The experimental results show a good behaviour of the architecture, concerning both the estimations of form parameters and of semiaxes' dimensions. Fig.5 shows the global performance of the architecture; the upper part shows the maximum error, while the bottom part shows the mean error. In both cases the estimate of the form parameter ε_1 and ε_2 is satisfactory, since they keep themselves limited for the entire test domain.

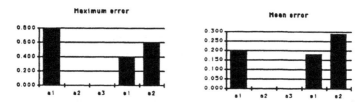

Fig.5: Histograms of the overall behaviour of the architecture BWE+SPS. The left histogram shows the max. error, while the right histogram shows the mean error in parameters estimate.

The estimate of the a_2 and the a_3 parameters, that are the sizes of the two superquadric semiaxes in the yz-plane orthogonal to the observer, is quite good. This was expected, since it is impossible to match boundary webs maps related to superquadrics with different sizes along the yz-plane, because of the presence of locations (i,j) in which there are elements active in a map and not active in the other one; so some differences in (7) can exhibit zero terms that cause the error function to take very high values. The incorrect estimation of the a_1 parameter, corresponding to the superquadric axis in front of the observer, is due to the difficulty of retrieving its size from the used view point.

4.3 A Comparison Between the Proposed Systems

The two architectures have been simulated and tested in C language on a HP9000/825 computer running under the HP-UX operating system and using the StarBase package to make up graphic interfaces; the backpropagation architecture was simulated using the Rumelhart's "bp" package [13]. The same images of single superquadrics have been used for the test: fig. 6 and fig. 7 show two examples of reconstruction of two superquadrics for both the systems. The original superquadric is shown on the left while the reconstructed shape is shown on the right. The original form factors are 0.5 and 1.5 in fig. 6 and 1.5 and 0.4 in fig. 7.

Results are quite satisfactory in all cases, but the BWE+SPS approach exhibits a better behaviour, even if it shares with other not neural shape-from-shading approaches some drawbacks. For example, it implies a considerable computational load, due to the need of generating the entire boundary webs map at every step and of accomplishing an exhaustive search in the parameter interval. On the contrary, the fully neural approach, even if executing a little less acceptable estimation of the shape parameters, is ever able to obtain a sub-optimal solution, generalising a few meaningful training examples. Moreover, after the learning phase, its computational cost is very low, being necessary only to calculate a rather simple in-out function. In particular it is to be pointed out that both approaches share the computation time nedeed by the BWE: about 30 minutes to train the network and derive a boundary webs map. The difference is in the second stage of the architectures: in fact the backpropagation net requires an off-line training of about 1 hour and exhibits an immediate response when tested, while the SPS system does'nt need to be trained, but requires about 10 minutes to perform a match.

Experiments have been carried out also to provide a comparison of the proposed architectures with the method proposed by Pentland [13], the most similar in literature to the authors' knowledge. The Pentland's method is based on the extraction of the needle diagram from the shaded image; then the superquadric shape factor ε_2 is found by executing a linear regression operation using the surface tilt information. The algorithm proposed by Horn [10] has been adopted to obtain the needle diagram. Note that only the estimate of e2 is significant in Pentland's case, while the proposed approaches are able to recover both the shape factors.

While the architectures proposed in this paper exhibit adequate estimates of form factors in their whole variation range, as shown in figs. 7 and 8, results of the Pentland's method are very good only when the form factor ε_2 is near 1, becoming poor when the form factor is far from this value. The proposed architectures are also less sensitive to the noise, since the BWE is more invariant to the environmental conditions than the needle diagram. In fig. 9 the boundary webs of the well known Lenna image and of the same image corrupted by a 40% random noise are shown: it is possible to note that the two maps are nearly the same.

Moreover, both the SPS generative method and the backpropagation allow for a better estimate than the linear regression: in particular, backpropagation can be considered as performing a non-linear regression, as stated in [9].

5. Conclusions

Only simple scenes made up by a single superquadric have been taken into account in the experimental paradigm. This is a not too serious limit, however, because the BWE gives a local estimation of an object's surface curvature. Therefore, even in the case of a complex scene made up by several objects, one has simply to carry out a series of local estimations, by using various portions of the whole boundary webs, corresponding to various portions of the surface of the objects present in the scene.

The authors are now trying to improve the performance of both architectures. As regards to the BWE+Backprop system, they are trying new topologies and learning paradigms, in order to obtain a more tuned estimate. As regards to the BWE+SPS architecture, they are implementing new versions of the SPS, based on search criterions inspired to the gradient descent philosophy.

The application of the proposed systems to the recognition of complex scenes is in an advanced experimental phase. The architectures will be integrated with other neural architectures capable to extract geometric information from the scene by using other paradigms, e.g. the visual motion [3], in order to obtain an optimum estimation of the geometric parameters of the objects present in the perceived scene.

Acknowledgements

This work has been partially supported by the "Consiglio Nazionale delle Ricerche" (CNR), Progetto Finalizzato "Robotica", and by the Italian "Ministero dell'Universita' e della Ricerca Scientifica e Tecnologica" (MURST).

References

[1]   Ardizzone, E., Gaglio, S., Sorbello, F. (1989). Geometric and Conceptual Knowledge Representation within a Generative Model of Visual Perception, *Journal of Intelligent and Robotic Systems*, 2, 381-409.

[2]   Ardizzone, E., Chella, A., Compagno, G., Pirrone, R. (1992). An Efficient Neural Architecture Implementing the Boundary Contour System, in: Aleksander, I., Taylor, J. (Eds.) *Artificial Neural Networks*, 2. North-Holland, Amsterdam.

[3]   Ardizzone, E., Chella, A., Gaglio, S., Pirrone, R., Sorbello, F. (1991), A Neural Architecture for the Estimate of 3-D Shape Parameters, in: Caianiello, E. (Ed.): *Parallel Architectures and Neural Networks - Fourth Italian Workshop*, World Scientific Publishers, Singapore, 270-275.

[4]   Ardizzone, E., Callari, F., Chella, A., Frixione, M. (1991), An Associative Link from Geometric to Symbolic Representations in Artificial Vision, in: Ardizzone, E., Gaglio, S., Sorbello, F. (Eds.): *Trends in Artificial Intelligence*, Springer Verlag, Berlin, 332-341.

[5]   Ardizzone, E., Chella, A., Pirrone, R., Sorbello, F. (1991), A System Based on Neural Architectures for the Reconstruction of 3-D Shapes from Images, in: Ardizzone, E., Gaglio, S., Sorbello, F. (Eds.): *Trends in Artificial Intelligence*, Springer Verlag, Berlin, 302-311.

[6]   Barr , A.H. (1981). Superquadrics and Angle-Preserving Transformations, IEEE *Computer Graphics and Applications*, 1, 11-23.

[7]   Callari, F., Chella, A., Gaglio, S., Pirrone, R. (1992). A New Hybrid Approach to Robot Vision, in: Aleksander, I., Taylor, J. (Eds.) *Artificial Neural Networks*, 2. North-Holland, Amsterdam.

[8]   Grossberg, S., Mingolla, E., (1987). Neural Dynamics of Surface Perception: Boundary Webs, Illuminants, and Shape-from-Shading. *Computer Vision, Graphics and Image Processing*, 37, 116-165.

[9]   Hecht-Nielsen, R. (1990) *Neurocomputing*, Addison-Wesley, Reading, MA, USA.

[10]   Horn, B.K.P. (1986). *Robot Vision*. MIT Press, Cambridge, MA, USA.

[11]   Marr, D.(1982) *Vision*, Freeman and Co., New York.

[12]   Pentland, A.P., Perceptual Organisation And The Representation Of Natural Form, *Artificial Intelligence*, 28, 293-331, 1986.

[13]   Rumelhart, D.E., Hinton, G.E. & Williams, R.J., Learning Internal Representations by Error Propagation, in: Rumelhart, D. E., McClelland, J. L. (Eds) & PDP Research Group (1986), Parallel Distributed Processing, Vol. 1, MIT Press, Cambridge, MA, USA.

[14]   Terzopoulos, D., Metaxas, D., Dynamic 3D Models with Local and Global Deformations: Deformable Superquadrics, *IEEE Trans. on PAMI*, 13, 7, July 1991, 703-714.

[15]   Ardizzone, E., Callari, F., Chella, A., Frixione, M. (1991), An Associative Link from Geometric to Symbolic Representations in Artificial Vision , in: Ardizzone, E., Gaglio, S., Sorbello, F. (Eds.): *Trends in Artificial Intelligence*, Springer Verlag, Berlin, 332-341.

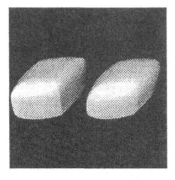 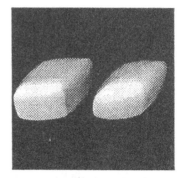

Fig.6 a, b): A reconstruction example: the original superquadric is on the left in both figures and has form factors 0.5 and 1,5; (a) the BWE+Backprop reconstruction obtains form factors 0.635 and 1.33; (b) the BWE+SPS reconstruction obtains form factors 0.7 and 1.4.

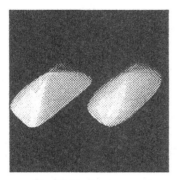 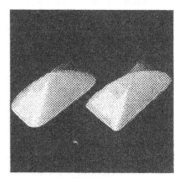

Fig.7 a, b): A reconstruction example: the original superquadric is on the left in both figures and has form factors 1.5 and 0.4; (a) the BWE+Backprop reconstruction obtains form factors 1.25 and 0.638; (b) the BWE+SPS reconstruction obtains form factors 1.3 and 0.2.

Fig.8 a, b) An example of BWE noise robustness: (a) the Lenna image and its boundary webs map; (b) the same image as in (a) but corrupted by a 40% random noise.

Projecting Sub-symbolic Onto Symbolic Representations in Artificial Neural Networks

Marco Gori   Giovanni Soda

Dipartimento di Sistemi e Informatica
Via di Santa Marta 3 - 50139 Firenze - Italy

Abstract. In this paper we introduce a novel approach to learning in artificial neural networks where the architecture is strongly involved and plays a central role. The function to be learned is supposed to be *partially determined* by prior rules and, therefore, the process of learning from examples consists of discovering solutions by taking this prior knowledge into account.

We discuss the basic ideas in the case of nondeterministic automata that can be injected in special architectures (*symbolic architectures*) by suitable constraints in the weight space. We consider fully-connected networks embedding these symbolic architectures. The learning is conceived in such a way that favorites the development of symbolic representations. This is very much related to many existing pruning techniques, but the pruning process we introduce forces the learning toward development of high level representations.

Index terms: Artificial Intelligence, connectionist models, learning from examples, pruning.

1 Introduction

In the last few years there has been a growing interest in the field of artificial neural networks that have been applied to solve successfully an impressive number of seemingly different tasks. Unfortunately neural networks seem scarcely adequate for dealing with highly structured tasks. It turns out that commonly used learning algorithms become very expensive in terms of computational resources. In the case of feedforward networks there have also been attempts to understanding the convergence of Backpropagation learning algorithm (see e.g.:

[4], [6]) and the generalization to new examples (see e.g. [1]) in the framework of *PAC learning*. These studies confirm the qualitative feeling developed by many researchers that "large" networks are required for coping with local minima during learning, whereas "small" ones seem necessary to attain high generalization. In many cases the function to be learned is *partially determined* in some points or by some prior rules. A "typical" connectionist approach in these cases is likely to lead to redundant architectures and, consequently, to low generalization. We consider the case in which a prior knowledge on a given task can be modeled by Nondeterministic Finite Automata (NFA) [5]. NFA can be injected into the connections of a neural networks in terms of proper architectures and weight constraints. The choice of a proper set of weights in the designed architecture leads to specify a particular finite automaton. As a result the wide range of behavior that is associated with neural networks is severely restricted by similar architectures (*symbolic architectures*) [1].

The process of learning in symbolic architectures consists of specifying the particular Finite Automaton that exhibits higher data fitting and can be place in the usual neural network optimization framework. One of the main concerns of this paper is that of considering the case in which also the partial function assumed by prior knowledge may be affected by errors. In this case the ordinary learning from examples approach may turn out to be useful for discovering additional rules not included in the prior knowledge model. Previous research in this direction has been carried out in [2]. In this paper we consider a more general embedding of the symbolic architecture into a sub-symbolic one. As for the learning, the main difference with respect to [2] is that we suggest to penalize the development of the sub-symbolic architectures by using a proper penalty function. The sub-symbolic representation turns out to be "projected" onto the symbolic one that is, to some extent, the reference used by the learning algorithm for framing as many examples as possible. As a matter of fact, high level representations are favorite during the learning thanks to a sort of pruning of the sub-symbolic architecture due to the way we penalize its development.

Most remarkable applications of this theory are in the field of high level perception (e.g. speech and image processing).

---

[1] The attribute given to similar neural networks is due to the possibility of extracting symbolic representations from neuron activities.

2   Connectionist models of partial functions

The limitations of the learning from examples approach in neural networks, that have been addressed in the previous section, suggest not to neglect eventual prior knowledge on a given problem. An open research problem is that of exploiting that knowledge in order to produce a biasing of the models that we use before learning from examples. This would improve significantly the chances to learn "difficult tasks" since the search for optimal solutions would take place in "biased models". A basic problem is that of giving the prior knowledge a representation that turns out to be natural for connectionist models. Since they are well-suited for describing functions, we suggest to represent prior information as *partial functions*.

In the case of static models, before learning takes place, one has a prior knowledge defined by $\mathcal{F}_p : \mathcal{X}_I \rightarrow \mathcal{X}_O$ partial function. This prior knowledge maps only a subset $\mathcal{P} \subset \mathcal{X}_I$ of the inputs onto the outputs. In order to be useful, this partial function must describe examples by simple and direct rules, and not just as a collection of input/output pairs [2]. The advantage of providing $\mathcal{F}_p$ in terms of "regular i/o pairs" is that one may look for architectures somewhat related to $\mathcal{F}_p$. Instead of assuming fully-connected networks, one may exploit the prior knowledge offered by $\mathcal{F}_p$ by looking for all networks and corresponding weight space that perform map $\mathcal{F}_p$ exactly. The prior knowledge and, therefore, the corresponding $\mathcal{F}_p$ makes it possible to begin learning using special networks $\mathcal{N}_p$ with weights constrained in a given weight space Ω_p. In the case of prior knowledge associated with sequential tasks a very interesting model is that of Nondeterministic Finite Automata (NFA) [5].

To some extent NFA give a "partial" i/o map of sequential task, although they do not act simply as partial maps. Formally they are represented by:

$$\Phi_n : Q \times \Sigma \longmapsto \mathcal{P}(Q) \tag{1}$$

being $\mathcal{P}(Q)$ the set of all subsets of Q (set of the states). In order to design a recurrent architecture based on NFA, we must define a state coding by neural activities. The state of the NFA can easily by coded by dynamic neurons. Among the many coding assumptions it is convenient to focus on those that simplify the architectural design. The details on this point, as well as on the design of the architecture are given in [2, 3] for a special case of NFA. The resulting architecture, shown in Fig. 1, is based on sigmoidal dynamic neurons as well as on locally tuned processing units commonly used in radial basis functions.

---

[2] It is quite obvious that if $\mathcal{F}_p$ is given only in terms of input/output pairs, it is not useful since it provides just additional data for learning from examples.

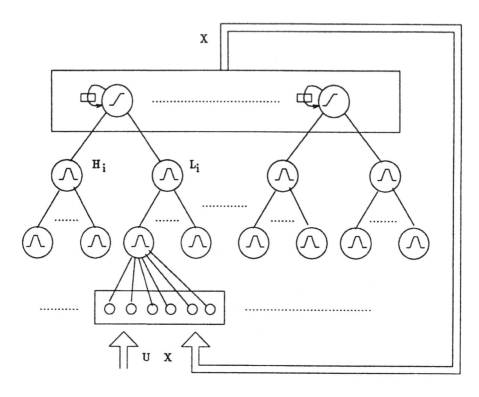

Fig. 1. The neural architecture implementing a given NFA

3 Learning as a projection onto structured architectures

In the previous section we have given a sketch on techniques that can be used for designing *symbolic architectures*. Once a set of weights compatible with the constraints is chosen, a symbolic network $\hat{\mathcal{N}}$ acts in a deterministic way. The selection of points in the admissible weight space $\hat{\Omega}$ that better fits a given set of examples can be performed learning from examples with parameters in that space. Using quite a restricted kind of nondeterminism, in [2] the process of learning is illustrated for applications to automatic speech recognition. The discussion presented in the previous section however, gives some more insights on the possibility of modeling nondeterministic automata, thus increasing significantly the possibility of expressing prior knowledge on a given problem. Obviously, the more "don't care conditions" we have in the prior knowledge model, the more the admissible weight space increases and the role of the learning becomes important.

Although learning is supposed to take place in the symbolic architectures for inferring the rules better suited for given examples, the application to tasks like automatic speech recognition suggests considering a more general architecture capable of coping with examples that can hardly be fitted using only a symbolic model. Hence, we suggest a natural extension of K-L proposed in [2] where the symbolic network $\hat{\mathcal{N}}$ is embedded into a fully-connected architecture $\mathcal{N} \doteq \hat{\mathcal{N}} \cup \tilde{\mathcal{N}}$. Unlike network $\hat{\mathcal{N}}$, the information is not represented by symbols in $\tilde{\mathcal{N}}$. The knowledge on the problem to be solved is represented at symbolic and sub-symbolic levels. The symbolic representation is compact and usually expresses rules where many examples are framed. That means the resulting networks are likely to be relatively small and to generalize very well to new examples. The limitations come out when representing any kind of knowledge that is difficult to make explicit. A sub-symbolic representation turns out to be more adequate in these cases, but is typically spread over many processing units and is not as compact as symbolic representations are. It turns out that in order to conceive models with good chances in generalization, one must favor symbolic knowledge and minimize development of sub-symbolic representations. This is possible by choosing the following cost function:

$$E_T \doteq \frac{1}{2} \sum_{t=1}^{T} \sum_{j=1}^{n} [d_j(t) - x_j(t)]^2 + \lambda \sum_{\tilde{w}_{ij} \in \tilde{\Omega}} \tilde{w}_{ij}^2, \tag{2}$$

where $d_j(t)$ is the target, $x_j(t)$ is the network's output, λ is a parameter weighting the penalty term, and $\tilde{\Omega}$ the space of the weights associated with $\tilde{\mathcal{N}}$. Let $X_h(t) \doteq [\hat{X}_h(t), \tilde{X}_h(t)]$ be the network status defined by collecting for each pattern t the associated representations by the hidden neurons. In the proposed framework the hidden neurons belong to the symbolic or to the sub-symbolic network. Because of the penalty function acting in $\tilde{\Omega}$, the learning process forces the reduction of $\tilde{X}_h(t)$ and, therefore, favors the *projection* of $X_h(t)$ onto $\hat{X}_h(t)$. High level representations are therefore favorite during learning since the penalty function of equation (2) inhibits connections $\tilde{w}_{i,j}$ toward "unuseful" neurons. The inhibition of this learning scheme can even be more stressed by *pruning* connections and removing "dangling neurons" as follows:

1. if $|\tilde{w}_{i,j}| < \delta_{\tilde{\Omega}}$ then remove i, j connection ($\delta_{\tilde{\Omega}}$ is the "pruning threshold").
2. remove all "dangling neurons" created by pruning connections.

Let us now consider two interesting particular cases that can be framed in the defined learning scheme. The first one is that in which we deal with "purely symbolic architectures" embedded into network $\mathcal{N}$. In that case we assume that learning by optimization of cost (2) is restricted to network $\tilde{N}$ and does not act on the symbolic architecture $\hat{N}$ [3]. Depending on the mutual connections between $\tilde{N}$ and $\hat{N}$ many different cases arise that have in common the high level processing carried out by $\hat{N}$.

The second one is that in which no prior knowledge is given. As in the previous case the process of learning takes place in $N \doteq \tilde{N}$ by following the classical optimization scheme. Notice that the presence of the penalty function acts, also in this case, to reduce the "overtraining phenomenon" and improve the generalization.

4 Conclusions

In this paper we have suggested a novel approach to integrate symbolic and sub-symbolic representations into connectionist models. The learning scheme proposed is based essentially on a pruning process that performs a sort of projection of the sub-symbolic onto the symbolic representation. This favors development of high level representations, thus making good generalization to new examples possible also in tasks with significant prior structure. The more the information is "projected" onto the symbolic representation, the higher generalization is likely to be attained on the test set.

References

1. E.B. Baum and D. Haussler, "What Size Net Give Valid Generalization?," Neural Computation, Vol. 1, No. 1, pp. 151-160
2. P. Frasconi, M. Gori, M. Maggini, and G. Soda, "Unified Integration of Explicit Rules and Learning by Example in Recurrent Networks," *IEEE Trans. on Knowledge and Data Engineering*, in press.
3. P. Frasconi, M. Gori, and G. Soda, "Injecting Nondeterministic Finite State Automata into Recurrent Neural Networks," Tech. Rep. RT.15/92, Universita' di Firenze, August 1992.
4. M. Gori and A. Tesi, "On the Problem of Local Minima in BackPropagation", *IEEE Trans. Pattern Anal. and Machine Intell.*, vol. 14, no. 1, pp. 76-86, 1991.
5. J.E. Hopcroft, J.D. Ullman, *Introduction to Automata Theory, Languages and Computation*, Addison-Wesley, Reading, Mass., 1979.
6. X.H. Yu, "Can Backpropagation Error Surface Not Have Local Minima?," IEEE Trans. on Neural Networks, Vol. 3, No. 6, November 1992, pp. 1019-1020

---

[3] In this case the symbolic architecture is not a neural network.

Integrating the Symbolic and the Sub-Symbolic Level in Sonar-Based Navigation

Alberto Braggiotti, Gaetano Chemello, Claudio Sossai and Gaetano Trainito

LADSEB-CNR, Corso Stati Uniti 4, I-35020 Padova, Italy

Abstract. Symbolic reasoning and data interpretation often coexist in Autonomous Systems as formally separate entities. In order to bridge the gap between them, a well-founded calculus based on a many-valued logic is introduced. This formalism preserves the ability to perform deductions on the exact abstract knowledge and it allows to reason on the uncertain knowledge acquired through a learning process. Sonar-sensorized mobile robotics provides a meaningful case study.

1 Introduction

The functionalities of an autonomous mobile system are commonly grouped into two levels, the *symbolic level* and the *sub-symbolic level*. The former corresponds to the ability to perform *high-level reasoning* on an abstract and static body of knowledge about the world; the latter refers to the capability of the system to deal with the *flow of information* coming from the real-world, intrinsically affected by uncertainty.

The symbolic level usually consists of some form of logic-deductive reasoning system. The sub-symbolic level can be viewed as the application of a minimum/maximum condition to the flow of information (minimum energy, minimum error, maximum gain function, maximum of some probability function, etc.). Although they often coexist in an autonomous system, the two levels are often considered "orthogonal" and report to separate and historically complementary disciplines.

In the line of previous work [2, 3] we propose a theoretical framework where both aspects can be treated using a uniform formalism. To obtain this, we introduce a *many-valued logic*, where the truth values are the elements of a Boolean algebra. Such semantics, being an extension of classical semantics, preserves the logical-deductive structure, i.e. all logical theorems are still true, and whatever is inferred from true statements is still true. In the same formalism, the uncertainty coming from real-world data can be accounted for by introducing an *interpretation function* which attributes truth values in the interval [0,1] to any formula.

To enable a global reasoning system to manipulate both the abstract and the uncertain knowledge, combined into a single knowledge base, we must adequately redefine the classical inference rules. Having done this, we obtain an extended reasoning mechanism for which we adopt the term *Adaptive Reasoning*.

In order to validate our approach we apply our formalism to an experiment in mobile robotics, where an autonomous vehicle must use its abstract knowledge about navigation to produce motion plans in a real-world unstructured environment. Here the sub-symbolic level is in charge of the interpretation of a sonar map. This is performed by an interpretation function learned by a neural network, which attributes truth values to the logical formulas describing the vehicle's perception of the environment.

2 A Boolean-Valued Semantics

A standard interpretation for a first-order logical language $\mathbf{L}$ generated by the set of predicates $\{P_1, \ldots, P_v\}$ is a pair $M = \langle A, \{R_1, \ldots, R_v\} \rangle$ where A is a set and every R_i is a relation over A (i.e. a subset of $A \times \cdots \times A$). An atomic sentence $P_i(a_1, \ldots, a_w)$ is true in M if and only if $\langle a_1, \ldots, a_w \rangle \in R_i$, where R_i is the relation corresponding to predicate P_i.

The set A is identified by its characteristic function $c_A(x)$:

$$c_A(x) = \begin{cases} 1 & if \ x \in A \\ 0 & if \ x \notin A \end{cases}$$

The set $\mathbf{2} = \{0, 1\}$ can be viewed as a Boolean algebra and we can extend $\mathbf{2}$ to a complete Boolean algebra $\mathbf{B}$ in such a way that the characteristic functions take value over $\mathbf{B}$. This is the main idea of Boolean-valued models of set theory [1]. The value of $c_A(x)$ can be viewed as the truth value of proposition $x \in A$, hence in this framework $x \in A$ may have a truth value $b = c_A(x)$ different from 0 and 1.

If we consider A not in the universe of standard sets but in the universe of Boolean-valued sets, the relation $\langle a_1, \ldots, a_w \rangle \in R_i$ can take a truth value $b \in \mathbf{B}$ different from 0 and 1, and we can adopt b as the degree of truth of $P_i(a_1, \ldots, a_w)$ and write:

$$\|P_i(a_1, \ldots, a_w)\| = b$$

If we know the truth values of the atomic sentences, then, by induction on the length of the formula, we can extend the interpretation function to all sentences by the following definition:

$$\|\neg\phi\| = \neg_B\|\phi\|$$
$$\|\phi \wedge \psi\| = \|\phi\| \wedge_B \|\psi\|$$
$$\|\exists x \phi(x)\| = \bigvee_{a \in A} \|\phi(a)\|$$

where $\wedge_B, \neg_B, \bigvee_B$ are the operations of the Boolean algebra.

In this way we have introduced an *interpretation function* (denoted by "$\| \ \|$") associating a truth value, in general different from 0 and 1, to each sentence of the language $\mathbf{L}$:

$$\mathbf{L} \xrightarrow{\| \ \|} \mathbf{B}$$

Let's now give a quick look at the link with probability theory.

A probabilistic space is made of a triplet $(X, \mathbf{B}, p)$, where X is a set, $\mathbf{B}$ is a Boolean σ-algebra and p is a probability measure, that is a function mapping the σ-algebra $\mathbf{B}$ to the closed interval of real numbers $[0, 1]$ [4]:

$$\mathbf{B} \xrightarrow{\ p\ } [0, 1]$$

By composing the interpretation function "$\| \ \|$" and the probability measure p, we can define the probability of the sentences of the logical language $\mathbf{L}$:

$$\mathbf{L} \xrightarrow{\ \| \ \|\ } \mathbf{B} \xrightarrow{\ p\ } [0, 1]$$

It is important to notice from now on that the following results are independent of the probability measure p and derive only from the logical structure.

We are now going to show how it is possible to use the formal structure just described to obtain a formalism suitable for reasoning with the uncertainty intrinsic to robotics.

3 Data Interpretation

Consider a mobile robot scanning the environment via a rotating ultrasonic sensor. At each location of the robot, due to the intrinsic imprecision of the sonar technique, the sensor returns an ordered set of points p_i, each of which in general differs from the actual point p_i', which originated the measurement, by an absolute distance $e_i = |p_i - p_i'|$.

The pairs $\langle p_i, e_i \rangle$ constitute the Informational State:

$$IS = \{\langle p_1, e_1 \rangle, \ldots, \langle p_n, e_n \rangle\}$$

We shall use this information to approximate the theoretical interpretation function "$\| \ \|$", but to achieve this we need a more complex model for the data contained in IS.

The raw sonar information is structured by a segmentation algorithm, inspired by [6], which partitions the n points p_i in IS into m sections S_j of contiguous points and then approximates each section by an arc called *Region of Constant Depth* or RCD [5]. An RCD s_j is identified by a pair $\langle \langle d_j, \sigma_j, l_j \rangle, e_j \rangle$ where d_j is the mean of the distances of the points in the corresponding section S_j from the robot, σ_j is the standard deviation, representing the dispersion of the points around s_j, l_j is the number of points in section S_j and e_j is the average of the distances of each observed point from the closest point in the environment.

The RCD's constitute the Learning Set LS:

$$LS = \{s_1, \ldots, s_m\} = \{\langle \langle d_1, \sigma_1, l_1 \rangle, e_1 \rangle, \ldots, \langle \langle d_m, \sigma_m, l_m \rangle, e_m \rangle\}$$

The next step consists in the algebraic representation of the errors. The basic idea is that $\|reliable(s_j)\|$ is *true*, i.e. its truth value is 1_B of the Boolean algebra **B**, if the corresponding error is 0, whereas it is *false*, i.e. 0_B, if the error is maximum; in general, the smaller is the error of the RCD and the larger is the truth value of $reliable(s_j)$.

All this can be formalized as follows: let **L** be a first-order logic language containing, among others, the atomic predicate $reliable(x)$ and let **B** be the Boolean algebra generated by the set of half-open intervals on the real axis (i.e. a Borel σ-algebra). Then we can define, for each RCD s_j belonging to LS:

$$\|reliable(s_j)\| = 1_B - [0, \hat{e}_j[= [\hat{e}_j, 1]$$

where $\hat{e}_j = e_j/E_{max}$ is the normalized error and $1_B = [0, 1]$.

What we are interested in is generalizing, via a learning mechanism, the set of information

$$\mathbf{I} = \{\|reliable(s_j)\| = [\hat{e}_j, 1] : 1 \le j \le m\}$$

to the interpretation function $\|reliable(s)\|$ defined for any RCD s.

Due to our semantics, to generalize the set of information **I** means to define $\|reliable(s)\| = [\hat{e}_s, 1] \in B$, for any s. This requires finding an appropriate function of s, or better of the three parameters characterizing s: distance, dispersion and number of points.

Such function must satisfy the constraint that $\|reliable(s_j)\| - [\hat{e}_j, 1]$, for all $1 \le j \le m$, be minimum, where "-" is the difference operator in the Boolean algebra **B**. This is equivalent to minimizing

$$\bigvee_{1 \le j \le m} (\|reliable(s_j)\| - [\hat{e}_j, 1]) =$$

$$= \bigvee_{1 \le j \le m} ((\|reliable(s_j)\| \wedge \neg [\hat{e}_j, 1]) \vee (\neg\|reliable(s_j)\| \wedge [\hat{e}_j, 1])) =$$

$$= \bigvee_{1 \le j \le m} [f(d_j, \sigma_j, l_j), \hat{e}_j]$$

For this it suffices that the distance between f and $\hat{e}_j$ be minimum, i.e. that $\sum_{1 \le j \le m} (f(d_j, \sigma_j, l_j) - \hat{e}_j)^2$ be minimum.

We draw attention on the fact that, as anticipated in the introduction, our semantics has allowed us to derive a typical sub-symbolic minimum condition (corresponding, in our case, to a problem of least-squares function approximation) starting from an algebraic condition. As described in the final section, a neural network provides an effective solution to the approximation problem.

4 Adaptive Reasoning

We cannot reduce the real-world information, coded using the technique just described, to a set of truth sentences, because it includes also sentences with truth values "less-than-true". For this reason the classical deduction algorithm is inadequate to handle in a complete way the available information. We can extend the deductive mechanism to less-than-true sentences by introducing a fuzzy-logic-like style of inference: a deduction rule r is a pair $r = (r', r'')$, where r' accounts for the syntactic part of the rule and r'' for the uncertainty propagation part.

The adoption of a truth-functional interpretation facilitates our task, because, as Bell has shown in [1], this allows to preserve the logical axioms, i.e. if ϕ is a logical axiom then $\|\phi\| = 1$ for any possible interpretation function $\| \|$. As derivation rules, we shall define:

$$r_1' = \frac{\phi \to \psi, \ \phi}{\psi}; \quad r_1'' = \frac{\|\phi \to \psi\| = a, \ \|\phi\| = b, \ \neg b \leq a}{\|\psi\| = a \wedge b}$$

$$r_2' = \frac{A(x)}{(\forall x) A(x)}; \quad r_2'' = \frac{\|A(x)\| = a}{\|(\forall x) A(x)\| = a}$$

where r_1' corresponds to Modus Ponens and r_2' corresponds to Generalization. We use the term *Adaptive Reasoning* to denote the reasoning mechanism based on the above rules.

5 Experimental Results and Conclusions

As mentioned earlier, we have applied the proposed approach to an experiment in mobile robotics. Preliminary navigation tests were carried out using a TRC LabMate mobile robot with a rotating sonar sensor. The robot's task was to move to a target location in an unknown, but stylized, office room, avoiding an obstacle.

The actual tests were preceded by a learning phase in which the robot would take various scans of the environment, calculate, for each scan, the RCD's with their parameters d, σ and l, and associate to each RCD the error of the sensor, measured manually, and therefore the RCD's reliability. At the end of the data acquisition process, all the data were fed to a neural network which would learn the function f. The network was a 3-layer feed-forward neural network, trained by backpropagation, with 3 input nodes, for d, σ and l, 20 nodes in the first layer, 10 in the second and 1 for the output (the estimated error).

At an early test phase, the robot was moved at random in the room and several new scans were taken. The truth values associated to the RCD's, now calculated using the trained neural network, seemed encouragingly close to a human observer's expectation, as shown in Fig. 1.

The network was then connected to a prototype adaptive reasoner, written in Prolog and specialized in navigation planning, and simple obstacle-avoidance tasks were carried out. Further experiments are in progress in a more complex environment, with more complex tasks and more complex planning.

However, what the experimental setup has already accomplished is to show how the truth value of a logical formula can be learned from uncertainty-affected real-world data and used by a reasoning system, equipped with an extended inference capability, in a uniform formal framework, to produce new knowledge, both certain and uncertain.

In that sense, we believe that the proposed approach already outlines a promising answer to the question of a formally sound symbolic/sub-symbolic integration.

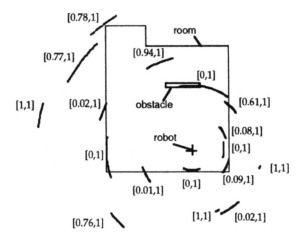

Fig. 1. A sonar scan coded into a set of RCD's, each shown with its truth value. The most reliable RCD's have a truth value of [0,1]

6 Acknowledgments

This research has been partially granted by the Italian Special Program on Robotics of the CNR (Progetto Finalizzato Robotica). Special thanks to Giangiacomo Gerla for his enlightening suggestions.

References

1. J.L. Bell: Boolean Valued Models and Independence Proofs in Set Theory, 2nd ed. Oxford: Oxford University Press 1985
2. G. Chemello, E. Pagello, C. Sossai, L. Stocchiero: Reasoning and Planning on Sensor Data: an Application of a Many-Valued Logic. Proc. 23rd ISIR, Barcelona 1992, 61-66
3. G. Chemello, C. Sossai, G. Trainito: A Homogeneous Formalism for Reasoning and Learning in Mobile Robotics. Proc. IROS '93, Yokohama 1993
4. P.R. Halmos: Measure Theory. New York: Van Nostrand 1950
5. J.J. Leonard, H.F. Durrant-Whyte: Mobile Robot Localization by Tracking Geometric Beacons. RA 7(3), 376-382, June 1991
6. J.J. Leonard, H.F. Durrant-Whyte: Directed Sonar Sensing for Mobile Robot Navigation. Boston: Kluwer Academic Publishers 1992

Randomness, Imitation or Reason Explain Agents' Behaviour into an Artificial Stock Market?

Pietro Terna

Istituto di Economia Politica, Università di Torino
Corso Unione Sovietica 218 bis, 10134 Torino, Italy.

Abstract. This paper shows that the effects of the interaction between simple artificial agents in a well defined economic environments, such as an artificial stock market, are useful to understand microeconomic events. We employ here the connectionist *cross-target* (CT) method [4] to build artificial neural subjects that make (i) guesses about their own actions and (ii) guesses about the effects of those actions. Each subject, learning and acting, develops the coherence between the two types of guesses. Our artificial interacting agents buy and sell shares, following cyclical behaviour (buying when the price rises and selling when the price diminishes) or developing risk aversion or true anti cyclical strategies. The last complex strategy can emerge from imitation between agents and randomness instead of reason.

1 Introduction

We are attempting to explain the behaviour of economic agents by substituting randomness or imitation to rationality. The work is founded on the interaction between simple agents instead of sophisticated representative ones [3]. We will employ the general framework of artificial adaptive agents [1] to make several experiments with two populations of agents. The first population acts with the goal of enrichment; in CT terminology this kind of goal is an external objective, or EO. The second population acts with no goals, but self developing a risk averse attitude on the basis of a simple mechanism generated by the learning; introducing randomness or imitation as suggestions (external proposals or EP) for the actions, unattended rationality emerges. Our agents act and simultaneously learn.

Section 2, after the presentation of the CT technique in a general way, introduces the specification of the equations describing the target for the training in these experiments; Section 3 presents simple results obtained with a stand alone agent, whose action has no counterpart and thus is unlimited; Section 4 is devoted to experiments with two populations of interacting agents, also adopting EP to influence the actions made by the second population. Section 4 also suggests future improvements.

2 The Cross-Target Technique and the Structure of the Model

CT method develops coherence between actions and effects, intended as guesses made by the artificial neural subject. Following also other authors' works [2], the choice of the neural approach is mostly due to the adaptive capabilities of neural functions (here: feed forward multilayer ones). Also genetic algorithms are highly flexible, but mainly if applied to neural network selection. So we here directly apply neural networks to simulate adaptive agents acting and simultaneously learning from their success and errors: the success is identified with the development of the coherence of agents' guesses. Other adaptive function or algorithm could be used, as classifier systems, but with a lack of objectivity in the work: The choice of a specific functional form or structure for classifier systems is less aseptic than neural adaptation. *We stress the fact that we do not have here any a priori economic rule.*

The targets necessary for training the neural network are generated by the artificial agent itself while it learns and acts, going from the actions to effects and from the effects to the actions, in a *crossed* way.

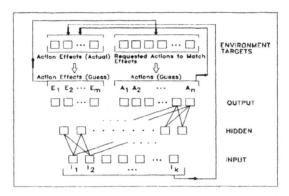

Fig. 1. The connectionistic structure of CT agents

Each neural agent produces (Fig. 1) guesses about both its own *actions* and their *effects*, following an information set (the input elements $I_1, ..., I_k$). Actual effects are estimated by environment rules on the basis of the guessed actions, taking account also of the consequences of interaction between agents, if any; the results are used to train the mechanism that guesses the effects. The evaluations of the actions necessary to match guessed effects are, on the contrary, employed to train the decision mechanism that guesses actions. In the last case we have to use inverse rules, with problems when the inverse is indeterminate. When the targets for some actions cannot be determinate separately due to the lack of inverse equations, we use a random separation of the inverse correction that is applied to the actions to obtain the desired effects. If one action determines multiple effects, they are included in several environmental accounting definitions; we have therefore more then one possible correction: The one with the largest absolute value is chosen.

EP and EO are external targets: EO substitute the cross one to train the specific output processing element, but the original CT target survives for the crossed training of actions; EP represents one of the multiple targets - from which the highest is chosen - used to train the side of the model that guesses the actions. External proposals suggest actions: in our case one source of suggestion is randomness, which is sufficient in Exp. B to explain in a radical way what apparently could be the effect of the reason. Another kind of EP is imitation, which is a powerful mean to exchange information between agents; imitation, well known by sociologists, but it is almost unknown in economic models, where agents exchange information by prices.

In the models shown here, the inputs of the neural artificial agents are: M_{t-1}, quantity of money at time $t - 1$; S_{t-1}, quantity of shares at the same time; W_{t-1}, global wealth (money and shares); A_{t-1}, V_{t-1}, A_{t-2}, V_{t-2} quantities of shares bought (A as acquisition) and sold (V as vendor) at the time $t - 1$ or $t - 2$; p_{t-3}, p_{t-2}, p_{t-1} prices at the specified time. On the side of the effects (following Fig. 1) the outputs are: Ac_t, Vc_t, guesses about actual contracts of purchase and sale of shares stipulated with another agent (the acts of sale and purchase are kept independent to verify deeply the artificial behaviour of the agents); M_t, S_t, W_t guesses about the effects of the subject's actions at time t. On the side of the actions the outputs are: A_t, V_t, guesses upon quantities of shares that the subject would buy and sell at time t. Globally we have 10 inputs, 13 hidden elements and 7 outputs.

We adopt the following non standard operators:

$H[\, x_1, x_2, \ldots x_n \,] = x_i$, where x_i is the highest x value in module;

C_i, ith random value uniformly distributed in the $0 \div 1$ range; we operate here with twenty subjects; the C operators (as C_{61} in Eqn. 1 or C_{81} in Eqn. 13) are numbered accounting for the presence of the other subjects;

$\{\, i\ n\ s_1\ s_2 \ldots s_n \,\}$ list operator number i, that chooses randomly between n subjects, avoiding the choice of the subject itself; the complete list is shown only in the first declaration; in subsequent uses the operator is written in the short form $\{\, i\, \}$; so $V_t\{\, i\ n\ s_1\ s_2 \ldots s_n \,\}$, or $V_t\{\, i\, \}$, means the value V_i of one of the n agents, randomly chosen. Several list operators can appear in a model, with different numbers. In each simulation period, or "day", the value of each list operator is kept constant.

The equations describing the targets are noted below; variables preceded by a little star are targets; they are eventually noted on the left with EO or EP. In the following experiments we have twenty agents. The complex notation adopted here is strictly related to the necessity of writing rules for CTs determination.

(1) $^{*}Ac_t = (V_t\, \{\, 1\ 20\ 1\ 2\ 3\ 4\ 5\ 6\ 7\ 8\ 9\ 10\ 11\ 12\ 13\ 14\ 15\ 16\ 17\ 18\ 19\ 20\ \}$

$\qquad - A_t) \cdot C_{61} + A_t$

(2) $^{*}Vc_t = (A_t\{\, 1\, \} - V_t) \cdot (1 - C_{61}) + V_t$

(3) $^{*}M_t = {}^{*}M_{t-1} + ({}^{*}Vc_t - {}^{*}Ac_t) \cdot p_{t-1}$

(4) $^{*}S_t = {}^{*}S_{t-1} + {}^{*}Ac_t - {}^{*}Vc_t$

(5) $^{*}W_t = {}^{*}M_t + {}^{*}S_t \cdot p_t$

(6) $^{*}A_t = H\,[(Ac_t - {}^{*}Ac_t), -C_1 \cdot (M_t - {}^{*}M_t)/p_{t-1}, C_2 \cdot (S_t - {}^{*}S_t), -C_3 \cdot (W_t - {}^{*}W_t)/(p_{t-1} - p_t)] + A_t$

(7) $^{*}V_t = H\,[(Vc_t - {}^{*}Vc_t), (1 - C_1) \cdot (M_t - {}^{*}M_t)/p_{t-1}, -(1 - C_2) \cdot (S_t - {}^{*}S_t),$

$\qquad (1 - C_3) \cdot (W_t - {}^{*}W_t)/(p_{t-1} - p_t)] + V_t$

This is the general framework of our agents, with neither EO nor EP. The implicit goal of this cross-target neural model is strictly the development of coherence between the effect side and the action one of the outputs. Everybody acts (buying or selling) at the price p_{t-1}, which is the closing price of the previous day, known by all agents; after the action - at the end of the day - the agents know the ending price of the day (p_t). The meaning of (1) and (2) is that of stating a random matching between the demand and the supply of any couple of exchanging subjects; other solutions (the min value, the arithmetic mean) do not give significant differences.

We can introduce in the model an external objective (EO) like that expressed in (8), with the obvious meaning of improving wealth at a daily fixed rate:

(8) $_{EO}W_t = {}_{EO}W_{t-1} \cdot 1.0005$

The cross-targets original equation (5) always runs to determine $^{*}W_t$ that is employed in (6) and (7). EO agents adjust the weights with which they guess their actions to improve the capability to make the difference between p_{t-1} and p_t fruitful. Remember that is the last price that is used in the determination of wealth W.

The experiments are conducted on the basis of an exogenous price, generated by a sinusoidal function with min 1.05, amplitude 0.9 and with a random perturbation of ±0.05, giving a complete range 1÷2; the starting price is about 1.5. In the equations (6, 7) the corrections are made upon A_t and V_t values as *proxies* of the correct Ac_t and $-Vc_t$ values, which are the effects upon which is founded the determination of all the other effects.

3 Independent Agents

The two introductory experiments are based on the independence of the agents. Only the graph of one agent per experiment is shown. All values other than p_t are noted -*gm* where g means guess and *m* is the number identifying the agent. *W-ex-p* (*ex post* value) is obtained, at p_t price, from $\dot{M}_t$ and $\dot{S}_t$. Due to independence of the agents, equations (1) and (2) are substituted by following equations:

(9) $\dot{A}c_t = A_t$

(10) $\dot{V}c_t = V_t$

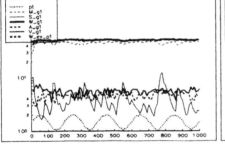
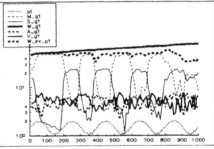

Fig. 2. Fig. 3.

To read the Figures 2÷7, we observe mainly the lines *M-g* (guess) and *S-g*, to discover their positive or negative relations with price cycle. Without EO we have (Fig. 2) all the agents acting to avoid risk: They sell all the shares and keep money, so greatly simplifying the task of developing coherence between the guesses of the actions and those of their effects. With EO of Eqn. (8), the agents are compelled to exploit the daily difference between p_{t-1} and p_{t-1} to augment W and thus they act in the short term (Fig. 3) selling when the price diminishes and vice versa.

4 Two Populations of Interacting Agents

Introducing the interaction, with twenty agents of two types (one population of ten agents acting with EO and without EP and the other without EO but in four cases with EP) we develop five Experiments (Table 1).

The new equations are the following:

(11) $\dot{A}_t = H\,[(Ac_t - \dot{A}c_t), -C_1 \cdot (M_t - \dot{M}_t)/p_{t-1}, C_2 \cdot (S_t - \dot{S}_t), -C_3 \cdot (W_t - \dot{W}_t)/(p_{t-1} - p_t),$

   $_{EP}z\,] + A_t$

(12) $\dot{V}_t = H\,[(Vc_t - \dot{V}c_t), (1 - C_1) \cdot (M_t - \dot{M}_t)/p_{t-1}, -(1 - C_2) \cdot (S_t - \dot{S}_t),$

   $(1 - C_3) \cdot (W_t - \dot{W}_t)/(p_{t-1} - p_t), _{EP}z\,] + V_t$

(13) $_{EP}z = C_{81} \cdot K$; K represents the max. amount of shares that can be daily bought or sold

(14) $_{EP}z = A_t$ { 2 20 1 2 3 4 5 6 7 8 9 10 11 12 13 14 15 16 17 18 19 20 } in (11);

   $_{EP}z = V_t$ { 2 } in (12)

(15) $_{EP}z = A_t$ { 2 10 1 2 3 4 5 6 7 8 9 10 } in (11); $_{EP}z = V_t$ { 2 } in (12)

(16) $_{EP}z = H[A_t$ { 2 10 1 2 3 4 5 6 7 8 9 10 }, $C_{81} \cdot K]$ in (11);

   $_{EP}z = H[A_t$ { 2 }, $C_{81} \cdot K]$ in (12)

In Exp. A the agents of the first population have no counterpart, being the second population risk averse and so are compelled, in the attempt of augmenting W, to keep shares (see Fig. 4). Those of the second population are risk averse, but having no EO are more oscillating in their behaviour, with spurious effect of constant, limited cyclical or limited anti cyclical behaviour (see in Fig. 5 an example of constant behaviour).

Exp.	EP or EO	Substituting Eqns. (6) and (7) for the second pop. with ...
A	first population with EO of Eqn. (8) - Second population without EP	no substitution
B	first population with EO of Eqn. (8) - Second population with EP of Eqn. (13), showing the *consequences* of *randomness*	(11) and (12), adopting (13)‡
C	first population with EO of Eqn. (8) - Second population with EP of Eqn. (14), showing the *consequences* of *generic imitation*	(11) and (12), adopting (14)‡
D	first population with EO of Eqn. (8) - Second population with EP of Eqn. (15), showing the *consequences* of *specific imitation*	(11) and (12), adopting (15)‡
E	first population with EO of Eqn. (8) - Second population with EP of Eqn. (16), showing the *consequences* of *generic imitation* plus *randomness*	(11) and (12), adopting (16)‡

Table 1. The five experiments. ‡We observe that the value produced by (13) influences (11) and (12) only if it represents the max. value in the H operator.

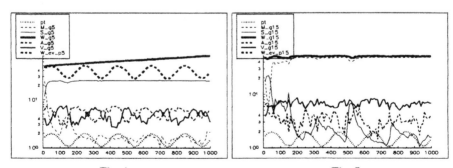

Fig. 4.   Fig. 5.

Introducing randomness (Exp. B), generic imitation from the second population to all the agents (Exp. C), specific imitation from the second population to the first one (Exp. D) and finally imitation plus randomness, we allow the agents of first population to find a counterpart for their exchanges, showing again the behaviour of Fig. 2; the agents of the second populations imitate or accept random suggestion and buy or sell against their natural risk aversion; then risk aversion newly prevails, determining anti cyclical behaviour (the whole effect is very complex). We show here two representative cases of Exp. E, in Fig. 6 and Fig. 7.

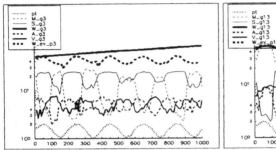
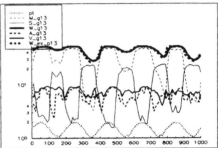

Fig. 6.   **Fig. 7.**

Summarising, agents $1 \div 10$ of the first population and agents $11 \div 20$ of the second population show opposite behaviour in almost all the Experiments (Table 2). It is very interesting to consider the importance of both imitation and randomness in the emergence of "rational" behaviour. Notice also that the concurrent effect is almost the sum of the two separated ones; so imitation here is essentially a source of noise as necessary instability of the economic system.

Ag. # .	Exp. A		Exp. B		Exp. C		Exp. D		Exp. E	
	M_g	S_g	M_g	S_g	M_g	S_g	M_g	S_g	M_g	S_g
$1 \div 10$	0.102	-0.069	-0.251	0.326	-0.275	0.316	-0.270	0.271	-0.631	0.634
$11 \div 20$	0.102	-0.164	0.350	-0.394	0.278	-0.323	0.236	-0.289	0.539	-0.605

Table 2. Mean correlation coefficients between pt and M_g, S_g, first and second population.

We stress the importance of these experiments, explaining what apparently is the consequence of the *reason* as the result of small random shocks and of imitation in a constrained environment. In other terms, *randomness and imitation vs. reason*.

The experiments shown here have been developed on the basis of an original software named CT. The program is under accomplishment and it will allow experiments with an *ex post* learning strategy reflecting the consequences of deep learning upon historical records of the subject's behaviour. Finally, models with endogenous price generation will be also developed.

5 References

1. J.H. Holland, J.H. Miller: Artificial Adaptive Agents in Economic Theory. American Economic Review, 365-370 (1991)
2. D. Parisi, F. Cecconi, S. Nolfi: Econets: Neural Networks that Learn in an Environment. Network, 149-168 (1990)
3. A.P. Kirman: Whom or What Does the Representative Individual Represent? Journal of Economic Perspectives, 117-136 (1992)
4. P. Terna: Labour, Consumption and Family Assets: A Neural Network Learning from Its Own Cross-Targets. In: T. Kohonen et al. (eds.): Artificial Neural Networks. Amsterdam: Elsevier 1991, pp. 1759-1762

Neural Networks for Constraint Satisfaction

Angelo Monfroglio

OMAR Institute of Technology, 28100 Novara, Italy

Abstract. Constraint Satisfaction Problems with finite domains for the variables (FCSPs) are considered. They play a central role in the real world and in Artificial Intelligence. FCSPs are in general NP-hard and a general deterministic polynomial time algorithm is not known. FCSPs can be reduced in polynomial time to the satisfaction of a Conjunctive Normal Form (CNF-SAT): we present here new techniques for solving CNF-SAT by means of three different neural networks. The results of significant tests are described and discussed.

1 Introduction and Related Work

Constraint Satisfaction Problems play a crucial role in AI.

We consider here only finite domains that is variables that range over a finite number of values, i.e. Finite Constraint Satisfaction Problems (FCSPs) [3]. Unfortunately, even FCSPs belong to the NP class of hard problems.

In his invited talk at ECAI'90 [2], M. Fox has described an approach to scheduling through a 'contention technique', which is analogous to ours about heuristic constraint satisfaction, as presented in [5]. Fox proposes a model of decision making that provides structure by combining constraint satisfaction and heuristic search. He introduces the concepts of topology and texture to characterize problem structure. The most important textures are:

-value contention: degree to which variables are contending for the same value;

-value conflict: degree to which a variable's assigned value is in conflict with existing constraints.

These textures are decisive for identifying bottlenecks in decision support. In the next section we will describe techniques we first introduced in [5], which use a slightly different terminology: for value contention we use shared resource index and for value conflict we adopt the term exclusion index. However, a sequential implementation of this approach for solving FCSPs continues to suffer from the 'sequential malady', i.e. only one constrain at a time is considered. Constraint satisfaction is an intrinsical parallel problem, and the same is the 'contention technique'. Distributed and parallel computations are needed for the 'contention computation'. In this paper we use this successful heuristic constraint satisfaction technique through connectionist networks.

2 The Shared Resource Allocation Algorithm (SRAA) and CNF-SAT

We will first study a resource allocation problem. The same approach is then used for the more difficult and more important CNF-SAT problem.

We assume the existence of a multitude of variables (or processes) and a multitude of shared resources. Each variable can obtain a resource among a choice of alternatives. Two or more variables may not have the same resource. As an example consider:

v1: E, C, B; v2: A, E, B; v3: C, A, B; v4: E, D, D; v5: D, F, B; v6: B, F, D

where v1,v2,v3,v4,v5,v6 are variables (or processes) and E, C, etc. are resources. Let us introduce our algorithm. Consider the trivial case: v1: B v2: C v3: A.

Obviously, the problem is solved, we say that each variable has a Shared Resource Index equal to zero. Now let us slightly modify the situation: v1: A, B v2: C v3: A.

Now v1 shares with v3 the resource A, we say that v1 has a Shared Resource Index greater than v2. Moreover the alternative A for v1 has a Shared Resource Index greater than B. Our algorithm is based on this simple observation and on the Shared Resource Index. It computes four Shared Resource Indexes:

1. the first Shared Resource Index (SRI) for the alternatives
2. the first SRI for the variables
3. the total SRI for the alternatives
4. the total Shared Resource Index for the variables.

Now we go back to our example of v1,v2,v3,v4,v5,v6 and we describe all the steps of our algorithm.

For v1 E is shared with v2 and v4, C with v3, B with v2,v3,v4,v6.

The algorithm builds the Shared Resource List for each alternative of each variable and then the length of each list that we name first Shared Resource Index for the alternatives.

We can easily verify that the first Share Indexes for the alternatives are:

v1: 2,1,4; v2: 1,2,4; v3: 1,1,4; v4: 2,2,2; v5: 2,1,4; v6: 4,1,2.

Then the algorithm builds the first Shared Resource Index for each variable as the sum of all the first Shared Resource Indexes of its alternatives:

v1: 7; v2: 7; v3: 6; v4:6; v5: 7; v6: 7.

Through the Shared Resource List for each alternative the system computes the total S.R. Index as the sum of the first Variable Indexes:

v1: 13,6,27 v2: 6,13,27 v3: 7,7,28 v4: 14,14,14 v5: 13,7,27 v6: 27,7,13.

For instance, in v1 we have the alternative E which is shared with v2 (Index 7) and v4 (Index 6) for a sum of 13.

Finally the algorithm determines the total Shared Resource Index for each variable as the sum of its total Shared Resource Indexes for the alternatives:

v1: 46; v2: 46; v3: 42; v4: 42; v5: 47; v6: 47.

Then it assigns for the variable with the lowest Share Index the alternative with the lowest Shared Resource Index: v3 with C (also v4 has the same Shared Resource Index).

The system updates the problem deleting the assigned variable with all its alternatives and the assigned alternative for each variable. Then the algorithm continues as a recursive call. In the example the assignments are:

v3: C; v1: E; v2: A; v4: D; v5: F; v6: B.

Since the SRAA algorithm was already published, for reason of space we will give only this brief description. The reader can consult [5].

The asymptotic complexity of the algorithm is $O(N^4)$. The real cost in significant tests was about $O(N^{3.4})$ in the dimension of the problem.

M. Fox has found that for a class of problems where each variable is contending for the same value, i.e., the same resource, it is beneficial to introduce a new type of graph: he calls it contention graph. It is needed to identify where the highest amount of contention is, so that it becomes clear where to make the next decision. The easy decisions are activities that don't contend for bottlenecked resources, the difficult decisions are activities that contend more. The Fox's contention graph is analogous to our techniques with the shared resource indexes.

A contention graph replaces disequality constraints (for example used in the conventional 'constraint graphs') by a node for each value under contention, and links these value nodes to the variables contending for it by a demand constraint.

It is very natural to think at this point that connectionist networks are well suited to encode the 'contention graph', or our shared resource indexes. It is straightforward to look at links between variables that share a resource or links between resources that share a variable as connections from a processing element to another. It is immediate to think of hidden layers as tools for representing and storing the meaning of our higher level indexes. This is the very idea of the paper. For more detail see [6].

Now let us consider a more difficult problem: the classic problem of the Satisfaction of a Conjunctive Normal Form (CNF-SAT). This problem is very important because all NP problems (and CSPs) may be reduced in polynomial time to CNF satisfaction. In formal terms the problem is:

Given a Conjunctive Normal Form, with n clauses, m literals per clause and n,m = 2, find an assignment for all variables that satisfies the conjunction. An example is: $(A + B).(C + D).(\sim B + \sim C).(\sim A + \sim D)$ where + means OR, . AND, $\sim$ NOT.

We reconduct the problem to a Shared Resource Allocation and we will then use a technique similar to SRAA. For space reason we will only outline the algorithm. Our algorithm procedes as follows:

-we name 'variables' v1, v2, etc, each clause (A + B), (C + D), etc. (not to be confused with the original variables A, B, C, etc.

-eachclause must be satisfied: since this term is a logical OR, it is sufficient that A or B is true

-we consider therefore as 'alternative' each literal A, B,..

-we use upper case letters for non-negated alternatives and lower case letters for negated alternatives.

So we achieve: v1: A, B; v2: C, D; v3: b, c; v4: a, d.

Of course, the choice of A for the variable v1, does not permit the choice of NOT A, that is the alternative a, for the variable 4.

If we find an allocation for the variables, we find also an assignment true / false for the CNF. For example: v1: A v2: C v3: b v4: d, leads to:

A = true, C = true, B = false, D = false.

There may be cases where the choices let undetermined some letter. In this case more than one assignment is possible.

Each upper case letter excludes the same lower case letter and viceversa. A with A, b with b, c with c, or B with B, etc. are not of course considered mutually exclusive.

We compute:

(1)the first Alternative Exclusion Index; (2)the first Variable Exclusion Index (3)the total Alternative Exclusion Index; (4)the total Variable Exclusion Index

Consider the example: $(A + B).(\sim A + \sim C + D).(\sim A + \sim B + C).(\sim D)$ which is transformed in: v1: A, B; v2: a, c, D; v3: a, b, C; v4: d. It gives:

v1: 2,1 v2: 1,1,1 v3: 1,1,1 v4: 1   v1: 3   v2: 3   v3: 3   v4: 1
v1: 6,3 v2: 3,3,1 v3: 3,3,3 v4: 3   v1: 9   v2: 9   v3: 7   v4: 3.

Now we assign the variable with the lowest Exclusion Index, and the alternative for that variable, with the lowest Excl.Ind. v4: d, i.e. D = false.

Note that this variable v4 is immediately instantiated even if the index is not the lowest because it has only one alternative.

Then we update the problem deleting all the alternatives not permitted by this choice, that is all the D alternatives. In our case, we find:

v1: A, B v2: a, b, C v3: a, c   v1: 2,1 v2: 1,1,1 v3: 1,1   v1: 3 v2: 3 v3: 6

v3: a, (A = false),   v2: a, v1: B (B = true)   C = undetermined.

For a formal description, the reader can consult [5].

3 Connectionist Networks for solving N-CNF-SAT problems

In the next sections we present three classes of connectionist networks that learn to solve CNF-SAT problems after a training phase with a supervised procedure. This work will show how some neural networks may be very useful for a high level symbolic computation problem such as CNF-SAT.

The neural network learns to choose the clause (variable) to satisfy in the next assignment, and the alternative for this clause among the possible choices. The network makes this choices on the basis of value contention, i.e. on the indices of section 2.

Of course, a good choice is the one that permits to satisfy all clauses (if this is possible, otherwise the greatest number of possible assignments).

The networks have been tested with some not previously used problems. Note we have adopted a training set of 15% of the total cases for learning and a testing set (of course not included in the training set) of 10% of the possible cases, for performance judgment. The performance results are that the networks always provide the 100% correct assignments for the problems which were used to train the network. For different cases, the networks provide the correct assignments in more than 90% of the tests.

We have chosen some networks among the most promising and appropriate. For each class of networks we give in the corresponding subsection a brief introduction with references. Within the space of a short paper we can report only three networks among the several NN we tested.

For the first network we have chosen the following architecture:

-Input layer: $2 * n^2$ PEs (processing elements)

-One Hidden layer: $2 * n^2$ PEs

-Output layer: $2 * n^2$ PEs

where n-CNF-SAT means n clauses and at most n literals per clause.

For instance, for a simple 2-CNF-SAT case such as the following

v1: A, b; v2: a, we have:

Input layer: 8 PEs, Hidden layer: 8 PEs, Output layer: 8 PEs

         v1   v2

      A B a b A B a b

Input: 1.0 0.0 0.0 1.0 0.0 0.0 1.0 0.0

Output: 0.0 0.0 0.0 1.0 0.0 0.0 1.0 0.0 (final solution).

This is a very compact representation: all the scores for all the choices are presented in the same instance of the training example. We have found this representation very efficient.

For the PNN paradigm, because of the categorization nature of these networks (only one category as winner), we have adopted the configuration:

Input Layer: $2 * n^2 + n$

Hidden Layer for LVQ: $2 * n$

Hidden Layer for PNN: = the number of training examples

Output Layer: 2 * n

because in the output only one is the winner (value of 1.0). Single instances should code all possible winners, and the representation is less compact, i.e. we should use in the above example the following data:

Instance 1   A   B   a   b   A   B   a   b   v1 v2

Input: 1.0 0.0 0.0 1.0 0.0 0.0 1.0 0.0 | 1.0 0.0

Output: 0.0 0.0 0.0 1.0

Instance 2   A   B   a   b   A   B   a   b   v1 v2

Input: 1.0 0.0 0.0 1.0 0.0 0.0 1.0 0.0 | 0.0 1.0

Output: 0.0 0.0 1.0 0.0.

For the CASC network, see the section 3.2.

3.1 Functional-link Fast Backpropagation Network (FL-F-BKP)

The functional-link network is a feed-forward network and uses back- propagation algorithms to adjust weights. The network has however additional nodes at the input layer that serve to improve the learning capabilities.

In the outer product (or tensor) model that we have used, each component of the input pattern multiplies the entire input pattern vector. This means an additional set of nodes with the combination of input items taken two at time. The number of additional nodes is: $n * (n -1) / 2$.

For example, in the 2-CNF-SAT with 8 inputs the number of additional nodes is $8 * 7 / 2 = 28$. The reader can consult [8] for reference.

Moreover, we have adopted here a variation of the back-propagation algorithm suggested by [9]: the fast model, which improves the convergence too.

As one can easily argue, these functional links are appropriate for our problem, because the input configuration is not as easy to learn as for instance a pattern in image understanding. Here, the pattern recognition task is a very "intelligent" one, as we said in the previous section on intelligent example database.

In addition, the learning speed is very important for networks which have to learn so much. Thus all attempts are made in the following paradigms to gain speed.

3.2 Cascade-Correlation Network, with 1 layer (CASC)

In the Cascade-Correlation network model, new hidden nodes are added incrementally, one at a time to predict the remaining output error. A new hidden node uses input PEs and previously trained hidden PEs. The paradigm was suggested by S. Fahlman and C. Lebiere of Carnegie Mellon University [2]. The advantages are that the network incrementally improves the performances following the course of learning and the errors. One hidden node at a time is trained.

Why have we used this paradigm? Our networks for solving n-CNF-SAT grow quadratically in the dimension n. So each attempt to reduce the number of neurons by incrementally adding only those that are necessary, is welcome. We have fixed a convergence value and the network has added only the neurons necessary to reach that convergence.

3.3 Probabilistic Neural Networks (PNN)

The PNN is a connectionist implementation of the statistical method called Bayesian Classifier. For details the reader can consult [10]. We tested this paradigm too, for the good categorization capabilities of the network: the network performes very well.

4 Performance summary and conclusions

The reported accuracy is relative to the CNF-SAT problems of the testing set, not included in the training set. As one can see, these networks have a very good performance. The accuracy is in percent of correct results to the total number of problems. The tests have been 10000 for N-CNF-SAT with $2 < N < 50$.

	# of learning cycles needed for convergence	% accuracy ((# correct results/total tests)*100)
Network		
FL-F-BKP	< 400	> 90
CASC	< 400	> 90
PNN	< 60	> 90

The main contributions of the present paper are that we have showed the successful use of three different connectionist networks to solve a high level symbolic computation problem and the knowledge representation that we have used for the input units. In particular, we have shown that some paradigms not usually chosen for search and combinatorial problems like FCSPs can in fact be used with success.

For lack of space in this short paper, we cannot report a comprehensive comparison with more traditional algorithms in solving CNF-SAT. In brief, we may say that in solving CNF-SAT these networks compare favourable with general problem solvers for FCSPs, but cannot compete with specialized ones. However, the present approach can be important and useful for several reasons:
it is very natural and more efficient to implement a constrained search technique as a neural network with parallel processing rather than using a conventional and sequential algorithm;
-we compare different connectionist paradigms for the same problem (CNF-SAT) through significant tests.

References

1. Fahlman S.E., C. Lebiere (1990) The Cascade Correlation Learning Architecture, Report CMU-CS-90-100, Carnegie Mellon Univ., 1990
2. Fox M. (1990) Why is scheduling difficult? A CSP Perspective, invited talk of ECAI'90, Proceedings, Stockholm, 1990
3. Mackworth A.K. (1992), The logic of constraint satisfaction, A.I. Vol.58, 1992
4. Matyas J. (1965) Random Optimization, Automation and Remote Control, Vol. 26, (1965) pp. 246-253
5. Monfroglio A. (1989) General Heuristics for Logic Constraint Satisfaction, in Proc. of the 1st AIIA Conference, Trento, Italy, 1989, pp. 306-315
6. Monfroglio A. (1991) Connectionist networks for constraint satisfaction, Neurocomputing, Vol. 3, N.1, (Elsevier Science Pub., Amsterdam, 1991), pp. 29- 50
7. Pao Y.H.,(1989) Adaptive Pattern Recognition and Neural Networks,(Addison-Wesley, 1989)
8. Samad T. (1989) Back-propagation Extensions,Honeywell SSDC Tech. Rep.,(MN, 1989)
9. Specht D.F. (1990) Probabilistic Neural Networks, Neural Networks, (1990)

Reasoning with Individuals in Concept Languages

Andrea Schaerf

Dipartimento di Informatica e Sistemistica
Università di Roma "La Sapienza"
Via Salaria 113, 00198 Roma, Italia
email: aschaerf@assi.ing.uniroma1.it

Abstract. One of the main characteristics of knowledge representation systems based on the description of concepts is the clear distinction between terminological and assertional knowledge. Although this characteristic leads to several computational and representational advantages, it usually limits the expressive power of the system. For this reason, some attempts have been done, allowing for a limited form of amalgamation between the two components and a more complex interaction between them. In particular, one of these attempts is based on letting the individuals to be referenced in the concept expressions. This is generally performed by admitting a constructor for building a concept from a set of enumerated individuals. In this paper we investigate on the consequences of introducing this type of constructor in the concept description language and we provide some complexity results on it.

1 Introduction

In *concept languages* (also called terminological languages), concepts are used to represent classes as sets of individuals, and roles are binary relations used to specify their properties or attributes. Typically concepts are structured into hierarchies determined by the properties associated with them. The hierarchical structure is defined in such a way that more specific concepts inherit the properties of the more general ones.

One of the main characteristics of *concept-based* knowledge bases is the clear distinction between terminological and assertional knowledge (see e.g.[14]). The former deals with concepts and roles and their relationship, the latter with individuals and their membership to concepts and roles. The two kinds of knowledge are stored in two different components of the knowledge base and each component has its specialized reasoner. Moreover, the inferences of each component can be combined in order to obtain more complex inferences, called hybrid inferences. The advantage of this architecture is that the specialized reasoners are usually able to process their specific knowledge more efficiently than a general purpose ones.

On the other hand, the strict separation of the two components limits the expressive power of the overall system. In order to recover some of the expressive power, some attempts have been done, which allow for a limited mixing of the two components and/or a more complex interaction between them.

One of these attempts is done by admitting the presence of the individuals, which are generally only present in the assertional component, also in the terminological component. This is usually done by introducing new constructors in the languages for defining the concepts. In particular, one of these constructors is obtained by building a concept from a set of enumerated individuals. This constructor, called ONE-OF in [3] and simply $\mathcal{O}$ in this paper, allows one to express many natural concepts. For example, the concept Permanent_onu_member can be defined as {china, france, russia, uk, usa}, where china,...,usa are individuals.

The demand for the constructor $\mathcal{O}$ in concept-based systems is due to the significant increase of the expressiveness of the language it provides, as shown in Section 3. It is also confirmed by the fact that it is included in both the proposals for a standard concept-based system in [16] and [1].

We investigate on the consequences of introducing $\mathcal{O}$ in the concept language. In particular in the following sections, we introduce concept languages and their reasoning services (Section 2); we give a survey of the various issues associated with the use of $\mathcal{O}$ (Section 3); we briefly describe one of the strategies chosen by the implementors of the actual systems in order to deal with $\mathcal{O}$ and (Section 4); we present several complexity results (Section 5); we propose a limited use of $\mathcal{O}$ (Section 6) and, finally, in Section 7 we draw some conclusions.

For the sake of brevity, the proofs are omitted. They can be found in [18].

2 Preliminaries

We consider a family of concept languages, called $\mathcal{AL}$-languages, which includes most of the concept languages considered in the literature. The simplest language of this family, called $\mathcal{AL}$, is an extension of the basic language $\mathcal{FL}^-$ introduced in [5], including a constructor for denoting the complement of primitive concepts and the two special concepts $\top$ and $\bot$. Given an alphabet of primitive concept symbols $\mathcal{C}$ and an alphabet of role symbols $\mathcal{R}$, $\mathcal{AL}$-concepts (denoted by the letters C and D) are built by means of the following syntax rule

$$
\begin{array}{lll}
C, D \longrightarrow & A \mid & \text{(primitive concept)} \\
& \top \mid & \text{(top)} \\
& \bot \mid & \text{(bottom)} \\
& \neg A \mid & \text{(primitive complement)} \\
& C \sqcap D \mid & \text{(intersection)} \\
& \forall R.C \mid & \text{(universal quantification)} \\
& \exists R & \text{(unqualified existential quantification)}
\end{array}
$$

where R denotes a *role*, that in $\mathcal{AL}$ is always primitive.

An *interpretation* $\mathcal{I} = (\Delta^{\mathcal{I}}, \cdot^{\mathcal{I}})$ consists of a nonempty set $\Delta^{\mathcal{I}}$ (the *domain* of $\mathcal{I}$) and a function $\cdot^{\mathcal{I}}$ (the *interpretation function* of $\mathcal{I}$) that maps every concept to a subset of $\Delta^{\mathcal{I}}$ and every role to a subset of $\Delta^{\mathcal{I}} \times \Delta^{\mathcal{I}}$ such that the following equations are satisfied:

$$\top^{\mathcal{I}} = \Delta^{\mathcal{I}}, \ \bot^{\mathcal{I}} = \emptyset, \ (\neg A)^{\mathcal{I}} = \Delta^{\mathcal{I}} \setminus A^{\mathcal{I}}, \ (C \sqcap D)^{\mathcal{I}} = C^{\mathcal{I}} \cap D^{\mathcal{I}}$$
$$(\forall R.C)^{\mathcal{I}} = \{d_1 \in \Delta^{\mathcal{I}} \mid \forall d_2 : (d_1, d_2) \in R^{\mathcal{I}} \rightarrow d_2 \in C^{\mathcal{I}}\}$$
$$(\exists R)^{\mathcal{I}} = \{d_1 \in \Delta^{\mathcal{I}} \mid \exists d_2 : (d_1, d_2) \in R^{\mathcal{I}}\}$$

An interpretation $\mathcal{I}$ is a *model* for a concept C if $C^{\mathcal{I}}$ is nonempty. A concept is *satisfiable* if it has a model and *unsatisfiable* otherwise. We say that C is *subsumed* by D if $C^{\mathcal{I}} \subseteq D^{\mathcal{I}}$ for every interpretation $\mathcal{I}$.

Other languages are obtained by adding to $\mathcal{AL}$ the following constructors:

- *qualified existential quantification* (indicated by the letter $\mathcal{E}$), written as $\exists R.C$, and defined by $(\exists R.C)^{\mathcal{I}} = \{d_1 \in \Delta^{\mathcal{I}} \mid \exists d_2 : (d_1, d_2) \in R^{\mathcal{I}} \wedge d_2 \in C^{\mathcal{I}}\}$;
- *union of concepts* (indicated by the letter $\mathcal{U}$), written as $C \sqcup D$, and defined by $(C \sqcup D)^{\mathcal{I}} = C^{\mathcal{I}} \cup D^{\mathcal{I}}$;
- *complement of general concepts* (indicated by the letter $\mathcal{C}$), written as $\neg C$, and defined by $(\neg C)^{\mathcal{I}} = \Delta^{\mathcal{I}} \setminus C^{\mathcal{I}}$;
- *number restrictions* (indicated by the letter $\mathcal{N}$), written as $(\geq n R)$ and $(\leq n R)$, where n range over the nonnegative integers, and defined by

$$(\geq n R)^{\mathcal{I}} = \{d_1 \in \Delta^{\mathcal{I}} \mid \ \mid \{d_2 \mid (d_1, d_2) \in R^{\mathcal{I}}\} \mid \ \geq n\},$$
$$(\leq n R)^{\mathcal{I}} = \{d_1 \in \Delta^{\mathcal{I}} \mid \ \mid \{d_2 \mid (d_1, d_2) \in R^{\mathcal{I}}\} \mid \ \leq n\},$$

Using these constructors, alone or in combination, it is possible to construct more expressive $\mathcal{AL}$-languages. Unfortunately, besides of the gained expressive power, such constructors usually increase the complexity of reasoning in concept languages. An extensive study of the complexity of computing subsumption in $\mathcal{AL}$-languages is performed in [8].

One further constructor have been considered in concept languages, which has the peculiarity of involving the elements of a new alphabet $\mathcal{A}$, called *individuals*:

- *collection of individuals* (indicated by the letter $\mathcal{O}$), written as $\{a_1, \ldots, a_n\}$, where each a_i belongs to $\mathcal{A}$.

In order to assign a meaning to $\mathcal{O}$, the interpretation function $\cdot^{\mathcal{I}}$ is extended to individuals in such a way that $a^{\mathcal{I}} \in \Delta^{\mathcal{I}}$ for each individual $a \in \mathcal{A}$ and $a^{\mathcal{I}} \neq b^{\mathcal{I}}$ if $a \neq b$ (Unique Name Assumption). The semantics of $\{a_1, \ldots, a_n\}$ is then defined by: $\{a_1, \ldots, a_n\}^{\mathcal{I}} = \{a_1^{\mathcal{I}}, \ldots, a_n^{\mathcal{I}}\}$.

From this point on, we will identify a language with a string of the form $\mathcal{AL}[\mathcal{E}][\mathcal{U}][\mathcal{C}][\mathcal{N}][\mathcal{O}]$ indicating which constructors are allowed in the language. We do not claim the list of the considered constructors to be exhaustive. The description of some other useful constructors can be found in [1] and in [16].

The construction of knowledge bases using concept languages is realized by permitting concept and role expressions to be used in assertions on individuals. Given a concept language $\mathcal{L}$, an $\mathcal{L}$-assertion is a statement of one of the forms:

$$C(a), \ R(a, b)$$

where C is a concept of $\mathcal{L}$, R is a role of $\mathcal{L}$, and a, b are individuals in $\mathcal{A}$. The semantics of the above assertions is straightforward: if $\mathcal{I} = (\Delta^{\mathcal{I}}, \cdot^{\mathcal{I}})$ is an interpretation, $C(a)$ is satisfied by $\mathcal{I}$ if $a^{\mathcal{I}} \in C^{\mathcal{I}}$, and $R(a,b)$ is satisfied by $\mathcal{I}$ if $(a^{\mathcal{I}}, b^{\mathcal{I}}) \in R^{\mathcal{I}}$.

A set Σ of $\mathcal{L}$-assertions is called an *$\mathcal{L}$-knowledge base*[1]. An interpretation $\mathcal{I}$ is said to be a *model* of Σ if every assertion of Σ is satisfied by $\mathcal{I}$. Σ is said to be *satisfiable* if it admits a model. We say that Σ *logically implies* α, where α is either an assertion or a subsumption relation, if α is satisfied by every model of Σ (written $\Sigma \models \alpha$).

Example 1. Let Σ_1 be the following $\mathcal{ALEO}$-knowledge base:

$$\Sigma_1 = \{\exists\texttt{FRIEND}.\{\texttt{susan},\texttt{peter}\}(\texttt{john}), \forall\texttt{FRIEND}.\texttt{Married}(\texttt{john})$$
$$\neg\texttt{Married}(\texttt{peter})\}$$

It is easy to see that Σ_1 is satisfiable. Moreover, some non-trivial conclusions can be drawn from Σ_1. For example, we can prove that $\Sigma_1 \models\texttt{FRIEND}(\texttt{john},\texttt{susan})$ and $\Sigma_1 \models\texttt{Married}(\texttt{susan})$. Intuitively, they can be explained by the following reasoning: Due to the last two assertions, Peter cannot be a friend of John; therefore, according to the first assertion, the friend of John must be Susan and, consequently, she must be married, too. □

There are several reasoning services to be provided by knowledge bases. Some of them are concerned with reasoning about concept expressions and they fall under the name of TBox-reasoning. Some others require to reason on a set of assertions, they are called ABox-reasoning. In this paper, we are mainly interested in the following basic reasoning tasks.

Definition 1. Let $\mathcal{L}$ be any concept language. Then, given an $\mathcal{L}$-knowledge base Σ, two $\mathcal{L}$-concepts C and D, and an individual a, we call:

- *concept satisfiability*: the problem of checking whether C is satisfiable;
- *terminological subsumption*: the problem of checking whether $C \sqsubseteq D$;
- *knowledge base satisfiability*: the problem of checking whether Σ is satisfiable;
- *instance checking*: the problem of checking whether $\Sigma \models C(a)$;
- *hybrid subsumption*: the problem of checking whether $\Sigma \models C \sqsubseteq D$;

Concept satisfiability and terminological subsumption are TBox-reasoning problems, whilst all the others are ABox-rasoning problems. The importance of TBox-reasoning has been stressed by several authors (see for example [14]).

---

[1] In actual systems, the knowledge base also includes an intensional part, called *terminology*, expressed in terms of concept definitions. However, almost all implemented systems assume that such definitions are acyclic, i.e. in the definition of concept C no reference, direct or indirect, to C itself may occur. It is well known that any reasoning process over knowledge bases comprising an acyclic terminology can be reduced to a reasoning process over a knowledge base with an empty terminology (see [15] for a discussion of this technique and its computational properties). For the above reason, in our analysis we do not take into account terminologies and, therefore, we conceive a knowledge base as just a set of $\mathcal{L}$-assertions.

Knowledge base satisfiability is used for verifying whether the information contained in a knowledge base is coherent. Hybrid subsumption is the problem of checking whether a subsumption relation holds with respect to the set of models of a knowledge base. Finally, instance checking is used to check whether an individual is an instance of a concept. It can be considered the central reasoning task for retrieving information on individuals in the knowledge-base. In fact, instance checking is a basic tool for more complex reasoning problems; for example, the problem of retrieving all the individuals which are instances of a concept can be easily reduced to instance checking.

3 On the role of $\mathcal{O}$ in the reasoning process

In this section we give an overview of the most relevant issues related to $\mathcal{O}$ and we give an intuition of how these issues can make the reasoning process more complex than in the corresponding language without $\mathcal{O}$ (called the *underlying language*). We do not claim that the list below is exhaustive. Some other issues can be found in [18].

3.1 Implicit Assertions

One of the characteristics of concept languages is the ability of describing incomplete knowledge. In particular, by means of existential quantification, it is possible to express information about objects that exist but whose identity is not known by the knowledge base. With regards to these unknown objects, it is also possible to state their membership to some concept. In particular, when $\mathcal{O}$ is used, it is possible to state the membership of an unknown object to a set of individuals. A consequence of this, is that the unknown object is bound to be one of the individuals of the set.

For example, consider the following $\mathcal{ALEO}$-assertion: $\exists R.(A \sqcap \{a\})(d)$. It explicitly states the membership of d in $\exists R.(A \sqcap \{a\})$, but it also implicitly states that a must be in the extension of A. In fact, it says that there exists an object in $A \sqcap \{a\}$, therefore this object must be a and it must be in the extension of A, that is equivalent to stating the assertion $A(a)$.

In the above example we have considered a collection formed by a single individual. If we consider collection formed by more the one element then the resulting implicit assertion can be disjunctive. For example, if we state the existence of an object in the concept $A \sqcap \{a, b\}$, then the resulting implicit assertion is $A(a) \vee A(b)$.

The following example shows how the implicit assertions play a role in the semantics of a concept.

Example 2. Consider the following $\mathcal{ALEO}$-concept formed by a conjunction of three existential quantifications

$$\exists R.(A \sqcap \{a, b\}) \sqcap \exists R.(\neg A \sqcap \{a\}) \sqcap \exists R.(\neg A \sqcap \{b\}).$$

Suppose that we want to check its satisfiability. The standard approach (e.g. [19, 2]) to this problem is to separately check for the satisfiability of the three concepts involved in the existential quantifications, namely $A \sqcap \{a, b\}$, $\neg A \sqcap \{a\}$, and $\neg A \sqcap \{b\}$. It is easy to see that this technique fails to recognize that the whole concept is unsatisfiable. In fact, although each of the conjuncts is separately satisfiable, the conjunction of their implicit assertion (i.e. $A(a) \vee A(b)$, $\neg A(a)$, and $\neg A(b)$) is unsatisfiable.

3.2 Mixing terminological and assertional knowledge

Another important characteristic of concept languages is that the reasoning process in the terminological component is in general not influenced by the assertional knowledge. More precisely, the following theorem holds for a large class of languages (in [14], here simplified slightly from the original version):

Theorem 2 [14]. *Given a satisfiable knowledge base Σ, for every pair of concepts C, D:*

$$\Sigma \models C \sqsubseteq D \quad \text{iff} \quad C \sqsubseteq D.$$

The above theorem states that hybrid subsumption can be trivially reduced to terminological subsumption (plus knowledge base satisfiability). In other words, it says that the knowledge base, if satisfiable, plays no role in the reasoning about concepts. The above property is crucial for the efficiency of reasoning in concept-based knowledge representation systems. In fact, it allows for the maintenance of a static hierarchy of concepts; which is not influenced by the evolution of the assertions. Unfortunately, such nice property does not hold when the language includes $\mathcal{O}$, as shown in the following example.

Example 3. Let $\Sigma_2 = \{A(a), A(b)\}$. It is easy to see that the following relation holds

$$\forall R.\{a, b\} \not\sqsubseteq \forall R.A.$$

In fact, given an interpretation $\mathcal{I}$ such that $R^\mathcal{I} = \{(d_1, d_2)\}$, $A^\mathcal{I} = \emptyset$, and $a^\mathcal{I} = d_2$ we have that $d_1 \in (\forall R.\{a, b\})^\mathcal{I}$ and $d_1 \notin (\forall R.A)^\mathcal{I}$. On the other hand, we have that

$$\Sigma_2 \models (\forall R.\{a, b\} \sqsubseteq \forall R.A).$$

3.3 Abstraction

Abstraction is a well known mechanism in reasoning about individuals in concept-based systems. It consists in retrieving all the assertions relevant to a given individual a and collecting them into a single concept. Such concept has the property of been the most specific concept expressible in the language such that the individual a is an instance of. For this reason it is generally indicated by $MSC(a)$ (Most Specific Concept).

Abstraction, together with subsumption, allows one to perform instance checking. In fact, an algorithm for checking whether $\Sigma \models C(a)$ can work as follows: Step 1. compute $MSC(a)$. Step 2. check whether C subsumes $MSC(a)$. This algorithm, called Abstraction/Subsumption, has been broadly exploited in actual systems (see [17, 14]).

However, the problem of exploiting this algorithm is that, in general, it is not possible to completely put the information relevant to an individual into a single concept of the language. Lets clarify this point by means of an example: Let Σ be the following $\mathcal{ALE}$-knowledge base $\Sigma = \{R(a,a), B(a)\}$. Now consider the individual a; the abstraction for a in $\mathcal{ALE}$ returns $MSC(a) = B \sqcap \exists R.B$. In $MSC(a)$, the information that the individual related to a is exactly a itself is lost. This fact has an impact on the completeness of the algorithm; for instance it fails to draw the conclusion that $\Sigma \models \exists R.\exists R.B(a)$.

In general, any time an individual is referred more than once in the knowledge base, the connection between the different occurrences may be lost. For this reason, the algorithms for instance checking based on abstraction are, in general, incomplete.

Nevertheless, if the language includes $\mathcal{O}$ it is possible to make a *lostless* abstraction. In the previous example, if the language is $\mathcal{ALEO}$ instead of $\mathcal{ALE}$, the abstraction for a gives $MSC(a) = \{a\} \sqcap B \sqcap \exists R.\{a\}$, and it is easy to see that the inference $\Sigma \models \exists R.\exists R.B(a)$ is captured because $\{a\} \sqcap B \sqcap \exists R.\{a\} \sqsubseteq \exists R.\exists R.B$ holds. In conclusion the use of $\mathcal{O}$ gives the possibility of doing complete reasoning using the Abstraction/Subsumption algorithm.

3.4 Epistemic Operator

In [9], the addition of an epistemic operator $\mathbf{K}$ to concept languages is investigated. Among other things, it is considered the instance checking problem, $\Sigma \models C(a)$, in which the language used to express the concept C is enhanced by means of that operator. In particular, the constructor $\mathbf{K}C$ is inserted in such query language denoting the set of individuals such that the knowledge base *knows* that are in the extension of C.

It that paper it is argued that a concept of the form $\mathbf{K}C$ is equivalent to the concept $\{a_1, \ldots, a_n\}$, where $a_1, \ldots, a_n$ are exactly the individuals for which $\Sigma \models C(a_i)$ holds. For this reason, as shown in [10], reasoning with $\mathcal{O}$ turned out to be a basic tool for reasoning with $\mathbf{K}$ and an analysis concerning $\mathcal{O}$ could shed light on the various issues related to $\mathbf{K}$.

3.5 Discussion

The above list of issues helps in understanding why reasoning with $\mathcal{O}$ is generally hard. This hardness has a twofold explanation: on one side, it is related to the implicit disjunction carried by the use of sets with more then one object. On the other side, it is due to the identification of unknown objects with individuals.

It is well known, that concept-based assertions can be translated into first-order formulae. The above explanation can be clarified looking at the translation in first-order formulae of assertions with $\mathcal{O}$. For example, an assertion of the form $\exists R.\{a_1, \ldots, a_n\}(b)$ is translated into the formula

$$R(b, x) \wedge (x = a_1 \vee \cdots \vee x = a_n).$$

This formula explicitly contains both disjunction and equality; they can be easily recognized as the causes of the hardness of reasoning with $\mathcal{O}$.

4 How CLASSIC deals with $\mathcal{O}$

It is interesting to see how actual systems deal with $\mathcal{O}$. To this aim, in this section we briefly describe the methods chosen by the implementors of CLASSIC for dealing with $\mathcal{O}$ and, in general, with individuals in the concept descriptions. A more detailed description of it can be found in [6] and [4].

In CLASSIC, individuals are treated with a non-standard semantics. The reason why the CLASSIC designers have left the standard semantics is mostly related to the drawbacks described in Section 3 (in particular in Subsections 3.1 and 3.2), and to the computational intractability of subsumption (see Section 6), which, in their opinion (see [4]), is not relegated only to few non practical worst cases.

Roughly speaking, the individuals appearing in concept descriptions are interpreted as primitive disjoint concepts, i.e. as subsets of the domain, instead of as single elements of it. This semantics eliminates the effects of implicit assertions. In fact the existence of an object in the concept $C \sqcap \{a\}$ does not tell that $a^{\mathcal{I}}$ is in $C^{\mathcal{I}}$ but only that $a^{\mathcal{I}}$ and $C^{\mathcal{I}}$ intersect each other. The fact that $a^{\mathcal{I}}$ and $C^{\mathcal{I}}$ intersect each other does not guarantee that $a^{\mathcal{I}} \subseteq C^{\mathcal{I}}$ and does not exclude the possibility that even $a^{\mathcal{I}}$ and $\neg C^{\mathcal{I}}$ intersect each other.

Moreover, in CLASSIC, the assertions on the individuals are not taken into account while reasoning with concepts. In other words, even when a knowledge base is involved the type of subsumption considered is always the terminological one. This semantics is weaker than the standard one, in fact it fails to draw several conclusions that are entailed in the standard semantics.

The following example is taken from [4, page 13]. The names are modified w.r.t. the original version.

Example 4. Let Σ_3 be the following CLASSIC-knowledge base:

$$\Sigma_3 = \{\forall \mathtt{FRIEND}.\{\mathtt{susan}\}(\mathtt{john}), \ \mathtt{Married}(\mathtt{susan})\}$$

The proposed semantics fails to draw the conclusion that $\Sigma_3 \models \forall \mathtt{FRIEND}.\mathtt{Married}(\mathtt{john})$.

5 Reasoning with $\mathcal{O}$

In [19, 11], a calculus based on constraint systems has been developed to design reasoning procedures for the various reasoning tasks in concept languages. In [18], we extend the proposed calculus obtaining a complete technique for reasoning with $\mathcal{O}$. For sake of brevity we don't propose it here. In this paper we analyze the relationship between the complexity of the various reasoning tasks in languages with $\mathcal{O}$.

In order to achieve our results, we present the transformation ϕ from a knowledge base to a concept defined as follows: Let $\mathcal{L}$ be a concept language including $\mathcal{O}$ and $\mathcal{E}$, Σ an $\mathcal{L}$-knowledge base, C, D two $\mathcal{L}$-concepts, and a, b two individuals, then:

$$\phi(C(a)) = \exists Q.(\{a\} \sqcap C)$$
$$\phi(R(a, b)) = \exists Q.(\{a\} \sqcap \exists R.\{b\})$$
$$\phi(\Sigma) = \sqcap_{(\alpha \in \Sigma)}\phi(\alpha)$$

where Q does not appear in Σ. Intuitively, ϕ "encodes" the knowledge base Σ in the implicit assertions of the concept $\phi(\Sigma)$. The following lemma states the relation between the satisfiability of Σ and $\phi(\Sigma)$.

Lemma 3. *Given a language $\mathcal{L}$ and an $\mathcal{L}$-knowledge base Σ, then Σ is satisfiable iff $\phi(\Sigma)$ is satisfiable*

Sketch of the proof. The concept $\phi(\Sigma)$ is a conjunction of existential quantifications of the form $\exists Q.C_i$. Such conjunction is satisfiable iff each concept C_i is satisfiable; moreover, due to the construction of $\phi(\Sigma)$, each C_i is satisfiable iff the corresponding assertion is Σ is satisfiable. In conclusion, $\phi(\Sigma)$ is satisfiable iff each assertion is Σ is satisfiable, i.e. iff Σ itself is satisfiable. □

Next lemma shows that in the languages with $\mathcal{O}$ and $\mathcal{E}$, instance checking can be reduced to terminological subsumption (without loss of generality, we assume that Q does not appear in C).

Lemma 4. *Give a language $\mathcal{L}$, an $\mathcal{L}$-knowledge base Σ, an individual a, and an $\mathcal{L}$-concept C then $\Sigma \models C(a)$ iff $\phi(\Sigma) \sqcap \{a\} \sqsubseteq C$*

From Lemmata 3 and 4 we obtain the following theorem

Theorem 5. *In any language including $\mathcal{O}$ and $\mathcal{E}$, knowledge base satisfiability is polynomially reducible to concept satisfiability and instance checking is polynomially reducible to terminological subsumption.*

In [18], it is shown that the above result holds even for smaller languages. In particular, it holds in every language including $\mathcal{O}$ and another constructor, not considered in this paper, called FILLS[2] (see [3]).

Regarding Theorem 5, in [11] it was already proved that for a large class of languages concept satisfiability and knowledge base satisfiability are in the same complexity class, and therefore the latter is reducible to the former. However, that result is achieved considering each language separately. The result obtained here is stronger, in the sense that it is proved independently of the single language (provided that $\mathcal{O}$ is included). This result is important, since it relates

---

[2] The semantics of FILLS, written as $R : a$, is $(R : a)^{\mathcal{I}} = \{d \in \Delta^{\mathcal{I}} \mid (d, a^{\mathcal{I}}) \in R^{\mathcal{I}}\}$.

the complexity of an ABox-problem to the complexity of a TBox-problem. Such a relationship is crucial for the design of efficient reasoning algorithms and it is still not completely clear.

In [11] it was also shown that there are languages such that instance checking and subsumption are in different complexity classes. In particular, it is shown that in $\mathcal{ALE}$ instance checking is PSPACE-complete, while subsumption is NP-complete. Therefore (assuming NP$\neq$PSPACE), such result proves that, in $\mathcal{ALE}$, instance checking is strictly harder than subsumption. On the other hand, the result in Theorem 5 ensures that, if $\mathcal{O}$ is included in the language, no result of that kind are possible since the two problems are reducible to each other.

In [18] we also investigate on the complexity of the various problems in the specific languages. In that paper, we consider various languages that do not use $\mathcal{O}$ and the corresponding languages obtained by adding them. In particular we focus on the languages $\mathcal{ALC}$, $\mathcal{ALE}$, and $\mathcal{AL}$, which are a good representative of the various degrees of expressiveness (and complexity), and we achieve some complexity results on the corresponding languages with $\mathcal{O}$. We summarize the result we obtained in that paper in Table 1, which also contain the previous known results on the underlying languages.

		without $\mathcal{O}$			with $\mathcal{O}$
	subsumption	instance checking			subsumption & inst. ch.
$\mathcal{AL}$	P [19]	P [12]	$\mathcal{ALO}$		coNP
$\mathcal{ALE}$	NP [7]	PSPACE [11]	$\mathcal{ALEO}$		PSPACE
$\mathcal{ALC}$	PSPACE [19]	PSPACE [2]	$\mathcal{ALCO}$		PSPACE

Table 1. Complexity of reasoning tasks

6 On the use of $\mathcal{O}$ in the query language

In the previous section we have shown that the use of $\mathcal{O}$ generally increases the complexity of reasoning. Despite this negative result, there exists one possibility of exploiting $\mathcal{O}$ in a useful way without increasing the complexity of reasoning: admitting it only in the query language, i.e. allowing $\mathcal{O}$ in the expression of the query concept but not in the assertions of the knowledge base.

Using $\mathcal{O}$ it is possible to express various forms of selection that can be usually admitted in database query languages, but are missing in standard concept languages. For example, it is possible to ask for the books whose author is Newton and whose subject it mathematics:

$$\text{Book} \sqcap \exists \text{AUTHOR.}\{\text{newton}\} \sqcap \exists \text{SUBJECT.}\{\text{math}\}$$

In [13], it is shown that it is possible to query an $\mathcal{AL}$-knowledge base using $\mathcal{ALO}$ concepts in polynomial time, in spite of the fact that reasoning in $\mathcal{ALO}$ is in general coNP-complete. Our conjecture is that this result is quite general, in the sense that for many languages $\mathcal{L}$, it is possible to query an $\mathcal{L}$-knowledge base using concepts in $\mathcal{L} + \mathcal{O}$ with the same computing resources of reasoning in $\mathcal{L}$.

7 Discussion and Conclusions

We have shown an analysis of the various issues related to the use of concept constructors involving individuals. This analysis gives an insight of the problem of reasoning with individuals and allows us to understand the intuitive aspects which makes reasoning difficult.

Moreover, we have presented a set of complexity results which formally confirm that reasoning with individuals is generally hard. In fact, in some languages, they increases the complexity of reasoning ($\mathcal{AL}$,$\mathcal{ALE}$). Whereas, in those cases in which reasoning is in the same complexity class as the underlying language ($\mathcal{ALC}$), the algorithms are generally more complex and less efficient (in term of both time and space) than in the underlying language (see [10]).

We have also identified an intuitive explanation of this intractability: on one side, it is related to the implicit disjunction carried by the use of sets with more then one object. On the other side, it is due to the implicit equality associated with individuals in concept expressions.

In our opinion, the solutions proposed in actual systems to overcome the computational intractability are not completely satisfying. Therefore a deeper insight of the problem can also be useful for the development of better incomplete reasoners.

Acknowledgements. I am indebt to Francesco Donini, Daniele Nardi, Werner Nutt and, in particular, to Maurizio Lenzerini, for their support and collaboration. I would like to thank Enrico Franconi, Marco Schaerf, and two anonymous referees for useful comments on earlier drafts of the paper. I also would like to thank Yoav Shoham for his hospitality at the Computer Science Department of Stanford University where part of this work has been done.

References

1. F. Baader, H.-J. Bürkert, J. Heinson, B. Hollunder, J. Müller, B. Nebel, W. Nutt, and H.-J. Profitlich. Terminological knowledge representation: A proposal for a terminological logic. Technical Report TM-90-04, Deutsches Forschungszentrum für Künstliche Intelligenz, Postfach 2080, D-6750 Kaiserslautern, Germany, 1991.
2. F. Baader and B. Hollunder. A terminological knowledge representation system with complete inference algorithm. In *Proc. of the Workshop on Processing Declarative Knowledge, PDK-91*, Lecture Notes in Artificial Intelligence. Springer-Verlag, 1991.

3. A. Borgida, R. J. Brachman, D. L. McGuinness, and L. Alperin Resnick. CLAS-SIC: A structural data model for objects. In *ACM SIGMOD*, 1989.
4. A. Borgida and P. F. Patel-Schneider. A semantics and complete algorithm for subsumption in the CLASSIC description logic. Submitted for publication, 1992.
5. R. J. Brachman and H. J. Levesque. The tractability of subsumption in frame-based description languages. In *Proc. of the 4th Nat. Conf. on Artificial Intelligence AAAI-84*, 1984.
6. R. J. Brachman, D. L. McGuinness, P. F. Patel-Schneider, L. Alperin Resnick, and A. Borgida. Living with CLASSIC: when and how to use a KL-ONE-like language. In J. F. Sowa, editor, *Principles of Semantic Networks*, pages 401–456. Morgan Kaufmann, 1991.
7. F. M. Donini, B. Hollunder, M. Lenzerini, A. Marchetti Spaccamela, D. Nardi, and W. Nutt. The complexity of existential quantification in concept languages. *Artificial Intelligence*, 2–3:309–327, 1992.
8. F. M. Donini, M. Lenzerini, D. Nardi, and W. Nutt. The complexity of concept languages. In J. Allen, R. Fikes, and E. Sandewall, editors, *Proc. of the 2nd Int. Conf. on Principles of Knowledge Representation and Reasoning KR-91*, pages 151–162. Morgan Kaufmann, 1991.
9. F. M. Donini, M. Lenzerini, D. Nardi, W. Nutt, and A. Schaerf. Adding epistemic operators to concept languages. In *Proc. of the 3nd Int. Conf. on Principles of Knowledge Representation and Reasoning KR-92*, pages 342–353, 1992.
10. F. M. Donini, M. Lenzerini, D. Nardi, W. Nutt, and A. Schaerf. Adding epistemic operators to concept languages. Technical report, Dipartimento di Informatica e Sistemistica, Università di Roma "La Sapienza", 1993. Forthcoming.
11. F. M. Donini, M. Lenzerini, D. Nardi, and A. Schaerf. From subsumption to instance checking. Technical Report 15.92, Dipartimento di Informatica e Sistemistica, Università di Roma "La Sapienza", 1992.
12. M. Lenzerini and A. Schaerf. Concept languages as query languages. In *Proc. of the 9th Nat. Conf. on Artificial Intelligence AAAI-91*, 1991.
13. M. Lenzerini and A. Schaerf. Querying concept-based knowledge bases. In *Proc. of the Workshop on Processing Declarative Knowledge, PDK-91*, Lecture Notes in Artificial Intelligence. Springer-Verlag, 1991.
14. B. Nebel. *Reasoning and Revision in Hybrid Representation Systems*. Lecture Notes in Artificial Intelligence. Springer-Verlag, 1990.
15. B. Nebel. Terminological reasoning is inherently intractable. *Artificial Intelligence*, 43:235–249, 1990.
16. P. Patel-Schneider and B. Swartout. Working version (draft): Description logic specification from the krss effort. January 1993. Unpublished Manuscript.
17. J. Quantz and C. Kindermann. Implementation of the BACK system version 4. Technical Report KIT-Report 78, FB Informatik, Technische Universität Berlin, Berlin, Germany, 1990.
18. A. Schaerf. Reasoning with individuals in concept languages. Technical report, Dipartimento di Informatica e Sistemistica, Università di Roma "La Sapienza", 1993. Forthcoming.
19. M. Schmidt-Schauß and G. Smolka. Attributive concept descriptions with complements. *Artificial Intelligence*, 48(1):1–26, 1991.

A Family of Temporal Terminological Logics

Claudio Bettini

Dipartimento di Scienze dell'Informazione
Università di Milano, Italy

Abstract. We present a family of temporal terminological logics that share the characteristic of having temporal operators on intervals as concept forming operators. These logics allow to represent concepts whose set of instances depends on the interval of time considered. Moreover, the temporal operators allow to define concepts by the pattern of change of properties of their instances. They are derived from the logic presented in [8], but differ in both their terminological and temporal expressiveness. The formalism and the semantics show a tight relation with propositional modal logics of time intervals. We also briefly present results on the problems of decidability of subsumption, relevance of the temporal structure and incomplete subsumption algorithms.

1 Introduction

In the last decade terminological logics have emerged among the several formalisms for knowledge representation, mainly for their clear model-theoretic semantics, the rigor imposed in building and maintaining knowledge bases and a set of useful inferential services that, typically, can be efficiently implemented. They have been experimented in several application areas among which natural language processing, information retrieval, configuration and planning. Many problems arising in these areas require temporal reasoning. When this is the case, terminological formalisms are often abandoned in favor of formalisms allowing the representation and reasoning on temporal knowledge. The extension of terminological systems to represent and manage this kind of knowledge can add the important feature of temporal reasoning to the recognized benefits of the terminological approach.

Most of the attempts to this extension have considered only the assertional component of a terminological system, basically associating temporal labels to assertions so that temporal relations between two assertions can be inferred by a separate temporal reasoner operating on the labels. While this extension can be actually useful, it is still unsatisfactory, since the representation of temporal aspects is limited to the assertional level and hybrid reasoning between that level and the terminological one cannot take advantage of the temporal information. Moreover, it is sometimes desirable to represent concepts identifying them by the temporal properties of their instances or by the changing of these properties along time. This requires a temporal extension of the terminological logic. The first principled way of integrating time in terminological logics was proposed by

A. Schmiedel in [8]. He extends a terminological logic with two temporal operators providing a limited universal and existential quantification over intervals of time. In the following we call this logic $\mathcal{TB}$ (Temporal BACK). The semantics is accordingly extended mapping each concept to a function from intervals to sets of individuals with the intuitive meaning of identifying for each time interval the set of individuals that are instances of that concept. However, crucial issues like the subsumption decision problem and the development of even incomplete algorithms were left unsolved. K. Schild in [7] proposes a much simpler extension augmenting the $\mathcal{ALC}$ logic with the temporal operators on time-points **since** and **until**, taken from *tense* logic. Subsumption in the resulting logic turns out to be decidable. We believe that the move from points to intervals advocated in many areas from philosophy to computer science is even more important for knowledge representation. It is not only a matter of having higher level temporal operators, but a really different perspective in associating events and propositions to time. The semantics of a concept in the point-based extension is a set of pairs (individual, time-point). It is possible to characterize instances having certain properties in time-intervals only imposing that in all time-points between a certain instant and a reference instant, those properties hold. Sometimes this is not what we want. For example, we want instances of events and actions to be associated to the time intervals where they occur, but not to any subinterval or instant inside them. We could know nothing about what happens there.

This is one of the main reasons why we follow the interval-based approach, even if we are aware of the greater difficulties it entails. In this paper we present a family of temporal terminological logics that are weaker in their temporal expressiveness than $\mathcal{TB}$, but closer to the terminological logics characteristics, like, for example, variable freeness. These logics also highlight their and $\mathcal{TB}$'s strong relation with known propositional modal logics of intervals. We report some of the results that we have obtained on the problem of computing subsumption in interval-based temporal extensions. They are extensively illustrated in [3].

2 Preliminaries

2.1 Terminological Logics

We consider the extension of terminological logics including the very simple $\mathcal{FL}^-$ logic [4] and those belonging to the so called $\mathcal{AL}$ family, adopting the standard definitions used in the literature (see for example [5]). We remind that concepts in $\mathcal{AL}$ are built out of primitive concepts and primitive roles (symbols) according to the syntax rule

$$C_1, C_2 \rightarrow A \mid \top \mid \bot \mid C_1 \sqcap C_2 \mid \neg A \mid \forall R.C_1 \mid \exists R.\top$$

where C_1 and C_2 are arbitrary concepts and A and R are respectively primitive concepts and roles. An interpretation structure $\langle \mathcal{D}, \mathcal{E} \rangle$ consists of a set $\mathcal{D}$ (the domain) and a function $\mathcal{E}$ that maps every concept to a subset of $\mathcal{D}$ and every role to a subset of $\mathcal{D} \times \mathcal{D}$ such that: $\mathcal{E}[\top] = \mathcal{D}$, $\mathcal{E}[\bot] = \emptyset$, $\mathcal{E}[C_1 \sqcap C_2] = \mathcal{E}[C_1] \cap \mathcal{E}[C_2]$,

$\mathcal{E}[\neg A] = \mathcal{D} \setminus \mathcal{E}[A]$, $\mathcal{E}[\forall R.C_1] = \{d \in \mathcal{D} : \forall d'\langle d, d'\rangle \in \mathcal{E}[R] \rightarrow d' \in \mathcal{E}[C_1]\}$ and $\mathcal{E}[\exists R] = \{d \in \mathcal{D} : \exists d'\langle d, d'\rangle \in \mathcal{E}[R]\}$.

The other logics in the $\mathcal{AL}$ family are obtained adding further operators. We shall give the semantics for the temporal extension of $\mathcal{ALCN}$ and, hence, of all its sublogics. $\mathcal{ALCN}$ can be obtained from $\mathcal{AL}$ adding *negation* on arbitrary concepts and *number restrictions*. Number restrictions allow to set a constraint on the number of role-fillers for a certain role. The basic reasoning task in these logics is subsumption. A concept C_1 is subsumed by concept C_2 iff $\mathcal{E}[C_1] \subseteq \mathcal{E}[C_2]$ for every interpretation structure.

2.2 Temporal Relations

Among the several formalisms used to represent temporal constraints, the Interval Algebra [1] defines a set of relations between two intervals and the operations of intersection and composition on these relations. Given two intervals defined over a linear temporal structure there are 13 mutual exclusive relations that can hold between them, considering the possible positions of the endpoints. They are extensively used in the temporal reasoning literature. Their names and their intuitive meanings are shown in Figure 1. These relations and the ones obtained as a disjunction of two or more of them form the set of relations in the Interval Algebra.

In this paper we consider also a particular subset of these relations known as the set of *pointisable* relations. A relation between two intervals is called pointisable if it can be expressed as a conjunction of constraints on the endpoints of the intervals using the binary relations: $<$, $>$, $\leq$, $\geq$, $=$ and $\neq$. Obviously, the 13 relations are pointisable, but not all the relations of the interval algebra are pointisable. For example, the translation into an expression on points of the constraint $x(b, bi)y$, asserting that interval x is before or after y, needs logical disjunction to say that the right endpoint of x is before ($<$) the left endpoint of y or after ($>$) the right endpoint of y. The set of pointisable relations is considered interesting because it retains good expressiveness and it allows efficient algorithms for the computation of consistency and transitive closure of sets of constraints. These problems are NP-complete for the full Interval Algebra. A list of pointisable relations and the main algorithms can be found in [10].

3 A Family of Logics

We define a family of temporal terminological logics adding to the set of terminological operators, provided by the logic taken as base, two temporal concept forming operators: $\Diamond TE$ and $\Box TE$. The intuitive meaning of the symbols $\Diamond$ and $\Box$ is respectively *sometime* and *alltime* and their quantification over intervals is constrained by TE. The temporal operators are very similar to those defined in $\mathcal{TB}$, but we do not allow variables for time-intervals. A TE, or *Time-Expression*, is a set of temporal constraints on two implicit interval variables: the *reference interval*, that we will denote with i and a so called *current interval* denoted by

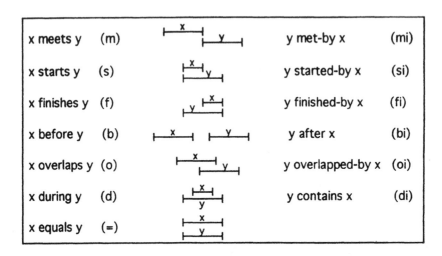

Fig. 1. The 13 interval relations

ci. These temporal operators can only have concepts as arguments, since we consider roles only as primitive entities.

Temporal expressiveness strongly depends upon the kind of constraints that we allow in time-expressions. The syntax of the different time-expressions that we are considering is given in Figure 2.

We distinguish our logics prefixing with $\mathcal{T}$ the terminological logic name and writing a subscript denoting the kind of temporal constraints allowed. For example, $\mathcal{TFL}_5^-$ is the temporal extension of the very simple logic $\mathcal{FL}^-$ allowing TE_5 as time-expressions in $\Diamond TE$ and $\Box TE$ operators.

3.1 Examples and Intuitive Semantics

A temporal domain of intervals is added to the standard semantic structure. The interpretation of a concept is a set of pairs $\langle i, d \rangle$ where i is a *time interval* and d is an *individual* of the interpretation domain. Intuitively, an individual can be an instance of a class (concept) in a set of time intervals and not in others. Similarly, a relation between individuals holds with respect to a time interval. The interpretation of a role is a set of triples $\langle i, d_1, d_2 \rangle$ with the meaning that the associated relation holds between d_1 and d_2 at the interval i. Given the interpretation of primitive terms, the meaning of complex definitions is defined inductively for each term forming operator.

Example 1. Consider the following definitional axiom:

engineer $\doteq$ person $\sqcap$
               ∃ education-level.engineering-degree

Intuitively this defines an engineer to be a person that has an education level characterized by an engineering degree. In our temporal logics, a definition without any temporal operator has a *reference interval* as implicit temporal context

$$\langle TE_1 \rangle ::= (\langle basic\_rel \rangle)$$
$$\langle TE_2 \rangle ::= (\langle single\_rel \rangle)$$
$$\langle TE_3 \rangle ::= (\langle pointisable\_multi\_rel \rangle)$$
$$\langle TE_4 \rangle ::= (\langle multi\_rel \rangle)$$
$$\langle TE_5 \rangle ::= \langle TE_3 \rangle \mid (\langle TE_3 \rangle \sqcap \langle MC \rangle) \mid (\langle MC \rangle)$$
$$\langle MC \rangle ::= (\langle TE_3 \rangle \langle int\_const \rangle) \mid (\langle dur\_rel \rangle \langle dur\_const \rangle) \mid$$
$$\langle MC \rangle \sqcap \langle MC \rangle$$
$$\langle basic\_rel \rangle ::= m \mid s \mid f \mid mi \mid si \mid fi$$
$$\langle single\_rel \rangle ::= \langle basic\_rel \rangle \mid b \mid o \mid d \mid bi \mid oi \mid di \mid =$$
$$\langle pointisable\_multi\_rel \rangle ::= \langle TE_2 \rangle \mid b, m \mid =, s, d, f \mid \ldots$$
$$\langle multi\_rel \rangle ::= \langle single\_rel \rangle \mid \langle single\_rel \rangle, \langle multi\_rel \rangle$$
$$\langle dur\_rel \rangle ::= < \mid = \mid > \mid \leq \mid \geq$$
$$\langle int\_const \rangle ::= k_1 \mid \ldots \mid k_s$$
$$\langle dur\_const \rangle ::= l_1 \mid \ldots \mid l_r$$

Fig. 2. BNF definition of time-expressions. The notation $(rel_1, \ldots, rel_n)$ denotes a disjunction among the relations.

and all of its concept and role components are defined with respect to this same interval. In particular, **engineer** denotes a set of pairs $\langle i, d \rangle$ such that d at interval i is a **person**, it exists another element d_1 of the domain such that $\langle i, d, d_1 \rangle$ is part of the interpretation of the **education-level** role and $\langle i, d_1 \rangle$ is part of the interpretation of **engineering-degree**.

Temporal operators are used to define time-dependent concepts. With the concept $\Diamond TE.C$ we denote the set of pairs $\langle i, d \rangle$ such that the individual d is a C at an interval i' satisfying $i' \, TE \, i$. For example, $\langle 1990, d_1 \rangle$ is in the set denoted by $\Diamond(bi)$.**engineer** if it exists an interval after 1990 at which d_1 is an **engineer** (e.g., if $\langle 1992, d_1 \rangle$ is an instance of the concept **engineer**). The $\Box$ operator is similar, but, for each *interval i*, the intervals satisfying TE with respect to i are universally quantified. This operator is similar to $\forall R.C$ quantifying over time intervals instead of quantifying over individuals. For example, $\Diamond(bi)$.(**engineer** $\sqcap \Box(mi, bi)$.**engineer**) intuitively denotes individuals that will be **engineer** in some future interval and that will remain **engineer** forever. In this definition we see an example of nesting of temporal terms. Note that, if the reference interval of the whole concept is i, the current interval, that is the interval *after i* defined by the external $\Diamond$ term, becomes the reference interval for the $\Box$ term. Obviously we can characterize sets of individuals having different properties at different times, like, for example, "all engineers having worked first for the government and then for a company". In natural language we can find many terms that are inherently temporal terms and they can be hardly defined without a notion of time. Consider, for example, the concept of **widow**, defined

as "a woman that sometime ago had an husband and now she has no husbands".
This can be expressed in our logics by:

woman $\sqcap \Diamond(b).\exists$ husband $\sqcap \forall$ husband.dead-person

The semantics does not assume the *homogeneity* of concepts. If an individual
is in the denotation of a certain concept at a certain interval i, it is not necessarily
in that denotation at different intervals, even if these intervals are subintervals
of i^1.

For this reason, with respect to extensions by operators on time-points, we
can represent concepts like, for example, $A \sqcap \Box(d).\neg A$ characterizing sets of
individuals that are instances of a concept A at a certain interval of time and
not in any subinterval of it. This expressiveness can be useful in several cases,
for example, for the representation of non-instantaneous events. Consider the
representation of a taxonomy of actions. We want concepts representing classes
of actions to denote sets of pairs where the second element is an action and the
first is its execution interval, taken as reference interval for the action description.
Actions are examples of non-homogeneous concepts: the fact that an action
with its execution interval belongs to a certain class does not imply that in a
subinterval of it the action belongs to the same class. On the counterpart, a
concept representing the state of a system is usually considered a homogeneous
concept.

It is possible to force a concept C to be homogeneous prefixing its definition
with a $\downarrow$ symbol, defined as follows: $\downarrow .C \equiv \Box(=, s, d, f).C$. This term denotes
pairs $\langle i, d \rangle$ such that $\langle i', d \rangle$ is in the denotation of C for all intervals i' *starting*,
during or *finishing* the interval i and even at i itself.

When the language allows the use of time-expressions of type TE_5 we can
specify temporal constraints on the duration of intervals and relations with constant intervals.

Example 2. The concept

$$\Diamond((b) \sqcap (> \text{ '2years'}) \sqcap ((bi) \text{ '1988'})). \downarrow .\text{widow}$$

represents persons that have been widows for more than 2 years after 1988^2.

The syntax allows more than one relation with a constant interval and constant
intervals have fixed durations. Hence, a time-expression can define a complex
set of constraints, possibly generating conflicts. In the above example, there are
no conflicts in the time-expression. However, imposing ci to be *after* '1988' and
also *before* the reference interval i, it constrains also the reference interval to be
after '1988'. This means that all pairs in the denotation of the above concept
will have an interval component that is necessarily *after* the '1988' constant
interval. To make explicit all of the constraints defined by a time-expression,
it is necessary to use constraint propagation techniques. We compute minimal
constraint networks corresponding to minimal time-expressions.

---

[1] An accurate classification of proposition types according to their property of inher-
iting validity on sub- and super- intervals can be found in [9].

[2] Note that, by our definition, we do not consider a remarried widow to be a widow.

4   Formal Semantics

A temporal structure $\langle \mathcal{UL}, < \rangle$ consists of a set of points and an order relation. Initially, we will not make any assumption about its properties, apart from being unbounded and linear. Intervals are characterized by their endpoints taken from the temporal structure. The intervals domain is defined by

$$\mathcal{I} \stackrel{def}{=} \{(t_1, t_2) | \, t_1 < t_2, \quad t_1, t_2 \in \mathcal{UL}\}$$

We assume a fixed model $\mathcal{M}$ that maps interval constants in pairs of points, duration constants in pairs of points (fixed reference intervals having that duration), duration relations in pairs of pairs of points (e.g., $<^{\mathcal{M}} = \{\langle (t_i, t_j), (t_r, t_s) \rangle :$ $t_j - t_i < t_s - t_r$ and $(t_i, t_j), (t_r, t_s) \in \mathcal{I}\}$). Obviously, speaking about durations is possible only if we have or define some kind of metric over the time structure. So, the above minus operator has to be intended as a measure of the distance between endpoints. Interval relations are mapped in sets of pairs of pairs of points:

$$m^{\mathcal{M}} = \{\langle (t_i, t_j), (t_r, t_s) \rangle : (t_j = t_r) \, \text{and} \, (t_i, t_j), (t_r, t_s) \in \mathcal{I}\}$$
$$s^{\mathcal{M}} = \{\langle (t_i, t_j), (t_r, t_s) \rangle : (t_i = t_r) \, \text{and} \, (t_j < t_s) \, \text{and} \, (t_i, t_j), (t_r, t_s) \in \mathcal{I}\}$$
$$f^{\mathcal{M}} = \{\langle (t_i, t_j), (t_r, t_s) \rangle : (t_j = t_s) \, \text{and} \, (t_i > t_r) \, \text{and} \, (t_i, t_j), (t_r, t_s) \in \mathcal{I}\}$$

About converse relations we can observe that $\langle (t_i, t_j), (t_r, t_s) \rangle \in z^{\mathcal{M}}$ iff $\langle (t_r, t_s), (t_i, t_j) \rangle \in zi^{\mathcal{M}}$ where z is any interval relation and zi its converse.

The semantics of TE is defined through the function $\mathcal{E}_t$ that given a TE and a reference interval (i) identifies a set of intervals in $\mathcal{I}$. $\mathcal{E}_t$ must satisfy the following equations, where $constr_j$ stays for an arbitrary constraint of type $\langle TE_3 \rangle$ or $\langle MC \rangle$ and rel is a single interval relation:

$$\mathcal{E}_t[(rel)]^i = \{i' : \langle i', i \rangle \in rel^{\mathcal{M}}\}$$

$$\mathcal{E}_t[(rel_1, \ldots, rel_n)]^i = \bigcup_{j=1}^{n} \mathcal{E}_t[(rel_j)]^i$$

$$\mathcal{E}_t[(constr_1 \sqcap \ldots \sqcap constr_n)]^i = \bigcap_{j=1}^{n} \mathcal{E}_t[constr_j]^i$$

$$\mathcal{E}_t[(\langle TE_3 \rangle \, int\_const)]^i = \mathcal{E}_t[\langle TE_3 \rangle]^{int\_const^{\mathcal{M}}}$$
$$\mathcal{E}_t[dur\_rel \, dur\_const]^i = \{i' : \langle i', dur\_const^{\mathcal{M}} \rangle \in dur\_rel^{\mathcal{M}}\}$$

These equations, together with a choice for $\mathcal{M}$, define the interpretation of the five types of time-expressions.

We interpret temporal terms in a structure $\langle \mathcal{D}, \mathcal{I}, \mathcal{E} \rangle$, where $\mathcal{D}$ is a set of individuals, $\mathcal{I}$ is the set of time intervals and $\mathcal{E}$ is an extension function. The function $\mathcal{E}$ assigns to each concept a set of pairs $\langle i, d \rangle$ and to each role a set of triples $\langle i, d_1, d_2 \rangle$. $\mathcal{E}$ is fully defined when its value is given for all primitive symbols (atomic concepts and roles). For $\langle \mathcal{D}, \mathcal{I}, \mathcal{E} \rangle$ to be a semantic structure of the logic, the function $\mathcal{E}$ must satisfy the equations[3] in Figure 3.

---

[3]   we give an equation for each common terminological operator. For a given logic, only those relative to the operators in that logic are required.

There are some equivalences among the logics that we have defined.

Proposition 1. *For all considered logics $T\mathcal{L}_i$, $T\mathcal{L}_1 \equiv T\mathcal{L}_2$*

This is true, since through the six temporal relations in TE_1 it is possible to define $\Diamond TE_2.C$ and $\Box TE_2.C$. For example, $\Diamond(b).C \equiv \Diamond(m).\Diamond(m).C$. However, it is sometimes desirable to avoid nesting of temporal operators.

Proposition 2. $T\mathcal{ALC}_1 \equiv T\mathcal{ALC}_2 \equiv T\mathcal{ALC}_3 \equiv T\mathcal{ALC}_4$

This equivalence can be easily proved observing that:
$$\Diamond(rel_1, rel_2).C \equiv (\Diamond(rel_1).C \sqcup \Diamond(rel_2).C)$$
So, if we have terminological disjunction in the logic, we can represent disjunction of temporal relations in time-expressions. Similarly:
$$\Box(rel_1, rel_2).C \equiv (\Box(rel_1).C \sqcap \Box(rel_2).C)$$

$$\mathcal{E}[C_1 \sqcap C_2] = \mathcal{E}[C_1] \cap \mathcal{E}[C_2] \tag{1}$$
$$\mathcal{E}[\top] = \mathcal{I} \times \mathcal{D} \tag{2}$$
$$\mathcal{E}[\bot] = \emptyset \tag{3}$$
$$\mathcal{E}[\neg C] = (\mathcal{I} \times \mathcal{D}) \setminus \mathcal{E}[C] \tag{4}$$
$$\mathcal{E}[\forall R.C] = \{\langle i, d \rangle : \forall d' \langle i, d, d' \rangle \in \mathcal{E}[R] \to \langle i, d' \rangle \in \mathcal{E}[C]\} \tag{5}$$
$$\mathcal{E}[\exists R] = \{\langle i, d \rangle : \exists d' \langle i, d, d' \rangle \in \mathcal{E}[R]\} \tag{6}$$
$$\mathcal{E}[\exists R.C] = \{\langle i, d \rangle : \exists d' \langle i, d, d' \rangle \in \mathcal{E}[R] \wedge \langle i, d' \rangle \in \mathcal{E}[C]\} \tag{7}$$
$$\mathcal{E}[\geq n R] = \{\langle i, d \rangle : \| \{d' : \langle i, d, d' \rangle \in \mathcal{E}[R]\} \| \geq n\} \tag{8}$$
$$\mathcal{E}[\leq n R] = \{\langle i, d \rangle : \| \{d' : \langle i, d, d' \rangle \in \mathcal{E}[R]\} \| \leq n\} \tag{9}$$
$$\mathcal{E}[\Diamond TE.C] = \{\langle i, d \rangle : \exists i' \ i' \in \mathcal{E}_t[TE]^i \wedge \langle i', d \rangle \in \mathcal{E}[C]\} \tag{10}$$
$$\mathcal{E}[\Box TE.C] = \{\langle i, d \rangle : \forall i' \ i' \in \mathcal{E}_t[TE]^i \to \langle i', d \rangle \in \mathcal{E}[C]\} \tag{11}$$

Fig. 3. Semantics of temporal concepts

4.1 A Simpler Semantics for a Subset of Logics

It is possible to give an equivalent much simpler semantics if we consider logics using only TE_2 or logics using TE_4 but having terminological disjunction. As noted above, temporal operators with disjunction of temporal relations can be translated into an equivalent form that is a disjunction (or conjunction) of temporal operators with a single temporal relation. The syntax for $T\mathcal{ALC}_i$ with $i \leq 4$, for example, can be described by the following formation rules:

$$C, C_1, C_2 \to \top \mid A \mid \neg C \mid C_1 \sqcap C_2 \mid \forall R.C \mid \Diamond\langle TE_1 \rangle.C$$

where C, C_1, C_2 are arbitrary concepts, A is an arbitrary atomic concept and R an arbitrary atomic role.

The semantics does not need the definition of $\mathcal{M}$ and $\mathcal{E}_t$, but it is simply given by the equations 1 through 5 in Figure 3, making explicit the representation of intervals by endpoints and adding the equations reported in Figure 4. This semantics is particularly interesting since it shows the strong correspondence with the interval-based propositional modal logics proposed in [6].

$$\mathcal{E}[\Diamond(s).C] = \{\langle(t_1,t_2),d\rangle : \exists t_3 \in \mathcal{UL} \quad t_1 < t_3 < t_2 \wedge \langle(t_1,t_3),d\rangle \in \mathcal{E}[C]\}$$
$$\mathcal{E}[\Diamond(si).C] = \{\langle(t_1,t_2),d\rangle : \exists t_3 \in \mathcal{UL} \quad t_2 < t_3 \wedge \langle(t_1,t_3),d\rangle \in \mathcal{E}[C]\}$$
$$\mathcal{E}[\Diamond(f).C] = \{\langle(t_1,t_2),d\rangle : \exists t_3 \in \mathcal{UL} \quad t_1 < t_3 < t_2 \wedge \langle(t_3,t_2),d\rangle \in \mathcal{E}[C]\}$$
$$\mathcal{E}[\Diamond(fi).C] = \{\langle(t_1,t_2),d\rangle : \exists t_3 \in \mathcal{UL} \quad t_3 < t_1 \wedge \langle(t_3,t_2),d\rangle \in \mathcal{E}[C]\}$$
$$\mathcal{E}[\Diamond(m).C] = \{\langle(t_1,t_2),d\rangle : \exists t_3 \in \mathcal{UL} \quad t_3 < t_1 \wedge \langle(t_3,t_1),d\rangle \in \mathcal{E}[C]\}$$
$$\mathcal{E}[\Diamond(mi).C] = \{\langle(t_1,t_2),d\rangle : \exists t_3 \in \mathcal{UL} \quad t_2 < t_3 \wedge \langle(t_2,t_3),d\rangle \in \mathcal{E}[C]\}$$

Fig. 4. Semantics of temporal concepts with single qualitative relations

4.2 Coherence and Subsumption

We are interested in evaluating subsumption relations between the concepts defined in a terminology using our logics. This is done evaluating formulae of the form $C_1 \sqsubseteq C_2$ with respect to temporal semantic structures.

Definition 3. $C_1 \sqsubseteq C_2$ is **true** in a structure $\langle \mathcal{D}, \mathcal{I}, \mathcal{E} \rangle$ iff $\mathcal{E}(C_1) \subseteq \mathcal{E}(C_2)$. We can use the notation: $\langle \mathcal{D}, \mathcal{I}, \mathcal{E} \rangle \models C_1 \sqsubseteq C_2$

Definition 4. A concept C is **coherent** iff the formula $C \sqsubseteq \bot$ is false in at least one structure. Formally:
C is coherent iff exist $\mathcal{D}, \mathcal{E}$ such that $\langle \mathcal{D}, \mathcal{I}, \mathcal{E} \rangle \not\models C \sqsubseteq \bot$.

Definition 5. A concept C_1 is **subsumed** by concept C_2 iff for all $\mathcal{D}, \mathcal{E}$ $\langle \mathcal{D}, \mathcal{I}, \mathcal{E} \rangle \models C_1 \sqsubseteq C_2$. We can use the notation: $\models C_1 \sqsubseteq C_2$

Definition 6. A concept C_1 is **equivalent** to concept C_2 iff $\models C_1 \sqsubseteq C_2$ and $\models C_2 \sqsubseteq C_1$

A concept is **incoherent**, or inconsistent, if it is equivalent to the empty concept ($\bot$).

Example 3. As a simple example of subsumption between temporal concepts, let us consider the following concept definitions:
$$C_1 \doteq \Diamond(d,bi).\text{engineer} \qquad C_2 \doteq \Box(=,s,d,f).\text{electrical-engineer}$$
Intuitively C_1 is the class of all persons that are engineers in a subinterval of the reference interval or that will be engineers in a future interval. C_2 is the class of persons that are engineers at the reference interval and at all intervals contained in it[4]. The subsumption of C_2 by C_1 is given by both temporal

---

[4] as it is natural for a *homogeneous* concept.

and terminological reasons. We concentrate on temporal subsumption assuming that **electrical-engineer** is subsumed by **engineer**, given an adequate definition of **electrical-engineer**. The subsumption of the $\Box$ term by the $\Diamond$ one can be formally checked referring to the semantics and can be intuitively motivated observing that, if an individual d is a C_2 at an interval i, then it is an **electrical-engineer** at i and at all intervals starting, finishing and during i. Hence, it exists an interval during i at which d is an **electrical-engineer** and, by the assumption, an **engineer**. This means that d is also a C_1 at interval i. Since d is an arbitrary individual and this reasoning does not depend from the function $\mathcal{E}$, the subsumption holds.

While computing subsumption is fairly trivial for this example, it gets hard when we consider complex terms with nesting of temporal operators.

5 The Subsumption Problem

As formally defined above, a concept C_1 is subsumed by another concept C_2 if for all semantic structures the value of the extension function for C_1 is a subset of that for C_2. For propositionally complete logics (where we have negation), this problem is equivalent to the incoherence of $C_1 \sqcap \neg C_2$. The fact that temporal operators seem to be a temporal counterpart of the terminological operators $\exists R.C$ and $\forall R.C$ suggests the extension of recent subsumption algorithms based on tableaux-like techniques as used, for example, in [5]. Our investigation in this direction reveals several problems due to deep differences between temporal relations and roles and to the fact of having a fixed unbounded interval domain. The non existence of such a complete and terminating algorithm, at least for some of the logics in our family, is confirmed by undecidability results.

Let us consider a slight variant of our $\mathcal{TALC}_1$ logic, adopting an interval domain admitting zero-length intervals, like (t, t). In this case we can represent individuals having certain properties not only at intervals but even at single instants. The semantics of temporal operators in Figure 4 must be slightly changed to include a point as a starting or finishing interval:

$$\mathcal{E}[\Diamond(s).C] = \{\langle (t_1, t_2), d \rangle : \exists t_3 \quad t_1 \leq t_3 < t_2 \wedge \langle (t_1, t_3), d \rangle \in \mathcal{E}[C]\}$$
$$\mathcal{E}[\Diamond(f).C] = \{\langle (t_1, t_2), d \rangle : \exists t_3 \quad t_1 < t_3 \leq t_2 \wedge \langle (t_3, t_2), d \rangle \in \mathcal{E}[C]\}$$

To distinguish logics interpreted on this domain with respect to our domain of proper intervals, we add the time structure and, respectively, the $\leq$ or $<$ sign between parenthesis at the end of the logic's name. It turns out that the propositional modal logics of intervals studied in [6] correspond to the $\mathcal{TALC}_1(\mathcal{UL}, \leq)$ logic, ignoring the value restriction operator ($\forall R.C$). This fact leads to the following theorems[5]:

---

[5] For lack of space, in this section we only report some of the results that we have obtained on the subsumption problem. A more detailed treatment with proofs can be found in [3].

Theorem 7. *The subsumption problem in $\mathcal{TALC}_i(\mathcal{UL}, \leq)$ with $1 \leq i \leq 5$ is undecidable (r.e.-hard). It is Π_1^1-hard if $\mathcal{UL}$ is a complete structure.*

$(\mathbb{R}, \leq)$ and $(\mathbb{Z}, \leq)$ are examples of complete structures. The proof of the theorem is based on a reduction from the satisfiability problem of the propositional interval logic, proved undecidable in [6], to the coherence problem in $\mathcal{TALC}_1(\mathcal{UL}, \leq)$.

Theorem 7 regards logics with interval domains admitting zero-length intervals. We proved its extension to the propositionally complete logic $\mathcal{TALC}_i(\mathbb{Z}, <)$, admitting only proper intervals defined on the integers.

This undecidability result is not limited to logics in our family.

Corollary 8. *The subsumption problem in $\mathcal{TB}$ extended with negation is Π_1^1-hard*

The proof is trivial, since the logics $\mathcal{TALC}_i(\mathbb{Z}, <)$ are essentially fragments of the $\mathcal{TB}$ logic[6]. We formally proved it by a reduction from the coherence problem in $\mathcal{TALC}_1(\mathbb{Z}, <)$.

Decidability of subsumption in the other logics is still an open problem. The limitation to proper intervals in the temporal domain is significant when considering a dense structure. We could not find any reduction from the subsumption problem in $\mathcal{TALC}_1(\mathbb{Q}, \leq)$ to the same problem in $\mathcal{TALC}_1(\mathbb{Q}, <)$. However, for logics with intervals defined over the rational numbers we get an interesting upper bound.

Theorem 9. *Subsumptions in $\mathcal{TALC}_4(\mathbb{Q}, <)$ and its sublogics are recursively enumerable.*

Note that, by Theorem 7, subsumptions in a similar logic, with integers in place of rational numbers, are not even recursively enumerable. The result is an extension of the one we presented in [2] and it is obtained by a translation in first order logic. This shows that, in principle, we can use first order resolution techniques for checking subsumption when intervals are defined on rational numbers. The translation has been implemented and we are conducting some experiments along these lines.

Regarding the logics of our family that do not allow negation, nor disjunction, we concentrated our efforts in the development of sound but incomplete algorithms. Most subsumption algorithms used in real terminological systems are incomplete and are implemented by a technique called *structural comparison*. We integrate this technique with temporal constraint propagation algorithms to compute minimal time-expressions that are essential to compare temporal terms. We have developed such an algorithm for the $\mathcal{TFL}_5^-$ logic, proving its soundness. Regarding incompleteness, we have identified in the nesting of temporal operators one of its main sources. Our experience shows that temporal nesting must be strongly limited and special *completion* rules must be added to the algorithm. While our basic algorithm has a polynomial time behavior, the price paid for

---

[6] The undecidability of $\mathcal{TB}$ with negation has been claimed also in [7] referring to the results in [6].

adding completion rules is a worst case exponential time complexity. In [3] we present an example of a completed algorithm for a fragment of $\mathcal{TFL}_5^-$ that can be used for the representation and management of taxonomies of actions.

Conclusions

In this paper we have presented a family of interval-based temporal terminological logics where the logics are differentiated by their set of terminological operators, their set of temporal operators and the temporal structure over which intervals are defined. This work can be considered an offspring of that of Schmiedel [8] where we address issues like the importance of the temporal structure, decidability of subsumption and the development of sound but incomplete algorithms.

We believe that there are application problems that really need the expressive power of such deep temporal extensions of terminological logics. However, we should be aware of the difficulties involved in implementing inferences. The results reported in the last section are a contribution to the understanding of these difficulties. Our work on incomplete algorithms shows that we can choose special fragments of these logics that are powerful enough for representing complex domains (like that of *actions*) and admit subsumption algorithms whose incompleteness can be reasonably restricted.

References

1. James F. Allen. Maintaining knowledge about temporal intervals. *Communications of the ACM*, 26(11):832–843, November 1983.
2. Claudio Bettini. A formalization of interval based temporal subsumption in first order logic. In *Workshop Notes of the ECAI Workshop on Theoretical Foundations of Knowledge Representation and Reasoning*, Vienna, Austria, 1992.
3. Claudio Bettini. *Estensioni temporali dei linguaggi terminologici.* PhD thesis, Dip. Scienze dell'Informazione - University of Milano, Italy, 1993. (in Italian).
4. Ronald J. Brachman and Hector J. Levesque. The tractability of subsumption in frame-based description languages. In *Proc. of the American National Conference on Artificial Intelligence (AAAI-84)*, pages 34–37, Austin, TX, 1984.
5. F. M. Donini, M. Lenzerini, D. Nardi, and W. Nutt. The complexity of concept languages. In *Proc. of the 2nd International Conference on Principles of Knowledge Representation and Reasoning*, pages 151–162, Cambridge, MA, 1991.
6. J. Y. Halpern and Y. Shoham. A propositional modal logic for time intervals. In *Proceedings of the Symposium on Logic In Computer Science*, 1986.
7. Klaus Schild. A tense-logical extension of terminological logics. Technical Report KIT Report 92, Computer Science Department, Technische Universität Berlin, 1991.
8. Albrecht Schmiedel. A temporal terminological logic. In *Proc. of the American National Conference on Artificial Intelligence (AAAI-90)*, pages 640–645, Boston, MA, 1990.
9. Y. Shoham. *Reasoning about Change.* The MIT Press, 1988.
10. P. van Beek and R. Cohen. Exact and approximate reasoning about temporal relations. *Computational Intelligence*, 6, 1990.

Logic Programming and Autoepistemic Logics: New Relations and Complexity Results*

Marco Schaerf

Istituto di Elettrotecnica, Università di Cagliari
Piazza d'Armi, 09123 Cagliari, Italia
and
Dipartimento di Informatica e Sistemistica,
Università di Roma "La Sapienza"
via Salaria 113, 00198 Roma, Italia
schaerf@assi.ing.uniroma1.it

Abstract. In recent years, many authors have pointed out the strict correlation between non-Horn logic programs and non-monotonic reasoning. As a result, many studies on the relations between various semantics for negation and non-monotonic logics have appeared in the literature. The analysis of these relations helps understanding the properties of the various systems and allows importing analysis from one formalism into another one. In this paper we show a one-to-one mapping between the positivistic models and moderately-grounded expansions of autoepistemic logic and a one-to-one correspondence between the minimally-supported models and the stable parsimonious expansions. These relations are then used to prove the computational complexity of reasoning with the positivistic and minimally-supported model semantics, as well as new complexity results for restricted subsets of autoepistemic logic.

1 Introduction

Since the pioneering work of Clark [5], the issue of correctly characterizing the behavior of logic programs with negation has always been a very important and controversial issue. More recently, people have started realizing that the problem of handling non-Horn logic programs is strictly related to the work done in Artificial Intelligence on non-monotonic reasoning. As a result, many studies on the relations between various semantics for negation and non-monotonic logics have appeared in the literature in recent years. Moreover, new semantics have been proposed that build directly on ideas from artificial intelligence. See, for example, the default model semantics of Bidoit and Froidevaux [2] that is inspired from Reiter's default logic [14].

The analysis of these relations is important for several reasons, first of all it helps clarifying the properties of the various systems and their correlations,

---

* Work partially supported by the ESPRIT Basic Research Action COMPULOG and the Progetto Finalizzato Informatica & Calcolo Parallelo of the CNR (Italian Research Council)

and secondly it helps importing analysis from one formalism into another one. One of the most important of these analysis is the study of the computational complexity of these formalisms, study that can take advantage of the known relations.

As an example, Marek and Truszczyński in [11, 12] have analyzed in great detail the properties of autoepistemic logics and, through established relations between the stable model (Gelfond and Lifschitz [8]) and supported model (Apt, Blair and Walker [1]) semantics with autoepistemic logics, have been able to completely characterize the computational complexity of the various reasoning tasks for these two semantics.

In this paper we establish two new relations between, on one side semantics for negation and on the other side variants of autoepistemic logic.

In particular, we show:

- A one-to-one correspondence between the positivistic models, introduced by Bidoit and Hull in [3, 4], and moderately-grounded expansions of autoepistemic logic introduced by Konolige in [9];
- A one-to-one correspondence between the minimally-supported models, introduced by Marek and Subrahmanian in [10] and the stable parsimonious expansions introduced by Eiter and Gottlob in [7].

These relations are then used to prove the computational complexity of reasoning with the positivistic and minimally-supported model semantics, as well as new complexity results for restricted subsets of autoepistemic logic.

The most important complexity result obtained is the following one: reasoning w. r. t. positivistic models is a problem at the second level of the polynomial hierarchy. In particular, deciding whether a literal is true in one positivistic model of a program is a Σ_2^p-complete problem, while deciding whether a literal is true in all the positivistic models of a program is Π_2^p-complete.

These complexity results are somehow surprising, since, to the best of our knowledge, the positivistic model semantics is the first semantics shown to be strictly harder than NP and co-NP (under the assumption that the polynomial hierarchy is proper).

2 Preliminaries

In this section we briefly review some semantics for negation in logic programming, autoepistemic logics and complexity results presented in the literature.

2.1 Supported Model Semantics

In this paper we will deal only with propositional languages. A program P is a set of rules of the form

$$a \leftarrow b_1 \wedge \ldots \wedge b_n \wedge \neg c_1 \wedge \ldots \wedge \neg c_m$$

where $a, b_1, \ldots, b_n, c_1, \ldots, c_m$ are propositional letters. a is called the head and $b_1 \wedge \ldots \wedge b_n \wedge \neg c_1 \wedge \ldots \wedge \neg c_m$ is the body of the rule. An interpretation I is a set of letters (those that are evaluated to *true*), while a model M of a program P is an interpretation which satisfies P, i. e. for all rules of P either the head is in M or one of the negative literals of the body is in M or one of the positive ones is not in M. A model M is minimal iff there exists no other model M' s. t. $M' \subset M$.

The supported models semantics has been introduced by Apt, Blair and Walker in [1]. The idea behind this semantics is very simple and appealing: Every interesting model of a program should be able to support itself. This idea is captured by the following definition:

Definition 1 Supported Model. Let P be a program and M one of its models. We say that M is a supported model of P iff $\forall l \in M$ there exists a rule $a \leftarrow b_1 \wedge \ldots \wedge b_n \wedge \neg c_1 \wedge \ldots \wedge \neg c_m$ in P s. t. $a = l$ and $M \models b_1 \wedge \ldots \wedge b_n \wedge \neg c_1 \wedge \ldots \wedge \neg c_m$.

Several variants of this semantics have been proposed in the literature, in particular Bidoit and Hull in [4] have introduced the positivistic model semantics.

Definition 2 Positivistic Model. Let P be a program and M one of its models. We say that M is a positivistic model of P iff it is at the same time a supported model and a minimal model of P.

Another interesting variant is the minimally supported model semantics proposed by Marek and Subrahmanian in [10].

Definition 3 Supp-minimal Model. Let P be a program and M one of its models. We say that M is a minimally-supported model of P (supp-minimal) iff it is a supported model of P and there exists no supported model M' of P s. t. $M' \subset M$.

Notice that the set of positivistic models and the set of supp-minimal models are distinct. For example, let $P = \{p \leftarrow p, p \leftarrow q, p \leftarrow \neg r, r \leftarrow p \wedge \neg q\}^2$, its only supported model is $\{p, r\}$ which is also supp-minimal, but it does not have any positivistic model since $\{p, r\}$ is not minimal. In fact, $\{r\}$ is a model of P.

2.2 Autoepistemic Logics

Autoepistemic logic has been introduced by Moore in [13] and is one of the most widely analyzed systems for non-monotonic reasoning. Its language is composed of the symbols of propositional logic plus a modal operator L. The intended reading of the formula $L\alpha$ is that α is believed. Formulae not containing the modal operator are called *objective*.

The semantics of autoepistemic logic is given through the notions of *stable set* and *stable expansion*.

---

[2] This example is taken from [4]

Definition 4 Stable Set. A set E is a stable set iff $E \supseteq \{\alpha | E \cup \{L\phi | \phi \in E\} \cup \{\neg L\psi | \psi \notin E\} \vdash \alpha\}$.

The intuition underlying this definition, is that a stable set of formulae should contain all the consequences of believing all its formulae and not believing all the formulae not in it.

The central notion in autoepistemic logic, is the concept of autoepistemic expansions of a set of formulae.

Definition 5 Stable Expansion. Given a set of formulae A, the initial assumptions, a set of formulae E is a stable expansion of A iff $E = \{\alpha | A \cup \{L\phi | \phi \in E\} \cup \{\neg L\psi | \psi \notin E\} \vdash \alpha\}$.

The objective part (denoted with $Ob(E)$) of a stable set or stable expansion E is the set of the objective formulae which belong to it. It is important to point out that the objective part uniquely characterizes a stable expansion, hence we frequently identify an expansion with the set of its objective formulae. While all stable sets are generally incomparable w. r. t. all the formulae they contain, they can be partially ordered w. r. t. their objective part.

Definition 6. Let E_1 and E_2 be two stable sets, $E_1 \preceq E_2$ iff $Ob(E_1) \subseteq Ob(E_2)$.

Konolige in [9] has defined a variant of autoepistemic logic based on moderately-grounded expansions.

Definition 7 Moderately-grounded Expansion. A stable expansion E of a set A is moderately-grounded iff there exists no stable set S such that $A \subseteq S$ and $S \prec E$.

A slightly different definition has been proposed by Eiter and Gottlob in [7], where they introduce the parsimonious expansions.

Definition 8 Parsimonious Expansion. A stable expansion E of a set A is parsimonious iff there exists no stable expansion E' of A such that $E' \prec E$.

2.3 Complexity Results

Throughout the paper we refer to the standard notation in complexity theory. In particular P^A (NP^A) corresponds to the class of decision problems that are solved in polynomial time by deterministic (nondeterministic) Turing machines using an oracle for A in polynomial time. All the problems we analyze reside in the *polynomial hierarchy*, introduced by Stockmeyer in [15], that is the analog of the Kleene arithmetic hierarchy. The classes Σ_k^p, Π_k^p and Δ_k^p of the polynomial hierarchy are defined by $\Sigma_0^p = \Pi_0^p = \Delta_0^p = P$, and for $k \geq 0$, $\Sigma_{k+1}^p = NP^{\Sigma_k^p}$, $\Pi_{k+1}^p = \text{co-}\Sigma_{k+1}^p$ and $\Delta_{k+1}^p = P^{\Sigma_k^p}$.

The computational complexity of reasoning with the supported model semantics has been analyzed by Marek and Truszczyński in [12], where they show that:

- deciding whether a formula is true in at least one supported model of a program is an NP-complete problem;
- deciding whether a formula is true in all the supported models of a program is a co-NP-complete problem.

Other complexity results we use in the following sections deal with the complexity of reasoning w. r. t. minimal models of propositional formulae and programs. Eiter and Gottlob in [6] show that:

- deciding whether a formula α is true in at least one minimal model of a propositional formula T is a Σ_2^p-complete problem. Σ_2^p-hardness holds even if α is a literal;
- deciding whether a formula α is true in all minimal models of a propositional formula T is a Π_2^p-complete problem. Π_2^p-hardness holds even if α is a literal.

These results can also be extended to the case of logic programs.

Theorem 9. *Let P be a program and α a propositional formula. Deciding whether α is true in all the minimal models of P is a Π_2^p-complete problem. Deciding whether a formula α is true in at least one minimal model of the program P is a Σ_2^p-complete problem. Π_2^p and Σ_2^p-hardness hold even if α is a literal.*

Proof. The first problem is known to be in Π_2^p as a consequence of the results of Eiter and Gottlob [6], we only need to show hardness. We prove it by a reduction from the problem of deciding whether α is true in all minimal models of a CNF formula T to deciding whether α is true in all minimal models of a program P.

Let p be a letter not occurring in T nor in α, $P = \{p \leftarrow \neg c |$ for any clause $c \in T\}$ and $\alpha' = \alpha \vee p$. There are three possibilities:

1. T is unsatisfiable. Hence α is true in all minimal models of T. Obviously P has a unique minimal model $M_1 = \{p\}$ and α' is true in M_1.
2. T has the unique minimal model $M_2 = \emptyset$. This will also be the unique minimal model of P and α' is true in M_2 iff α is true in M_2.
3. the set of minimal models of P is equal to the union of M_1 and the set of all minimal models of T. If α is true in all minimal models of T obviously α' will be true in all minimal models of P and viceversa.

Hence, Π_2^p-completeness follows. For the proof of Σ_2^p-completeness, notice that α is true in all minimal models of P iff it is not the case that exists a minimal model of P which makes $\neg\alpha$ true. Therefore, this problem is in the complementary complexity class Σ_2^p-complete. $\qquad\Box$

In our analysis we also use the study of the computational complexity of reasoning in autoepistemic logics with moderately-grounded and parsimonious expansions done by Eiter and Gottlob in [7].

3   New Relations and Complexity Results

The strict relations linking autoepistemic logics and semantics for negation have been pointed out by several authors. In particular, several translations of logic programs into autoepistemic theories have been defined. Here we recall one of them. Given a program rule r

$$c \leftarrow a_1 \wedge \ldots \wedge a_n \wedge \neg b_1 \wedge \ldots \wedge \neg b_m$$

its translation $tr(r)$ is the autoepistemic formula

$$La_1 \wedge \ldots \wedge La_n \wedge \neg Lb_1 \wedge \ldots \wedge \neg Lb_m \Rightarrow c$$

Given a program P we define its translation $tr(P)$ as the set of autoepistemic formulae that are translations of rules in P.

In the following, given an interpretation $M = \{a_1, \ldots, a_k\}$ we denote with $E(\{M\})$ the minimal (w. r. t. $\preceq$) stable set whose objective part is $\{\alpha | \alpha$ is objective and $a_1 \wedge \ldots \wedge a_k \vdash \alpha\}$. Notice that such a set is always consistent.

Given a clause $c = a_1 \vee \ldots \vee a_k \vee \neg b_1 \vee \ldots \vee \neg b_m$, we denote with c^* the formula $a_1 \vee \ldots \vee a_k \vee \neg Lb_1 \vee \ldots \vee \neg Lb_m$. Using these notations we can establish the relation between truth in an interpretation and belonging in the corresponding stable set.

Corollary 10. *Let M be an interpretation and c a clause. Then $M \models c$ iff $c^* \in E(\{M\})$.*

The existence of a relation between supported models and stable expansions has been proven by Marek and Subrahmanian in [10] and further discussed by Marek and Truszczyński in [12].

Theorem 11 Marek-Subrahmanian. *Let P be a logic program and M an interpretation, then M is a supported model of P iff $E(\{M\})$ is a stable expansion of $tr(P)$.*

We now show that similar relations also hold between moderately-grounded and parsimonious expansions on one side and positivistic and supp-minimal models on the other side.

Theorem 12. *Let P be a logic program and M an interpretation, then M is a model of P iff $E(\{M\})$ is a stable set such that $tr(P) \subseteq E(\{M\})$.*

Proof. ($\Longrightarrow$) Since M is a model of P we have that M satisfies all rules $a \leftarrow b_1 \wedge \ldots \wedge b_n \wedge \neg c_1 \wedge \ldots \wedge \neg c_m$ of P. We now have three cases:

1. $a \in M$. In this case, $a \in E(\{M\})$ and hence $(Lb_1 \wedge \ldots \wedge Lb_n \wedge \neg Lc_1 \wedge \ldots \wedge \neg Lc_m \Rightarrow a) \in E(\{M\})$;
2. $\exists c_i$ s. t. $0 \leq i \leq m$ and $c_i \in M$. Since $c_i \in E(\{M\})$ then $Lc_i \in E(\{M\})$ and, therefore, $(Lb_1 \wedge \ldots \wedge Lb_n \wedge \neg Lc_1 \wedge \ldots \wedge \neg Lc_m \Rightarrow a) \in E(\{M\})$;

3. $\exists b_j$ s. t. $0 \leq j \leq n$ and $b_j \notin M$. Since $b_j \notin E(\{M\})$ then $\neg Lb_j \in E(\{M\})$ and, therefore, $(Lb_1 \wedge \ldots \wedge Lb_n \wedge \neg Lc_1 \wedge \ldots \wedge \neg Lc_m \Rightarrow a) \in E(\{M\})$.

$(\Longleftarrow)$ Since $E(\{M\})$ is a stable set containing $tr(P)$ for any translated rule $tr(r)$ of $tr(P)$ we have that either:

1. $a \in E(\{M\})$. In this case, $a \in M$ hence $M \models r$;
2. $\exists Lc_i$ s. t. $0 \leq i \leq m$ and $Lc_i \in E(\{M\})$. Therefore, $c_i \in M$ hence $M \models r$;
3. $\exists \neg Lb_j$ s. t. $0 \leq j \leq n$ and $\neg Lb_j \in E(\{M\})$. Therefore, $b_j \notin M$ hence $M \models r$.

By applying the same argument to all the rules of P, it follows the thesis. $\square$

Using this result we can prove the one-to-one relation between positivistic models and moderately-grounded expansions.

Theorem 13. *Let P be a logic program and M an interpretation, then M is a positivistic model of P iff $E(\{M\})$ is a moderately-grounded expansion of $tr(P)$.*

Proof. $(\Longrightarrow)$ Since M is a positivistic model of P it is at the same time minimal and supported. Hence, $E(\{M\})$ is a stable expansion of $tr(P)$ and no stable set containing $tr(P)$ is smaller of it, therefore it is moderately-grounded.

$(\Longleftarrow)$ Since $E(\{M\})$ is a moderately-grounded expansion of $tr(P)$ then it is at the same time a stable expansion of $tr(P)$ and there is no smaller stable set containing $tr(P)$. Hence, M is supported and minimal and therefore positivistic. $\square$

Similarly, we have the one-to-one relation between supp-minimal models and parsimonious expansions.

Theorem 14. *Let P be a logic program and M an interpretation, then M is a supp-minimal model of P iff $E(\{M\})$ is a stable parsimonious expansion of $tr(P)$.*

Proof. $(\Longrightarrow)$ Since M is a supp-minimal model of P it is at supported and no other supported model is smaller of it. Hence, $E(\{M\})$ is a stable expansion of $tr(P)$ and no other stable expansion containing $tr(P)$ is smaller of it, therefore it is parsimonious.

$(\Longleftarrow)$ Since $E(\{M\})$ is a stable parsimonious expansion of $tr(P)$ then it is a stable expansion and there is no smaller stable expansion containing $tr(P)$. Hence, M is supported and no other supported model is smaller of it, therefore it is supp-minimal. $\square$

The relation between truth of a formula in a positivistic (supp-minimal) model and belonging in a moderately-grounded (stable parsimonious) expansion is provided by Corollary 10.

An example is now in order. Let's look again at the example used in the previous section. Let $P = \{p \leftarrow p, p \leftarrow q, p \leftarrow \neg r, r \leftarrow p \wedge \neg q\}$, then $tr(P) = \{Lp \Rightarrow p, Lq \Rightarrow p, \neg Lr \Rightarrow p, Lp \wedge \neg Lq \Rightarrow r\}$.

This set of autoepistemic formulae has only one stable expansion, that is $E(\{p, r\})$. As a consequence, $E(\{p, r\})$ is also parsimonious, but it is not moderately-grounded since there is a stable set $E(\{r\})$ s. t. $tr(P) \subseteq E(\{r\})$ and $Ob(E(\{r\})) \prec Ob(E(\{p, r\}))$. Notice that the stable set $E(\{r\})$ is not a stable expansion of $tr(P)$, since $E(\{r\}) \supset \{\alpha | A \cup \{L\phi | \phi \in E(\{r\})\} \cup \{\neg L\psi | \psi \notin E(\{r\})\} \vdash \alpha\}$. In fact, $r \in E(\{r\})$ but $r \notin \{\alpha | A \cup \{L\phi | \phi \in E(\{r\})\} \cup \{\neg L\psi | \psi \notin E(\{r\})\} \vdash \alpha\}$.

There are several positive outcomes of these results, first of all they give us a more complete picture of the relation between logic programming and non-monotonic reasoning, but, secondly they also help us in the analysis of the computational complexity of reasoning under the positivistic and supp-minimal model semantics. These problems have never been, to the best of our knowledge, addressed in the literature. The main result is the following:

Theorem 15. *Let P be a logic program and α a clause. Deciding whether α is true in at least one positivistic (supp-minimal) model of P is a Σ_2^p-complete problem. Deciding whether α is true in all the positivistic (supp-minimal) models of P is a Π_2^p-complete problem. Π_2^p and Σ_2^p-hardness hold even if α is a literal.*

Proof. We prove Σ_2^p-hardness (Π_2^p-hardness) by reducing the problem of deciding whether a literal u is true in at least one (all) minimal models of a program P'. This problem is Σ_2^p-complete (Π_2^p-complete) as shown by Theorem 9.

Let P' be $P \cup \{l \leftarrow l|$ for all literals l occurring in $P\}$. Notice that P and P' have the same models and that all models of P' are supported, hence the set of positivistic (supp-minimal) models of P' is exactly equal to the set of minimal models of P'. Hence, u is true in at least one (all) minimal model of P iff u is true in at least one (all) positivistic (supp-minimal) model of P'.

The fact that this problem belongs to the class Σ_2^p (Π_2^p) is an immediate consequence of the results of Eiter & Gottlob [7]. In fact, Theorem 3.6 for parsimonious expansions and Theorem 5.5 for moderately-grounded expansions give us the upper bounds.   □

These results are somehow surprising and put in serious doubt the feasibility of adopting these two semantics. As a term of comparison, notice that the same reasoning tasks are polynomial under the well-founded semantics of Van Gelder, Ross and Schlipf ([16]), NP and co-NP-complete under the stable/default semantics (Gelfond & Lifschitz [8] and Bidoit & Froidevaux [2]) and the supported model semantics, as shown in the previous section.

The above results also allow us to obtain tighter lower bounds for autoepistemic reasoning. A set of autoepistemic sentences is an *epistemic program* iff each sentence is of the form:

$$La_1 \vee \ldots \vee La_n \vee \neg Lb_1 \vee \ldots \vee \neg Lb_m \vee c$$

where $a_1, \ldots, a_n, b_1, \ldots, b_m, c$ are propositional letters (positive literals). It immediately follows from Theorems 13, 14 and 15 that:

Corollary 16. *Let A be an epistemic program and l a literal. Then deciding whether l* is true in at least one moderately-grounded (parsimonious) expansion of A is a Σ_2^p-complete problem. Deciding whether l* is true in all the moderately-grounded (parsimonious) expansions of A is a Π_2^p-complete problem.*

Notice that l^* is either a propositional letter or $\neg La$ where a is a propositional letter.

4 Conclusions

In this paper we have further investigated the relations between the various semantics for negation in logic programming and non-monotonic logics. In particular, we have established two strict relations, one between positivistic models and moderately-grounded expansions and the second one between minimally-supported models and stable parsimonious expansions.

These relations have also been used to prove new complexity results, some of which turn out to be very interesting and somehow surprising. In particular, the positivistic model semantics has been shown to be highly intractable from a computational point of view.

References

1. K. R. Apt, H. A. Blair, and A. Walker. Towards a theory of declarative knowledge. In J. Minker, editor, *Foundation of Deductive Databases and Logic Programming*, pages 89–142. Morgan Kaufmann, 1988.
2. N. Bidoit and C. Froidevaux. General logic databases and programs: default logic semantics and stratification. *Information and Computation*, 91:15–54, 1991.
3. N. Bidoit and R. Hull. Positivism versus minimalism in deductive databases. In *Proceedings of the Fifth Conference on Principle Of Database Systems (PODS-86)*, pages 123–132, 1986.
4. N. Bidoit and R. Hull. Minimalism, justification and non-monotonicity in deductive databases. *Journal of Computer and System Sciences*, 38:290–325, 1989.
5. K. L. Clark. Negation as failure. In H. Gallaire and J. Minker, editors, *Logic and Data Bases*, pages 293–322. Plenum, 1978.
6. T. Eiter and G. Gottlob. Propositional circumscription and extended closed world reasoning are Π_2^p-complete. Technical Report CD-TR 91/20, Technische Universität Wien, Vienna Austria, Christian Doppler Labor für Expertensysteme, May 1991. To appear in *Theoretical Computer Science*.
7. T. Eiter and G. Gottlob. Reasoning with parsimonious and moderately grounded expansions. *Fundamenta Informaticae*, 17(1,2):31–54, 1992.
8. M. Gelfond and V. Lifschitz. The stable model semantics for logic programming. In *Proceedings of the Fifth Logic Programming Symposium*, pages 1070–1080. MIT Press, 1988.
9. K. Konolige. On the relationship between default and autoepistemic logic. *Artificial Intelligence Journal*, 35:343–382, 1988.

10. W. Marek and V. S. Subrahmanian. The relationship between logic program semantics and non-monotonic reasoning. In *Proceedings of the Sixth International Conference on Logic Programming (ICLP-89)*, pages 600–617, 1989.
11. W. Marek and M. Truszczyński. Autoepistemic logic. *Journal of the ACM*, 38(3):588–619, 1991.
12. W. Marek and M. Truszczyński. Computing intersection of autoepistemic expansions. In *Proceedings of the First International Workshop on Logic Programming and Non Monotonic Reasoning*, pages 37–50. The MIT press, 1991.
13. R. C. Moore. Semantical considerations on nonmonotonic logic. *Artificial Intelligence Journal*, 25:75–94, 1985.
14. R. Reiter. A logic for default reasoning. *Artificial Intelligence Journal*, 13:81–132, 1980.
15. L. J. Stockmeyer. The polynomial-time hierarchy. *Theoretical Computer Science*, 3:1–22, 1976.
16. A. van Gelder, K. A. Ross, and J. S. Schlipf. The well-founded semantics for general logic programs. *Journal of the ACM*, 38:620–650, 1991.

Inferring in Lego-land: an Architecture for the Integration of Heterogeneous Inference Modules

Mauro Gaspari[1], Enrico Motta, and Arthur Stutt

Human Cognition Research Laboratory
The Open University
Walton Hall,
Milton Keynes, MK7 6AA, UK
email: e.motta@open.ac.uk

Abstract: The VITAL-KR provides the basic sub-structure for integrating a number of representation and inference paradigms as a means towards experimenting in the design of hybrid systems. In this paper we give an overview of the VITAL-KR, in particular illustrating how it supports the development of hybrid applications, as well as the integration of new inference systems. We believe that the VITAL-KR provides a number of advantages over alternative hybrid AI programming environments. Its communication primitives are *generic*, as they do not depend on the structure of a particular knowledge representation system; it is *extendible*, as it provides well-defined mechanisms for integrating new inference systems; it enjoys a formal, unambigous specification; and it comprises mechanisms to ensure the consistency of the overall, hybrid KB.

1 Introduction

1.1 The Rationale for Hybrid Systems

Over the past few years there has been quite a lot of interest in *hybrid* systems - i.e. systems which integrate multiple representation and inference paradigms (Allen & Miller, 1991; Corkill, 1991). An important reason underlining these efforts is that there is now widespread consensus in the AI community that "there is no single knowledge representation that is best for all problems, nor is there likely to be one" (Neches et al., 1991). Therefore, researchers are developing environments which can offer the user 'more choice' in terms of AI programming paradigms.

At the same time, researchers working on methodologies for AI system design (Reichgelt & Van Harmelen, 1986; Schreiber et al., 1988; Inder et al., 1990) are developing guidelines to help knowledge engineers to select the right knowledge representation technique for a given problem, or part of it. Obviously, to put these guidelines into practice, it is necessary to build hybrid knowledge engineering toolkits, supporting a wide choice of representation alternatives.

Finally, the current interest in hybrid systems has also been stimulated by the need to facilitate the reuse of knowledge-based (KB) components. In fact, as the number and size of KB applications grow, it is becoming more and more important that pre-existing KB components can be reused in the development of new applications. An

---

[1] Mauro Gaspari's current address is: Dipartimento di Matematica, Universita' di Bologna, Piazza S. Donato 5, Bologna, Italy. E-mail address is gaspari@csr.unibo.it

important prerequisite for this to happen is the development of open architectures supporting the interoperability of heterogeneous inference systems[2].

Testbeds such as MACE (Gasser, Braganza and Herman, 1987) have been introduced in order to facilitate the development of distributed and parallel systems. The recent interest in hybrid systems suggests there is also a need for a testbed supporting the development of non-distributed but hybrid inference systems. The VITAL-KR[3] (Motta et al., 1992) is a programming environment which provides the basic substructure for integrating a number of representation and inference paradigms as a means towards such experimentation. In this paper we give an overview of its architecture, we provide a formal account of its communication primitives and control components, and we discuss how it supports the development of hybrid applications as well as the integration of new inference systems.

1.2 Approaches to Hybrid Architectures

Commercial, hybrid knowledge engineering environments such as KEE™ and KnowledgeWorks™ are limited in terms of the numbers of paradigms they support (usually just rules and frames). More importantly, they are not easily extendible, to embed alternative inference mechanisms. In other words these systems are 'closed'.

In the GBB-OPS5 architecture (Corkill, 1991) it is possible to extend the reasoning mechanisms (at least in theory) by the specification of new types of GBB knowledge sources. While systems of this type are therefore extendible, they remain *embedded* in that the communication primitives and the integrating structure are *kernel-specific*. This means that even if a number of engines are integrated into the GBB framework, as far as the programmer of the resulting hybrid environment is concerned, the architecture remains that of an albeit extended blackboard.

Embedded architectures are currently the principal way in which hybrid programming environments are defined. The main problem with embedding as the integration technique for hybrid systems is that the resulting cooperation between the two reasoners depends on the design of the kernel, rather than on a generic and principled cooperation protocol. That is, because the emphasis is on integrating the component tools with the kernel, only kernel-dependent mechanisms for cooperation are provided. This aspect limits both the generality and the extendibility of these approaches.

In contrast with the aforementioned programming environments, a lot of work on distributed AI - for instance HECODES (Zhang & Bell, 1991) and the Contract Net organization described in (Davis and Smith, 1983) - is characterized by the adoption of a non-embedded, more extendible approach, where the system components are 'democratically organized' (i.e. there is no component in which all the others are embedded). Current work on a standard for communicating agents, KQML (Finin, et al., 1992), also presupposes a loose, 'horizontal' kind of organization. These non-embedded architectures do not suffer from the limitations we ascribe to embedded approaches. Because all components cooperate at the same level, and are only loosely

---

2   This is, however, only a necessary condition - see (Patil et al., 1992) for a complete analysis of requirements for reusable knowledge bases.

3   This research was part-funded by the Commission of the European Communities ESPRIT-II Project 5365 - VITAL. The partners in the VITAL project are the following: Syseca Temps Reel (F), Bull Cediag (F), Onera (F), The Open University (UK), University of Nottingham (UK), Royal PTT Netherland (NL), Nokia (SF), University of Helsinki (SF), and Andersen Consulting (E)

integrated, they are more suitable than embedded ones for supporting the sort of 'pick and mix' approach to KBS design mentioned earlier. Moreover, because the control and communication aspects of a non-embedded architecture do not depend on the embedding kernel, the communication language used by the components of the hybrid application can be truly generic and diverse cooperation strategies can be supported.

The non-embedded approach is therefore the one we have adopted for designing the VITAL-KR, which provides a hybrid AI programming environment as part of the VITAL workbench (Domingue et al, 1993). The VITAL-KR uses a horizontal, extendible organization for integrating a number of representation and inference paradigms (*engines*). However, in contrast with the aforementioned non-embedded systems, our primary aim is to provide a 'testbed' (or 'experimental workbench'), where AI programmers can develop systems which make use of a number of heterogeneous representations, as well as carrying out experiments in the design of hybrid systems. The adoption of a non-embedded organization allows us to define a generic (implementation-independent or *knowledge-level*) communication language, and enables users/designers to experiment with a range of configurations. Moreover, it also enables us to specify a simple and general framework for integrating additional engines, thus supporting implementation-level reusability.

Because non-embedded approaches only afford loose integration of components, it is normally difficult for this class of architectures to guarantee the consistency of the hybrid KB, and to describe its behaviour formally. In the design of the VITAL-KR we have addressed these two problems by i) defining the communication primitives so that it is possible for a justification-based truth maintenance system (*JTMS*) (Doyle, 1979) to monitor the consistency of the integrated, hybrid KB; and by ii) providing a formal account of the architecture.

2. An Overview of the VITAL-KR

The VITAL-KR 'shell' consists of three main (sets of) components which support the design of hybrid KBS. These are: an *Inference Scheduler* (IS), which is the main control and communication component; a set of default (i.e. predefined) engines which provide the VITAL-KR user with a range of representation and inference capabilities; and a JTMS, which can be used to ensure the consistency of the overall hybrid KB, and/or to provide default truth maintenance facilities to those engines which do not implement their own ones.

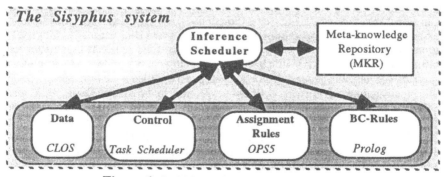

Figure 1. Architecture of the Sisyphus System.

Any particular hybrid system developed with the VITAL-KR consists of a number of *Inference Modules* (IMs). Each IM can be regarded as an internally homogeneous component of the overall hybrid KB and is therefore associated with a particular engine. As an example, we show in figure 1 the architecture of a simple application developed with the VITAL-KR, which solves the Sisyphus room allocation problem (Linster, 1992). This application comprises four inference modules, which make use of four different engines (in italics in the figure). Support for truth maintenance was not deemed necessary in this system, so the JTMS was not used

2.1 Communication in the VITAL-KR: the Functional Interface

IMs in a VITAL-KR based application communicate through a *functional interface*, which plays three roles. First, it defines the range of messages that can be exchanged by the IMs. Second, because the user or external tools can also be seen as IMs, it defines at a black-box level the range of functionalities that the VITAL-KR can provide. Third, because the VITAL-KR can only provide the functionalities supported by its components, it provides a functional framework for integrating IMs or for adding new engines to the engine library. Thus, it provides a non-ambiguous specification for those VITAL-KR users who wish to integrate additional engines. The functional interface does not depend on a particular configuration of the VITAL-KR, nor on the internal structure of an IM.

The functional interface supports a number of classes of *generic* operations, which include support for: entering new data (TELL); retracting existing data (RETRACT); querying the VITAL-KR (ASK); and interacting with the JTMS.

The primitives in the functional interface have been chosen by following two main criteria. On the one hand we want to have a set of primitives which enable us to deal with IMs and KBs as black boxes. In other words, "they are characterized not in terms of the structures they use to represent knowledge, but in terms of what they can be asked or told about some domain" (Levesque, 1984). On the other hand, because the aim is to provide a practical testbed for building large, hybrid KBS, a more fine grained breakdown has been used than would have been strictly necessary from a logical point of view. This can be seen in the case of the ASK class of primitives, which distinguishes between requests that are simple data retrieval operations (fetch, fetchall), and those which may require IMs to perform inferences (prove, proveall, establish, establishall).

All communication within, from, and to the VITAL-KR is centralized through the IS, and mediated by the functional interface. Messages have the structure: (<functional-interface-command> <c-expression>). A *c-expression* (or expression in the common language) is of the form: (<predicate> {<arg1>... <argn>}), with n ≥1. The predicate of a c-expression is a lisp symbol, and the optional arguments are arbitrary lisp S-expressions which can contain logical variables. A ground c-expression (i.e. one which does not contain variables) is called a *g-expression*.

The predicate in a c-expression defines its *type*, and, in the case of TELL, ASK, and RETRACT operations, this information is used by the IS to decide which IMs can deal with the operation in question. For example, in the Sisyphus problem the IM BC-rules contains Prolog clauses which enable the problem solver to decide which of the currently available rooms provides maximum access to the head of the group and the secretaries. Hence, the definition of IM BC-rules also specifies that this IM deals with queries of type 'maximum-access-to'. This information enables the IS to dispatch this class of queries correctly.

The advantage of having a simple type-based dispatching mechanism is that it minimizes the dispatching overhead. The mapping from types to IMs is stored in the *Meta-knowledge Repository* (MKR), which also contains knowledge on how to order the dispatching when more than one IM can deal with a particular message.

The IS associates an *agenda* with each IM and the JTMS, and uses these to manage the flow of messages to and from each of these components. Each agenda stores all messages dispatched to the corresponding component but not yet processed. Before a message is processed by a particular IM, its agenda is cleared - i.e. all pending messages are executed. This is done to ensure that the query is processed in an up-to-date environment.

This centralized model of communication (i.e. IS-mediated) makes for a more modular architecture, as both the communication between the VITAL-KR and the external world, and the communication between components of the VITAL-KR do not depend on the particular configuration of the system. A particular IM need not 'know' which IM (if any) can deal with a message which it originates. IMs send generic messages to the IS, this finds out those which can deal with them, and dispatches *concrete* messages to the interested IMs. Thus, in the Sisyphus example, we could substitute BC-rules with another (perhaps more efficient) IM, without this change affecting the rest of the system[4].

An important aspect of the specification of the functional interface is that, at a black box level, there is no difference between generic and concrete operations, for example between a generic and a concrete `prove`. The only difference is that generic messages operate on a virtual hybrid KB, while concrete ones operate on a IM-specific one. In the rest of the paper, we'll prefix generic messages with "c_", to construct the associated concrete message.

Because of space limitations we will skip the formal specification of the functional interface which can be found in (Motta et al., 1992).

2.2 Extendibility in the VITAL-KR System

Currently, the engine library provided by the VITAL-KR includes: a CLOS-based (Keene, 1989) object-oriented representation; a task scheduler; a Prolog engine; an OPS5 implementation (Brownston et al, 1985); a Ground Repository (GR), which is a simple flat working memory like structure; and the rule interpreter from the KEATS system (Motta et al., 1991). Additional engines can be added, by supplying a file of definitions for the functional interface operations. In fact, a particular engine does not need to support all operations. Typically, these definitions translate a generic communication primitive into an engine-specific operation. The main requirements on the integrability of an engine in the VITAL-KR are the following.

1. *An engine must support (a subset of) the Functional Interface.* This is an obvious requirement. However, sometimes it can be tricky to decide how a particular functional interface primitive should be instantiated in a particular engine. For this reason we provide a formal, non-ambiguous specification of the functional interface.

2. *An engine must support multiple instantiations of itself.* This is a very important requirement needed to enable the VITAL-KR user to map multiple

---

[4] It is important to emphasize that the fact that the IS plays a control role does not imply that the VITAL-KR is an embedded architecture. The IS does not impose any particular inference paradigm, it only plays a 'mediating' role.

IMs to the same engine, and to enable IMs to deal with multiple, recursive queries.

3. *An engine must be able to do IO in terms of c-expressions.* That is to say that it must either use c-expressions internally or be able to translate from c-expressions to its internal formalism and vice versa. This is not a very limiting requirement, as the large majority of AI tools use symbolic representation[5]. However, in some cases some programming work is needed to ensure smooth translation.

3 A Formal, Operational Account of the VITAL-KR

In addition to the specification of the functional interface, a precise account of the VITAL-KR also requires a description of the behaviour of its main control component, the IS. In particular, a formal account of its behaviour enables us to discuss how the various IMs and the JTMS are integrated, under what conditions the VITAL-KR behaves correctly, and how an efficient implementation can be achieved. These issues are discussed in the next section, where we give a formal account of the behaviour of the VITAL-KR in terms of Structural Transition Systems (TSs), a formalism introduced in (Plotkin, 1981).

3.1 Basic Definitions

All components of the VITAL-KR can be modelled as agents which perform autonomous computation and communicate using the VITAL-KR functional interface.

Definition 1 - State of the VITAL-KR. The state of the VITAL-KR is composed of the states of the IMs, the IS, and the JTMS. These are defined as follows:

IS_{State}:	ISstack
IM_{State}:	<Name, CS, agenda>
$JTMS_{State}$:	<DR, agenda>

ISstack is a stack used by the IS to control the dispatching of queries and results, agendas are queues, CS is a computation stack associated with each IM, Name is a string naming the associated IM, and DR is the repository of dependencies handled by the JTMS[6].

The IS stack contains triples such as (msg, IMq, IM^{List}), where msg is the functional interface primitive which has just been invoked by an IM, IMq, and IM^{List} is an ordered list of IMs which can deal with the message. The reason why a stack is needed is that recursive calls are possible between IMs.

A CS contains pairs of the form (C, state), where C is a computation local to the IM in question, and state can be **wait** or **busy**. Local computations are represented as sequences of actions. The concatenation operator, "." is associative and

---

5   Exceptions include neural-network based applications, and diagrammatic approaches (Funt, 1980)

6   Stacks and agendas are represented in the following using the standard Prolog notation for lists: [] represents the empty stack (agenda), and [H|T] represents the stack (agenda) with first element H and rest T. New elements, say H, are inserted in an agenda, say [Front], using the constructor ":" and the notation [Front:H].

non-commutative. The empty computation is represented by the symbol λ. To simplify the notation, when the state field of a pair (C, state) is **busy**, only the local computation field will be shown. For instance, the notation [fetch(σ).C|CS] will be used instead of the more laborious [(fetch(σ).C, busy)|CS]. The notation IM$\hat{}$CS is used to access a particular field of a configuration (in this case CS of IM). In the rest of the paper we'll make use of the abbreviations, predicates, and functions shown in the table below.

---

execute_agenda(IM) represents a local computation of an IM related to the execution of the actions stored in its agenda.

type(σ) is a function that returns the type of a c-expression.

idle(IM) is a function that tests whether an IM is currently idle. More precisely: idle(IM) **iff** (IM$\hat{}$CS = [(C,wait)|CS'] **or** IM$\hat{}$CS = λ)

ddd(type, IM^{List}) and **qdd(type, IM^{List})** are relations mapping the type of a c-expression with the associated ordered list of interested IMs. **ddd** deals with TELL and RETRACT operations, while **qdd** deals with ASK operations. They express the knowledge encoded in the MKR.

Table 1. Some useful abbreviations.

3.2 Operational Semantics of ASK Primitives

Definition 2 - TS modelling the evolution of the IMs and the IS. A transition system modelling the evolution of the IMs and the IS is a pair $\langle\Gamma_{IM\&IS}, \rightarrow_{IM\&IS}\rangle$, where $\Gamma_{IM\&IS}$ is a set of configurations with the following structure: $IM^1+...+IM^n+IS$, and $\rightarrow_{IM\&IS} \subseteq \Gamma_{IM\&IS} \times \Gamma_{IM\&IS}$ is a transition relation[7].

In the rest of the paper we'll use the symbol σ to denote an arbitrary c-expression, the symbol γ to denote an arbitrary g-expression, and the notation IMq to indicate the agent invoking the functional interface primitive being modelled.

Rules R1-R3 and axiom A1 model the primitive fetch.

$$\frac{idle(IM') \text{ and } ddd(type(s),[IM'|IML])}{\langle IMq,[fetch(\sigma).C|CS],[]\rangle+\langle IM',CS',A'\rangle+...+IS} \quad \textbf{R1}$$

$$\rightarrow_{IM\&IS}$$
$$\langle IMq,[(C, wait)|CS],[]\rangle+\langle IM',[C_{c\_fetch*}|CS'],[]\rangle+...+$$
$$+[(fetch(s),IMq,IML)|IS]$$

where C_{c_fetch*} = execute_agenda(IM').c_fetch(σ)

Rule R1 specifies that when a fetch primitive is invoked by an IM (IMq), the IMs which can handle the query are retrieved, ordered, and the concrete message c_fetch(σ) is sent to the first one which can handle it, say IM'. In order to handle this query, IM' must be free. Because we are assuming a sequential model of operations, this is always the case. The new local computation of IM', C_{c_fetch*}, is defined as the concatenation of the evaluation of the pending messages in the agenda and the execution of the concrete message c_fetch. The state in which IM' was

---

7   To be more precise we should say that $\rightarrow_{IM\&IS}$ is the smallest transition relation satisfying the list of rules and axioms required to model it. However, because we don't have enough space to give all the required definitions, we can't be totally rigorous.

when the query was dispatched, is saved into the associated computation stack CS'. The triple $(\texttt{fetch(}\sigma\texttt{)}, \texttt{IMq}, \texttt{IM}^L)$ is inserted at the top of the IS stack, so that, depending on the evaluation of $C_{\texttt{c\_fetch}*}$, the IS can either return the result from IM' back to IMq, or try out the next IM in $\texttt{IM}^L$.

Rule R2 below describes the case in which IM' successfully answers the fetch query. In this case the result, R, is sent back to IMq. The notation C(R) is used to indicate that the computation C is passed result R as argument.

$$R \neq false$$
$$\rule{10cm}{0.4pt} \quad \textbf{R2}$$
<IMq,[(C,wait)|CS],A>+<IM',[answer(R)|CS'],[]>+...+
          [(fetch(σ),IMq,IM^L)|IS]
$$\rightarrow_{\text{IM\&IS}}$$
<IMq,[C".C(R)|CS],[]>+<IM',CS',[]>+...+IS

where C"= execute_agenda(IMq)

If IM' fails to answer the query, the next IM in the list is tried. This case is described by rule R3.

$$idle(H)$$
$$\rule{10cm}{0.4pt} \quad \textbf{R3}$$
<IM',[answer(false)|CS'],[]>+<IM",CS,A>+...+
          [(fetch(σ),IMq,[IM"|IM^L])|IS]
$$\rightarrow_{\text{IM\&IS}}$$
<IM',CS',[]>+<IM",[C$_{\text{c\_fetch}*}$|CS],[]>+...+[(fetch(σ),IMq,IM^L)|IS]

where $C_{\text{c\_fetch}*}$ = execute_agenda(IM").c_fetch(σ)

Finally, the axiom A1 below describes the case in which no IM can successfully answer the query and false is returned to IMq.

<IM",[answer(false)|CS"],[]>+<IMq,[C,wait|CS],A>+...+
          [(fetch(σ),IMq,[])|IS]
$$\rightarrow_{\text{IM\&IS}} \qquad\qquad \textbf{A1}$$
<IM",CS",[]>+<IMq,[C'.C(false)|CS],[]>+...+IS

where C'= execute_agenda(IMq)

There is no difference between prove and fetch as far as the operational semantics of the VITAL-KR is concerned. The difference only concerns the internal computation of the IMs. Establish is the combination of a prove followed by an assert, which is described in the next section.

3.3 Operational Semantics of Assertions

In order to give the operational semantics of assertions in the VITAL-KR, we also need to take the JTMS into account. So, we introduce a new transition system.

Definition 3. TS modelling the evolution of the IMs and the JTMS. A transition system, modelling the evolution of the IMs and JTMS, is a pair $\langle \Gamma_{\text{IM\&JTMS}}, \rightarrow_{\text{IM\&JTMS}} \rangle$, where $\Gamma_{\text{IM\&JTMS}}$ is a set of configurations with the following structure: $\text{IM}^1 + ... + \text{IM}^n + \text{JTMS}$, and $\rightarrow_{\text{IM\&JTMS}} \subseteq \Gamma_{\text{IM\&JTMS}} \times \Gamma_{\text{IM\&JTMS}}$ is a transition relation.

The next rule defines the operational semantics of assert. The relevant IMs are retrieved, and the assert message is dispatched to them. If a justification, say J, is associated with the assert, the message newj(J) is sent to the JTMS.

$$\frac{\texttt{idle(JTMS)} \textbf{ and } \texttt{ddd(type(}\gamma\texttt{),[IM}^i\texttt{...])} \textbf{ and } \texttt{idle(IM}^i\texttt{)}}{\begin{array}{c}\texttt{<IMq,[assert(}\gamma\texttt{,J).C|CS],[]>+<IM}^i\texttt{,CS}^i\texttt{,A}^i\texttt{>+...+<DR,A}_{\texttt{JTMS}}\texttt{>}\\ \xrightarrow{\texttt{IM\&JTMS}}\\ \texttt{<IMq,[C|CS],[]>+<IM}^i\texttt{,CS}^i\texttt{,[A}^i\texttt{:c\_assert(}\gamma\texttt{)]>+...+<DR,[A}_{\texttt{JTMS}}\texttt{:newj(J)]>}\end{array}} \qquad \textbf{R4}$$

The only thing left to do is to show how the JTMS copes with new justifications. Because of space limitations we will have to skip the discussion of the relevant formal rules and axioms, and we simply assume that its operational semantics can be modelled through a transition system: $\langle \Gamma_{\texttt{JTMS}}, \rightarrow_{\texttt{JTMS}} \rangle$, whose configurations have the structure $\langle \texttt{DR, agenda} \rangle$, and that its behaviour consists of popping messages from the top of the agenda, and executing them. In practice, when a JTMS node changes its state from in to out, the JTMS sends an `unassert` message to the relevant IMs (`assert` messages are sent in the opposite case).

Definition 4. TS modelling the evolution of the VITAL-KR. A transition system for the VITAL-KR is a pair $\langle \Gamma_{\texttt{VITAL-KR}}, \rightarrow_{\texttt{VITAL-KR}} \rangle$, where $\Gamma_{\texttt{VITAL-KR}}$ is a set of configurations with the following structure: $\texttt{IM}^1 + ... + \texttt{IM}^n + \texttt{JTMS} + \texttt{IS}$, and $\rightarrow_{\texttt{VITAL-KR}} \subseteq \Gamma_{\texttt{VITAL-KR}} \times \Gamma_{\texttt{VITAL-KR}}$ is the transition relation defined as the smallest relation satisfying the rules R5-R7. In the rules below we assume that a transition system, $\langle \Gamma_{\texttt{IM}}, \rightarrow_{\texttt{IM}} \rangle$, has been defined to model the internal behaviour of an IM.

$$\frac{\texttt{idle(JTMS)} \textbf{ and } \texttt{IM}_1 \rightarrow_{\texttt{IM}} \texttt{IM}_1\texttt{'}}{\texttt{JTMS+IM}_1 + ... + \texttt{IM}_n + \texttt{IS} \rightarrow_{\texttt{VITAL-KR}} \texttt{JTMS+IM}_1\texttt{'} + ... + \texttt{IM}_n + \texttt{IS}} \qquad \textbf{R5}$$

$$\frac{\texttt{JTMS+IM}_1 + ... + \texttt{IM}_n \rightarrow_{\texttt{IM\&JTMS}} \texttt{JTMS'+IM}_1\texttt{'} + ... + \texttt{IM}_n\texttt{'}}{\texttt{JTMS+IM}_1 + ... + \texttt{IM}_n + \texttt{IS} \rightarrow_{\texttt{VITAL-KR}} \texttt{JTMS'+IM}_1\texttt{'} + ... + \texttt{IM}_n\texttt{'} + \texttt{IS}} \qquad \textbf{R6}$$

$$\frac{\texttt{idle(JTMS)} \textbf{ and } \texttt{IM}_1 + ... + \texttt{IM}_n, \texttt{IS} \rightarrow_{\texttt{IM\&IS}} \texttt{IM}_1\texttt{'} + ... + \texttt{IM}_n\texttt{'} + \texttt{IS'}}{\texttt{JTMS+IM}_1 + ... + \texttt{IM}_n + \texttt{IS} \rightarrow_{\texttt{VITAL-KR}} \texttt{JTMS+IM}_1\texttt{'} + ... + \texttt{IM}_n\texttt{'} + \texttt{IS'}} \qquad \textbf{R7}$$

R5 specifies that the local computations of IMs can be executed indipendently. R6 specifies that the IM&JTMS transition system can proceed without involving the IS. R7 specifies that the computation of the IM&IS transition system for queries can proceed only if the JTMS is idle. In other words queries must wait until the JTMS terminates its computation.

3.4 Discussion

The formalization outlined above specifies a unique sequence of operations and defines the correct behaviour of the VITAL-KR. In view of the efficiency to be gained through a parallel implementation, we should consider whether non-deterministic but still correct accounts can also be provided. Because IMs can do their internal computations in parallel, the main bottleneck appears to be the JTMS, which has to be idle for IMs to be able to make assertions, retract data, or pose queries. So, we want to investigate whether a correct account of the VITAL-KR can be given, in which (some of) these JTMS-related bottlenecks are relaxed.

If the JTMS were not idle when queries were performed, these will produce incorrect results. Therefore, this is a constraint which cannot be relaxed. Let's assume then that we allow assertions and retractions to be carried out while the JTMS is running.

Because the JTMS sends `assert` and `unassert` messages to the other IMs, relaxing the constraint implies that the order in which these messages are inserted in the agenda of a particular IM cannot be determined. Unfortunately, this creates problems. For instance, let's assume that, according to the specification given in the previous section, an IM, say IM', reaches a state in which its agenda looks like: [c_assert(γ_1), c_assert(γ_2), c_unassert(γ_1)]. Introducing non-determinism in the handling of assertions and retractions implies that [c_unassert(γ_1), c_assert(γ_1), c_assert(γ_2)] is a legal, alternative state for the agenda of IM'. Unfortunately, executing the latter sequence will result in γ_1 not being removed from IM', in contrast with the previous case. So, implementers cannot increase efficiency by relaxing these JTMS-related bottlenecks.

4 Related Work

CYC. The CYC system (Lenat & Guha, 1990) comprises a number of inference mechanisms (heuristic level) which are integrated by means of a homogeneous representation (epistemological level). A translator between the two levels ensures that CYC programmers need only concern themselves with the epistemological level of representation. In the context of hybrid architectures, the main difference between CYC and the VITAL-KR is that the integration in the former is achieved by writing compilers from the homogeneous language to the inference mechanisms, while in the latter it is achieved by defining the range of messages which IMs can exchange. So, it is much easier to integrate new engines in VITAL than it is in CYC. Furthermore, CYC does not specify a clear protocol to do this, nor gives requirements. Because of the looser form of integration, developers of hybrid KBs in the VITAL-KR can experiment with cooperation strategies and configurations which might be difficult to emulate in CYC.

KQML. KQML is a language which is being developed with the aim of providing a standard for applications in distributed AI. For this reason it follows a somewhat more general approach than we do, as it handles not only the problem of integrating KB modules, but also that of interfacing these to standard software tools such as database management systems (Cutkosky, 1992). Moreover, it also deals with lower level communication issues, such as the type of communication, or the kind of transport used. In contrast with KQML, the functional interface of the VITAL-KR is only concerned with knowledge-level primitives, and handles these in more detail than KQML. This is because we mainly concern ourselves with hybrid AI programming, rather than applications in distributed AI. Moreover, we also tackle truth maintenance and formal issues which are not addressed in the KQML effort.

Software Engineering Approaches. The issue of interoperability has also been extensively approached by the software engineering community. Top-down approaches (Gisi & Kaiser, 1991) can be seen as analogous to embedded ones, while the bottom-up ones - such as Forest (Garlan & Ilias, 1990) - can be regarded as the non-embedded counterpart. Bottom-up approaches in software engineering provide a looser form of integration than non-embedded AI architectures. Typically there is no attempt at understanding the cooperation strategies which are needed, and at classifying the communication primitives. When this is attempted, as in Forest, *ad hoc* protocols are defined, which are at a lower level than the ones used in AI. Top-down approaches provide means to specify precisely the interaction between components, but, as it is the case with embedded AI approaches, they are limited by the formalism and environment used, and by the master-slave cooperation framework.

5 Conclusions and Future Work

The specification of the VITAL-KR has now been completed and the first prototype is running in Common Lisp on SUN workstations. The system has been tested on a couple of small domains, such as Sisyphus, and the results have been encouraging, both from a methodological and an efficiency related point of view. A number of support tools are being developed, including visualization tools, debuggers, and editors.

From a methodological point of view the VITAL-KR framework encourages designers to organize a KB in a 'principled way', by encouraging them to determine its functionalities, specify the relevant IMs, and map them to AI languages. This process also has positive repercussions on efficiency, as the mapping IMs-engines is usually driven by performance-related considerations. This methodological aspect is particularly important as the aim of the VITAL workbench is to support a comprehensive methodology for KBS development.

An issue which will require further research concerns the level of complexity of the communication. Given the current specification of the functional interface any attempt to add IMs which need to communicate more complex information than data and queries, such as rules, will fail, as primitives such as `assert` only deal with g-expressions. In order to allow IMs to communicate arbitrary formulas, we need to modify both the functional interface, and the communication language. An obvious candidate for the latter is KIF (Genesereth & Fikes, 1992), for which translators to a number of knowledge representation tools are being developed.

References

Allen, J.F. and Miller, B.W. (1991). The RHET System: A Sequence of Self-Guided Tutorials. TR 325, Computer Science Dept, University of Rochester, July 1991.

Brownston, L., Farrell, R., Kant, E., and Martin, N. (1985). *Programming expert systems in OPS5: An Introduction to rule based programming.* Reading, MA: Addison-Wesley.

Corkill, D.D. (1991). Embedable Problem-Solving Architectures: A Study of Integrating OPS5 with UMass GBB. *IEEE Transactions on Knowledge and Data Engineering,* 3(1), March 1991.

Cutkosky, M,. Engelmore, R., Fikes, R., Gruber, T., Genesereth, M., Mark, W., Tenenbaum, J., Weber, J. (1992). PACT: An Experiment in Integrating Concurrent Engineering Systems, 1992.

Davis, R. and Smith, R.D. (1983). Negotiation as a Metaphor for Distributed Problem Solving. *Artificial Intelligence,* 20(1), pp 63-109.

Domingue, J., Motta, E. and Watt, S. (1993). The Emerging VITAL Workbench. *Proceedings of the 7th European Knowledge Acquisition Workshop,* Toulouse, France, September 1993.

Doyle, J. (1979). A Truth Maintenance System. *Artificial Intelligence,* 12.

Finin, T., Fritzon, R. and McKay, D. (1992). An Overview of KQML: A Knowledge Query and Manipulation Languag, Technical Report, Department of Computer Science, University of Maryland Baltimore County, 1992.

Funt, B.V. (1980). Problem-Solving with Diagrammatic Representations. *Artificial Intelligence*, 13(3), pp 201-230.

Garlan, D. and Ilias, E. (1990). Low-Cost, Adaptable Tool Integration Policies for Integrated Environments, *Proceedings 4th ACM SIGSOFT Symposium on Software Development Environments*, Irvine, December, 1990.

Gasser, L., Braganza, C. and Herman, N. (1987). MACE: A Flexible Testbed for Distributed AI Research. In Huhns (Ed.), *Distributed Artificial Intelligence*, Pitman, London.

Genesereth, M.R. and Fikes, R.E. (1992). Knowledge Interchange Format, Reference Manual, Version 3.0. Technical Report, Computer Science Department, Stanford University, 1992.

Gisi, M., Kaiser G.(1991). Extending a tool integration language. *Proceedings First Int. Conference on the Software Process*, IEEE Computer Society Press, October 1991, pp 218-229.

Inder, R., Aylett, R., Bental, D., Lydiard, T. and Rae, R. (1990). Study on the Evaluation of Expert Systems Tools for Ground Segment Infrastructure: Final Report. TR84, AI Application Institute, University of Edinburgh.

Keene, S. (1989). *Object-Oriented Programming in Common Lisp*. Addison-Wesley, Reading, Massachussets.

Lenat, D.B. and Guha, R.V. (1990). *Building Large Knowledge-Based Systems: Representation and Inference in the Cyc Project*. Addison-Wesley, Reading, MA.

Levesque, H.J. (1984). Foundations of a Functional Approach to Knowledge Representatio. *Artificial Intelligence*, 23(2), 1984.

Linster, M. (1992). Sisyphus '92: Models of Problem Solving. GMD Technical Report.

Motta, E., Stutt, A., O'Hara, K., Kuusela, J., Toivonen, H., Reichgelt, H., Watt, S., Aitken, S., and Verbeck, F. (1992). VITAL Knowledge Representation Language Specification: Final Deliverable. VITAL Technical Report , OU/DD412/W/1.

Motta, E., Rajan, T., Domingue, J., and Eisenstadt, M. (1991). Methodological Foundations of KEATS, The Knowledge Engineers'Assistant. *Knowledge Acquisition*, 3(1), March 1991.

Neches, R., Fikes, R., Finin, T., Gruber, T., Patil, R., Senator, T. and Swartout, W. (1991). Enabling Technology for Knowledge Sharing. *AI Magazine*, vol 12(3).

Patil, R.S., Fikes, R.E., Patel-Schneider, P.F., Makay, D., Finin, T., Gruber, T., Neches, R. (1992) The DARPA Knowledge Sharing Effort: Progress Report, *Principles of Knowledge Representation and Reasoning: Proceedings of the 3rd International Conference*, Morgan Kaufmann, 1992.

Plotkin, G.D. (1981). A Structural Approach to Operational Semantic. Technical Report DAIMI FN-19, Computer Science Department, Aarhus University, Denmark, September 1981.

Reichgelt, H., and Van Harmelen, F. (1986). Criteria for choosing representation languages and control regimes for expert systems. *The knowledge engineering review*. 1(4).

Schreiber, G., Breuker, J., Bredeweg, B., and Wielinga, B. (1988). Modelling in KBS Development. *Proceedings of the 3rd European Knowledge Acquisition Workshop,*, EKAW '88, Bonn.

Zhang, C. and Bell, D.A. (1991). HECODES: a framework for HEterogeneous COoperative Distributed Expert Systems. *Data & Knowledge Engineering*, 6, 1991.

MAP - a Language for the Modelling of Multi-Agent Systems

Giovanni Adorni and Agostino Poggi

DII - University of Parma,
Viale delle Scienze, 43100 Parma, Italy

Abstract. This paper presents a distributed object-oriented language, called Multi-Agent Programming language, whose features are suitable to develop multi-agent systems. This language is based on an object, called agent, (i) performing private actions, (ii) communicating with other agents, and (iii) re-configuring system structure through the creation of other agents and changing its behaviour. The main feature of this language is the use of a large set of communication primitives, defined on the spirit of Speech Act theory, which are suitable to model agent interactions and which can be specialised to implement specific communication protocols. In particular, the paper shows how these primitives are suitable to model negotiation protocols.

1 Introduction

In recent years there has been a growing interest in Distributed Artificial Intelligence (DAI) systems: that is a consequence of the development of powerful distributed computers and of the proliferation of computer networks, as well as the recognition that the solution of most of the AI problems, serialises by traditional AI, are naturally composed of parallel/concurrent tasks (see, for example, [4]).

A common view of a DAI system is given by a collection of intelligent agents cooperating to solve a task. This view has shown the need of languages and tools for the development of DAI systems offering adequate means for the coordination of the different agents. Distributed object-oriented languages present some interesting features that make them attractive for DAI systems development. In fact, object-oriented programming is a good technique to design high-level and modular systems, and message exchange is a natural framework for parallelism and task's synchronisation (see, for example, [3, 13, 5]). Nevertheless, current distributed object-oriented languages do not offer a set of primitives suitable for multi-agent programming, making the development of such kind of applications difficult. Moreover, some DAI testbeds have been developed (see, for example, MACE [6] and MICE [9]). These testbeds allow to partially use abstract formal languages for the system modelling, while most of their actual implementations are based on conventional AI languages (e.g., Lisp). However, they offer limited means for the definition of agent behaviours.

A step in the direction of the definition of a multi-agent programming language has been done by Shoham[11]. He defined a language, called Agent0, whose purpose is not only the analysis, but also the design of a distributed computational system. The purpose of Shoham is to give raise a new computational framework, called agent oriented programming, which can be viewed as a specialisation of object-oriented programming. Agent0 makes use of an interpreter working on agent's state. An agent updates its state on the basis of private actions, and on the basis of information and requests of action's execution received by other agents. The communication between agents is possible through a set of primitives that allow to an agent to inform another agent about something and to (possibly) require the execution of some actions to another agent. Nevertheless, Agent0 does not take advantage of inheritance to specialise agents and their methods, making its use in application development rather limited.

This paper presents a language, called Multi-Agent Programming (MAP) language, which tries to integrate features of current distributed object-oriented languages with Agent0's ones. The next section describes MAP features. Section three shows as MAP communication primitives are suitable to model negotiation protocols. In the last section some concluding remarks and some implementation notes are sketched.

2 MAP

MAP is a distributed object-oriented language derived from the Actor model [3], ABCL/1 [13], ABCDL [2] and CUBL [1]. This language is based on an object called agent, composed of a local state, one or more scripts, and some methods (actions), allowing the modification of its local state and the communication with other agents. Agents are classified in classes and they take advantage of inheritance for their specialisation and for the specialisation of their methods.

An agent can assume one of the following modality: i) sleeping, ii) waiting, or iii) active. Usually, an agent is sleeping and becomes active when it receives a message. When it is active, it applies its script to the received message, performing methods and sending other messages. In particular, when its execution requires a message that is not yet arrived, it becomes waiting. When an agent is waiting, each time a new message arrives, it test if it is the waited answer, becoming active in the affirmative. The messages, arrived while the agent is active, are queued and served in a FIFO order.

The definition of an agent class has the following form:

```
<agent> ::= (defclass <agent_name> <superclass>
              <local_state> { <action> } { <script> } )
```

A local state contains agent internal variables. Its declaration is given by indicating variable names. Actions are represented by methods either working on the agent's local states (private actions) or performing communication with other agents (communicative actions). Its declaration has the following form:

```
<action> ::= (action <actionname>
               ( { <parameter> } ) { <command> } )
```

The metaclass agent (i.e., the superclass at the top of the hierarchy) defines six communicative actions, eventually used to inform the agents about facts and events, to request an action, to commit an action, to retreat the request (unrequest) of an action, to accept an action, and to reject an action from an agent. They have the following form:

```
<inform>    ::= (inform ( { <agent> } ) <fact> [ <rest> ])
<requese>   ::= (request ( { <agent> } ) <action>
                         <wait_cond> } ) [ <rest> ])
<commit>    ::= (commit ( { <agent> } ) <action> [ <rest> ])
<unrequest> ::= (unrequest ( { <agent> } ) <action> [ <rest> ])
<accept>    ::= (accept ( { <agent> } ) <action> [ <rest> ])
<reject>    ::= (reject ( { <agent> } ) <action> [ <rest> ])
```

where:

- <agent> is the name of an agent;
- <fact> is a couple, variable - value, which can modify agent local state;
- <rest> is an optional information that can be sent to <agent>s.
- <action> is a list containing the name of the action to be executed and its arguments, if any;
- <wait_cond> is a condition that is used to terminate the execution of the action request.

While the actions of inform, commit, retreat a request, accept and reject correspond to the sending of one or more messages, the action of request is more complex; it sends messages and waits for answers until <wait_cond> becomes true. When it happens it returns the list of answers. For example:

(request 'ag1 '(act1) '(< (time self) ,(+ (time self) 120)))

waits for all the answers arriving within two minutes and then returns the answers. Note that the form (time self) indicates the agent time, and the time is expressed in seconds.

These communicative actions derive from Speech Act theory [10] and, in particular, from the communicative actions of Agent0. Nevertheless, they offer some advantages with respect to Agent0 communicative actions: i) they support broadcasting (an agent can communicate with more than one agent through a single action), and ii) they can be specialised to implement a specific communication protocol (see the next section).

Agent performance is driven by script. When an agent receives a message, it processes the message through one of its scripts that performs private actions, communicates with other agents, creates other agents, and changes its own behaviour. Agent behaviour is defined by the script processing messages, therefore, an agent modifies its own behaviour changing the script processing messages. A script declaration has the form:

```
<script> ::= (script <script_name> { <command> } )
```

An agent manages input messages through a predicate, called received, whose purpose is to accept messages. Its form is the following:

```
<received>    ::= (received <agent> <msgtype> <fact_action>)
<fact_action> ::= (<fact_action_name> { <arg> } )
```

where <msgtype> indicates one among the communicative actions, and <arg> indicates an argument of <fact_action>. These arguments can be either constant or variable. Constant indicates a message element that must have a fixed value, while variable indicates a message element that can assume any value. For example:

(received *ag* 'commit ('solve *problem*))

accepts the message (ag1 commit (solve p1)) binding ag1 and p1 to the two variables *ag* and *problem*, but it does not accept, for example, the two following messages: (ag1 request (solve p1)) and (ag1 commit (do act1)).

3   Negotiation

The expressive power of MAP communicative actions allows an easy definition of a negotiation protocol, like Contract Net Protocol [12], between an agent, *manager*, and a set of candidate agents, *contractors*. The manager looks for a candidate agent able to do its task, *action*, and accepting to perform the task. This protocol is modelled as follows:

1. The *manager* announces a task to the contractors through a message indicating the information, *bid_requirement*, that a contractor must send to the manager. A contractor sends its answer (bid) to the manager. When bids arrive, the manager selects a contractor on the basis of the bids through a selection *criterion*. If the manager does not receive bids verifying the criterion within a *cycle_time*, then it sends again the request to the contractors:

   (request *contractors action*
     :bid *bid_requirement* :selection *criterion* :cycle *cycle_time*)

2. A *contractor* receiving a task announcement may answer submitting a bid to the manager. The form of the answer is:

   (accept *manager action bid_description*)

3. The *manager* chooses one of the contractors, informs it about its decision (contract assignment), and asks it a *result* report. The form of the request is as follows:

   (commit *contractor action* :inform *result*)

4. The *contractor* may reject the task, using the form:

   (reject *manager action*)

5. The *manager* may terminate the contract, using the form:

   (unrequest *contractor action*)

6. The *contractor* concludes the assigned task and sends a final report, result, to the manager:

(inform *manager result*)

The previous protocol can be used by a class of agents (*neg_agent*) which specialises the action request as follows:

```
(defclass neg_agent (agent)
  ....
  (action request(agents actions w_cond &rest args)
    (let (answers)
      (do () (answers (eval (nth 3 args)))
        ; if there are answers, then they are filtered through a
        ; criterion (nth 3 args) and the selected answer is
        ; returned. Otherwise, a new request is sent out.
        (super ; calls the method request of its superclass.
          agents actions
          (list 'or w_cond
                '(> (time self) (+ ,(time self) (nth 5 args)))))))
        ; (time self) indicates the agent current time.
        ; wait_cond is w_cond or the timeout given
        ; by the cycle_time.
        (nth 0 args) ; the keyword :bid.
        (nth 1 args) ; the value of bid_requirement.
        )))
  .... )
```

The above action (request) sends a request every cycle_time until the arrival of some answers. This task is performed through the action inherited by the metaclass agent. When an answer arrive, the action filters the answers through a selection criterion.

4   Conclusions

This paper presented a distributed object-oriented language, called MAP (Multi-Agent Programming) language. This language supports system reconfigurability through the creation of new agents and the changing of behaviour of others. It also allows an easy management of agent interactions through a set of communication primitives derived from Shoham's communicative actions. These primitives allow broadcasting, and they can be specialised to define specific communication protocols taking advantage of method inheritance. In particular, the paper shows as the simple specialisation of one of these methods allows to use negotiation protocols to manage agent interactions.

MAP kernel has been written in CLOS [8], while its compiler has been created using YACC [7]. The compiler translates agent classes into CLOS classes, and agent procedures and scripts into CLOS methods. MAP integrates pseudo-parallelism with real parallelism, allowing the execution of different parts of a MAP program on different Sun workstations connected through an ethernet network. Concurrency and communication among agents on a same workstation are managed through the *Multitasking Facility* of Sun Common Lisp, while concurrency and communication among agents on different workstations are managed through UNIX sockets. To support data transmission and object reference across different machines, data (messages) sent to external objects are translated into strings; objects are referenced both through its pointer and through a name string address whose value is the same for all the machines. Therefore, local objects are accessible both through object pointers and name string address, while remote objects are only accessible through name string address.

Our current research involves both MAP improvement and its use for the development of applications. In particular, we are developing some applications to test new cooperation protocols and a DAI testbed based on two programming level (object and agent levels).

References

1. G. Adorni and A. Poggi. CUBL: A language for the development of dai systems. In *Proc. AI*IA - Incontro di lavoro su: Intelligenza Artificiale Distribuita*, pages 41–49, Roma, 1992.
2. G. Adorni and A. Poggi. An object-oriented language for Distributed Artificial Intelligence systems. *Int. Journal of Man-Machine Studies*, (38):435–453, 1993.
3. G. Agha. *Actors, A Model of Concurrent Computation in Distributed Systems*. The MIT Press, Cambridge, MA, 1986.
4. A.H. Bond and L. Gasser. *Readings in Distributed Artificial Intelligence*. Morgan Kaufmann, San Mateo, CA, 1988.
5. J. Ferber and P. Carle. Actors and agents as reflective concurrent objects: a Mering IV perspective. *IEEE Trans. on SMC*, 21(6):1420–1436, 1991.
6. L. Gasser, C. Braganza, and N. Herman. Implementing distributed artificial intelligence systems using MACE. In *Proc. of the Third IEEE Conference on Artificial Intelligence Applications*, pages 315–320, 1987.
7. S.C. Johnson. Yacc - yet another compilers compiler. Technical Report 32, AT&T Bell Laboratory, Murray Hill, NJ, 1975.
8. S. Keene. *Object-Oriented Programming in Common Lisp - A Programmer's Guide to CLOS*. Addison Wesley, Reading, MA, 1989.
9. T.A. Montgomery and E.H. Durfee. Using mice to study intelligent dynamic coordination. In *Proc. 2nd Conference on Tools for AI*, pages 215–220, 1990.
10. J.R. Searle. *Speech Acts: An Essay in the Philosophy of Language*. Cambridge University Press, Cambridge, U.K., 1969.
11. Y. Shoham. Agent oriented programming. Technical Report STAN-CS-1335-90, Robotics Lab. - Computer Sci. Dept. - Stanford University, Stanford, Ca, 1990.
12. R.G. Smith. The contract net protocol: High level communication and control in a distributed problem solver. *IEEE Trans. Computers*, 29(12):1104–1113, 1980.
13. A. Yonezawa. *ABCL: An Object-Oriented Concurrent System*. The MIT Press, Cambridge, MA, 1990.

Developing Co-operating Legal Knowledge Based Systems

George Vossos and John Zeleznikow

Database Research Laboratory, Applied Computing Research Institute, La Trobe University, Bundoora, Victoria, 3083, Australia.

Daniel Hunter

Law School, University of Melbourne, Parkville, Victoria 3052, Australia.

Abstract. In attempting to build intelligent litigation support tools, we have moved beyond first generation, production rule legal expert systems. Our work supplements rule-based reasoning with case based reasoning and intelligent information retrieval. This research, specifies an approach to the case based retrieval problem which relies heavily on an extended object-oriented / rule-based system architecture that is supplemented with causal background information. Machine learning techniques and a distributed agent architecture are used to help simulate the reasoning process of lawyers. In this paper, we outline our implementation of the hybrid IKBALS II Rule Based Reasoning / Case Based Reasoning system. It makes extensive use of an automated case representation editor and background information.

1. Introduction

Current legal tools provide very little "intelligence" and so have grave limitations as to the support they can give to lawyers. Recently, some first generation knowledge based tools have recognised that the old methodology is inflexible and inadequate. Their developers have taken steps to add enhanced features. For example, in the realm of legal information retrieval, West Publishing Co, the proprietors of Westlaw, are undertaking serious research in advanced, non-boolean, information retrieval. The first such product may be seen in WIN (Westlaw Is Natural), a natural language front-end to the Westlaw database, [3].

We aim to build intelligent legal tools which do not seek to replicate human reasoning, but rather assist lawyers to improve their performance. This paper details our approach to constructing more sophisticated Legal Knowledge Based Systems (LKBS) by using an Intelligent Cooperating Information Systems (ICIS) architecture. Our previous work, [10] has led to the development of the IKBALS Project (*I*ntelligent *L*egal *K*nowledge *B*ased *S*ystems). The original prototype IKBALS I was a hybrid/object oriented rule based system. We discuss its descendant, IKBALS II, which adds case based reasoning and intelligent information retrieval to the rule based reasoner.

1.1. Reasoning Strategies in LKBS

There are a number of techniques which have been used to enhance legal knowledge based systems, by reasoning with experience. These include Case Based Reasoning (CBR), Neural Networks (NN) and extending Rule Based Reasoning systems to interface to CBR or NN (hybrid reasoning). We have chosen CBR as the best means for implementing additions to straight RBR systems since CBR provides flexibility, allows for machine learning (via a customised induction algorithm) and mimics many features of legal reasoning. The use of neural nets in legal reasoning, whilst superficially attractive because of their similarities with human cognitive processes must be carefully examined in the legal domain. One of the features with which lawyers are concerned is the ability to explain why the case or form of argument is relevant. This is a feature of which neural nets are currently incapable of providing, and hence at this stage we have not included neural nets in this system.

Of the techniques discussed in the preceding paragraph, in our view the three basic components necessary for useful intelligent legal tools are rule based reasoning, case based reasoning and information retrieval. This is because lawyers approaching a legal research question must deal with the enunciated rules (RBR) and with precedents which change or add to these rules (CBR), and must have access to a range of information where either the rules or precedents are not clear (IR). We decided, in implementing such a combined system, to use a distributed artificial intelligence (DAI) approach in order to allow statutes, heuristic knowledge and precedents to be accessed as independent heterogeneous modules. These knowledge sources in all their disparate forms interact via the medium of agents [4].

We chose this approach rather than the blackboard architecture used by CABARET [5] with their adoption of the GBB product and PROLEXS [8]. We do so because we believe that the blackboard approach is too constraining in a domain which will inevitably involve linking heterogeneous cases, rules and databases using parallel architectures. Whilst blackboard systems do allow for the above-mentioned linking of cases, rules and databases, reasoning is confined to one of a serial nature. Admittedly, it is possible to re-design this architecture to facilitate for parallel processing, but we believe our approach of tackling the problem via a distributed agent architecture bypasses inherent inadequacies in serial answers to parallel solutions. However, blackboard architectures in the legal are valuable and significant work is being done in attempting to overcome their inadequacies, as can be seen in [7].

Many of the details of our customised induction algorithm and agent architecture, are, due to space restrictions, only discussed in generalities. Full details may be found in the journal article of [12] and the Phd thesis of [9].

1.2 The Legal Domain

IKBALS I and II both deal with statutory interpretation of the *Accident Compensation (General Amendment) Act* 1989 (Vic). The Act allows a worker who has been injured during employment to gain compensation for injuries suffered. These compensation payments are called WorkCare entitlements, and IKBALS focuses on elements giving rise to such an entitlement.

An example of the sort of problem that a lawyer may find is this area is as follows. A person who works for a company is injured while not on the company premises. She suffered the injury at a union meeting which was convened to discuss whether her union was going to strike. The worker upon leaving the meeting is run over by a truck and suffers brain damage. Her parents consult a lawyer and ask whether she is able to recover worker's compensation payments to help alleviate her condition.

IKBALS will, like any production rule system, fire rules based upon information input in this the Current Input Case (CIC). However, it will eventually run out of rules to fire. It is then that the CBR module will be invoked, and where this fails to assist, the IR module will be invoked, in order to help the lawyer find the answer.

Before discussing the way in which these modules are invoked, it is necessary to look at the way in which we have determined the knowledge representation.

2. Designing the IKBALS Case Representation

While current research examines CBR and legal information retrieval, it does not address the recurrent problem in case representation. In order to overcome the case representation bottleneck experienced during CBR development, we propose to automate the generation of case representations using an Intelligent Legal Cooperating Information System (ILCIS) architecture. That is, given a set legal domain, we hope to automate the process of determining what attributes need to be included in a case representation, in order for a particular application to handle CBR successfully in that domain, using agents.

After examining existing CBR systems, is seems apparent that irrespective of whether the researcher was looking at the problem from a standard frame/slot/schema representation [1], or indeed even from the 'deep structure' standpoint [6] all were relying upon an encyclopedic understanding of the legal domain. Leaving aside the difficult and as yet unresolved problems of Natural Language Processing in the legal domain, it is apparent that even in these so-called 'automatic' systems the legal expert must define the schema. To do so requires an overall understanding and appreciation of the legal domain which is being modelled. This is why we have a legal expert involved in building expert systems—without her overall understanding of the field it would be impossible to determine what elements should be included in the case schema.

We approached the knowledge representation issue from a different perspective. We concluded that the task of a the person who enters the case representation ('case-enterer') would be greatly simplified if she could represent each case on its own merits. That is, the case-enterer should be able to enter new cases independently of any other case existing in the system. She would determine the attributes which are relevant to the particular case under study at the time and then assign values to these attributes. The attributes and values are committed to the case base and the process is repeated for every case that needs to be entered.

Since each case is analysed in isolation, each frame representing the cases will differ not only in the values which attributes take (which is the normal situation in CBR) but in the *attributes* coded in the frame. Example representations for two cases are shown in figure 1.

Case name	Johansen v Accident Compensation Commission
Judge	Judge Read
Court	Accident Compensation Tribunal
Date of judgment	22 February 1990
Worker at union meeting	Yes
Worker on strike	Yes
Contract of Employment Terminated	No
Injury in Course of Employment	No
Action incidental to employment	No
Holding	Respondent

Case name	Riego v Accident Compensation Commission
Judge	Judge Boyes
Court	Accident Compensation Tribunal
Date of judgment	1 March 1990
Worker at union meeting	Yes
Meeting approved by employer	Yes
Travel incidental to employment obligations	Yes
Injury in Course of Employment	Yes
Holding	Applicant

Fig. 1 Example representations for two cases.

The case frame attributes will differ from case to case. Having all this information would ordinarily be useless, since it is not in a form which is computationally tractable. Having hundreds of different case schemes means that we have a significant amount of information, but very little knowledge. However, by virtue of the customised Induction algorithm described below, IKBALS II can interpret this data into knowledge.

However, with so much information, particularly so many attributes, the induction algorithm may branch at inappropriate points. For example, suppose that we have three properties: *injury, mental_incapacity, and hand_incapacity.* An expert would quickly see the attribute should be *injury* and the value which this attribute can take should include *mental_incapacity* and *hand_incapacity*. Thus, the two latter attributes are in fact values which the first attribute can take. Therefore, we need an algorithm which allows a human expert to form the necessary associations between the attributes. Our algorithm allows attributes to be instances of another attributes, or a synonym for a related attributes. In this way the induction algorithm can use the semantic net which the expert generates in an attempt to reduce the amount of branching, and thus retrieve the most on point cases.

In the current implementation of this system, we need a human expert to form the associations which make up the semantic net. However, this is somewhat automated in that each time a unique attribute is associated with other attributes, all other related attributes are associated. We believe that this system is an advance in knowledge representation because while not doing away with the human expert, it greatly reduces the amount of work which the expert need perform. This speeds up the coding of the knowledge base, and reduces the knowledge representation bottleneck described above. It also automates knowledge representation to a degree which has not previously been seen in expert systems.

The benefit of the induction algorithm and the association algorithm in IKBALS II is that inconsistencies in indexing are no longer as great a problem. The first reason for this is that all the attributes are displayed in the association algorithm, and one human expert can check for consistency and associate attributes where necessary. The second reason is that the more information one has, the more the induction algorithm provides accurate knowledge. A related feature is that this system does away with a charge that the LKBS is merely a reflection of an expert's idiosyncratic approach to the law. Since the cases are indexed in isolation from each other, and are not indexed according to one expert's view of what is important, it is less likely that important information is omitted.

The associations which make up the semantic net are held separately from the CKB. This has the advantage that the CKB is kept inviolate and is not affected by the association algorithm. This form of knowledge representation requires an existing vocabulary. In the legal domain there exist many fine indices and case representations which have been created for manual searching, but which are not very useful for automatic systems. The methodology described above allows re-use of these indices and representations. Given the amount of manual information and indices available in the legal domain, we believe that a system of automatically adapting the manual data is of great use in building practical systems.

Within the IKBALS II architecture, hypertext is used to represent the sources of the law in a textual form. Amongst other things we represent cases, sections of the act and definitions using this technology. In addition to supplementing RBR and CBR with hypertext, we have found it very useful to utilise hypertext as a standalone knowledge representation language. In particular, one is able to represent in-house expert commentary within legal firms using this technology. The advantage of this approach is that legal opinions can be accessed by pointing and clicking at relevant terms, bypassing the need to further burden the RBR or CBR modules. Navigating through the hypertext network of cases, sections of the Act, and definitions can be performed either independently of the reasoning system (the RBR and CBR modules) or help supplement reasoning with these reasoners.

3. The IKBALS Case Based Reasoning Retrieval Engine

Crucial to the success of any CBR system are the algorithms used by the retrieval engine to identify candidate relevant cases. These algorithms need to retrieve relevant cases quickly and accurately from a database of stored cases. Determining when a case should be selected for retrieval in similar future situations is the goal of the case-indexing problem. Case indexing processes usually fall into one of two categories: nearest neighbour or inductive.

Our retrieval engine utilises a customised induction algorithm which references domain specific background knowledge during the generation of the index into the case-base. Background information is stored in the form of causal networks that represent generalisations / specialisations of properties and values. Access to these class/object hierarchies during the building of the decision tree helps refine the final index by making it more precise. To help prune the decision tree further, certain heuristics have been incorporated into the inductive algorithm to help filter noise. For example when an attribute has been included in the learning process and the values for that attribute exceed a certain threshold, then if there is no background information which will generalise the attribute (and hence reduce the branching factor of the tree), a warning is posted. The developer can then proceed to either exclude the attribute, go back and define some background information or ignore the message. The multi-way decision tree produced by the algorithm is represented in the system by an object hierarchy. This hierarchy is then translated into rule-objects which are subsequently used to index cases at run-time.

It is important to note the huge benefit of the use of the induction algorithm within the legal domain. The induction algorithm can only work where the knowledge engineer/user specifies an outcome field, on which the cases are to be indexed. Litigated cases in this domain always have a clearly enunciated outcome field, to wit, who prevailed in the current case. Therefore the induction algorithm can very quickly index upon the outcome field *'finding*. All properties will be relevant (to varying degrees) to this one outcome field. There is an added benefit within the domain of workers compensation: the prevailing party can only ever be the worker or the insuring body, the Accident Compensation Commission. Therefore there are only two possible values which the *'finding* property can take. This simplifies the work of the algorithm, but even if there were multiple party actions which we were representing, the induction algorithm could manage.

4. The IKBALS II 'Agent' Architecture

Intelligent Information Systems of the twenty first century will need to be both distributed and heterogeneous, [2]. [4] discuss in detail how to construct ICISs. The construction of ICISs is only at a developmental stage, and as yet, there are no clearly enunciated techniques for building ICISs. The methodology used on the project embraces the concepts of ICIS. In particular, our approach uses a combination of Object Oriented Programming, machine learning algorithms, Rule Based Reasoning and Case Based Reasoning to construct legal knowledge based systems.

In brief, there are three active agents in our implementation of IKBALS II: the *Case Representation Editor agent* (CaRE), the *Rule Based deductive Agent* (RuBA) and the *Case Based Agent* (CaBA). Each of these agents has been designed and implemented using a common object-oriented / AI architecture of objects and rules. Our system has been designed to adhere to the principles of DAI by supporting design autonomy and communication autonomy. Association autonomy (the agents alone decide whether to participate in the problem solving process) was not required as our model of reasoning in the accident compensation domain assumes reasoning with statutes before any reference is made to the case law.

CaRE has been designed to be used by developers of case-based reasoning systems. It is responsible for supporting the input and modification of cases into the case-base in addition to the generation of attribute and value associations as described previously. The CaRE automated agent interfaces directly with the user agent (Human-computer cooperative systems consist of heterogeneous agents, including the user, which cooperate in solving a problem), who with the aid of CaRE helps construct both the knowledge representation to be used when accessing cases as well as background and causal information. This supplementary knowledge is exploited by CaBA when building the decision tree and generating the index rules. Once the developer has finished defining and indexing the case-base, the end user of the system can then begin to use the case-base to supplement reasoning with rules: cases, indices and causal information are used to categorise and explain open-textured legal predicates encountered in the rule-base.

An IKBALS consultation begins when the user sends a message to the RuBA agent specifying the type of statutory provisions to be analysed. In our CIC the relevant statutory rules are invoked from the information presented by the user. This then engages the user and the RuBA automated agent into a cooperative framework in which RuBA leads the consultation between the two. The RuBA agent can also communicate with the CaBA agent under the supervision of the user. It is hence the responsibility of RuBA to consider, intelligently but systematically, all options when assessing the merits of any claim under the Accident Compensation Act. When it is uncertain on how it should act it requests the assistance of CaBA. For example, in the CIC there are statutory rules which provide that a worker can receive compensation if the injury was sustained in the course of employment. However, there is no statutory rule which provides whether attending a union meeting is within the course of employment. RuBA would therefore at this point invoke the CaBA in order to retrieve relevant cases to aid the user's determination of this question. This is achieved by i) retrieving similar cases and ii) identifying the arguments pro and con that were associated with these cases.

In order to provide a context for the problem, RuBA needs to gather details concerning the circumstances of the legal claim. This is performed through a dialogue in which RuBA asks questions and the human agent replies. In our CIC example, a question which RuBA may ask is 'Was the injury suffered in the course of employment?' Answers to questions are stored within the RuBA instance, and questions are only asked if they cannot be determined from existing facts. In addition, both RuBA and CaBA support explanation and provides links to hypertext facilities that enable the user to reference items such as a) the section of the statute that a particular question has been derived from, or b) expert commentary by leading figures in this area of law. This consultation is typical of many deductive expert system consultations that support hypertext. IKBALS accomplishes its task by using a meta-slot control strategy to direct its reasoning. This type of modelling has the benefit that it can simulate deductive behaviour without the need for an inference engine [11].

During the RuBA consultation, the user agent can answer questions by volunteering either a Yes, No or Unknown answer. A Yes or No answer confines the reasoning exclusively to RuBA. An Unknown answer shifts control to the CaBA agent which retrieves relevant similar cases for the human agent to peruse. So, if the user does not know whether attending a union is in the course of employment, then RuBA requests the assistance of CaBA to help the human user determine an answer to the question posed. The RuBA agent can then continue with the consultation. Before CaBA can process the request, it needs RuBA to define a context for the inductive retrieval. This is achieved by RuBA passing to CaBA the following parameters: the open textured predicate, the case-base and the user-defined association networks. CaBA then proceeds to use the generated index to retrieve the relevant cases & arguments. The memorandum produced at this stage includes a summary of the most relevant cases and the arguments that favoured and hurt the plaintiff. After the human agent has browsed the relevant case-law, she then has a better understanding as to how the courts have decided the disputed point of law in circumstances similar to those described. In the CIC example, the cases disclose that the important principle is whether the worker had the employer's permission to attend the meeting. The user then returns to the RuBA consultation and answers the question in a more informed manner.

5. Conclusion

We have described how first generation legal expert systems need to be enhanced with case based reasoning, machine learning and intelligent information retrieval. Our approach has been to construct intelligent legal cooperating information systems using a distributed framework, which includes some automation of knowledge representation. Our architecture involves three active agents, the Case Representation Editor, Rule Based deductive Agent and the Case Based Agent. The benefits of our architecture and methodology include:

1. Provides a comprehensive architecture for integrating rule based and case based reasoning;
2. Relevant to large parallel processing knowledge based systems;
3. Mimics some of the reasoning processes of lawyers; and
4. Reduces the case representation bottleneck.

Further work will look at performance issues and scalability for large knowledge bases.

References

1. Ashley, K.D., and Rissland, E.L., 1988, 'A Case-Based Approach to Modelling Expertise', in IEEE Expert, Fall 1988, pp 70-77

2. Brodie, M., 'The Promise of Distributed Computing and the Challenge of Legacy Information Systems', in Hsiao, D., Neuhold, E.J. & Sacks-Davis, R. (eds.) DS-5 Semantics of Interoperable Database Systems, Lorne, Victoria, Australia, November 1992, pp. 1-32; to be published by Elsevier in February 1993

3. Croft, W.B., Smith, L.A. & Turtle H.W., 'A Loosely Coupled Integration of a Text retrieval System and an Object-Oriented Database System', SIGIR92, pp. 223-232, ACM Press, New York

4. Papazoglou, M.P. and Zeleznikow, J.(eds), 1992, The Next Generation of Information Systems: From Data to Knowledge, Lecture Notes in Artificial Intelligence, 611, Springer Verlag, Berlin.

5. Rissland, E.L. and Skalak, D.B., 1991, 'CABARET: Rule Interpretation in a Hybrid Architecture', International Journal of Man Machine Studies, 34(6) 1991, pp. 839 -

6. Smith,J.C., & Deedman,C., 1987, ' The Application of Expert Systems Technology to Case-Based Law', Proceedings of the First International Conference on Artificial Intelligence and Law, ACM Press, pp 84-93.

7. Walker, R. F., 'An Expert System Architecture for Heterogeneous Domains: a case study in the legal field', PhD thesis, Department of Computer Science, Vrije Universiteit Amsterdam, 1992.

8. Walker,R.F., Oskamp,A., Schrickx,J.A., Opdorp,G.J., Berg,P.H. van den, 1991, 'PROLEXS: Creating Law and Order in a Heterogeneous Domain', International Journal of Man Machine Studies 35(1), pp. 35-68.

9. Vossos, G., 'Multi - modal reasoning in legal knowledge based systems', PhD thesis, La Trobe University, 1993.

10. Vossos, G., Dillon, T., Zeleznikow, J. and Taylor, G., 1991, 'The Use of Object Oriented Principles to Develop Intelligent Legal Reasoning Systems', Australian Computer Journal, Vol. 23, No. 1, February, pp 2-10.

11. Vossos, G., Zeleznikow, J. & Moore, A., 1993, 'The Credit Act Advisory System (CAAS): Conversion From an Expert System Prototype to a C++ Commercial System', to appear in Proceedings of Fourth International Conference on Artificial Intelligence and Law, Amsterdam, June 16-18 1993.

12. Zeleznikow, J., Vossos, G. and Hunter, D., 'The IKBALS Project: Multi-modal reasoning in Legal Knowledge Based Systems ', submitted to Artificial Intelligence and Law Journal.

Negation as a Specializing Operator

Floriana Esposito, Donato Malerba and Giovanni Semeraro*

Dipartimento di Informatica, Università di Bari
Via Orabona 4, 70126 Bari, Italy

Abstract. This paper proposes a novel operator, based on the negation, for specializing the hypotheses inductively generated by any system that learns structural descriptions from positive and negative examples or, equivalently, learns intensional definitions of logical relations. Such a specializing operator adds the negation of one or more literals of a misclassified example to the Horn clause representation of an *inconsistent* hypothesis, after having properly turned constants into variables. The search for the literals to be added is firstly performed in a set named *reduced base of consistent specializations* and, in case of failure, it is extended to the *augmented base of consistent specializations*. Indeed, two theorems prove that clauses generated by adding literals in the former set preserve the consistency property and are most general specializations of the inconsistent hypothesis. On the contrary, the consistency property of clauses generated by adding literals in the latter set has to be checked on the misclassified example. The search strategy takes advantage of the structure of the set of the *linked* Horn clauses, $\mathbf{1}$, ordered by the generality relation ($\leq$). Some clarifying examples and experimental results are also presented.

1 Introduction

Incremental capability is an important characteristic of many existing learning systems, such as ID5 [1], AQ15 [2], COBWEB [3], UNIMEM [4], VS [5], ARCH [6], THOTH [7], SPROUTER [8], RULEMOD [9], and INDUCE 4 [10]. However, most of them, namely ID5, AQ15, COBWEB, UNIMEM and VS, adopt a zero-order representation language, such as propositional calculus formulas, feature vectors or attribute-value pairs. Thus they are unable to deal with more complex descriptions of real objects (*structural descriptions*). Also the applicability of THOTH and SPROUTER is strongly limited since they can only learn maximally-specific conjunctive hypotheses from positive examples. As to RULEMOD, it should be noted that it is strongly task-oriented, even if it can learn disjunctive rules from both positive and negative examples. The other systems suffer from several problems due to poor incremental strategies. For instance, INDUCE 4 suffers from the problem of overgeneralization and uses a specialization rule, named *stripping the reference*, which is strongly dependent on the language in which descriptions are represented. Also ARCH implements a weak learning algorithm since it strongly relies on the assumption that training instances are provided in a "good order" so that a negative example following a very different positive example leads to poor results. Even more so, its specializing operator is not sound, even though Winston never told it.

This paper proposes a novel operator for specializing the hypotheses inductively generated by any system that learns structural descriptions from positive and negative examples. Section 2 describes the representation language used by the learning system. In section 3, the problem of specialization is cast as a search problem in the quasi-ordered space of linked Horn clauses, then a formal definition of a specializing operator is provided. Section 4 presents an analysis of the computational complexity of the specializing operator. An example of application of such operator to the toy-world domain of the

---

* Currently at the Department of Information and Computer Science, University of California, Irvine, CA 92717.

geometric figures is shown in section 5.

The operator proposed in this paper is absolutely independent of the adopted representation language. The only assumption is that the descriptions are expressed as well formed formulas (*wff's*) in disjunctive normal form of a First Order Predicate Logic (*FOPL*). Nevertheless, in the following we will refer to the VL_{21} representation language [11] only because it is the language used to represent knowledge in INDUBI [12, 13], the model-driven system for multiple concept learning used to perform the experimentations presented in the paper.

2 The Representation Language

The VL_{21} system is a variable-valued extension of a FOPL. The main difference with respect to FOPL consists in the definition of atomic formulas: in VL_{21} the equivalent of atom is the notion of *selector*, which is written as [L = R], where L, known as the *referee*, is a functional symbol with its arguments and R, known as the *reference*, is a (*internal*) disjunction of values in the referee's domain. Function symbols of referees are called *descriptors* and they are *n*-ary typed functions ($n \geq 1$) mapping onto one of three different kinds of domains: *nominal, linear*, and *tree-structured* [11]. Both examples and hypotheses are expressed as *Horn clauses*, where a *literal* is a selector or the negation of a selector. Semantically, we adopt negation-as-failure rule to define the meaning of a negated selector [14]. The negation of a selector that presents variables occurring in non-negated selectors can also be rewritten as a positive selector whose reference is the complement to the function domain. Henceforth, we will indifferently use both the set notation and the Prolog notation for Horn clauses. Moreover, non-negated selectors in the Prolog notation for Horn clauses will be called *positive* literals.

The differences existing between examples and hypotheses are the following:

i) Each example is represented by just one *ground* Horn clause with only positive literals.

ii) Each hypothesis is a set of *constant-free* Horn clauses, having the same *head*.

iii) The reference of each selector in any example is made up of exactly one value.

iv) In the examples, false predicates are omitted while all the attributes are specified.

v) In the hypotheses, every omitted selector is assumed to be a function taking any value of its domain.

vi) Variables with different names denote distinct objects.

We will adopt the convention of omitting the reference of a predicate when it is true.

Let FU^0={obj1, obj2, ..., objk, p1, p2, ...,pn} ($k,n \geq 1$) be a set of constants (0-ary functions), VARS={x1, x2, ...,xm, ..., y1, y2, ..., yl ...} a set of variables, FU={contain (cont), ontop (on), touch, orientation (or), shape (sh)} a set of function symbols, where "contain", "ontop" and "touch" are binary predicates, "orientation" and "shape" are attributes whose nominal domains are {horizontal (hor), vertical (ver), not_applicable (NA)} and {rectangle (rect), triangle (tri), circle (cir)}, respectively. Suppose that a learning problem is given in which the goal is to find decision rules that allow us to discriminate between two classes of objects. Let us denote as *arch* and *non-arch* the concepts related to the classes. An instance of the class *arch* could be the following (Fig. 1a):

A_1 [class(obj1)=*arch*] :- [cont(obj1,p1)], [cont(obj1,p2)], [cont(obj1,p3)],
[on(p1,p2)], [on(p1,p3)], [or(p1)=hor], [or(p2)=ver], [or(p3)=ver],
[sh(p1)=rect], [sh(p2)=rect], [sh(p3)=rect]

The hypothesis for the class *arch* produced by a learning system could be the following:

G_{arch}[class(y1)=*arch*] :- [cont(y1,x1)], [on(x1,x2)], [or(x1)=hor], [or(x2)=ver], [sh(x1)=rect]

or equivalently, in the corresponding set notation of the clause:

G_{arch}= { ¬[cont(y1,x1)], ¬[on(x1,x2)], ¬[or(x1)=hor], ¬[or(x2)=ver], ¬[sh(x1)=rect],

[class(y1)=*arch*] }

whose graphical representation is given in Fig. 1b. According to the assumption vi) made on VL_{21} constant-free Horn clauses, G_{arch} is equivalent to:

G_{arch}= { ¬ [y1 ≠ x1], ¬[y1 ≠ x2], ¬[x1 ≠ x2], ¬[cont(y1,x1)],

¬ [on(x1,x2)], ¬[or(x1)=hor], ¬[or(x2)=ver], ¬[sh(x1)=rect], [class(y1)=*arch*] }

All the descriptions, such as A_1 and G_{arch} above, belong to a particular kind of Horn clauses, namely *linked Horn clauses* [15].

Definition 1. A Horn clause is *linked* if all of its positive literals are. A positive literal is linked if at least one of its arguments is. An argument of a literal is linked if either the literal is the head of the clause or another argument in the same literal is linked.

Henceforth, we will assume that our rule space is the set of all linked Horn clauses, in order to avoid meaningless hypotheses. Before presenting the methodology, further useful definitions should be given.

Definition 2. A *substitution* σ is a function from variables into terms.

A substitution can also be viewed as a function from clauses to clauses via its *application* to each variable that occurs in a clause.

Note that, given a clause φ, we will be interested in substitutions σ defined as follows:

$$σ: vars(φ) → FU^0 ∪ VARS$$

where *vars(φ)* denotes the set of variables occurring in the clause φ. This is due to the particular form of the atomic formulas of our language. Another relevant observation is that substitutions are necessarily injective functions (see assumption vi)), that is, only one-to-one variable bindings are allowed, instead of many-to-one variable bindings.

Definition 3. A clause φ *θ-subsumes* a clause ψ if and only if there exists a substitution σ such that (s.t.) σ(φ) ⊆ ψ.

For example, G_{arch} θ-subsumes A_1 since σ(G_{arch}) ⊂ A_1, where σ = {y1 ← obj1, x1 ← p1, x2 ← p2} is the substitution that replaces the variables y1, x1 and x2 with the constants obj1, p1 and p2 respectively. However, σ is not the only substitution that meets this requirement, since also the substitution σ' = {y1 ← obj1, x1 ← p1, x2 ← p3} satisfies the following condition: σ'(G_{arch}) ⊂ A_1.

When the reference of one or more selectors of a hypothesis G is made up of a disjunction of multiple values, the notion of θ-subsumption should be clarified. In fact, in this case, G can be split into several Horn clauses, one for each distinct value in the multiple-valued references. For example,

G^i_{arch}[class(y1)=*arch*] :- [cont(y1,x1)], [on(x1,x2)], [or(x1)=hor, NA], [or(x2)=ver], [sh(x1)=rect,tri]

should be converted before testing θ-subsumption through an equivalent transformation, called *Splitting the Condition Part*, into the following set of *single-valued* clauses:

G^i_{arch} = { G^i_{arch1}, G^i_{arch2}, G^i_{arch3}, G^i_{arch4} } where

$G^i_{arch 1}$[class(y1)=*arch*] :- [cont(y1,x1)], [on(x1,x2)], [or(x1)=hor], [or(x2)=ver], [sh(x1)=rect]

$G^i_{arch 2}$[class(y1)=*arch*] :- [cont(y1,x1)], [on(x1,x2)], [or(x1)=hor], [or(x2)=ver], [sh(x1)=tri]

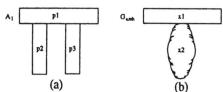

Fig. 1. The class *arch*: (a) an instance and (b) a hypothesis.

$G^i_{arch\,3}$[class(y1)=*arch*] :- [cont(y1,x1)], [on(x1,x2)], [or(x1)=NA], [or(x2)=ver], [sh(x1)=rect]
$G^i_{arch\,4}$[class(y1)=*arch*] :- [cont(y1,x1)], [on(x1,x2)], [or(x1)=NA], [or(x2)=ver], [sh(x1)=tri]

Note that a (VL_{21}) single-valued clause is a Horn clause, while a *multiple-valued* clause is equivalent to a finite set of Horn clauses. Generally speaking, a multiple-valued clause $\varphi = \{\varphi_1, \varphi_2, ..., \varphi_n\}$ θ-subsumes a multiple-valued clause $\psi = \{\psi_1, \psi_2, ..., \psi_m\}$ if and only if $\exists \sigma$ s.t. $\forall i \in \{1,2, ..., m\}$ $\exists j \in \{1,2, ..., n\} : \sigma(\varphi_j) \subseteq \psi_i$.

The definition of θ-subsumption induces a quasi-ordering upon the space of the Horn clauses. We say that φ is *more general* (less specific) than or equal to a clause ψ if and only if φ θ-subsumes ψ, and denote it $\psi \leq \varphi$.

Generally, the canonical inductive paradigm requires the fulfilment of the properties of completeness and consistency for the learned rules. More formally we introduce the following definitions:

Definition 4. Given two clauses, φ and ψ, we say that φ is *inconsistent* with respect to (w.r.t.) ψ if and only if there exists a substitution σ s.t.:
1) $\sigma(\text{body}(\varphi)) \subseteq \text{body}(\psi)$
2) $\sigma(\text{head}(\varphi)) \neq \text{head}(\psi)$
where *body(η)* and *head(η)* denote respectively the *body* and the *head* of a clause η.

Definition 5. Given two clauses, φ and ψ, we say that φ is *incomplete* w.r.t. ψ if and only if there exists no substitution σ s.t.:
1) $\sigma(\text{head}(\varphi)) = \text{head}(\psi)$
2) $\sigma(\text{body}(\varphi)) \subseteq \text{body}(\psi)$.

Given a hypothesis φ, that is complete and consistent w.r.t. a set of training examples, and a new negative example ψ s.t. φ is inconsistent w.r.t. ψ, it becomes necessary to specialize φ so that the new hypothesis φ' is complete and consistent w.r.t. both the previous set of training examples and the new negative example ψ.

3 The Methodology

3.1 Specialization as Search

The problem of specialization can be investigated in the framework of search problems. We can define the search space as the quasi-ordered (q.o.) set ($\mathcal{L}, \leq$), where $\mathcal{L}$ is the set of the linked constant-free Horn clauses and $\leq$ is the quasi-ordering defined in section 2.

The problem of specialization is a subtask of the more general problem of concept learning based on Horn clauses. Most of the work in this area refers to Plotkin's framework [16] to define the space in which the search for concept descriptions is performed. Unfortunately, the properties of the lattice $\mathcal{C}$, defined by Plotkin considering general clauses, are not preserved when the proper subset of Horn clauses is considered. In particular, Plotkin's operator for computing the greatest lower bound (*glb*) of two clauses is not closed for Horn clauses, thus the set of Horn clauses $\mathcal{H}$ is not a sublattice of $\mathcal{C}$. Even more so, the ordered set of the linked Horn clauses, ($\mathcal{L}, \leq$), is not a sublattice of $\mathcal{C}$. Furthermore, ($\mathcal{L}, \leq$) is not a lattice at all, since there may exist a finite set of *most specific generalizations*[1] (*msg*) or *least general generalizations* (*lgg*) of any pair of elements in $\mathcal{L}$ instead of at most a single and unique msg, due to assumption vi) in section 2.

By dropping assumption vi), ($\mathcal{L}, \leq$) becomes a lattice because any two clauses φ_1 and φ_2 in $\mathcal{L}$ have a least upper bound (*lub*) or *join*, $\varphi_1 \vee \varphi_2$, that corresponds to the only msg of φ_1 and φ_2 and a glb or *meet*, $\varphi_1 \wedge \varphi_2$, obtained by performing the union of the two clauses

---

1. A most specific generalization of two clauses is a generalization which is not more general than any other such generalization. Formally, given $\varphi_1, \varphi_2 \in \mathcal{L}$:

$$msg(\varphi_1, \varphi_2) = \{\ \varphi \mid \varphi_i \leq \varphi, i=1,2 \text{ and } \forall \psi \text{ such that } \varphi_i \leq \psi, i=1,2 : \text{not}(\ \psi < \varphi\ )\ \}$$

under the condition that their heads are unifiable (the precise definition of the glb of two any Horn clauses is beyond the scope of this paper). Two special clauses, called *universal* (or *empty*) *clause* (⊤) and *inconsistency* or *empty program* (⊥), denote the top and the bottom of the q.o. set, respectively. The former is the clause to which all pairs of clauses can generalize, the latter is the one θ-subsumed by all pairs of clauses. Fig. 2 shows a portion of the q.o. space ($\mathbf{1}$, ≤). In this space there exist only finite strictly ascending chains since the set of all generalizations of a single-valued clause φ corresponds to the set of all subsets of the literals of φ, thus each (proper) generalization of φ has a number of literals less than the number of literals of φ [17]. Conversely, when many-to-one variable bindings are allowed, there exist infinite strictly ascending chains in the lattice of the linked Horn clauses.

The search strategy used to solve the problem of specialization takes advantage of the particular structure of the search space. Given a hypothesis φ which is complete w.r.t. the positive examples φ^+_1, φ^+_2, ..., φ^+_n and inconsistent w.r.t. ψ, the search process aims at finding one of the *most general specializations*[2] (*mgs*) of φ against ψ given φ^+_1, φ^+_2, ..., φ^+_n, *mgs(φ,ψ)*, that is still complete w.r.t. the positive examples φ^+_1, φ^+_2, ..., φ^+_n. Formally:

$$\text{mgs}(\varphi,\psi \mid \varphi^+_1, \varphi^+_2, ..., \varphi^+_n) = \{\ \varphi^i \in \text{mgs}(\varphi,\psi) \mid \varphi^+_j \leq \varphi^i, j=1,2,...,n\ \}.$$

Each φ^i in mgs($\varphi,\psi \mid \varphi^+_1, \varphi^+_2, ..., \varphi^+_n$) is the highest bound of a finite strictly descending chain consisting of the clauses χ, χ≤φ, s.t. $\varphi^+_j \leq \chi$, j=1,2,...,n and not(body(ψ)≤body(χ)).

3.2 The Specializing Operator

Throughout this section we shall refer to a simple example for a better understanding of the formal explanation of the methodology. Suppose a learning problem is given, in which the goal is to find a decision rule that allows us to learn the description of the concept *arch* from positive and negative examples. Let:

G^i_{arch} [class(y1)=*arch*] :- [cont(y1,x1)], [on(x1,x2)], [or(x1)=hor,NA], [or(x2)=ver], [sh(x1)=rect,tri]

be the decision rule learned in a previous step by INDUBI from the examples reported in Fig. 3. Let us suppose now that an instance of *non-arch*, denoted by N_3, becomes available:

N_3 [class(obj5)=*non-arch*] :- [cont(obj5,p13)], [cont(obj5,p14)], [cont(obj5,p15)],
                               [on(p13,p14)], [on(p13,p15)], [touch(p14,p15)],
                               [or(p13)=hor], [or(p14)=ver], [or(p15)=ver],
                               [sh(p13)=rect], [sh(p14)=tri], [sh(p15)=rect]

whose graphical description is given in Fig. 4. It follows straightforwardly that N_3 is wrongly classified as an *arch*, since σ_1 (body(G^i_{arch})) ⊂ body(N_3) and σ_2 (body(G^i_{arch})) ⊂ body(N_3),

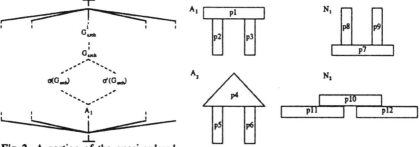

Fig. 2. A portion of the quasi-ordered space of the linked Horn clauses.

Fig. 3. Training set for the problem *arch*.

2. Formally, mgs(φ,ψ)={ φ^i | φ^i≤φ and not(body(ψ) ≤ body(φ^i)) and ∀χ such that χ≤φ and not(body(ψ) ≤ body(χ)) : not(φ^i<χ) }

where σ_1 and σ_2 are the following substitutions:

$\sigma_1 = \{$ y1 $\leftarrow$ obj5, x1 $\leftarrow$ p13, x2 $\leftarrow$ p14 $\}$, $\sigma_2 = \{$ y1 $\leftarrow$ obj5, x1 $\leftarrow$ p13, x2 $\leftarrow$ p15 $\}$.

More precisely, $\sigma_1 (\text{body}(G^i_{arch\,1})) \subset \text{body}(N_3)$ and $\sigma_2 (\text{body}(G^i_{arch\,1})) \subset \text{body}(N_3)$. Therefore, G^i_{arch} is no longer consistent with the available examples and a proper knowledge refinement mechanism is desirable. As a consequence, the *body* of the inconsistent clause needs to be subjected to a suitable process of *specialization* in order to restore the consistency property. The specialization process proposed in this section uses a novel operator, that is strongly based on the application of the negation. In order to present this operator, it is necessary to give the following definitions:

Definition 6. Given two single-valued linked Horn clauses φ and ψ and a substitution σ_j s.t. φ is inconsistent w.r.t. ψ, the *difference* between ψ and φ under the mapping σ_j, denoted by $\psi \, \Delta_j \, \varphi$, is the following set of literals: $\psi \, \Delta_j \, \varphi = \text{body}(\psi) \setminus \sigma_j(\text{body}(\varphi))$ where $\setminus$ denotes the usual set difference.

As concerns the example of the concept *arch*, we have two substitutions σ_1 and σ_2 that meet both the conditions required by definition 4.

Thus we have two distinct differences between N_3 and $G^i_{arch\,1}$. They are:

$N_3 \Delta_1 \, G^i_{arch\,1}$ = $\{$ $\neg[\text{cont(obj5,p14)}], \neg[\text{cont(obj5,p15)}], \neg[\text{on(p13,p15)}], \neg[\text{touch(p14,p15)}],$ $\neg[\text{or(p15)=ver}], \neg[\text{sh(p14)=tri}], \neg[\text{sh(p15)=rect}]$ $\}$,

$N_3 \Delta_2 \, G^i_{arch\,1}$ = $\{$ $\neg[\text{cont(obj5,p14)}], \neg[\text{cont(obj5,p15)}], \neg[\text{on(p13,p14)}], \neg[\text{touch(p14,p15)}],$ $\neg[\text{or(p14)=ver}], \neg[\text{sh(p14)=tri}], \neg[\text{sh(p15)=rect}]$ $\}$

Definition 7. An *antisubstitution* γ is a mapping from terms into variables.

When a clause φ θ-subsumes a clause ψ through a substitution σ_i, then it is possible to define a corresponding antisubstitution, σ_i^{-1}, which is exactly the inverse function of σ_i. In fact, σ_i is an injective function due to condition vi) in section 2, which defines the equality theory underlying the adopted representation language. Then σ_i^{-1} maps some constants and/or variables in ψ to variables in φ, that is: $\sigma_i^{-1}: \sigma(\text{vars}(\varphi)) \rightarrow \text{vars}(\varphi)$.

It is worthwhile to note that the antisubstitutions involved in a process of specialization map some constants (never variables) in ψ to variables in φ. This is due to the fact that ψ is always a ground Horn clause in a problem of specialization. Indeed, in the previous example, $\sigma_1^{-1} = \{$ obj5 $\leftarrow$ y1, p13 $\leftarrow$ x1, p14 $\leftarrow$ x2 $\}$.

It should be observed that not all constants in N_3 have a corresponding variable according to σ_1^{-1}. Therefore, for our purposes, we introduce the extension of σ_1^{-1}, defined on the whole set of constants occurring into ψ, $FU^0(\psi)$, and taking values in *VARS*:

$$\underline{\sigma}_i^{-1}(c_n) = \begin{cases} \sigma_i^{-1}(c_n) & \text{if } c_n \in \sigma(\text{vars}(\varphi)) \\ \_n & \text{otherwise} \end{cases}$$

Henceforth, variables denoted by _n as in Prolog notation will be called *new* variables. As to the example of the concept *arch*, $\underline{\sigma}_i^{-1}$ is the following function:

$$\underline{\sigma}_i^{-1} = \{ \text{obj5} \leftarrow \text{y1, p13} \leftarrow \text{x1, p14} \leftarrow \text{x2, p15} \leftarrow \_15 \}.$$

Definition 8. Let $\varphi = \{ l_1, l_2, ..., l_n \}$, $n \geq 1$, be a *single-valued* clause. Then $neg(\varphi)$ denotes the negation of the dual clause of φ, i.e., the clause:

$$neg(\varphi) = \{ \neg l_1, \neg l_2, ..., \neg l_n \}$$

Definition 9. Given a single-valued hypothesis φ, an example ψ and a substitution σ_j s.t. φ is *inconsistent* w.r.t. ψ, the *base* $\mathcal{B}_j$ of *consistent specializations* under the mapping σ_j is the following set of literals: $\mathcal{B}_j = neg(\underline{\sigma}_i^{-1}(\psi \, \Delta_j \, \varphi))$.

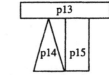

Fig. 4. A *near-miss* of arch.

Henceforth, we will call *clause generated by* $\mathcal{B}_j$ any clause obtained by adding a literal in $\mathcal{B}_j$ to the inconsistent clause φ.

In the example of *arch*, there are two bases of consistent specializations, i.e., $\mathcal{B}_1 = \text{neg}(\sigma_1^{-1}(N_3 \Delta_1 \ G^i_{\text{arch 1}}))$ and $\mathcal{B}_2 = \text{neg}(\sigma_2^{-1}(N_3 \Delta_2 \ G^i_{\text{arch 1}}))$:

$\mathcal{B}_1 = \{ \quad \neg[\text{cont}(y1,x2)], \ \neg[\text{cont}(y1,\_15)], \ \neg[\text{on}(x1,\_15)], \ \neg[\text{touch}(x2,\_15)],$
$\qquad \neg[\text{or}(\_15)=\text{ver}], \ \neg[\text{sh}(x2)=\text{tri}], \ \neg[\text{sh}(\_15)=\text{rect}] \qquad \}$

$\mathcal{B}_2 = \{ \quad \neg[\text{cont}(y1,\_14)], \ \neg[\text{cont}(y1,x2)], \ \neg[\text{on}(x1,\_14)], \ \neg[\text{touch}(\_14,x2)],$
$\qquad \neg[\text{or}(\_14)=\text{ver}], \ \neg[\text{sh}(\_14)=\text{tri}], \ \neg[\text{sh}(x2)=\text{rect}] \qquad \}$

Theorem 1 *Let φ be a single-valued hypothesis, ψ an example and $\sigma_j, j=1,2,\ldots,k$, the set of all substitutions s.t. φ is inconsistent w.r.t. ψ. Any linked Horn clause*
$$\varphi' = \varphi \cup \{ l_{n+1} \} \quad \text{with } l_{n+1} \in \bigcap_{j=1,2,\ldots,k} \mathcal{B}_j, \text{ is consistent w.r.t. } \psi.$$

Note that l_{n+1} is an element of $body(\varphi')$, since it is a negative literal.

Theorem 2 *φ' is one of the most general specializations of φ against ψ.*

A proof of theorems 1 and 2 is given in [18]. Theorems 1 and 2 easily extend to any literal l_{n+1} which introduces new variables, due to negation-as-failure rule.

In the previous example we have $\mathcal{B}_1 \cap \mathcal{B}_2 = \{ \ \neg[\text{cont}(y1,x2)] \ \}$, thus the following linked Horn clause:

$G^{ii}_{\text{arch 1}}$ [class(y1)=*arch*] :- [cont(y1,x1)], [on(x1,x2)], [or(x1)=hor], [or(x2)=ver], [sh(x1)=rect],
$\qquad \neg[\text{cont}(y1,x2)]$

results consistent w.r.t. N_3 and, in addition, it represents one of the most general specializations of $G^i_{\text{arch 1}}$ against N_3. This clause can be equivalently transformed into:
$G^{ii}_{\text{arch 1}}$ [class(y1)=*arch*] :- [cont(y1,x1)], [cont(y1,x2)=false], [on(x1,x2)],
$\qquad$ [or(x1)=hor], [or(x2)=ver], [sh(x1)=rect]

and we have the following specialization of G^i_{arch}: $G^{ii}_{\text{arch}} = \{ \ G^i_{\text{arch 1}}, G^i_{\text{arch 2}}, G^i_{\text{arch 3}}, G^i_{\text{arch 4}} \ \}$.

Of course, adding further selectors to $G^{ii}_{\text{arch 1}}$ does not prejudice the consistency property of the clause. Nevertheless, there is no guarantee that the original property of completeness of G^i_{arch} still holds for G^{ii}_{arch}. Actually, such completeness property is not satisfied by the hypothesis G^{ii}_{arch}, since it θ-subsumes neither A_1 nor A_2. Thus, in this case, a search for complete and consistent hypotheses should be performed in a wider space than $\mathcal{B}_1 \cap \mathcal{B}_2$.

Generally speaking, we can say that, given a clause φ and an example ψ s.t. φ is inconsistent w.r.t. ψ due to some substitutions $\sigma_j, j=1,2,\ldots,k$, the search for a complete and consistent hypothesis can be viewed as a two-staged process, in which the second stage is characterized by an enlarged search space. In the example, after the failure of the search in $\mathcal{B}_1 \cap \mathcal{B}_2$, the wider space $\mathcal{B}_1 \cup \mathcal{B}_2$ should be considered.

$\mathcal{B}_1 \cup \mathcal{B}_2 = (\mathcal{B}_1 \cap \mathcal{B}_2) \cup \{ \quad \neg[\text{cont}(y1,\_15)], \ \neg[\text{on}(x1,\_15)], \ \neg[\text{touch}(x2,\_15)],$
$\quad \neg[\text{or}(\_15)=\text{ver}], \ \neg[\text{sh}(x2)=\text{tri}], \ \neg[\text{sh}(\_15)=\text{rect}], \ \neg[\text{cont}(y1,\_14)], \ \neg[\text{on}(x1,\_14)],$
$\quad \neg[\text{touch}(\_14,x2)], \ \neg[\text{or}(\_14)=\text{ver}], \ \neg[\text{sh}(\_14)=\text{tri}], \ \neg[\text{sh}(x2)=\text{rect}] \quad \}$

This space deserves to be analyzed in depth. Firstly, we can notice that four literals in $\mathcal{B}_1 \cup \mathcal{B}_2$, namely $\neg[\text{or}(\_14)=\text{ver}], \ \neg[\text{or}(\_15)=\text{ver}], \ \neg[\text{sh}(\_14)=\text{tri}], \ \neg[\text{sh}(\_15)=\text{rect}]$, produce incomplete clauses when added to $G^i_{\text{arch 1}}$. Secondly, two literals in $\mathcal{B}_1 \cup \mathcal{B}_2$, namely $\neg[\text{sh}(x2)=\text{tri}]$ and $\neg[\text{sh}(x2)=\text{rect}]$, give rise to as many inconsistent clauses. This happens because theorem 1 is no longer valid in the search space $\mathcal{B}_1 \cup \mathcal{B}_2$. Thus, in such a space, an additional consistency test is required. Henceforth, the set $\mathcal{S}_r = \bigcap_{j=1,2,\ldots,k} \mathcal{B}_j$ will be named *reduced base of consistent specializations*. The first stage of the search process concerns just $\mathcal{S}_r$, since theorem 1 answers for the consistency of the explored clauses. In fact, we aim at finding a complete and consistent hypothesis with the minimum effort and, by exploring the clauses generated by $\mathcal{S}_r$ first, we will not need to check for the consistency property of the specialized rules. Search in this space is very simple, since exactly one literal of $\mathfrak{S}_r$ is added to the inconsistent clause. However a check on completeness property has to be performed. If an explored clause results to be complete then the search process succeeds, otherwise the search space should be enlarged since further exploration of more specific clauses generated by $\mathfrak{S}_r$ would fail in finding complete hypotheses. This last consideration comes from the fact that the search strategy takes advantage of the structure of the q.o. space ($\mathfrak{X}, \leq$). When the search in the reduced base of consistent specializations fails, a breadth-first search is performed in the *augmented base of consistent specializations* $\mathfrak{S}_a = \underset{j=1,2\ldots k}{\cup} \mathfrak{B}_j$. In this case, a further check on the explored clauses has to be considered, namely the consistency check *with respect to only the negative example that caused the inconsistency*, since the addition of one or more literals in a $\mathfrak{B}_j$ does not guarantee the consistency w.r.t. all the other substitutions σ_k, $k \neq j$. During the search process, three different cases can occur:

1) The explored clause is *incomplete*, that is, it does not θ-subsume all the positive examples: Search has reached a dead end since further addition of literals will never restore the completeness property

2) The explored clause is *complete* but *inconsistent*: Search will continue since the addition of further literals may restore the consistency property while hopefully preserving the completeness

3) The explored clause is *complete* and *consistent*: Search terminates successfully.

In Fig. 5, the explored portion of the q.o. space generated by $\mathfrak{S}_a$ for the example given above is shown. Clauses $G^{iii}_{arch\,1}$ through $G^{vi}_{arch\,i}$ have the following descriptions:

$G^{iii}_{arch\,1}$ [class(y1)=arch] :- [cont(y1,x1)], [on(x1,x2)], [or(x1)=hor], [or(x2)=ver], [sh(x1)=rect], ¬[cont(y1,_15)]

$G^{iv}_{arch\,1}$ [class(y1)=arch] :- [cont(y1,x1)], [on(x1,x2)], [or(x1)=hor], [or(x2)=ver], [sh(x1)=rect], ¬[on(x1,_15)]

$G^{v}_{arch\,1}$ [class(y1)=arch] :- [cont(y1,x1)], [on(x1,x2)], [or(x1)=hor], [or(x2)=ver], [sh(x1)=rect], ¬[sh(x2)=tri]

$G^{vi}_{arch\,1}$ [class(y1)=arch] :- [cont(y1,x1)], [on(x1,x2)], [or(x1)=hor], [or(x2)=ver], [sh(x1)=rect], ¬[touch(x2,_15)]

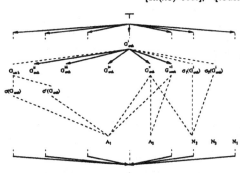

and $G^k_{arch} = \{ G^k_{arch\,1}, G^i_{arch\,2}, G^i_{arch\,3}, G^i_{arch\,4} \}$, k=iii, iv, v, vi. It is easy to see that G^{iii}_{arch} and G^{iv}_{arch} fall in case 1), G^v_{arch} is complete but inconsistent w.r.t. N_3 (case 2)), and finally G^{vi}_{arch} is complete and consistent, thus it represents the goal of the search.

In general, there is no guarantee of success of the search in the enlarged space $\mathfrak{S}_a$. When a failure occurs, a further attempt to specialize the inconsistent hypothesis consists in dropping all the single-valued clauses that caused inconsistency. This is equivalent to specialize the original multiple-valued clause according to the *dropping an alternative* rule [19]

Fig. 5. The explored portion of the search space. Each node denotes the body of the corresponding clause, e.g., N_3 means $body(N_3)$. A plain edge from φ to ψ denotes the fact that $\psi \leq \varphi$ and there is no χ such that $\psi \leq \chi \leq \varphi$. A path between two nodes is represented by a dashed line.

and may sometimes result into rules in which the reference of one or more literals has been *stripped*. This further step of the search is justified by the fact that model-driven learning systems might have produced overgeneralized rules.

It is worthwhile to note that the application of the specializing operator proposed in this paper needs to keep a record of the only past positive examples.

4 Computational Complexity of the Specializing Operator

In order to evaluate the computational complexity of the proposed operator, we have to distinguish the cost of specialization in the three subsequent steps of the search:
1) Search in the reduced space of consistent specializations, $\mathbf{S}_r$
2) Search in the augmented space of consistent specializations, $\mathbf{S}_a$
3) Dropping a single-valued clause.

As to the first point, let p denote the number of possible substitutions that make a hypothesis φ inconsistent w.r.t. a negative example ψ. In the worst case:

$$p = |consts(\psi)| \cdot (|consts(\psi)|-1) \cdot \ldots \cdot (|consts(\psi)|-|vars(\varphi)|+1) = P(|consts(\psi)|, |vars(\varphi)|)$$

where $consts(\psi)$ denotes the set of constants occurring in ψ and $P(n, m)$ is the number of permutations of m objects out of n. Of course, in many practical situations p is much less than $P(|consts(\psi)|, |vars(\varphi)|)$, otherwise the conditions expressed in $body(\varphi)$ should be true for any permutation of $|vars(\varphi)|$ objects in ψ. This means that, in the worst case, there are p distinct bases of consistent specializations $\mathbf{B}_j$. If q denotes the cardinality of the difference between ψ and φ under any mapping σ_j (q is the same for all possible mappings that make φ inconsistent w.r.t. ψ), then the construction of $\mathbf{S}_r$ has a complexity of $p \times q$ in the worst case, that is when $\mathbf{S}_r$ contains q literals. Consequently, the maximum cost to explore such a space is given by:

$$p \times q + q \times cost\ of\ completeness\ check\ on\ all\ positive\ examples$$

where the completeness check on all positive examples has a cost comparable to a join on as many relations as the number of literals in the specialized clause φ'. In the second step, the cost to generate the space $\mathbf{S}_a$ can be neglected since we can exploit information on the intersection computed in the previous step. However, $\mathbf{S}_a$ may contain up to $p \times q$ literals, so that the maximum cost to explore $\mathbf{S}_a$ is given by:

$$p \times q \times (cost\ of\ completeness\ check\ on\ all\ positive\ examples + cost\ of\ consistency\ check\ on\ \psi).$$

Finally, the third step requires a completeness check on all positive examples for the hypothesis obtained by dropping all the single-valued clauses that caused inconsistency.

An alternative approach to specializing a previously generated hypothesis is learning a new hypothesis from scratch by exploiting the training set, the new examples correctly classified (if any) and the negative example which caused inconsistency. This approach would generally be much more expensive if INDUBI [12, 13], that implements the STAR methodology [19], were used. Indeed, STAR methodology performs a beam search by generating *partial stars* that are pruned according to a user's *preference criterion*, named *Lexicographic Evaluation Functional* (LEF). For each partial star, there are at most *VLMAXSTAR × ALTER* hypotheses to be tested, where *VLMAXSTAR* is the beam size and *ALTER* is the branching factor. The test of a hypothesis involves all positive and negative examples since the properties of completeness and consistency have to be checked. The number of times a partial star is updated depends on a user defined parameter, *NCONSIST*, that represents the number of consistent hypotheses to generate before choosing the best one. However, the number of partial stars is never lower than the number of selectors in the shortest consistent hypothesis that covers at least a positive example. Since the search strategy is a separate-and-conquer at the highest level, the whole process of induction may start again if the best consistent hypothesis is not complete. In the worst case, the number of times the induction process is restarted is given by the number of positive examples.

To sum up, by learning from scratch it is necessary to search through a wider space since both information contained in the misclassified example and regularities discovered in all the positive examples are neglected. Since it is costly, such a process should be delayed as long as possible, in particular until no specialization of a hypothesis can restore the original properties.

5 An Example of Application

In order to evaluate the specializing operator proposed in section 3.2, we ran two experiments in the toy-world domain of the geometric figures. Fig. 6 shows fifteen examples of geometric figures, that belong to three classes - C_a, C_b and C_c - each of which has five examples. Table 1 describes the representation language used for this problem. **First experiment.** INDUBI was run on the first three examples for each class and produced the following hypotheses in 30 seconds:

G_a [class(y1)=C_a] :- [cont(y1,x1)], [on(x1,x2)], [size(x1)=medium,large],
                  [shape(x2)=square, ellipse, circle]   (10 sec.)

G_b [class(y1)=C_b] :- [cont(y1,x1)], [size(x1)=large], [texture(x1)=clear],
                  [shape(x1)=square, circle]

       [class(y1)=C_b] :- [cont(y1,x1)], [texture(x1)=shaded], [shape(x1)=ellipse]   (13 sec.)

G_c [class(y1)=C_c] :- [cont(y1,x1)], [on(x1,x2)], [size(x1)=small],
                  [size(x2)=small, medium]   (7 sec.)

The hypotheses above are both complete and consistent w.r.t. the training instances. Events *ev4, ev5, ev9, ev10, ev14,* and *ev15* were used to test the predictive accuracy of the decision rules produced by INDUBI. Results provided by the system were:

Class	Events
C_a	ev4, ev5, ev10
C_b	ev9, ev10
C_c	ev14, ev15

As a consequence, the system detected a classification error imputable to one of the six single-valued clauses that make up the rule $G_a = \{G_{a1}, G_{a2}, G_{a3}, G_{a4}, G_{a5}, G_{a6}\}$, namely: G_{a1} [class(y1)=C_a] :- [cont(y1,x1)], [on(x1,x2)], [size(x1)=medium], [shape(x2)=ellipse]

Fig. 6. Examples from the domain of geometric figures.

Descriptor	Type	Domain	Meaning
CONTAIN(x,y)	Nominal	{False, True}	Object x is a part of y
ONTOP(x,y)	Nominal	{False, True}	Object x is on y
SIZE(x)	Linear	{Small, Medium, Large}	Size of the object x
TEXTURE(x)	Nominal	{Clear, Shaded}	Texture of the object x
SHAPE(x)	Nominal	{Triangle, Square, Circle, Rectangle, Ellipse}	Shape of the object x

Table 1: The representation language for the problem of geometric figures.

Indeed, this clause resulted to be inconsistent w.r.t. the event *ev10*. Thus, the process of rule specialization produced the following mgs of G_{a1}:

G^i_{a1} [class(y1)=C_a] :-   [cont(y1,x1)], [on(x1,x2)], [size(x1)=medium], [shape(x2)=ellipse],
                          ¬[shape(x1)=triangle]   (1 sec.)

that makes G_a = { G^i_{a1}, G_{a2}, G_{a3}, G_{a4}, G_{a5}, G_{a6} }, both complete and consistent w.r.t. all the fifteen examples available.

Second experiment. INDUBI was run with all the fifteen examples. The hypotheses produced in 64 seconds were:

G_a [class(y1)=C_a] :-   [cont(y1,x1)], [on(x1,x2)], [size(x1)=medium,large],
                          [shape(x2)=square, circle]

    [class(y1)=C_a] :-   [cont(y1,x1)], [texture(x1)=clear], [shape(x1)=ellipse]

G_b [class(y1)=C_b] :-   [cont(y1,x1)], [on(x1,x2)], [size(x2)=medium, large],
                          [texture(x2)=shaded], [shape(x1)=triangle, ellipse, circle]

    [class(y1)=C_b] :-   [cont(y1,x1)], [on(x1,x2)], [size(x1)=small], [shape(x2)=square]

G_c [class(y1)=C_c] :-   [cont(y1,x1)], [on(x1,x2)], [size(x1)=small], [size(x2)=small, medium]

Comparing these results to the ones obtained from the first experiment, we can observe that total CPU time required to learn *from scratch* is more than twice the time required by the incremental process (64 vs. 31 sec.). However, it is worthwhile to note that there is no guarantee of success for the search performed in order to specialize an inconsistent rule. The failure of the search process is used by the learning system to *decide* a new invocation of the model-driven process in order to produce inductive hypotheses from scratch.

6 Conclusions

The problem of specialization is central to structural incremental learning. As the related problem of generalization, it can be cast as a search through the space of the well formed hypotheses, that can be structured by a generality relation. We propose an algorithm for inductive specialization that takes advantage of the particular structure of the search space to restore the consistency property, thus producing new concept descriptions that are both complete and consistent with respect to all the available training examples. A computational analysis and an initial experimentation in the domain of geometric figures have shown that the computational costs of learning decision rules generated through an incremental process are lower than those required by a single step learning process. More extensive experimentation in the domain of office document analysis and classification [20] has already been planned. Future work will also concern the following aspects:

1) The use of a syntactic distance to select the *most promising* example when more than one instance causes inconsistency in the rule base [21, 22].

2) The implementation of some data-driven generalizing operators in order to cope also with the dual problem of incomplete rules. Several papers have already addressed this problem, but seldom generalization and specialization have been integrated in an efficient and effective methodology to learn structural concept descriptions incrementally.

Acknowledgements

The authors would like to thank Lorenza Saitta, Attilio Giordana, Michael Pazzani and Cesare Tinelli for their useful suggestions on earlier drafts of the paper.

References

1. P.E. Utgoff: Incremental Induction of Decision Trees. Machine Learning 4, 161-186 (1989)
2. J. Hong, I. Mozetic, R.S. Michalski: AQ15: Incremental Learning of Attribute-Based Descriptions from Examples, the Method and User's Guide. Department of Computer Science, University of Illinois at Urbana-Champaign, Urbana, Illinois, UIUCDCS-F-86-949 (1986)
3. D.H. Fisher: Knowledge Acquisition Via Incremental Conceptual Clustering. Ph.D. dissertation, University of California, Irvine (1987)
4. M. Lebowitz: Experiments with Incremental Concept Formation: UNIMEM. Machine Learning 2, 103 - 138 (1987)
5. T.M. Mitchell: Generalization as Search. Artificial Intelligence 18, 203-226 (1982)
6. P.H. Winston: Learning Structural Descriptions from Examples. In: P.H. Winston (ed.): The psychology of computer vision. New York: McGraw Hill 1975
7. S.A. Vere: Induction of concepts in the predicate calculus. In: Proceedings of the 4th IJCAI. Tbilisi, USSR: Morgan Kaufmann 1975, pp. 281-287
8. F. Hayes-Roth: Schematic classification problems and their solution. Pattern Recognition, 105-113 (1974)
9. B.G. Buchanan and T.M. Mitchell: Model-directed learning of production rules. In: D.A. Waterman and F. Hayes-Roth (eds.): Pattern-Directed Inference Systems. New York: Academic Press 1978
10. J.A. Bentrup, G.J. Mehler, J.D. Riedsel: INDUCE 4: A Program for Incrementally Learning Structural Descriptions from Examples. Department of Computer Science, University of Illinois at Urbana-Champaign, Urbana, Illinois, UIUCDCS-F-87-958 (1987)
11. R.S. Michalski: Pattern Recognition as Rule-Guided Inductive Inference. IEEE Transactions on Pattern Analysis and Machine Intelligence PAMI-2, 4, 349-361 (1980)
12. F. Esposito: Automated acquisition of production rules by empirical supervised learning methods. In: M. Schader (ed.): Data, Expert Knowledge and Decisions, (Vol. II). Heidelberg: Springer-Verlag 1990
13. G. Semeraro: Un Sistema per l'Apprendimento Induttivo Concettuale da Esempi con Logica Variable-Valued. Laurea dissertation (also available as LACAM Technical Report, Dipartimento di Informatica, Università di Bari) (1988)
14. K.L. Clark: Negation as failure. In: H. Gallaire and J. Minker (eds.): Logic and Databases. New York: Plenum Press 1978
15. N. Helft: Inductive Generalization: A Logical Framework. In: I. Bratko, N. Lavrac (eds.): Progress in Machine Learning - Proceedings of EWSL 87. Wilmslow: Sigma Press 1987
16. G.D. Plotkin: A Note on Inductive Generalization. In: B. Meltzer and D. Michie (eds.): Machine Intelligence 5. Edinburgh: University Press 1970, pp. 153-163
17. K. VanLehn: Efficient Specialization of Relational Concepts. Machine Learning 4, 99-106 (1989)
18. F. Esposito, G. Semeraro and D. Malerba: Inductive Specialization: An Analytic Approach. LACAM Technical Report, Dipartimento di Informatica, Università di Bari (1992)
19. R.S. Michalski: A Theory and Methodology of Inductive Learning. Artificial Intelligence 20, 111-161 (1983)
20. F. Esposito, D. Malerba, G. Semeraro, E. Annese, G. Scafuro: Empirical Learning Methods for Digitized Document Recognition: An Integrated Approach to Inductive Generalization. In: Proceedings of the 6th Conference on Artificial Intelligence Applications. Santa Barbara, CA: IEEE Comp. Soc. Press 1990, pp. 37-45
21. F. Esposito, D. Malerba and G. Semeraro: Flexible Matching for Noisy Structural Descriptions. In: Proceedings of the 12th IJCAI. Sydney, Australia: Morgan Kaufmann 1991, pp. 658 - 664
22. F. Esposito, G. Semeraro and D. Malerba: A Syntactic Distance for Partially Matching Learned Concepts Against Noisy Structural Object Descriptions. International Journal of Expert Systems 4, 409-451 (1992)

Constructing Refinement Operators
by Decomposing Logical Implication

Shan-Hwei Nienhuys-Cheng[1],
Patrick R.J. van der Laag[1,2], Leendert W.N. van der Torre[1,3]

[1] Department of Computer Science, Erasmus University of Rotterdam,
P.O.Box 1738, 3000 DR Rotterdam, the Netherlands
[2] Tinbergen Institute, same address
[3] EURIDIS, same address

Abstract. Inductive learning models [15] [18] often use a search space
of clauses, ordered by a generalization hierarchy. To find solutions in the
model, search algorithms use different generalization and specialization
operators. In this article we introduce a framework for deconstructing
orderings into operators. We will decompose the quasi-ordering induced
by logical implication into six increasingly weak orderings. The difference between two successive orderings will be small, and can therefore be understood easily. Using this decomposition, we will describe
upward and downward refinement operators for all orderings, including
θ-subsumption and logical implication.

1 Introduction

It is well known that logical implication can be considered as an ordering on
clauses. In this article, three questions are discussed. Each answer will give us a
starting point for the next question. The answers to these questions serve as a
framework for deconstructing logical implication into refinement operators.

1. How can we weaken the ordering, induced by logical implication?
2. How can we split up logical derivations into simple operations?
3. How can we find generalizations and specializations of a clause?

Logical implication can be described by *resolution*. This will be the starting point
of our investigations to answer the first question. We propose a decomposition of
the ordering induced by logical implication into six increasingly weak orderings.
Every ordering lacks one feature of the former and is less flexible, but more
mechanical and manageable.

To answer the second question, we will use our decomposition. If we analyze
how the orderings are defined, we will notice that different operations like substitution, permutation and addition of literals are introduced in different orderings.

Example 1. Consider
$C = p(f(X)) \leftarrow p(X),$
$D = p(f(f(X))) \leftarrow p(X),$
$E = p(f(f(X))) \leftarrow p(X), q(Y)$ and
$F = p(f(f(a))) \leftarrow p(a), q(b).$

Clause F can be logically derived from clause C. Our analysis will show this by observing there is a resolution step (from C to D), an addition of a literal (from D to E) and a substitution step (from E to F).

The motivation of the first two questions is to find an answer for the third question. First we will define operators that find refinements (generalizations or specializations) of a clause for the weakest ordering. For each stronger ordering, we split up the new operations into small steps. By extending the operators with these small steps, refinement operators for all orderings are found.

1.1 Related work

Questions related to orderings on clauses and refinements have received a lot of attention within machine learning, especially within Inductive Logic Programming (ILP). Logical derivations are used as explanations of examples by a theory: a theory T explains positive E^+ and negative E^- examples iff $T \models E^+$ and $T \not\models E^-$. Machine learning algorithms like the well-known algorithms ID3 and AQ11 construct a theory using the examples. Within ILP, people focus on *incremental* learning which makes the construction of a theory a search process [8].

In this article we focus on *orderings on clauses*. Search algorithms usually try to find individual clauses of the theory instead of the whole theory at once. This simplifies the generalization hierarchy, which becomes an ordering on clauses only. To deal with background knowledge, these orderings are made relative to a logical theory [15] [16] [2]. Constructive operators for these relative orderings use inverse resolution [9] or a translation to background knowledge consisting of ground atoms (called a model of the theory) [11] [10].

Lapointe and Matwin [5] were the first to define a generalization operator for *logical implication*. Their operator finds a generalization of two examples in two steps: the construction of a recursive clause from the two examples and the generalization of this recursive clause. Muggleton [10] generalizes the second step such that it is possible to find any generalization. Many people within the ILP community use θ-*subsumption* (e.g. Shapiro [18]) because it is more manipulable than resolution. Plotkin [14] introduced θ-subsumption as a kind of explanation. He used this ordering to compute a least general generalization (lgg). With relative orderings, both the logical implication and subsumption rlgg do not have to exist [12], which prompted Niblett to question the advantages of θ-subsumption over logical implication. *Substitution* is a basic operation of θ-subsumption, introduced in machine learning for ordering atoms by Reynolds [17]. He showed that computing an lgg of atoms is a kind of dual to unification.

In [4], Laird has described a general framework for upward and downward *refinement operators* which can respectively find more general and more specific clauses. (Downward) refinement operators were introduced by Shapiro [18]. In his Model Inference System, refinement operators are used to replace clauses by more specific ones if the theory is too strong. In Ling's system SIM [7], abstraction operators do the opposite if the theory is too weak.

2 Decomposing Logical Implication

In this section, we will decompose the ordering on clauses induced by logical implication into six increasingly weak quasi-orderings, $\succeq_6, \ldots, \succeq_1$.

2.1 Definitions

Definition 1. Given a set clauses S and clauses $C, D, E \in S$, we use the following related notions:

- A partially defined binary relation $\geq$ on S is called a *partial ordering* on S iff it is reflexive ($C \geq C$), transitive ($C \geq D$ and $D \geq E$ imply $C \geq E$) and antisymmetric ($C \geq D$ and $D \geq C$ imply $C = D$).
- A partially defined binary relation $\succeq$ on S that is reflexive and transitive but not necessarily antisymmetric is called a *quasi-ordering*.
- If $\succeq_1$ and $\succeq_2$ are two quasi-orderings then $\succeq_2$ is *stronger* than $\succeq_1$ if $C \succeq_1 D$ implies $C \succeq_2 D$. If also for some C, D, $C \not\succeq_1 D$ and $C \succeq_2 D$ then $\succeq_2$ is *strictly stronger* than $\succeq_1$.
- If $C \succeq D$ or $D \succeq C$ then C and D are called *comparable*.
- C *covers* D iff $C \succ D$ ($C \succeq D$ and $D \not\succeq C$) and there exists no E such that $C \succ E \succ D$. If C covers D then C is called an *upward cover* of D, and D is called a *downward cover* of C. We denote the set of all downward and upward covers of a clause C by $dc(C)$ and $uc(C)$.
- For every quasi-ordering $\succeq$ we can define an *equivalence* relation: $C \sim D$ iff $C \succeq D$ and $D \succeq C$.

Within the logical language used in this article there is an explicit distinction between the representation of a clause as a set and as a sequence of literals. This is necessary to describe our new orderings. When we say 'clause C' we mean a sequence of literals: $C = L_0 \leftarrow L_1, \ldots, L_n$. The set representation is common in ILP and will, in this article, sometimes be used to facilitate definitions. By writing $\dot{C}$ we mean that clause C is implicitly considered as a set of literals and thus the internal ordering and repetition of literals play no role. For example, the clauses $p(X) \leftarrow q(X), r(X), r(X)$ and $p(X) \leftarrow r(X), q(X)$ have the same set representation $\dot{C} = \{p(X), \neg q(X), \neg r(X)\}$.

Whenever we say clauses we mean Horn clauses. The results of this article however are easily generalized to clauses.

2.2 The Logical Implication and θ-Subsumption Ordering

Definition 2. In the *logical implication ordering* $\succeq_6$, $C \succeq_6 D$ iff $C \models D$.

The logical implication ordering is defined model-theoretically. To work with this ordering, we need a proof-theoretic counterpart. This was given by Muggleton and Bain (a reproof of Lee [6]) and uses the resolution closure of Robinson.

Definition 3. Let T be a set of clauses. The *resolution closure* $\mathcal{L}^*(T)$ is defined by the function $\mathcal{L}$:
1. $\mathcal{L}^0(T) = T$
2. $\mathcal{L}^n(T) = \{C \mid D_1 \in \mathcal{L}^{n-1}(T),\ D_2 \in T$ and C is a resolvent of D_1 and $D_2\}$
3. $\mathcal{L}^*(T) = \mathcal{L}^0(T) \cup \mathcal{L}^1(T) \cup \ldots$

Theorem 4 [1]. $C \succeq_6 D$ *iff* D *is a tautology or there is a* $D' \in \mathcal{L}^*(\{C\})$ *and a substitution* θ *such that* $\dot{D}'\theta \subseteq \dot{D}$.

This ordering can be naturally divided into two parts: the construction of D' using resolution and the derivation of D from D'.

Clause C and D of Example 1 (also in [3] and [12]) illustrate that logical implication is strictly stronger than θ-subsumption. The difference between θ-subsumption and logical implication is characterized exactly by the operations involving self-resolution [10].

Definition 5. In the θ-*subsumption ordering* $\succeq_5$, $C \succeq_5 D$ iff $\dot{C}\theta \subseteq \dot{D}$ for some substitution θ.

Definition 6 [14]. A clause C is *reduced* iff $\dot{D} \subseteq \dot{C}$ and $D \sim_5 C$ imply $\dot{D} = \dot{C}$.

In words, a clause is reduced iff it is not equivalent to a proper subset of itself when regarded as a set. If a clause C is not reduced, Plotkin's reduction algorithm returns a reduced clause D such that $\dot{D} \subset \dot{C}$. We call all literals in $\dot{C} \setminus \dot{D}$ *redundant*. Plotkin proved the following proposition.

Proposition 7 [14]. $C \sim_5 D$ *iff after reduction* $\dot{C}$ *and* $\dot{D}$ *are renamings.*

From the previous proposition, it follows that addition of non-redundant literals to reduced clauses as well as applying substitutions that are not renamings result in proper specializations in the θ-subsumption ordering.

In the two following sections, we will weaken θ-subsumption, $\dot{C}\theta \subseteq \dot{D}$, to $\dot{C}\theta = \dot{D}$, in two steps.

2.3 The Restricted θ-Subsumption Ordering

Example 2. Consider
$$C = p(X) \leftarrow q(f(X)),$$
$$D = p(X) \leftarrow q(f(X)), q(Y),$$
$$E = p(X) \leftarrow q(f(X)), q(g(V)) \text{ and}$$
$$F = p(X) \leftarrow q(f(X)), r(W).$$
We have $C \sim_5 D$, $C \succ_5 E$ and $C \succ_5 F$.

Definition 8. [14] Two literals are called *compatible* iff they have the same predicate symbol and sign.

It can be verified that adding to a clause C a literal L that is incompatible with each literal in C always results in a proper specialization ($\succ_5$). In the new ordering we exclude the case of addition of incompatible literals:

Definition 9. In the *restricted θ-subsumption ordering* $\succeq_4$, $C \succeq_4 D$ iff there exists a substitution θ such that $\dot{C}\theta \subseteq \dot{D}$ and every literal in D is compatible with a literal in C.

Revisiting the last example, we see that in the restricted θ-subsumption ordering C and F have become incomparable. So $\succeq_5$ is strictly stronger than $\succeq_4$.

If $C \sim_5 D$, then C and D cannot contain a literal that is incompatible with each literal in the other clause. Therefore, equivalence in the θ-subsumption and restricted θ-subsumption ordering amounts to the same.

Proposition 10. $C \sim_4 D$ *iff after reduction $\dot{C}$ and $\dot{D}$ are renamings.*

2.4 The Set Ordering

Definition 11. In the *set ordering* $\succeq_3$, $C \succeq_3 D$ iff there exist a substitution θ such that $\dot{C}\theta = \dot{D}$.

Example 3. Consider
$$C = p(X) \leftarrow q(X,Y), q(Y,Z), q(Z,X),$$
$$D = p(X) \leftarrow q(X,Y), q(Y,X), q(X,X) \text{ and}$$
$$E = p(X) \leftarrow q(X,X).$$
In the restricted θ-subsumption ordering we have $C \succ_4 D \sim_4 E$. In the set ordering we have $C \succ_3 D \succ_3 E$.

Proposition 12 [13]. $C \sim_3 D$ *iff $\dot{C}$ and $\dot{D}$ are renamings.*

We can also express this proposition without the use of the set-notation of clauses. We call a clause *set reduced* iff it contains no duplicate literals. Thus, clauses remain equivalent after set reduction ($\sim_3, \ldots, \sim_6$). Clauses are equivalent in the set ordering iff their set reduced equivalents are permuted renamings.

In the two following sections, the set properties of the orderings are removed. Firstly the introduction (and removal) of duplicate literals and secondly permutation is prohibited.

2.5 The Permutation Ordering

Definition 13. In the *permutation ordering* $\succeq_2$, if $C = L_0 \leftarrow L_1, \ldots, L_m$ and $D = M_0 \leftarrow M_1, \ldots, M_n$, then $C \succeq_2 D$ iff $m = n$ and there exist a permutation π of $\{1, \ldots, m\}$ and a substitution θ such that $L_0\theta = M_0$ and $L_{\pi(i)}\theta = M_i$, $i = 1, \ldots, m$.

Example 4. Given $C = p(X) \leftarrow q(X,Y), q(Y,X)$, $D = p(X) \leftarrow q(X,X)$. In the set ordering, $C \succ_3 D$, but C and D are incomparable w.r.t. $\succeq_2$.

From the definition of $\succeq_2$ it follows directly that addition of literals results in incomparable clauses. Furthermore, permutations preserve equivalence:

Proposition 14 [13]. $C \sim_2 D$ *iff C and D are permuted renamings.*

2.6 The Substitution Ordering

To obtain the last, weakest and simplest ordering, we remove the free exchange of positions of literals from the permutation ordering.

Definition 15. In the *substitution ordering* $\succeq_1$, if $C = L_0 \leftarrow L_1, \ldots, L_m$ and $D = M_0 \leftarrow M_1, \ldots, M_n$, then $C \succeq_1 D$ iff $m = n$ and there exists a substitution θ such that $L_i\theta = M_i$, $i = 0, \ldots, m$.

Example 5. $C = p(X) \leftarrow q(X,Y), r(Y,X)$, $D = p(X) \leftarrow r(X,X), q(X,X)$. We had $C \succ_2 D$ but C and D are incomparable w.r.t. $\succeq_1$.

This ordering is a generalization of Reynolds' [17] ordering on atoms. Clauses are only comparable iff there exists a substitution such that every literal in one clause is mapped onto the corresponding literal in the other clause. The following proposition is a direct generalization of Lemma 1 in [17]. As a consequence, substitutions that are not renamings result in proper specializations.

Proposition 16. $C \sim_1 D$ iff C and D are renamings.

2.7 Summary

In this section we have defined six increasingly weak orderings on clauses, by deleting generality relations at each stage. Every ordering lacks one feature of the former, it is less flexible but more mechanical and manageable. The whole decomposition gives us a clearer view on logical implication and θ-subsumption.

A side-effect of this approach is that along the decomposition steps the number of clauses in an equivalent class decreases. Equivalence classes are partitioned into smaller equivalence classes of weaker orderings.

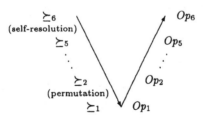

Fig. 1. Deconstruction framework

Now we are ready to answer the second question of this article: How can we split up logical derivations into simple operations? To answer this question we approach the orderings from weak to strong. From the substitution ordering to the restricted θ-subsumption ordering, equivalence classes melt together by 'recognizing' equivalent clauses that differ in the operations permutation, repetition of literals and addition of redundant literals respectively. In these first three strengthenings substitutions determine the comparability of clauses; if $C \succeq_i D$ then there exists $C' \sim_i C$ and $D' \sim_i D$ such that $C' \succeq_1 D'$, $i = 2, 3, 4$. In the last two strengthenings, two new operations are involved in comparability: in the θ-subsumption ordering the addition of incompatible literals and in the logical implication ordering self-resolution.

The last question of this article – how to find generalizations and specializations – will be answered in the next section, using this decomposition. For every ordering, the results of the weaker orderings can be used and only the new operation has to be examined. Thus, our deconstruction framework (Fig. 1) can be used to find operators for all orderings.

3   Constructing Refinement Operators

Refinement operators can be used to find specializations and generalizations of clauses. If $C \succ D$, then a clause equivalent with D can be derived from C or vice versa.

3.1   Definitions

The following definitions are related to refinement operators.

Definition 17. Given a set of clauses S, some quasi-ordering $\succeq$ on S and clauses $C, D \in S$, we use the following related notions:

- For every C, $\{D | C \succeq D\}$ is the set of *downward refinements* of C. If $C \succeq D$ and $D \not\succeq C$ then D is a *proper downward refinement* of C. (Proper) upward refinements are defined dually.
- A *downward (upward) refinement operator* ρ (δ) is a mapping from S to 2^S such that for every $C \in S$: $\rho(C)$ $(\delta(C))$ is a subset of the downward (upward) refinements of C.

The terminology of downward and upward refinements is adopted from Laird [4]. Shapiro's refinement operators [18] are downward refinement operators, and Ling's abstraction operators [7] are upward refinement operators.

The following definitions are in terms of downward refinement operators ρ but hold similarly for upward refinement operators δ.

Definition 18. Let ρ be a downward refinement operator, then

- $\rho^0(C) = \{C\}$ and $\rho^n(C) = \{D | \exists E \in \rho^{n-1}(C)$ such that $D \in \rho(E)\}$.
- $\rho^*(C) = \rho^1(C) \cup \rho^2(C) \cup \ldots \cup \rho^i(C) \cup \ldots$.

Definition 19. Let ρ be a downward refinement operator for clauses ordered by $\succeq$. Then

- ρ is called *complete for the ordering* $\succeq$ iff for every pair of clauses C, D, if $C \succ D$ then $\exists E: E \in \rho^*(C)$ and $E \sim D$.
- ρ is called *downward cover complete* iff $\forall D \in dc(C) \exists E : E \in \rho(C)$ and $E \sim D$.

It is easy to see that if ρ is complete for $\succeq$, then for any C, $\rho^*(C)$ must contain equivalents of all downward covers of C. If ρ is complete and returns proper refinements only, then ρ returns all these covers (may return more) in one refinement step, i.e., completeness implies cover completeness. The reverse however does not hold. All refinement operators in the rest of this section will be cover complete. In Sect. 3.8 we will discuss restricting the search space.

3.2 The Substitution Ordering

We will define a downward refinement operator ρ_1 using Reynolds' cover-relation for atoms. By Theorem 4 of Reynolds [17], ρ_1 returns exactly all downward covers. δ_1 is obtained by inverting the substitution of ρ_1, and returns exactly the upward covers.

Definition 20. Let C be a clause, then
- $D \in \rho_1(C)$ iff one of the following holds:
    1. $D = C\theta$, where $\theta = \{Y/X\}$, $X \neq Y$ and both X and Y occur in C.
    2. $D = C\theta$ where $\theta = \{X/c\}$, c is a constant symbol and X occurs in C.
    3. $D = C\theta$ where $\theta = \{Y/f(X_1, \ldots, X_n)\}$, f is a n-ary function symbol, Y occurs in C and all X_i's are distinct variables not occurring in C.
- $D \in \delta_1(C)$ iff one of the following holds:
    1. D is C after some (not all) occurrences of a variable X in C are replaced by a variable Y not in C.
    2. D is C after some or all occurrences of a constant c are replaced by a variable X not in C.
    3. D is C after all occurrences of $f(X_1, \ldots, X_n)$ are replaced by a variable Y, where f is a n-ary function symbol, Y does not occur in C and all X_i's are distinct variables not occurring elsewhere in C besides in terms $f(X_1, \ldots, X_n)$.

The downward refinement operator ρ_1 corresponds with Shapiro's [18] refinement operator for atoms (also named ρ_1).

In [7], Ling describes an upward refinement operator for atoms. This so-called abstraction operator replaces arbitrary terms by variables. He also omits anti-unification which implies that some proper upward refinements cannot be derived. E.g., $p(X, Y)$ cannot be derived from $p(X, X)$. However, all generalizations of ground atoms can be derived.

3.3 The Permutation Ordering

If D covers C in the substitution ordering, we may expect that D is no longer a cover in the permutation ordering because $\succeq_2$ is stronger than $\succeq_1$, i.e., there may exist a clause E such that $D \succ_2 E \succ_2 C$. However, this cannot happen as is shown in [13] by Nienhuys-Cheng. It is proved that D is a cover of C in the permutation ordering iff we can find a clause $D' \sim_2 D$ such that D' is a cover of C in the substitution ordering. From this it follows that ρ_1 and δ_1 also return all covers for the permutation ordering.

Example 6. Consider $C = p(X) \leftarrow q(Y), r(Y)$, $D = p(X) \leftarrow r(X), q(X)$. $C \succ_2$ D, but D is not derivable from C by applying ρ_2. However, if we define $D' = p(X) \leftarrow q(X), r(X)$, then $D' \sim_2 D$ and $D' \in \rho_2(C)$.

3.4 The Set Ordering

In the set ordering as well as in all stronger orderings, clauses may be regarded as sets of literals.

Example 7. We revisit the clauses of Example 4, $C = p(X) \leftarrow q(X,Y), q(Y,X)$, $D = p(X) \leftarrow q(X,X)$. In the permutation ordering C and D are incomparable, but $C \succ_3 D$. We cannot derive C from D using δ_2. However, if we define $D' = p(X) \leftarrow q(X,X), q(X,X)$ then $D' \sim_3 D$ and $C \in \delta_2(D')$. This motivates our definition of δ_3 later on.

In the case of downward refinement operators, equal literals are of no use since equal literals remain equal after substitution. Hence there is no need to duplicate literals at any time and they can be removed as soon as they appear.

As the last example showed for the case of upward refinement, literals sometimes should be repeated before inverse substitutions can be applied. By $eq_3(C)$ we denote the operation of duplicating one of the body literals of C. By repeatedly applying eq_3, $eq_3^*(C)$ contains infinitely many clauses $C' \sim_3 C$ such that $C' = L_0 \leftarrow L_1, \ldots, L_1, L_2, \ldots, L_2, \ldots, L_n, \ldots, L_n$.

Definition 21. Let C be a set reduced clause, then
  – $D \in \rho_3(C)$ iff there is a $D' \in \rho_1(C)$, $D \sim_3 D'$ and D is set reduced.
  – $D \in \delta_3(C)$ iff there are $C' \in eq_3^*(C)$, $D \in \delta_1(C')$ and D is set reduced.

3.5 The Restricted θ-Subsumption Ordering

Example 8. We revisit the clauses of Example 3,
  $C = p(X) \leftarrow q(X,Y), q(Y,Z), q(Z,X)$,
  $D = p(X) \leftarrow q(X,Y), q(Y,X), q(X,X)$ and
  $E = p(X) \leftarrow q(X,X)$.
In the set ordering, $C \succ_3 D \succ_3 E$, $D \in \delta_3(E)$, $C \in \delta_3(D)$ and both upward refinement steps generate proper refinements.

In the restricted θ-subsumption ordering, D and E are equivalent, since the literals $q(Y,X)$ and $q(X,Y)$ are redundant in D. If we want proper refinements only, then, for defining δ_4, we must add the redundant literals before applying δ_3.

We must also add redundant literals for proper downward refinement:

Example 9. $C = p(X) \leftarrow q(X,Y)$, $D = p(X) \leftarrow q(X,Y), q(U,V), q(V,W)$. $C \succ_4 D$, but by substitutions and removal of duplicate literals, D cannot be derived from C. If we first add the redundant literals $q(U,V)$ and $q(Z,W)$ to C, then D can be derived by ρ_3.

In [20], an inverse reduction algorithm is presented. Given a reduced clause C and a bound n, this algorithm returns all clauses that contain C and has at most n redundant literals. By $eq_4(C)$ we denote the operation of adding one redundant literal to C. By repeatedly applying eq_4, $eq_4^*(C)$ contains all clauses that contain C and arbitrary many redundant literals.

Definition 22. Let C be a reduced clause, then
- $D \in \rho_4(C)$ iff there are $C' \in eq_4^*(C)$, $D' \in \rho_3(C')$ such that $D' \not\prec_4 C'$ and D is the reduced equivalent of D'.
- $D \in \delta_4(C)$ iff there are $C' \in eq_4^*(C)$, $D' \in \delta_3(C')$ such that $D' \not\prec_4 C'$ and D is the reduced equivalent of D'.

3.6 The θ-Subsumption Ordering

In [20], a downward refinement operator for the θ-subsumption ordering is described in detail. It differs from ρ_4 in the operation of adding incompatible literals such that we can derive $p(X) \leftarrow q(f(X)), r(W)$ from $p(X) \leftarrow q(f(X))$.

Definition 23. Let C be a reduced clause, then
- $D \in \rho_5(C)$ iff $D \in \rho_4(C)$ or
  D is C after a literal that is incompatible with each literal in C is added. This literal has only new and distinct variables as arguments.
- $D \in \delta_5(C)$ iff $D \in \delta_4(C)$ or
  D is C after a literal that is incompatible with each other literal in C is removed. This literal has only distinct variables as arguments that do not occur in elsewhere in C.

For the θ-subsumption ordering, a number of refinement operators are known. Shapiro[18] has defined a downward refinement operator (ρ_0) for reduced first order clauses, Laird did the same [4] for not necessarily reduced first order clauses. Shapiro's operator ρ_0 is not complete, and Laird's operator does not return proper refinements only [19].

3.7 The Logical Implication Ordering

It was noted before that self-resolution characterizes exactly the difference between θ-subsumption and logical implication. Although these operations were described in an (inverse) resolution context, since they describe implication relations between clauses, they can also be regarded as refinement operators.

Definition 24. Let C be a reduced clause, then
- $D \in \rho_6(C)$ iff $D \in \rho_5(C)$ or
  D is the reduced equivalent of $D' \not\prec_6 C$ for some $D' \in \mathcal{L}^n(\{C\})$, $n \geq 1$
- $D \in \delta_6(C)$ iff $D \in \delta_5(C)$ or
  D is the reduced equivalent of $D' \not\prec_6 C$ for some $C \in \mathcal{L}^n(\{D'\})$, $n \geq 1$

3.8 Restricting the Search Space

Two problems with refinement operators have not been discussed. We will solve these problems by restricting the search space.
1. Some refinement operators are not locally finite.
2. Cover complete operators do not have to be complete.
An operator is *locally finite* iff it returns finitely many clauses in finite time. Using a restricted, finite search space S, we can easily see that all refinement operators are locally finite because we consider only the intersection of $eq_3^*(C)$ and $eq_4^*(C)$ with S.

In Sect. 3.1 we have shown that cover completeness is a necessary condition for complete refinement operators that return proper refinements only. It is, however, not a sufficient condition. Problems arise if $C \succ D$ and there exists an infinite chain of proper refinements $C \succ C_1 \succ C_2 \succ \ldots$ such that every C_i satisfies $C_i \succ D$. Then, if we keep on refining C_i's, D will never be derived.

However, if we limit our search to a finite set of clauses S, then S cannot contain infinitely long chains of proper refinements. In [20] we have introduced a new complexity measure to bound S. We have proved that ρ_5 is complete for every fixed bound.

In [19], we have used our framework to define refinement operators for an *unrestricted search space*. In the article we show that we need only a finite part of eq_3^* for unrestricted upward refinement in the set ordering. We can also use this finite part to define an (improper) upward refinement operator for the θ-subsumption ordering.

4 Conclusions and Future Research

In this article we have introduced a framework for orderings and operators. We have decomposed logical implication into six increasingly weak quasi orderings. The restricted θ-subsumption, set and permutation ordering are new. Another, the substitution ordering, is new in its usage. We think that they help to clarify properties of θ-subsumption and logical implication.

By reversing the decomposition, and looking at the small differences with the former weaker orderings, we were able to incrementally describe upward and downward refinement operators for all orderings including θ-subsumption and logical implication.

The results of the decomposition of logical implication are subject of further research. We are presently looking at least general generalizations (lgg's) of sets of clauses. Following Plotkin's definition, lgg's are unique if they exist, e.g. in the substitution and (restricted) θ-subsumption ordering. We want to loose the requirement of uniqueness and consider sets of incomparable minimal generalizations. So far, we can compute these sets for all other orderings except logical implication.

We are also extending the framework to obtain a classification of refinement operators. They will be categorized according to their properties (local finiteness, (local) completeness and properness) and according to whether the search space is restricted or not and how it is ordered.

References

1. M. Bain and S.H. Muggleton. Non-monotonic Learning. *Machine Intelligence*, 12, 1991.
2. W. Buntine. Generalised Subsumption and its Applications to Induction and Redundancy. *Artificial Intelligence*, 36(2):149–176, 1988.
3. N. Helft. Inductive Generalization: A Logical Framework. In I. Bratko and N. Lavrac, editor, *EWSL-87*, pages 149–157. Sigma Press, Wilmslow, England, 1987.
4. P.D. Laird. *Learning from Good and Bad Data*. Kluwer Academic Publishers, 1988.
5. S. Lapointe and S. Matwin. Subunification: A Tool for Efficient Induction of Recursive Programs. In *ML-92*, pages 273–280, Aberdeen, 1992. Morgan Kaufmann.
6. C. Lee. *A completeness theorem and a computer program for finding theorems derivable from given axioms*. PhD thesis, University of California, Berkely, 1967.
7. C. Ling and M. Dawes. SIM the Inverse of Shapiro's MIS. Technical report, Department of Computer Science, University of Western Ontario, London, Ontario, Canada., 1990.
8. T.M. Mitchell. Generalization as Search. *Artificial Intelligence*, 18:203–226, 1982.
9. S.H. Muggleton. Inductive logic programming. In *First Conference on Algorithmic Learning Theory*, Ohmsha, Tokyo, 1990. Invited paper.
10. S.H. Muggleton. Inverting Logical Implication. preprint, 1992.
11. S.H. Muggleton and C. Feng. Efficient Induction of Logic Programs. In *First Conference on Algorithmic Learning Theory*, Ohmsha, Tokyo, 1990.
12. T. Niblett. A Study of Generalisation in Logic Programs. In *EWSL-88*, pages 131–138. Pitman, 1988.
13. S.H. Nienhuys-Cheng. Generalization and Refinement. Technical report, Erasmus University Rotterdam, Dept. of Computer Science, August 1992. Preprint.
14. G.D. Plotkin. A Note on Inductive Generalization. *Machine Intelligence*, 5:153–163, 1970.
15. G.D. Plotkin. A Further Note on Inductive Generalization. *Machine Intelligence*, 6:101–124, 1971.
16. G.D. Plotkin. *Automatic Methods of Inductive Inference*. PhD thesis, Edinburgh University, Edinburgh, August 1971.
17. J.C. Reynolds. Transformational Systems and the Algebraic Structure of Atomic Formulas. *Machine Intelligence*, 5:135–153, 1970.
18. E.Y. Shapiro. Inductive Inference of Theories from Facts. Technical Report 192, Department of Computer Science, Yale University, New Haven. CT., 1981.
19. P.R.J. Van der Laag and S.H. Nienhuys-Cheng. A Locally Finite and Complete Upward Refinement Operator for θ-Subsumption. In *Benelearn-93*, Artificial Intelligence Laboratory, Vrije Universiteit Brussel, 1993.
20. P.R.J. Van der Laag and S.H. Nienhuys-Cheng. Subsumption and Refinement in Model Inference. In *ECML-93*, pages 95–114, 1993.

Learning Relations: Basing Top-Down Methods on Inverse Resolution

F. Bergadano[1] and D. Gunetti[2]

[1]University of Catania, via A. Doria 6/A,
95100 Catania, Italy, bergadan@mathct.cineca.it

[2]University of Torino, corso Svizzera 185,
10149 Torino, Italy, gunetti@di.unito.it

Abstract

Top-down algorithms for relational learning specialize general rules until they are consistent, and are guided by heuristics of different kinds. In general, a correct solution is not guaranteed. By contrast, bottom-up methods are well formalized, usually within the framework of inverse resolution. Inverse resolution has also been used as an efficient tool for deductive reasoning, and here we prove that input refutations can be translated into inverse unit refutations. This result allows us to show that top-down learning methods can be also described by means of inverse resolution, yielding a unified theory of relational learning.
Keywords: Machine learning, Automated reasoning, Relational Learning.

1   Introduction

Recently, in the Machine Learning community there has been a growing interest on *relational learning algorithms*, which learn restricted first order formulas from positive and negative examples. Early work is well represented by Plotkin's study on least general generalizations [8] and Shapiro's Model Inference System [10]. The former is related to the problem of generalizing clauses, as a basis for the bottom-up induction of logic formulas: the least general generalization of a number of examples will serve as a compressed description. The latter is based on the top-down specialization of clauses, until a set of Horn formulas which is consistent with the available examples is produced. These works have guided much of the recent research. Plotkin's idea of least general generalizations of logic formulas has inspired later work on "inverse resolution" [6], while providing the basis for most bottom-up approaches to the induction of logic programs [7].

Shapiro's use of a refinement operator is a natural reference for recent top-down clause induction methods [9, 2].

Early and more recent methods must now be analyzed w.r.t. some criterion of inductive success. The most natural property one may require is that the learned description P behaves correctly on the given examples E:

Definition 1 *A description P is complete w.r.t. E, iff* $\forall e^+ \in E \ P \vdash e^+$.

Definition 2 *A description P is consistent w.r.t. E, iff* $\forall e^- \in E \ P \not\vdash e^-$.

If we suppose that an inductive method accepts as input a set of examples and prior information (an inductive bias) in the form of a set $\mathcal{P}$ of allowed descriptions, the two properties defined below are desirable:

Definition 3 *An induction procedure M is correct iff whenever M terminates successfully and M(E,P)=P, then P is complete and consistent w.r.t. E.*

Definition 4 *An induction procedure M is sufficient iff whenever a complete and consistent description w.r.t. E exists in $\mathcal{P}$, then M(E,P) will output one such description.*

Completeness and consistency of the learned descriptions was considered important in previous Machine Learning research and is easily obtained for propositional and non-recursive relational rules. However, when we move to recursive clauses, or to the problem of learning multiple predicates, the above requirements are not always met. In fact, most systems generate candidate program clauses one at a time in a top-down fashion, and check them against the examples independently of one another. For instance, the clause "p(X) :- q(X,Y), p(Y)." is normally said to cover the example p(a) if there is a positive example q(a,b) of q such that p(b) is a positive example of p. Other clauses for p and q (e.g. those learned previously) are not used to try a derivation for q(a,b) and p(b). In other words, clauses are evaluated extensionally at the time of learning. However, when the final description has been learned, at the time of testing, it will be used intensionally and this may yield unexpected results, e.g. positive examples that were found to be covered may not be derived, while valid proofs for negative examples may become possible [1]. As a consequence, well known systems such as Foil [9] and Golem [7] are not correct nor sufficient [1]. Some systems do solve the problem while keeping the extensional evaluation of clauses by asking queries to the user, so that missing examples are provided and unexpected derivations cannot be found [10]. However, these systems are incremental, and added examples may require backtracking.

A consequence of the above considerations is that top-down methods, which evaluate clauses extensionally, are considered to be empirical and heuristic, without a strong formal basis. This is aggravated by the fact that most top-down systems do not explore the whole hypothesis space, but use statistical information in order to guide the search. This is usually contrasted with Bottom-up methods based on inverse resolution, which can proved to be theoretically well founded [7]. In this paper we show that it is possible to give a theoretical basis to extensional top-down learning methods by restating them in terms of a special kind of inverse resolution not employing inverse unifiers.

Here is the plan of the paper: in the second section we briefly review the extensional learning approach. In the third section we describe the basics of inverse resolution in theorem proving and clarify the relationship between input and linear resolution, as first pointed out by Chang. In the fourth section we use the results of section three to show how extensional methods can be rewritten in terms of theorem proving with inverse resolution.

2 Relational Learning Algorithms based on Extensionality

Many systems, such as Foil [9] and Golem [7] learn concepts described by means of Horn clauses. Clauses are evaluated extensionally, since in this way candidate clauses can be generated directly from the examples one at a time and independently of one another. The basic learning algorithm of such systems can be described as follows:

Let P be the target concept and pos_examples(P) and neg_examples(P) the given positive and negative examples of P (in the following, α and γ represent generic conjunction of literals).

Extensional top-down learning method:
while pos_examples(P) $\neq \emptyset$ do
    Generate one clause "P($\vec{X}$) :- $\alpha(\vec{X},\vec{Y})$";
    pos_examples(P) $\leftarrow$ pos_examples(P) $-$ pos(α)

Generate one clause:
$\alpha \leftarrow$ true;
while pos(α) $\neq \emptyset$ do
    if neg(α) $= \emptyset$ then return(P($\vec{X}$) :- α)
        else choose a predicate Q and its arguments Args;
            $\alpha \leftarrow \alpha \wedge$ Q(Args)

where pos(α) and neg(α) are the sets of positive and negative examples of P covered by P:-α, i.e. the examples P($\vec{a}$) such that T $\cup$ E $\cup$ P($\vec{X}$):-$\alpha \vdash$ P($\vec{a}$). Where E is the set of given examples and T is a user-given Horn Theory. The presence of E means that some predicates (in particular the one representing the target concept) are not derived from T but immediately found among the given examples.

The choice of the literal Q(Args) to be added to the partial antecedent α of the clause being generated is guided by heuristic information. It might nevertheless be a wrong choice in some cases, in the sense that it causes the procedure

"Generate one clause" to fail by exiting the while loop without returning any clause. This problem can be remedied by making the choice of Q(Args) a backtracking point.
We illustrate the method on the task of learning the *append* relation:

pos(*append*) = {append([],[b],[b]), append([a],[b],[a,b]).}
neg(*append*) = {append([],[b],[]), append([a],[b],[b]).}

we also know that *append* depends on the following set of predicates, with their usual definition supplied (except for *append*, of course):

null, head, tail, cons, assign, append.

This is an important information, but obviously still very far away from the actual description that we want to learn: we need to associate variables to these predicates, and divide the obtained literals among the unknown number of clauses that will be necessary.

The algorithm starts to generate the first clause - the antecedent α is initially empty. We need to choose the first literal Q(Args) to be added to α. As we have left the heuristics unspecified, we will choose it so as to make the discussion short. Variables are taken from the clause head, or from a finite set of additional typed variables.

Let α=*assign*(Y,Z). A positive example is covered, but we cannot accept the clause
append(X,Y,Z) :- *assign*(Y,Z) as it is, because its body is true for the negative example *append*([],[b],[b]), so more literals need to be added.
Let α=*assign*(Y,Z) $\wedge$ *null*(X); the first example is covered and no wrong outputs can be computed. A clause is generated and the covered example *append*([],[b],[b]) is removed from examples(*append*).

We proceed to the generation of another clause; α is empty again. Suppose we have already generated α=*head*(X,H) $\wedge$ *tail*(X,T); the remaining positive example is covered, but again we have to specialize because α is true for the second negative example.
Let α = *head*(X,H) $\wedge$ *tail*(X,T) $\wedge$ *append*(T,Y,W); this clause again extensionally covers the remaining example. In fact, we have that *head*([a],a) and *tail*([a,],[]) are true, and *append*([],[b],[b]) is a given example. However, the second negative example is still covered (moreover, the output variable Z is not instantiated), and the procedure needs to be continued.
At the next step, suppose we add the literal *cons*(H,W,Z), obtaining, e.g.,
α = *head*(X,H) $\wedge$ *tail*(X,T) $\wedge$ *append*(T,Y,W) $\wedge$ *cons*(H,W,Z)
which covers all positive examples and none of the negative ones.
The final solution turns out to be:

$append(X,Y,Z) :- assign(Y,Z), null(X).$
$append(X,Y,Z) :- head(X,H), tail(X,T), append(T,Y,W), cons(H,W,Z).$

3 Inverse Refutations and the Relationship between Input and Unit Resolution

Inverse Resolution has been used as an effective tool for learning Horn Clauses from examples [6]. The basic idea is that a clause C_2 is "learned" from an example C and a clause C_1 given in the background knowledge if C is the resolvent of C_1 and C_2. In [4] we show that inverse resolution can also be the basis for efficient forms of deductive reasoning, with a procedure which we shall call *inverse refutation*. The idea is simply to invert the refutation process based on resolution, in order to go from the empty clause to the given clause set instead of vice versa. This results in a strongly guided refutation process, because it is based on the form of the given clauses. Intuitively, a clause is generated by means of inverse resolution only if it is a subset (proper or not) of a given clause. The process of inverse refutation ends when all clauses (or at least a minimally unsatisfiable subset of them) have been reconstructed, and if read in its turn in reverse order it appears just like a usual classical refutation of the given set. in the following, we assume familiarity with the basic concepts of resolution and theorem proving as in [5]. We remember that in unit deductions at least one of the parent clauses involved in a resolution step is a unit clause, while in input deductions at least one of the parent clauses is one of those given initially. We illustrate the method on the following set S of clauses.

c1 = ACH, c2 = AD, c3 = ¬A, c4 = B¬C, c5 = ¬B, c6 = ¬H.

Just as resolution of two complementary unit clauses is the last step in a classical deduction, it is the first step of the inverse resolution deduction. Initially we have the empty clause; we open two branches and label them with two complementary unit clauses consisting of the first two complementary literals (say A and ¬A) found in the given set (we will build the inverse refutation from bottom to top, so it reads from top to bottom as a classical resolution refutation - see Fig. 1a, first step). Now we focus attention on the two unit clauses. If a refutation for S exists in which the last step resolves these two units, then there must exist an (inverse) deduction of each of them separately. Hence we have decomposed the problem of deriving the empty clause into the two independent subproblems of deriving the chosen unit clauses. Obviously, both of these subproblems must be solved, so they share an *and* relationship. On the other hand, we could have chosen different pairs of complementary literals to start the deduction, and a solution stemming from any of those choices is sufficient, so there we see an *or* relationship. Hence, our search for an inverse deduction will take the form of a typical and-or search tree.

Consider A. Since there are two clauses in the given set containing A (namely, c1 and c2), we open from A two new pairs of branches. The first pair corresponds to clause c1 and one of its branches is labeled AC (intuitively A with C added) because C is the next unexplored literal of c1. The other branch is labeled with ¬C, the unit clause built from the complementary of the literal added (Fig. 1a, second step). The second pair of branches corresponds to c2 and is labeled with AD and ¬D via a similar analysis. In general, corresponding to every given clause that contains the literal of the clause to be derived, there is a possible derivation. These derivations are or-related subproblems. Each of these subproblems corresponds to a choice of one such given clause and is, in turn, expressed as two and-related tasks: in one, a new literal from the given clause under consideration is added to the clause to be derived (thus this new vertex is labeled with a larger subset of the given clause chosen). The other is the problem of deriving the unit clause consisting of the complement of the added literal. So in our example, the two pairs of branches opened from A are two *or* tasks, and the branches in each pair are *and* tasks. In this example, to give a derivation of A we must demonstrate that there exists a derivation of the two clauses AC and ¬C, or that there exists a derivation of AD and ¬D.

Now again we must give attention separately to the two pairs of opened branches trying to build a complete (inverse) derivation of A. Let us concentrate only on the first pair of branches. On the right branch we are rebuilding the clause c1, so from the current clause AC (a subset of c1) we open two branches. One of them is labeled with AC to which we add H, the remaining literal of c1, and the other is labeled with its complementary ¬H (Fig. 1a, third step). But now the two new generated clauses belong to the given set and so there is nothing more to do with their subtasks. Now, only an *and* branch remains to be considered, the one labeled with ¬C, and we note that there is only one given clause containing it, so at its top we open a new pair of branches labeled with B¬C and ¬B respectively (Fig.1a, fourth step). We note that these two clauses belong to S, and because also clause ¬A is a given one, the inverse refutation is completed and all the other *or* branches opened while trying to derive A can be discarded. If read from top to bottom, the inverse refutation represents a classical unit derivation of the empty clause from the given set.

It should be noted that the strategy described here only builds unit refutations. See [4] for the complete strategy. In 1970 Chang proved an interesting relationship between unit and input resolution: a set of ground clauses S has a unit proof if and only if it has an input proof [5] (we recall that an input derivation is also a linear one). Here we clarify this relationship via inverse resolution, with the following theorems (Proofs can be found in [3]).

Theorem 1. For every input refutation of an unsatisfiable set S of propositional clauses there exists an inverse unit refutation for S where the same literals are introduced in the same order they are resolved in the input refutation.

The above relationship is much more easy to understand visually. Fig. 1b reports the input refutation corresponding to the inverse unit refutation of Fig. 1a. Equally numbered operations involve the same occurrences of the same literals (Fig. 1b must be read from top to bottom).

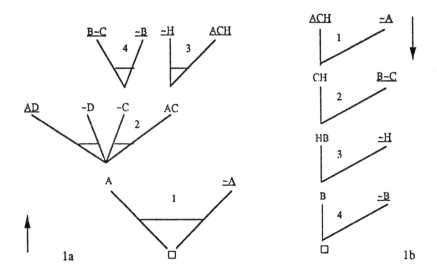

Fig. 1a and 1b. (Inverse) unit and input refutation for S.

Extending inverse resolution to first order logic requires, in principle, the use of *inverse substitutions*, as in [6], whose computation can have exponential complexity. The next theorem shows that this is not the case if we limit ourselves to input deductions without factoring (in fact, an equivalent property for deductions using factoring can be easily obtained from the next theorem).

Definition 5 In our framework, we define *inverse resolution refutations* in first order logic as follows (for simplicity we always assume literals l and ¬l' to have disjoint variables. Let |l| denote the atom of literal l).
At the first step, if there exist in the given set of clauses two literals l and ¬l' and a substitution σ_1 such that $|l\sigma_1| = |\neg l'\sigma_1|$, then we can open from the empty clause two branches labeled respectively $|l\sigma_1|$ and $|\neg l'\sigma_1|$.
Suppose now that the first literal of a clause A has been introduced at the j-th step in an inverse refutation using substitution σ_j. Then, at the k-th step it is allowed to add a literal l to the subset of A built up to that point via inverse resolution using a complementary literal ¬l' if and only if $\exists \sigma_k$ such that $|l\sigma_j\sigma_{j+1}...\sigma_k| = |\neg l'\sigma_k|$, where $\sigma_j,...,\sigma_{k-1}$ are the unifiers used between steps j and k-1.
The inverse refutation is completed when all branches are labeled with clauses from the given set, ignoring the introduced unifiers.

The above definition of inverse refutation in first order logic is justified by the following theorem:

Theorem 2. For every input refutation of an unsatisfiable set S of clauses there exists a inverse unit refutation of S where complementary literals are introduced in the same order they are resolved within the input refutation and where the same unifiers are involved.

Observe that, while in propositional calculus inverse deductions read from top to bottom appear to be ordinary deductions, in first order logic this is no longer true. In Fig. 2a an input refutation for an unsatisfiable set of clauses is shown, while Fig. 2b reports the corresponding inverse unit refutation. Note how the inverse refutation, if read from top to bottom, does *not* turn out to be an ordinary refutation (for simplicity, first order literals are represented with only capital letters, without reporting their terms. But two literals A and ¬A are considered to be complementary only if there exists a substitution σ such that $|A\sigma| = |\neg A\sigma|$).

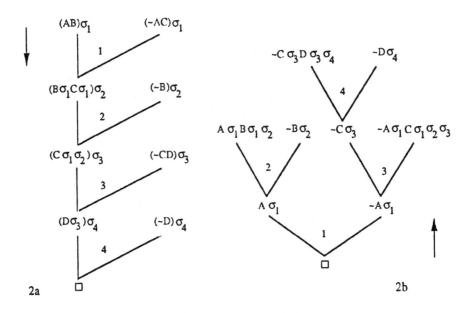

Fig. 2a and 2b. An input refutation an the corresponding inverse unit refutation

4   Learning Horn Theories

An important subset of first order logic which admits input (and hence unit) refutation is the set of Horn clauses, and because inverse resolution builds clauses, theorem 2 seems to suggest a way to build (i.e. to learn) Horn theories from ground examples. If P(a,b) is a positive example of a concept P, then there exists an input refutation of P $\cup$ ¬P(a,b) with ¬P(a,b) as top clause. But, by theorem two, there exists also a corresponding inverse unit refutation of P $\cup$ ¬P(a,b) which, in fact, rebuilds the clauses of P (or, at least, those effectively involved in the refutation).

Now, suppose we do not have a Horn description of a concept P. We only know that P may depend on a given set of predicates, where every predicate can be defined by means of logical rules or with a set of positive and negative ground instances. Obviously, at least P is only defined by a set of positive and negative instances. Then, applying inverse resolution as in the previous section, we can build an inverse unit refutation starting with a positive example P(a,b) of P and where the leaves of the proof tree represent a possible (partial) description of P. We can stop the inverse refutation (in this case, the learning process) for that example when that partial description does not entail any of the given negative examples of P.

In this section we show that the learning process of section two can be re-stated in the above terms of clause construction via inverse resolution (in the following, the empty clause will be indicated with ":-", T will be the set of intensional definitions and E the given positive examples. C will be the clause we are currently learning).

As we have seen in section two, given a positive example P(a,b), where P is an inductive predicate (i.e. the concept to be learned) we start *guessing* the unit clause C = P(X,Y). In terms of inverse refutation, this means to start from the empty clause ":-", opening one branch labeled ¬P(a,b) and the other labeled $C\sigma_1$ (where $\sigma_1 = \{X/a, Y/b\}$). Because obviously C derives negative examples of P, (in this case, ($\forall e^-$) $C \cup T \cup E \vdash e^-$) we must specialize (i.e. add literals to) its body.

At the next step, we choose a literal $Q_1(Args)$ such that the body of C = P(X,Y) :- $Q_1(Args)$ is extensionally evaluated to true on example P(a,b). Within inverse resolution, this means that there exists a substitution σ_2 such that $Q_1(Args)\sigma_1\sigma_2$ is a given positive example of Q_1 (if it is defined extensionally) or it is derivable from its definition (if it is defined by means of logical rules - in fact, in this case we have not to start an inverse derivation for $Q_1(Args)$, because we already have a definition for Q_1).

In general, at the k+1-th step, we can add literal $Q_k(Args)$ to the body of C if there exists a substitution σ_{k+1} such that $Q_k(Args)\sigma_1, ..., \sigma_{k+1}$ is a positive example of Q_k or it is derivable from its definition.

In extensional top-down learning methods we stop when C does not cover any of the negative examples, and still P(a,b) is covered. If no such C can be found, then backtracking occurs. Within inverse resolution this means that it must not be the case that $C \cup T \cup E \vdash e^-$ for any negative example e^-. Otherwise, alternative paths from the empty clause for example P(a,b) must be tried.

We clarify the above relationship by restating the learning task of *append* in terms of inverse resolution. Suppose we are given the following ground unit clauses, which are the positive examples of *append*:

$e_1^+ = $ append([],[b],[b]), $e_2^+ = $ append([a],[b],[a,b]),

and the two negated clauses

$e_1^- = \neg$append([],[b],[]), $e_2^- = \neg$append([a],[b],[b]),

which are negative examples of *append*. We are also given the following set L of literals, that make it possible to build a description of *append* (we assign variables to literals in order to make the discussion short):

{null(X), head(X,H), tail(X,T), cons(H,W,Z), assign(Y,Z), append(T,Y,W)}

where predicates, except for *append*, are defined as follows (call T this set of definitions):

null([],[]).
head([A|_],A).
tail([_|B],B).
cons(C,D,[C|D]).
assign(E,E).

Now we start the learning task by looking for a clause C such that $C \cup T \cup \{e_1^+\} \cup \{\neg e_2^+\}$ is unsatisfiable (again for brevity, we do not consider alternative paths).

We start from the empty clause and generate two branches, one labeled $\neg$append([a],[b],[a,b])σ_1 and the other one labeled $C = $ append(X,Y,Z)σ_1, with $\sigma_1 = \{X/[a], Y/[b], Z/[a,b]\}$. Because $(\forall e^-) \, C \cup T \cup \{e_1^+\} \vdash e^-$, we must continue the inverse derivation.

At the next step, suppose we select from L the literal head(X,H). From C we open two branches, one labeled head([A|_],A)σ_2 and the other one labeled

$C = $ append(X,Y,Z)σ_1 :- head(X,H)$\sigma_1 \sigma_2$
with $\sigma_2 = \{A/a, H/a\}$.

At the third step, tail(X,T) is selected, and from C we open one branch labeled tail([_|B],B)σ_3 and the other labeled:
$C = $ append(X,Y,Z)σ_1 :- head(X,H)$\sigma_1 \sigma_2$, tail(X,T)$\sigma_1 \sigma_2 \sigma_3$

with $\sigma_3 = \{B/[], T/[]\}$.

At the fourth step append(T,Y,W) is selected, and from C we open a branch labeled append([],[b],[b])σ_4 and the other one labeled

C = append(X,Y,Z)σ_1 :- head(X,H)$\sigma_1\sigma_2$, tail(X,T)$\sigma_1\sigma_2\sigma_3$,
$\qquad\qquad\qquad$ append(T,Y,W) $\sigma_1\sigma_2\sigma_3\sigma_4$
with $\sigma_4 = \{T/[], W/[b]\}$.

Finally, cons(H,W,Z) is selected, and from C we open one branch labeled: cons(C,D,[C|D])σ_5 and the other one labeled:

C = append(X,Y,Z)σ_1 :- head(X,H)$\sigma_1\sigma_2$, tail(X,T)$\sigma_1\sigma_2\sigma_3$,
$\qquad\qquad\qquad$ append(T,Y,W)$\sigma_1\sigma_2\sigma_3\sigma_4$, cons(H,W,Z) $\sigma_1\sigma_2\sigma_3\sigma_4\sigma_5$.
with $\sigma_5 = \{C/a, D/[b]\}$.

At this point it is the case that $\forall \, e^- \; C \cup T \cup \{e_1^+\} \not\vdash e^-$. It can be easily verified that there exists an input refutation of $C \cup T \cup \{e_1^+\} \cup \{\neg e_2^+\}$ where at the first step C is resolved against $\neg e_2^+$ and where the substitutions $\sigma_1,...,\sigma_5$ are employed, in that order.
By removing substitutions introduced along the inverse refutation,

C= *append*(X,Y,Z) :- *head*(X,H), *tail*(X,T), *append*(T,Y,W), *cons*(H,W,Z)

represents the first learned clause for *append*. It should be noted that the used substitutions correspond to the assignment of values to variables performed in the extensional evaluation of the body of C, in section two.
A similar procedure could then be followed to learn the non-recursive clause of *append*.

5 Conclusion

We have argued that theorem proving with inverse resolution represents a theoretical basis for top-down extensional learning methods. Our result can have many interesting consequences.

First, the method suggests how to query the user for missing examples, by possibly asking for the truth values of the unit clauses used in every inverse resolution step. Obviously, the number of queries depends on the size of the hypothesis space and on the chosen variabilization for the various predicates. However, it has been shown [10, 2] that queries provide the basis for inductive methods which are efficient if appropriate syntactic restrictions are adopted.

Second, such methods can also be proved to be correct and sufficient as defined in the introduction [2], and the present paper can also be seen as an alternative argument for proving the same results. In fact, if a correct Horn theory exists in the hypothesis space, an input refutation from all the given and queried examples is possible. But then these clauses may be learned by means of some inverse unit refutation. The argument of section 4 will then imply that top-down learning of a complete and consistent program is also possible.

Third, some computational problems of inverse resolution, as developed in [6], are avoided because inverse substitutions need not be computed.

Finally, our results suggest that one initial given positive example is sufficient to learn all the clauses necessary to derive it (if they exist in the hypothesis space). This means that, most of the time, one well chosen example is sufficient to learn a complete description of a concept. This should be contrasted with classical extensional methods, where a lot of examples are required.

Acknowledgments: This work was in part supported by BRA ESPRIT III Project 6020 on Inductive Logic Programming.

References

[1] F. Bergadano. Inductive Database Relations. *IEEE Trans. on Data and Knowledge Engineering*, 5(4), 1993.

[2] F. Bergadano and D. Gunetti. An interactive system to learn functional logic programs. In *Proc. 13th Int. Joint. Conf. on Artificial Intelligence*, Chambery, France, 1993. Morgan Kaufmann.

[3] F. Bergadano and D. Gunetti. Unifying Top-Down and Inverse Resolution Approaches to Inductive Logic Programming. *Tech. Rep. 93.3.28, CS Dept., Univ. of Torino*, 1993.

[4] D. Gunetti. Efficient proofs in propositional calculus with inverse resolution. In P. Dewilde and J. Vanderwalle, editors, *Proc. of the CompEuro, 1992*, The Hague, Netherlands, 1992. IEEE Comp. Soc. Press.

[5] D. W. Loveland. *Automated Theorem Proving: a Logical Basis*. North Holland, 1978.

[6] S. Muggleton. Machine Invention of First Order Predicates by Inverting Resolution. In *Proc. of the Fifth Int. Conf. on Machine Learning*, pages 339–352, Ann Arbor, MI, 1988.

[7] S. Muggleton. Inductive Logic Programming. *New Generation Computing*, 8(4):295–318, 1991.

[8] G. Plotkin. A note on Inductive Generalization. In B. Meltzer and D. Michie, editors, *Machine Intelligence 5*, pages 153–163, 1970.

[9] R. Quinlan. Learning Logical Definitions from Relations. *Machine Learning*, 5:239–266, 1990.

[10] E. Y. Shapiro. *Algorithmic Program Debugging*. MIT Press, 1983.

Complexity of the CFP, a Method for Classification Based on Feature Partitioning

H. Altay Güvenir and İzzet Şirin

Computer Engineering and Information Science Department Bilkent University,
Ankara 06533 TURKEY

Abstract. This paper presents a new methodology for learning from examples, called *Classification by Feature Partitioning* (CFP). Learning in CFP is accomplished by storing the objects separately in each feature dimension as disjoint partitions of values. A partition is expanded through generalization or specialized by subdividing it into sub-partitions. It is shown that the CFP algorithm has a low sample and training complexity.

1 Introduction

Several representation techniques have been used to describe concepts for supervised learning tasks. Exemplar-based learning techniques store only specific examples that are representatives of other several similar instances. Previous implementations of this approach usually extended the nearest neighbor algorithm, which use some kind of similarity metric for classification. The classification complexity of such algorithms is proportional to the number of objects stored.

This paper presents another form of exemplar-based learning, called *Classification by Feature Partitioning* (CFP). The CFP makes several significant improvements over other exemplar-based learning algorithms, where the examples are stored in memory without any change in the representation. For example, IBL algorithms learn a set of instances, which is a representative subset of all training examples [1]. On the other hand, the CFP partitions each feature into segments corresponding to concepts. Therefore, a concept description learned by the CFP is a collection of feature partitions.

The CFP algorithm can be seen to produce a special kind of decision trees (e.g., ID3, [3]). Unlike ID3, the CFP probes each feature exactly once. An important difference between decision tree approach and the CFP is that the classification performance of the CFP does not depend critically on any small part of the model. In contrast, decision trees are much more susceptible to small alterations. Similar to CFP and ID3, the *probabilistic learning system* called PLS1, also creates orthogonal hyperrectangles by inserting boundaries parallel to instance space axes [4]. The PLS1 system starts from the most general description and applies only specializations.

The CFP algorithm is briefly described in the next section. Section 3 presents the *sample complexity* and the *training complexity* analysis of the CFP algorithm with respect to *Probably Approximately Correct* (PAC) learning theory [6]. The final section discusses the applicability of the CFP and concludes with a general evaluation of the algorithm.

2 The CFP Algorithm

The CFP algorithm learns the projection of the concepts over each feature dimension. An example is given as a vector of feature values plus a label that represents its class. A partition is the basic unit of representation in the CFP algorithm. For each partition, lower and upper bounds of the feature values, the associated class, and the representativeness value (the number of instances it represents) are maintained. Initially, a partition is a point (lower and upper limits are equal) on the line representing the feature dimension. For instance, suppose that the first example e_1 of class C_1 is given during the training phase. If the value of e_1 for feature f is x_1, then the set of possible values for feature f will be partitioned into three partitions: $< [-\infty, x_1], U, 0 >$, $< [x_1, x_1], C_1, 1 >$, $< [x_1, \infty], U, 0 >$; where U stands for *undetermined* partition. A partition can be extended towards a neighboring point of the same class in an undetermined partition. Assume that the second example e_2 with class C_1 is close to e_1 in feature f. In that case the CFP will generalize the partition at x_1 on f into an extended partition: $< [x_1, x_2], C_1, 2 >$.

Since partitions are disjoint the CFP algorithm pays attention to avoid over generalization. In order to generalize a partition in feature f to cover a new example, the distance between them must be less than a given *generalization limit* (D_f). Otherwise, the new example is stored as another point partition in the feature dimension f. If the feature value of a training example falls in a partition with the same class, then simply the representativeness value of the partition is incremented by one. However, if the new training example falls in a partition with a different class than that of the example, the CFP algorithm specializes the existing partition by dividing it into two range partitions and inserting a point partition (corresponding to the new example) in between them.

The training process of the CFP has two steps: (1) learning the feature weights, (2) learning feature partitions. In order to learn appropriate feature weights, for each training example, the prediction of each feature is compared with the actual class of the example. If the prediction of a feature is correct the weight of that feature is incremented by Δ (global feature weight adjustment rate) percent; otherwise, it is decremented by the same amount (all weights are initially set to 1).

Classification in the CFP is based on a voting taken among the predictions made by each feature separately. For a given instance e, the prediction based on a feature f is determined by the value of e_f. If e_f falls properly within a partition with a known class then the prediction is the class of that partition. If e_f falls in a point partition then among all the partitions at this point the one with the highest representation count is chosen. If e_f falls in a partition with undetermined class value, then no prediction for that feature is made. The effect of the prediction of a feature in the voting is proportional with the weight of

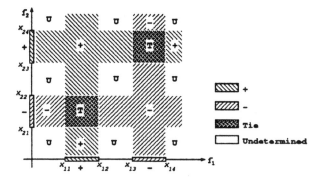

Fig. 1. An example concept description in a domain with two features.

that feature. The predicted class of a given instance is the one which receives the highest amount of votes among all feature predictions.

In order to illustrate the form of the concept descriptions, let us consider a domain with two features, f_1 and f_2. Assume that during the training phase, positive ($+$) instances with f_1 values in $[x_{11}, x_{12}]$ and f_2 values in $[x_{23}, x_{24}]$, and negative ($-$) instances with f_1 values in $[x_{13}, x_{14}]$ and f_2 values in $[x_{21}, x_{22}]$ are given. The resulting concept description is shown in Fig. 1. The corresponding concept description for the class ($+$) can be written as:

class $+$: $(x_{11} \leq f_1 \;\&\; f_1 \leq x_{12} \;\&\; f_2 < x_{21})$ or $(x_{11} \leq f_1 \;\&\; f_1 \leq x_{12} \;\&\; f_2 > x_{22})$ or
$(x_{23} \leq f_2 \;\&\; f_2 \leq x_{24} \;\&\; f_1 < x_{13})$ or $(x_{23} \leq f_2 \;\&\; f_2 \leq x_{24} \;\&\; f_1 > x_{14})$

The CFP does not assign any classification to an instance, if it could not determine the appropriate class value. This may result from having seen no instances for a given set of values or having a tie between two or more possible contradicting classifications. If the features have different weights, the ties are broken in favor of the class predicted by the features with the highest weights during the voting process.

The CFP algorithm has been implemented and empirically evaluated in several standard domains and its performance has been compared with similar algorithms. In most of these domains the CFP algorithm attained higher accuracy than the other algorithms. The details of the CFP algorithm and the empirical comparisons can be found in [5].

3 Complexity of the CFP

This section presents an analysis of the CFP algorithm with respect to *PAC-learning* theory [6]. The intent of the PAC (Probably Approximately Correct) model is that successful learning of an unknown target concept should entail obtaining, with high probability, that it is a good approximation of the concept.

Since the classification in the CFP is based on a voting taken among the individual classifications of each attribute, it can learn a concept if each attribute, independently from other attributes, can be used in the classification. We will define what we mean by "learn" in a way that preserves the spirit of the Valiant (1984) definition of learnability, but modifies it for the voting based classification used in the CFP. We first determine the minimum number of training instances required to learn a given concept. Using this sample complexity we derive the training complexity of the CFP algorithm. In the following analysis we assume that all feature values are normalized to the interval [0,1].

Definition 1. Let X be a subset of $\Re^n$ with a fixed probability distribution and d is positive integer less than or equal to n. A subset S of X is an $< \varepsilon, \gamma, d >$ $-net <$ for X if, for all x in X, with probability greater than γ, there exist an s in S such that $|s_f - x_f| < \varepsilon$ at least for d values of f ($1 \le f \le n$).

Lemma 2. *Let ε, δ, and γ be fixed positive numbers less than one and d is positive integer less than or equal to n. A random sample S containing $m > (\lceil 1/\varepsilon \rceil / \gamma) \times (n \ln 2 + \ln(\lceil 1/\varepsilon \rceil / \delta))$ instances, drawn according to any fixed probability distribution from $[0,1]^n$, will form an $< \varepsilon, \gamma, d >$-net with confidence greater than $1 - \delta$.*

Proof. We prove this lemma by partitioning the unit interval for each feature dimension, into k equal length sub-intervals, each with length less than ε, such that all pairs of points[1] in the sub-interval are within ε distance of each other. The idea of the proof is to guarantee that, with high confidence, at least for d dimensions out of n, each of k sub-intervals contains at least one point of m instances, with sufficient probability.

Let $k = \lceil 1/\varepsilon \rceil$, S_{1f} be the set of sub-intervals with probability greater or equal to γ/k and S_{2f} be the set of remaining sub-intervals of a dimension f. The probability that an arbitrary point in $[0,1]$ will not lie in a selected sub-interval of S_{1f} is $(1-\gamma/k)$. The probability that none of the m sample points will lie in a selected sub-interval of S_{1f} is $(1-\gamma/k)^m$. Therefore, the probability that any sub-interval of S_{1f} is excluded by all m instances is at most $p = k(1-\frac{\gamma}{k})^m$.

The probability that, for more than $n-d$ dimensions, any sub-interval of S_1's are excluded by all m instances is at most $\sum_{i=n-d+1}^{n} C(n,i)p^i$.[2] To make sure this probability is small, we force it to be less than δ, that is, $\sum_{i=n-d+1}^{n} C(n,i)p^i < \delta$.

Recall the *binomial theorem*: $(a+b)^n = \sum_{i=0}^{n} C(n,i)a^i b^{n-i}$. With $a = p$ and $b = 1$, $\sum_{i=0}^{n} C(n,i)p^i = (p+1)^n$. Since n is a positive integer, $(p+1)^n - 1 = \sum_{i=1}^{n} C(n,i)p^i$ and it is greater than $\sum_{i=n-d+1}^{n} C(n,i)p^i$, our requirement can be written as $(p+1)^n - 1 < \delta$. On the other hand, $(1-\gamma/k)^m < e^{-m\gamma/k}$ and, since the value of p is greater than zero and less than one, $2^n p > (p+1)^n - 1$. If we solve the requirement $2^n k e^{-m\gamma/k} < \delta$ for m, and substitute $\lceil 1/\varepsilon \rceil$ for k, it yields $m > \lceil 1/\varepsilon \rceil / \gamma \times (n \ln 2 + \ln(\lceil 1/\varepsilon \rceil / \delta))$.

Consequently, with confidence greater than $1 - \delta$, each sub-interval in S_{1f} of d or more dimensions, contains some sample point of an instance of S. $\qquad \square$

---

[1] a point here represents the value of an instance for a feature for that dimension
[2] $C(n,r)$ represents the number of combinations of r objects out of n.

Theorem 3. *Let ε, δ, and γ be fixed positive numbers less than one and S a sample set with n features. If $\lceil \frac{n+1}{2} \rceil$ of features of the elements of S form an $< \varepsilon, \gamma, \lceil \frac{n+1}{2} \rceil >$-net then, the CFP algorithm with equal feature weights and generalization limit $D_f \geq 2\varepsilon$ for all features, will learn a concept C for S with confidence $1 - \delta$.*

Proof. Since, the CFP algorithm does not use distance metric for classification, the idea of the proof is to ensure that the CFP can construct ε length partitions with high confidence, at least one of the m sample instances lies in each sub-intervals of $\lceil \frac{n+1}{2} \rceil$ features with sufficient probability. The CFP algorithm employs a majority voting scheme in the classification. Hence, only $d = \lceil \frac{n+1}{2} \rceil$ of the features must agree on the classification. Following the proof of the lemma, if S form an $< \varepsilon, \gamma, d >$-net, then it is guaranteed that each sub-interval contains at least one instance of S with high confidence. The CFP algorithm will generalize two points into one partition, if the distance between them is less than or equal to D_f. Therefore, if $D_f \geq 2\varepsilon$ then the points will be generalized into one partition, corresponding to a projection of the concept on that feature. □

Theorem 4. *Let ε, δ, and γ be fixed positive numbers less than one. If a random sample set S with n features forms an $< \varepsilon, \gamma, \lceil \frac{n+1}{2} \rceil >$-net with confidence greater than $1 - \delta$, then CFP with $D_f \geq 2\varepsilon$ constructs at most $n\lceil 1/\varepsilon \rceil$ partitions.*

Proof. Since S is an $< \varepsilon, \gamma, \lceil \frac{n+1}{2} \rceil >$-net with with confidence greater than $1-\delta$, each feature line is divided in to ε length sub-intervals and each one contains at least one sample point and the CFP algorithm constructs at most one (due to $D_f \geq 2\varepsilon$) partition for each sub-interval. Thus, for n features, the CFP constructs at most $n\lceil 1/\varepsilon \rceil$ partitions. □

Theorem 5. *Given ε, δ, and γ fixed positive numbers less than one. If random sample S is an $< \varepsilon, \gamma, \lceil \frac{n+1}{2} \rceil >$-net with confidence greater than $1 - \delta$, then classification complexity of the CFP with $D_f \geq 2\varepsilon$ is $O(n \log(\lceil 1/\varepsilon \rceil))$ and the training complexity is for m sample instances is $O(mn \log(\lceil 1/\varepsilon \rceil))$.*

Proof. Proof of the theorem 2 shows, that the CFP constructs at most $\lceil 1/\varepsilon \rceil$ partitions for each feature. In CFP algorithm the classification is composed of a search and a voting. The complexity of the search operation is $O(\log(\lceil 1/\varepsilon \rceil))$ for each feature. Since the complexity of voting is $O(n)$, the classification complexity of the CFP algorithm is $O(n log(\lceil 1/\varepsilon \rceil))$ for n features. Consequently, with m training instances, the training complexity of the CFP algorithm is $O(mn \log(\lceil 1/\varepsilon \rceil))$. □

The classification process in exemplar-based learning algorithms which use some form of the nearest neighbor algorithm involves computing the Euclidean distance (or similarity) of the instance to each stored exemplar in each dimension. Therefore, if there are M exemplars stored in the memory, and n features are used, then the complexity of the classification is $O(nM)$. On the other hand, since the partitions are naturally sorted for each feature dimension, the classification process in the CFP algorithm is only $O(n \log M)$, which significantly reduces the classification complexity.

4 Conclusion

The CFP algorithm is applicable to concepts, where each feature, independent of the others, can be used to classify the concept. This approach is a variant of algorithms that learn by projecting into one feature dimension at a time. The novelty of CFP is that it retains a feature-by-feature representation and uses voting to categorize. Algorithms that learn by projecting into one dimension at a time are limited in their ability to find complex concepts.

The analysis of the CFP shows that it requires small number of examples and a small amount of memory to learn a given concept, compared to many other similar algorithms. Another outcome of the analysis is that, the CFP has also a low training complexity.

The real-world data sets usually contain missing attribute values. Most of the learning systems usually overcome this problem by either filling in missing attribute values, or looking at the probability distribution of values of attributes. In contrast, the CFP solves this problem very naturally. Since the CFP treats each attribute value separately, in the case of an unknown attribute value, it simply leaves the partitioning of that feature intact.

The CFP uses feature weights to cope with irrelevant attributes. Introducing feature weights protects the algorithm's performance, when attributes have different relevances. In the CFP the feature weights are dynamically adjusted according to the global Δ adjustment rate, which is an important parameter for the predictive accuracy of the algorithm. Another important component of the CFP is D_f generalization limit for each attribute, which controls the generalization process. Δ and D_f are domain dependent parameters to the CFP, and their selection affects the performance of the algorithm. Determining the best values for these parameters is an optimization problem for a given domain. A version of CFP, called GA-CFP, has been implemented to learn these parameters using genetic algorithms [2].

References

1. D. W. Aha, D. Kibler and M. K. Albert, Instance–Based Learning Algorithms. *Machine Learning* 6 37–66, 1991.
2. H. A. Güvenir and İ. Şirin, A Genetic Algorithm for Classification by Feature Partitioning, *Proceedings of the ICGA'93*, Illinois, 1993.
3. J. R. Quinlan, Inductions of Decision Trees. *Machine Learning* 1, 81-106, 1986.
4. L. Rendell and H. Cho, Empirical Learning as a function of Concept Character, *Machine Learning* 5 267–298, 1990.
5. İ Şirin and H. A. Güvenir, *An Algorithm for Classification by Feature Partitioning.* Technical Report CIS-9301, Bilkent University, Dept. of Computer Engineering and Information Science, Ankara, 1993.
6. L.G. Valiant, A Theory of the Learnable. *Communications of the ACM*, 27 (11) 1134-1142, 1984.

Genetic Algorithms Elitist Probabilistic of Degree 1, a generalization of Simulated Annealing *

P. Larrañaga , M. Graña ,A. D'Anjou, F.J. Torrealdea
Dept.of Computer Science and Artificial Intelligence
University of the Basque Country
649 p.k. E-20080 . Donostia-Spain
e-mail: ccplamup@si.ehu.es

June 21, 1993

Abstract

This paper describes an Abstract Genetic Algorithm (AGA) that generalizes and unifies Genetic Algorithms (GA) and Simulated Annealing (SA), showing that the latter belongs to a family of genetic algorithms which we have called elitist probabilistic.

1 Introduction

The underlying idea - and the name - of Genetic Algorithms (GA), and Simulated Annealing (SA) originates from Nature. Both algorithms have been applied in learning [3], artificial vision [8] , VLSI design [18], artificial neural networks [12, 16], classifiers systems [4, 5], as well as search algorithms to handle combinatorial optimization problems [2, 10, 19, 20, 21].

A combinatorial optimization problem can be showed as a pair (E, C) ,where E is a finite (or numerable) set of possible configurations (search space) and C is a cost function that assigns a real number to each possible configuration. If we define the cost function, the problem is reduced to find a configuration i_0 where C takes his optimal value, $C_{opt} = C(i_0)$.

One possible way to solve a combinatorial optimization problem is by an optimization algorithm, that arrives at an exact solution. Many times the computational effort associated to such an algorithm can be unbearable. For this

---

*This work was supported by grant PGV 9220 from the Gobierno Vasco - Departamento de Educación , Universidades e Investigación

reason approximation algorithms are very often used in practice . In this case we try to obtain a solution, which is near to the optimun, whit a reasonable effort.

Whithin this perspective both GA and SA can be considered as general approximation algorithms that are not dependent on the problem.

The organization of the paper is as follows: In Section 2 we describe the basic operators that constitute an Simple Genetic Algortihm (SGA), introducing in Section 3 the pseudo-code for the Simulated Annealing (SA) algorithm. In Section 4 an Abstract Genetic Algorithm (AGA) is proposed , of which as one can see in the next Section, the Simple Genetic Algortihm (SGA) is an instance. Section 6 presents the fundamental result of the paper, that is, that the Simulated Annealing (SA) algorithm can be seen as an particular case of a family of Genetic Algorithms, which we have called elitistic probabilistc of degree 1. Finally , in Section 7, we collect the conclusions of the work .

2 Genetic Algorithms (GA)

Genetic algorithms are search algorithms based on the mechanics of natural selection and natural genetics [9, 15]. They combine survival of the fittest among string structures with a structured yet randomized information exchange to form a search algorithm which evolves to the optimum with probability 1 [6].

In each generation we have a new set of artificial strings, using bits and blocks of bits , which provided good fittness in the former generations. They used historical information to speculate new points in the search space with characteristics that hoped to be better than the formers. Genetic algorithms are theoretically and empirically proved to provide robust search in complex spaces.

A Simple Genetic Algorithm (SGA) is composed of three operators:

1. Reproduction.

2. Crossover

3. Mutation.

Reproduction is a process in which strings are selected according to their fitness. Each individual has a probability to contribute to the next offspring that is proportional to its fitness. Once the individuals have been selected for reproduction, a copy of them is produced which will be used in the crossover.

Simple crossover may proceed in two steps. First members of the newly reproduced strings in the mating pool are mated at random. Second, each pair of
strings undergoes crossing over as follows: an integer position l along the string
is selected uniformly at random between 1 y $k - 1$ (where k is the length of
the string). Two new strings are created by swapping all characters between
positions $l + 1$ and k. These new strings are individuals of the next generation.
It is clear, that the objective is the construction of new solutions from the best
former solutions.

The third operator, the mutation, plays a secondary role in the SGA. In
the SGA, mutation is the ocasional (with small probability) random alteration
of the value of a string position. Used in combination with the reproduction
and the crossover, it is a mechanism against the premature loss of important
solutions.

3 Simulated Annealing (SA)

The algorithm known as Simulated Annealing (SA) [1, 2, 7, 11], Statistical
Cooling, Stochastic Relaxation,.. is based on the analogy between the physical
annealing of solids - finding low energy states- and combinatorial optimisation
problems.

Once the paralelism between cost and energy was done, Kirkpatrick y col.
[14] produced a combinatorial optimization algorithm, that they called Simulated Annealing, consisting in running the Metropolis algorithm - which emu-
lates the evolution of a solid to thermodynamic equilibrium - with a decreasing
succesion of temperatures values.

The Metropolis algorithm or Descent algorithm can be described in the following pseudo-code:

begin Descent algorithm
    Select an initial state $i \epsilon E$
    Repeat
        Generate at random state j , a neighbour of i
        If $C(j) - C(i) \leq 0$ *then* $i := j$
    Until $C(j) \geq C(i)$ for all j in the neighbourhood of i
end Descent algorithm

One way of improving the solution is to run the descent algorithm several times
starting from diferent initial solutions, and take the best of the local minima
found. In SA, instead of this strategy, the algorithm attempts to avoid becoming trapped in a local optimun by sometimes accepting a neighbourhood move

which increases the value of C. The acceptance or rejection of an uphill move is determined by a sequence of random numbers, but with controlled probability. The probability of accepting a move which causes an increase δ in C is normaly set to $\exp(-\delta/T)$, where T is a control parameter which corresponds to temperature in the analogy with the physical annealing. The algorithm is started with a relatively high value of T, to avoid being prematurely trapped in a local optimum.

Two fundamental questions to execute the SA algorithm are the definition of a topology in the search space, as well as the determination of the annealing or cooling schedule, which consists in the determination of the initial temperature, the rate at which the temperature is reduced, the number of iterations at each temperature and the criterion used for stopping.

A pseudo-code for the SA algorithm in minimization problems is the following:

begin SA
     Select an initial state $i \epsilon E$
     Select an initial temperature $T > 0$
     Set temperature change counter $t = 0$
     Repeat
     Set repetition counter $n = 0$
       Repeat
       Generate state j, a neigbhour of i
       Calculate $\delta = C(j) - C(i)$
       If $\delta < 0$ *then* $i := j$
         else if random(0,1) $\leq exp(-\delta/T)$ *then* $i := j$
       $n := n + 1$
       until $n = N(t)$
     $t := t + 1$
     $T := T(t)$
     until stopping criterion true
end SA

4   Abstract Genetic Algorithm (AGA)

Taking into account our objective, we present a modification of the notation and definitions introduced in [6], first defining an Abstract Genetic Algorithm (AGA) which generalizes and unifies Genetic Algorithms (GA) and Simulated Annealing (SA).

A raw version of this AGA can be as follows:

begin AGA
    Make initial population at random
    WHILE NOT stop DO
      BEGIN
      Select parents from the population
      Let the selected parents *Produce children*
      Extend the population by adding the children to it
      Mutate the children with a probability near zero
      Reduce the extended population to the original size
      END
    Output the optimum of the population.
end AGA

Suppose we are working with a mimimization problem, of cost function C, defined over a search space E.

Trying to formalize the former abstract algorithm we introduce some notation and definitions, from where we will specify the AGA.

Definitions:

- *a size of the initial population*, will be proportional to the cardinality of the search space E.

- S_a *set of well sized populations*. Its elements are populations with a individuals.

- S_{a+} *set of oversized populations* . Its elements are populations with more than a individuals.

- A *selection function* f_{SPI} :$\{1,\ldots,a\} \rightarrow E$, from which the initial population from the search space E is obtained.

- A, B, H, D, 4 sets, $\alpha \epsilon A$, $\beta \epsilon B$, $\gamma \epsilon H$, $\delta \epsilon D$, parameters randomizing respectively the following functions f_{SP}, f_{RP}, f_M, f_R which we define next.

- A *selection function* $f_{SP}(\alpha, x)$ dependent on one randomized parameter α working over well sized populations, $x \epsilon S_a$, in order to select a set of parents able to produce offspring.
  $f_{SP} : A \times S_a \rightarrow \mathcal{P}(P), f_{SP}(\alpha, x) = y \subseteq x$

- A *reproduction function* $f_{RP} : B \times S_a \rightarrow \mathcal{P}(E)$ dependent on one randomized parameter β operating over populations $y \epsilon S_a$ with the objetive of producing children z getting from the parents y . That is $f_P(\beta, y) = z$, $z \epsilon S_a$.

- A *mutation function* $f_M : H \times E \to E$ dependent on one randomized parameter γ. His objective is to escape from local mimima, $f_M(\gamma, z) = z'$ where $z' \epsilon$ neighbourhood of z

- A *reduction function* $f_R \colon D \times S_{a+} \to S_a$ from which oversized populations are reduced to well sized populations. $f_R(\delta, t_+) = t$.

- A *boolean evaluation function* $f_e(x)$ dependent on one extern parameter, which controls the stopping of the algorithm.

Using this notation the AGA can be expressed as follows:

begin AGA(Abstract Genetic Algorithm)
    Get one initial population $f_{SPI}(1, \ldots, a) = x \epsilon S_a$
    While not $f_e(x)$ do
      Begin
        Get $\alpha, \beta, \gamma, \delta$
        $y = f_{SP}(\alpha, x)$
        $z = f_{RP}(\beta, y)$
        $z' = f_M(\gamma, z)$
        $t = x \cup z'$
        $x = f_R(\delta, t)$
      End
    Output the current population
end AGA

5 SGA as an instance of AGA

Next we will provide the form of the functions defined in the former section, in order to make it clear how the SGA can be seen as an special case of the AGA.

- The selection function , f_{SPI}, of the initial population can be considered as one simple random sampling with size a being carried out from a population sized $cardE$.

- The selection function of the parents ,f_{SP} , works as an stratified randomized sample with probabilities proportional to size of strata (cost function -or inverse- of each individual of the population, if we are maximizing -minimizing-).

- The reproduction function $f_{RP} : B \times S_2 \to S_2$
  $f_{RP}(\beta, (p_1, p_2)) = (h_1, h_2)$.

If we suppose that we need k bits for representing, in binary notation, the individuals of the E space, we will have:

$$f_{RP}(\beta, (p_1^1, \ldots, p_1^k; p_2^1, \ldots, p_2^k)) = (h_1^1, \ldots, h_1^k; h_2^1, \ldots, h_2^k)$$

If we denote by j an integer number taken at random from the set $\{1, \ldots, k-1\}$, we will have that the children's components will be obtained in the following way:

$$h_w^s = p_w^s \Leftrightarrow 1 \leq s \leq j$$
$$h_w^s = p_z^s \Leftrightarrow j+1 \leq s \leq k-1$$
$$w, z = 1, 2 \; ; w \neq z$$

- The mutation function f_M depending on the γ parameter, mutation probability, will remain constant in each iteration, taking values near to zero.

- The reduction function f_R, no elitist -as will be clear from the definitions in the next section- that is, the population in each iteration are constituted of the descendant of the former population.

6 SA as a special case of the genetic algorithms elitist probabilistic of degree 1

In the following we will introduce some definitions that will be used to show that the SA algorithm can be seen as belonging to a family of genetic algorithms that we have called elitist probabilistic of degree 1.

- Suppose that t_{l+} denotes the outcoming population at time l before the reduction have been done. That is: $t_{l+} = t_{l-1} \cup d_l = \{i_1^{l-1}, \ldots, i_a^{l-1}\} \cup \{i_{d_1}^l, \ldots, i_{d_a}^l\}$ where
i_j^{l-1} the individual number j of the population at time $l-1$
$i_{d_j}^l$ the descendant number j of the population at time l
We denote $t_l = f_R(\delta; t_{l+})$

- The reduction function f_R will be called *non elitist* $\Leftrightarrow t_l = d_l$,
that is, the population at time l is constituted by the l-th descendant.

- The reduction function will be called *elitist of degree a* $\Leftrightarrow$
$i_j^{l-1} \epsilon t_l \Leftarrow rg(C(i_j^{l-1})) \leq a$ with $j = 1, \ldots, a$
$i_{d_j}^l \epsilon t_l \Leftarrow rg(C(i_{d_j}^l)) \leq a$ with $j = 1, \ldots, a$
where $rg(C(i))$ denotes the rank of the cost function, extended the rank over the $2a$ individuals (population at time $l-1$, and descendants at time l)

That means that the reduction function is elitist of degree a if and only if the population at time t is constituted of the a individuals with better cost functions.

In order to approach the SA algorithm we define the concept of *reduction function elitist probabilist of degree a*, trying to control the behaviour of the reduction function by means of a conjunction between elitism and probability, in a way in which the h_j^l individual getting from the descendant at time t will have a probability to belong to the population at time t that will be proportional to the improvement in the cost function provided by this individual in comparision with the cost functions of its parents.

That is:

$P(h_j^l \epsilon t_l) = 1$ if $\Delta C \leq 0$
$P(h_j^l \epsilon t_l) = f(\Delta C)$ if $\Delta C > 0$

An instance of a reduction function that is probabilistic and elitist, and that reduced to populations with only one individual coincides with the criterium used in the SA algorithm, is the following:

If we denote by p_1^{l-1} and p_2^{l-1} the parents of the children h_1^l and h_2^l in the $l-1$ iteration of the algorithm, and by $\Delta C(p_1^{l-1}, p_2^{l-1}; h_1^l)$ the improvement in the cost function quantified as the diference between the semisum of the cost function assigned to the parents and the cost function relative to the first children, that is

$$\Delta C(p_1^{l-1}, p_2^{l-1}; h_1^l) = \frac{C(p_1^{l-1}) + C(p_2^{l-1})}{2} - C(h_1^l).$$

Similarly we define $\Delta C(p_1^{l-1}, p_2^{l-1}; h_2^l)$.

The conjunction between elitism and probability can be accomplished in this example, in order to define a reduction function that is elitist and probabilist of degree a, using the following criterium:

$$\Delta C(p_1^{l-1}, p_2^{l-1}; h_1^l) < 0 \Rightarrow h_1^l \epsilon t_l$$

$$\Delta C(p_1^{l-1}, p_2^{l-1}; h_1^l) > 0 \& random(0,1) \leq \exp\frac{-\Delta C(p_1^{l-1}, p_2^{l-1}; h_1^l)}{T_{l-1}} \Rightarrow h_1^l \epsilon t_l$$

, where $\{T_l\}$ is a decreasing succession of real numbers with limit 0.

And if anyone of the former conditions is verified,
$p_w^{l-1} \epsilon t_l$,where $w/p_w^{l-1} = \max_{w=1,2} C(p_w^{l-1})$.

Taking into account the former definitions, the SA algorithm can be seen as belonging to a family of genetic algorithms elitist probabilistic of degree 1, if we choose the following functions:

- f_{SPI} choose only one individual.

- f_{SP} and f_{RP} are reduced to the identity function

- f_M the mutation function, depends on one parameter that as in the Simple Genetic Algorithm (GSA) is constant for all the iterations, and in the SA take the value 1, with the following restriction:
  $f_R(1; z) = d$ where $d\epsilon$ Neighbourhood z, taking into account the topology thas has been defined in E.

- f_R, the reduction function, is elitist probabilistic of degree 1.

7 Conclusions

We have presented an Abstract Genetic Algorithm, from which we have obtained as particular cases, the Simple Genetic Algorithm, and the Simulated Annealing Algorithm, showing how the latter can be seen as an special case of a family of Genetic Algorithms, that we have called elitist probabilistic of degree 1.

References

[1] Aarts E.H.L., Korst J.H.M. (1989). *Simulated Annealing and Boltzmann Machines*. Wiley, Chichester.

[2] Aarts E.H., Van Laarhoven P.J.M. (1985). Statistical Cooling: A general approach to combinatorial optimization problems. *Philips J. Res.* 40, 193-226.

[3] Baba N. (1992). Utilization of stochastic automata and genetic algorithms for neural network learning. *Parallel Problem Solving from Nature, 2* 431-440.

[4] Booker L.B., Goldberg D.E., Holland J.H. (1989) . Classifiers systems and genetic algorithms. *Artificial Intelligence* 40, 235-282.

[5] Chockalingam T., Arunkumar S. (1992). A randomized heuristics for the mapping problem: The genetic approach. *Parallel Computing* 18, 1157-1165.

[6] Eiben A.E., Aarts E.H.L., van Hee K.M. (1990). Global Convergence of Genetic Algorithms: an Infinite Markov Chain Analysis. *Computing Science Notes*. Eindhoven University of Technology.

[7] Eglese R.W. (1990). Simulated annealing: A tool for operational research. *European Journal of Operational Research* Vol. 46 271-281.

[8] Geman S., Geman D. (1984). Stochastic relaxation, Gibbs distributions, and the Bayesian restoration of images. *IEEE Transactions on pattern analysis and machine intelligence.* Vol. PAMI-6, No. 6, 721-741.

[9] Goldberg D.E. (1989). *Genetic algorithms in search, optimization , machine learning.* Addison-Wesley

[10] Grefenstette J.J. (1989). *Genetics Algorithms and their applications: Proceedings of the Second International Conference on Genetics Algorithms, ICGA'89.*

[11] Haario H., Saksman E. (1991). Simulated annealing process in general state space . *Adv. Appl. Prob.* Vol. 23, 866-893.

[12] Hancock P.J.B.(1992). Recombination operators for the design of neural nets by genetic algorithm. *Parallel Problem Solving from Nature ,2* 441-450.

[13] Holland, J.H. (1975). *Adaptation in Natural and Artificial Systems.* Univ. of Michigan Press, Ann Arbor.

[14] Kirkpatrick S., Gelatt C.D., Vecchi M.P. (1983). Optimization by simulated annealing. *Science* 220, 671-680.

[15] Langley P. (1987) *Machine Learning. Special Issue on Genetic Algorithms.* Volume 3, Nos. 2/3.

[16] Polani D., Uthmann T. (1992). Adaptation of Kohonen feature map topologies by genetic algorithms. *Parallel Solving from Nature,2* 421-429

[17] Rajasekaran S., Reif J.H. (1992). Nested annealing: a provable improvement to simulated annealing. *Theorical Computer Science* 99, 157-176.

[18] Sugai Y., Hirata H. (1991). Hierarchical algorithm for a partition problem using simulated annealing: application to placement in VLSI layout. *Int. J. Systems Sci.* Vol. 22, No. 12, 2471-2487

[19] Tam K.Y. (1992). Genetic algorithms, function optimization and facility layout design . *European Journal of Operational Research* 63, 322-346.

[20] Tan H.L., Gelfand S.B. (1991). A cost minization approach to edge detection using simulated annealing. *IEEE Transactions on Pattern Analysis and Machine Intelligence.* Vol. 14, No. 1, 3-18.

[21] Venugopal V., Narendran T.T. (1992). Cell formation in manufacturing systems through simulated annealing: An experimental evaluation. *European Journal of Operational Research.* 63, 409-422.

Learning Relations Using Genetic Algorithms

A. Giordana, L. Saitta, M.E. Campidoglio and G. Lo Bello

Dipartimento di Informatica, Università di Torino
Corso Svizzera 185, 10149 Torino (Italy)

Abstract. Inducing concept descriptions from examples requires a large space of hypotheses to be explored. Genetic algorithms offer an appealing alternative to traditional search algorithms, because of their multi-point search strategy. In this paper, the new system REGAL is described: it uses genetic algorithms to learn first order logic concept descriptions. Moreover, it can be easily integrated with a deductive component, in order to exploit a domain theory. Two approaches to learning disjunctive concept descriptions are presented: the first one is a modification of the classical method of learning one disjunct at a time, whereas the second one is based on the idea of fitness sharing and tries to let subpopulations be spontaneously formed, according to the theory of the niches and species. The approaches have been compared on an artificial domain.

1 Introduction

Inducing concept descriptions from examples and background knowledge is a fundamental machine learning task which can be formulated as a search problem [1]. However, Genetic Algorithms offer a powerful, domain-independent search method: they have been first used in machine learning associated to the "classifier" model [2], but, recently, they have also been used for concept induction, both in propositional calculus [3,4] and in first order logic [5]. From these first experiments, genetic algorithms proved to be an appealing alternative for traditional search algorithms, because of their great exploration power, useful to escape local minima, and their suitability to exploit massive parallelism.

The system REGAL, described in this paper, is an evolution of GA-SMART [5] and adopts the same method of encoding first order logic (FOL) formulas into bit strings. GA-SMART was a straightforward evolution of the *Simple Genetic Algorithm* proposed by De Jong [7]. By restricting the hypothesis representation language L in such a way that it becomes finite, first order logic formulas can be represented using a bitstring in orde to be handled by the standard genetic operators. In particular, the complexity of L is defined through a *language template* Λ, which represents the maximally complex formula in L. Any other well formed formula is obtained by deleting some literal from Λ.

In GA-SMART, formulas in L were in conjunctive normal form and negation was not explicitly allowed. The richer language used in REGAL allows the system to learn the same set of formulas as other systems do [6]. Another important advantage of REGAL is its suitability to be integrated with a deduction system and used to refine, by induction, inconsistent concept descriptions generated by EBG [9] with an incomplete and/or inconsistent domain theory. Finally, a further improvement introduced in REGAL is the use of a new kind of sharing functions [11] allowing the formation of sub-populations. Crowding was already used in GA-SMART in order to learn many concepts at the same time. Here, the technique is modified in order to learn concept descriptions expressed as disjunctions of Horn clauses.

2. Knowledge Representation and Encoding

The language L, used by REGAL, is a first order logic language containing conjunction, disjunction, negation, internal disjunction [11] and existential and universal quantification. The building blocks of the language are "internally disjunct" atoms, such as, for instance:

$$colour(x, yellow \vee green) \qquad (2.1)$$

in which one of the arguments of a predicate is a disjunction of constants. Formula (2.1) is semantically equivalent to:

$$colour(x, yellow) \vee colour(x, green) \qquad (2.2)$$

but is more compact and readable. More in general, a predicate P of arity m is specified using the following syntax:

$$P(x_1, x_2, ..., x_m, [v_1, v_2, ..., v_n]) \qquad (2.3)$$

here the complex term $[v_1, v_2, ..., v_n]$ denotes the maximal internal disjunction, i.e., the set of all the possible values the feature P can assume on the tuple of variables $< x_1, x_2, ..., x_m>$. Any other disjunction inside P is represented by a subset of the set $[v_1, v_2, ..., v_n]$. If the set $[v_1, v_2, ..., v_n]$ does not exhaust the possible values of P, this set is completed by means of the symbol "$*$". Then, in the formula $P(x_1, x_2, ..., x_m, [v_1, v_2, ..., v_n, *])$ the symbol "$*$" denotes "no one of the values $v_1, v_2, ..., v_n$". In other words, "$*$" is an abbreviation for the expression $\neg v_1 \wedge \neg v_2 \wedge ....\wedge \neg v_n$. Therefore, the symbol "$*$" allows a restricted form of negation to be implemented. As an example, let us consider the predicate colour(x, [yellow, green, blue, grey, $*$]. Then, colour(x, [yellow, $*$]) is equivalent to colour(x, yellow $\vee$ [$\neg$ yellow $\wedge$ $\neg$ green $\wedge$ $\neg$ blue $\wedge$ $\neg$ gray]) or, equivalently, to $\neg$ colour(x, green) $\wedge$ $\neg$ colour(x, blue) $\wedge$ $\neg$ colour(x, grey).

Deleting a term from an internal disjunction is a specialization operation. For instance[1] : $P(x, [v_1])$ $|< P(x, [v_1, *])$ $|< P(x, [v_1, v_2, *])$

In particular, a predicate is said in maximally specific form (*msf*) when its internal disjunction contains only one term, and in maximally general form (*mgf*), when its internal disjunction contains all the possible values, including " * ". We notice that, owing to the completeness hypothesis, a predicate with an empty internal disjunction has to be considered illegal and one in mgf is tautologically true.

A second form of negation, greatly increasing the power of the language L, is the negation of existentially quantified formulas. This form of negation, widely used in logic programming, can be learned by systems such as ML-SMART [6]. A negated existentially quantified formula has, in L, the following syntax:

$$\neg \exists y_1,..., y_m [\psi(x_1, ..., x_n, y_1, ..., y_m)] \tag{2.4}$$

where ψ is a disjunction of (possibly internally disjunct) predicates, each one containing at least one variable in the set $y_1, y_2, ..., y_m$. The genetic operators can deal with negated formulas in a similar way as they do with positive ones. Deleting a term from the internal disjunction of a predicate occurring in ψ is a generalization operation, as it appears from the equivalence of formulas (2.5) and (2.6):

$$\neg \exists x [(P(x, [a \lor b]) \lor (Q(x, [e \lor f])] \tag{2.5}$$

$$\forall x [\neg P(x, a) \land \neg P(x, b) \land \neg Q(x, a) \land \neg Q(x, b)] \tag{2.6}$$

Finally, the occurrence inside ψ of a predicate in *mgf* leads to an *absurdum*, owing to the completeness hypothesis, whereas a predicate with an empty internal disjunction leads to a tautology.

The knowledge base acquired by REGAL consists of a flat set of concept descriptions in disjunctive normal form:

$$\varphi_1 \lor \varphi_2 \lor .... \lor \varphi_n \to h \tag{2.7}$$

where h denotes a concept and the φ_i's $(1 \leq i \leq n)$ are conjuctions of predicates, possibly containing, in turn, internal disjunctions. In the following we will describe the language template and the method for mapping each conjunction φ_i to a fixed-length bit string.

2.1. The Language Template

As mentioned in Section 2, the language L is characterized by a language template Λ, which is a conjunctive formula such that every other conjunctive

---

[1] The relation "ψ is more general than φ" is denoted by $\varphi |< \psi$, according to Michalski [10].

formula φ_i of L can be obtained by deleting some literal from Λ^2. In REGAL the template Λ obeys the following syntax:

$$\Lambda \equiv \varphi(x_1, \dots, x_n) \wedge \neg \exists\, y_1, \dots, y_m\, [\psi(x_1, \dots, x_n, y_1, \dots, y_m)]. \tag{2.8}$$

In (2.8) both φ and ψ denote conjunctions of predicates; moreover, each predicate in ψ must contain at least one variable in the set $y_1, y_2, \dots, y_m$, as in (2.4). The template Λ is, then, partitioned into two subformulas, Λ^+ and Λ^-, corresponding to the positive and negated parts of Λ, respectively. In Fig. 2.1 an example of a language template is reported, for the sake of illustration.

$\Lambda \equiv$ colour(x, [red, blue, *]) $\wedge$ shape(x, [square, triangle, *]) $\wedge$

$\qquad \neg\, \exists y$ [colour(y, [red, blue, *]) $\wedge$ far(x, y, [0, 1, 2, 3, *])]

$\Lambda^+ \equiv$ colour(x, [red, blue, *]) $\wedge$ shape(x, [square, triangle, *])

$\Lambda^- \equiv \neg\, \exists y$ [colour(y, [red, blue, *]) $\wedge$ far(x, y, [0, 1, 2, 3, *])]

Fig. 2.1 – Example of a language template including the unary predicates "colour" and "shape" and the binary predicate "far". The template describes a scene in which no object y, of any color, is at any distance from an object x of any color and shape.

Any predicate occurring in φ or ψ is in mgf. Each φ_i, occurring in any concept description (2.7), is a particular instantiation of Λ. For example, the formula:

color(x, [red]) $\wedge$ shape(x,[square]) $\wedge \neg\, \exists y$ [color(y, [blue]) $\wedge$far(x, y, [2,3])] (2.9)

is an instantiation of the template reported in Fig. 2.1. Formula (2.9) describes a scene in which no blue object has a distance value of 2 or 3 from a red square.

As discussed before, each predicate in Λ^+ is tautologically true, and, thus, Λ^+ is also tautologically true. On the contrary, Λ^- is tautologically false and, hence, Λ is tautologically false. As a consequence, a predicate in *mgf* can be deleted from the positive part of a formula without changing its extension, whereas a predicate with an empty internal disjunction can be deleted from the negated part of a formula without changing its extension.

In the language L there may also exist predicates which do not have internal disjunction (for instance, equal(x,y)). These predicates are suggested and added to the language template by the background knowledge, but are not considered during the inductive learning process, because they represent *necessary constraints* that must always be present in every concept description and are not processed by the generalisation mechanism of REGAL.

---

2 In this paper "literal" is used to refer to a single constant in an internal disjunction, because this last can be transformed into a disjunction of literals, as shown by (2.1) and (2.2)

2.2. Mapping Formulas to Bit Strings

The language template can be represented using a bit string s(Λ), where each literal (term) occurring in the maximal internal disjunction of a predicate in Λ is associated to a corresponding bit in s(Λ). Predicates in Λ which do not have internal disjunction (necessary constraints) do not need to be associated to any bit in the string.

By keeping adjacent in s(Λ) the bits corresponding to literals that are adjacent in the template, s(Λ) will be partitioned into two parts s(Λ$^+$) and s(Λ$^-$), corresponding to Λ$^+$ and Λ$^-$, respectively. The bit string associated to the template of Fig. 2.1 is reported in Fig. 2.2. Any other formula in L, obtained by deleting some literal from Λ, can be represented by the bit string s(Λ), in which the values of the bits have been properly set. This last point needs a separate discussion for the positive and negative parts of the template.

The semantic interpretation of the alleles in the bit string has been defined on the basis of the previous considerations. In particular, for the positive part of a formula, if the bit corresponding to a given term v in a predicate P is set to 1, then v belongs to the current internal disjunction of P, whereas if it is set to 0, it does not belong to it. Hence, a substring containing all 0's for a predicate is illegal and it is automatically rewritten as a string of all 1's. On the contrary, for the negated part of a formula, the semantic interpretation is the opposite: setting to 1 a bit corresponding to a given term v means that v is absent from the corresponding internal disjunction, whereas setting it to 0 means that it is present. Again, a substring containing all 0's for a predicate is illegal, whereas a substring containing all 1's corresponds to the maximal generality for aconjunct. Then, the system again replaces a string of all 0's with a string containing all 1's, whenever it occurs. In Fig. 2.2 tan example of bitstring for a formula obtaned from the template in Fig 2.1 is reported.

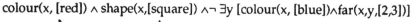

colour(x, [red]) ∧ shape(x,[square]) ∧¬ ∃y [colour(x, [blue])∧far(x,y,[2,3])]

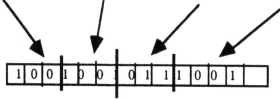

Fig. 2.2 – Bit string corresponding to a formula obtained by the template of Fig. 2.1.

3. The Fitness Function

The fitness function gives an evaluation of how well a formula φ describes a concept h. Three main criteria are usually adopted to evaluate the quality of a concept description: consistency, completeness and simplicity [10]. The same criteria are adopted here and are combined in the fitness function. In the following, a family of empirical fitness functions, new with respect to the one used in GA-SMART, is presented and analysed.

Let F be the set of learning examples, and let φ be a candidate description of the concept h; let, moreover, $M^+(h)$ and $M^-(h)$ denote the numbers of positive and negative instances of h in F, respectively. Finally, let $m^+(\varphi)$ and $m^-(\varphi)$ be the numbers of positive and negative instances of h, respectively, belonging to F and verifying φ.

As a measure of completeness the ratio $x = m^+(\varphi)/M^+(h)$ is used, whereas the consistency is evaluated by $w = m^+(\varphi)/[m^+(\varphi) + m^-(\varphi)]$, i.e., as the ratio between the number of positive instances and the global number of instances verifying φ [6]. However, w tends to give a too optimistic evaluation, especially when the number of available negative instances is small in comparison to that of positive ones. Suppose, for instance, that $M^+(h) = 750$ and $M^-(h) = 250$; a formula covering all positive instances and all negative instances will have $w = 0.75$, even if it is totally useless. Therefore, we looked for a measure more severely penalising inconsistency. The currently adopted measure is:

$$y = \text{Max} \left\{ 1-w, \ \frac{m^-(\varphi)}{M^-(\varphi)} \right\} \tag{3.1}$$

Finally, the simplicity of a formula is equated to its syntactic generality and is measured by $z = n(1)/n(s)$, where $n(1)$ is the number of 1's in a string $s(\Lambda)$, and $n(s)$ is the total number of bits in $s(\Lambda)$. This may seem a simplistic evaluation, but proved to work well in several test cases.

The three measures introduced above are combined into a unique function $f(\varphi)$, defined as follows:

$$f(\varphi) = x^\alpha (1 - y^\beta) + A (e^{B \times z} - 1) + D \tag{3.2}$$

where A, D << 1 and B, α, β < 1 are user-defined parameters. The resulting surface representing $f(\varphi)$ in a domain with $M^-(h) = 250$ and $M^+(h) = 750$ is reported in Fig. 3.3. We notice that the actual syntactic definition of the function f is not fundamental. What is important is the qualitative shape of the corresponding surface. The proposed function is the result of a series of trials; its computation time is irrelevant with respect to the matching time required to evaluate $m^+(\varphi)$ and $m^-(\varphi)$. The small value D has been added for the following reason: when the population is randomly initialized, it is possible that x be zero, thus making $f(\varphi)$ zero, which hinders φ from being selected for reproduction. A value of $f(\varphi)$ different from zero, even if small, gives to φ a chance of being selected by the reproduction operator.

4. Genetic Operators

The fundamental genetic operators used by REGAL are the classical ones used in the literature, with the addition of two non-standard crossovers and a new form of mutation called *seeding*,. Crossover operators are inherited by GA-SMART, and the reader can find a detailed description in [6]; in particular, they are the *two-point crossover* and the *uniform crossover,* previously used in the literature [8], and the *generalising* and *specialising crossovers,* specifically designed for the task at hand [6].

The *seeding operator* is primarily used to initialise the population in order to start with a set of formulas covering at least some examples in F. In fact, the concept description language characterised by a template can be so large that a randomly generated population may have no one individual matching any element in F. In this case, the fitness is close to zero for all individuals and the search reduces to a random walk for a long initial phase, until formulas covering a few examples are discovered by chance. The seeding operator receives in input a string s (corresponding to a formula φ) and returns a modified string s', which covers at least one instance randomly selected from F. Therefore, the action performed by this operator resembles the selection of the seed in the Star methodology [10]. Seeding operator can also be used by REGAL, in alternative to classical mutation, in order to reintegrate genetic information lost during the evolution of the program.

5. Learning Multimodal Concepts

The fundamental novelty of REGAL is its ability to learn disjunctive concepts. Learning disjunctive concepts is a problem inherently deceptive for a genetic algorithm. In fact, each separate disjunct in the concept description corresponds to a local maximum of the fitness function. Therefore, the genetic algorithm will frequently try to apply crossover between individuals representative of different disjuncts, creating thus offsprings that are necessarily worst than the parents (because a consistent common generalization does not exist).

Two strategies have been experimented in order to deal with this problem. The first one is an adaptation of a commonly used technique, which suggests to learn a disjunct at a time [5]. The second one, based on the theory of the niches and species [11] tries to learn a set of complete and consistent disjunctive descriptions by encouraging the formation of subpopulations. Both techniques will be discussed and compared using an artificial domain, where a difficult mutimodal concept has been constructed.

5.1. Learning one Disjunct at a Time

The test application has been designed by extending the well known train set used by Michalski [10]. Also in the present case, we have two concepts to distinguish: trains going East and trains going West. Therefore, each learning event is represented as a sequence of items (coaches), each one described by a vector of attributes referring to shape, colour, position, length, number of wheels and number of loads. Thousands of trains have been generated by a program which selects at random the values of the attributes. Then, each train has been classified using a set of disjunctive rules. The challenge for REGAL was to discover the original rules or a set of equivalent ones.

The rules for classifying trains going East (the first concept) are reported in the following:

Class 1 - Trains going East
Rule 1: In second position there is an open-top small coach, carrying one load, followed by an open-top small coach.
Rule 2: In third position there is a closed-top small coach carrying one load and an open top small coach in fifth position.
Rule 3: In position two, three or four there is a small coach, with two wheels and carrying one load, immediately followed by a long white coach carrying one load.

The learning set used for the experiment contained 500 instances of Class 1 and 500 instances of Class 2. Rule 1 covered 98 instances of Class 1, Rule 2 covered 206 and Rule 3 covered 209. The three subsets were slightly overlapping, because 13 instances verified more than one rule.

The concept description language used by REGAL is very similar to the one described in [11] and is reported in Table I.

Using the strategy of learning a disjunct at a time, REGAL was able to solve the problem. In particular, it learned a complete and consistent description of Class 1, consisting of three disjuncts, covering 216, 200 and 90 positive examples and roughly corresponding to Rule 3, 2 and 1, respectively. For example, the description of the largest disjunct (216 examples), is the following:

$coach(x) \land coach(y) \land follows(x,y) \land length(x, [1]) \land Nload(x, [1]) \land$
$length(y,[2]) \land Nload(y, [1,3]) \land colour(y, [white])$

These results have been obtained using a population of 800 individuals initialized by the seeding operator. The genetic evolution has been controlled using a linear fitness scaling mechanism [9] and a generation gap of 35%, i.e., only about one third of the individuals was replaced at each generation.

The system was ran repeatedly, in order to find a single partial definition each time, until all the training instances of the target concept were covered. In particular, at each run, the system was let free to converge to some concept definition φ, which, of course, covered only one subset φ^* of the positive instances of Class 1. Then, the instances in φ^* were removed from F and the system was restarted.

the older ones that are most similar to them, according to a given similarity measure. In this way, sub-populations are likely to grow up because genetic pressure tends to manifest itself primarily among similar individuals. Both in GA-SMART and in REGAL this method proved to work well to learn many concepts at one time, but was unable to allow a stable formation of subpopulations, representative of disjunctive definitions of the same concept. In all the experiments performed, in the long term there was a disjunct overcoming the other ones. The interpretation we give, in terms of the deceptiveness of the problem, is that stronger disjuncts inhibit the reproduction of the other ones by means of unfruitful matings.

The method based on sharing functions, unlike crowding, tries to act on the reproduction probability in order to inhibit the excessive growth of the genetic pressure of a subpopulation. This is done by reducing the fitness of an individual, depending on the number of existing individuals similar to it. In the initial formulation, proposed by Goldberg & Richardson (1987), genotypical sharing was considered. The fitness value $f(\varphi)$, associated to an individual φ, was considered as a reward from the environment to be shared with other individuals, proportionally to their similarity degree with φ. Similarity between two individuals φ and φ' was evaluated as the Hamming distance $d(s,s')$ between the corresponding bit strings s and s'.

However, in many cases it is better to consider a semantic distance, i.e., the phenotypical distance, rather than the syntactic one, as it has been discussed in [12]. For instance, by referring to our problem, it is easy to find formulas apparently similar but having a very different extension of the learning set F. Therefore, we tried to design a proper mechanism for sharing fitness, being the one described in [12] not suitable to our task. The philosophy underlying the sharing function approach is that subpopulations (species) live by exploiting environmental niches. If a species proliferates too much, it will be limited by the implicit reduction of the pro-capite incoming from the niche it exploits.

In REGAL, learning events are considered as life sources that are exploited by the formulas covering them. A formula φ matching $m^+(\varphi)$ positive events takes its support from them in order to evaluate its fitness. However, if the same events are matched also by other formulas, the fitness of φ is consequently reduced, because φ is not essential to cover such events. In this way, the reproduction rate decreases when formulas become too redundant.

The algorithm used to evaluate the fitness, shared by competing formulas, can be easily understood using the following metaphor: concept instances are cakes and formulas are living being eating cakes:

1) After crossover, mutation and seeding, formulas are evaluated using the function described in Section 4 for computing their absolute fitness.

2) Formulas, sorted according to their absolute fitness, are allowed to eat cakes. Each one takes one serving from each one of the cakes associated to the positive instances it covers. If all servings have been already eaten, it will not have any.

3) For each formula φ the shared fitness $f_{sh}(\varphi)$ is evaluated according to the following expression:

$$f_{sh}(\varphi) = f(\varphi)\, E/m^+(\varphi) \tag{5.1}$$

where E represents the total amount of serving eaten by φ and $m^+(\varphi)$ the number of positive instances covered by φ.

If an individual cannot eat at all, it will have a shared fitness equal to zero and then will not reproduce.

Experimentation with the test case described above showed that the method was able to control reproduction rate in order to allow the formation of stable subpopulations. The results obtained running REGAL through 200 generations and with a global population of 800 individuals, are reported in Fig. 5.1. Black columns in the histogram represent the numbers of positive instances covered by each one of the first 21 disjuncts, sorted as follows: first, the consistent disjuncts (1-16) are sorted according to decreasing completeness and, then, inconsistent disjuncts (17-21) are sorted according to increasing inconsistency. Dashed (dotted) columns report the global number of positive (negative) instances covered by all the disjuncts from the first until the current one.

It is worth noting that the first six disjuncts cover 450 of the 500 positive instances of Class 1. They are in a static equilibrium, being positioned on F in such a way that each one exploits a good amount of instances without competitors. Such disjuncts were present in the population since the 60th generation. On the contrary, the 12 disjuncts from 9 to 21 were in a kind of dynamic equilibrium, being in hard competition for survival. They some time disappeared, to reappear later, when regenerated by the genetic evolution. In particular, the presence of the small disjuncts from 10 to 16 is due to the continuous creation of the seeding operator. We notice that several large disjuncts are present, some of them corresponding approximately to the definitions given by Rules 2 and 3; others were discovered by performing alternative kinds of generalization. For instance, the first disjunct corresponds to the following definition obtainable by generalising Rule 3:

$$coach(x)\wedge\ length(x,\ [1])\wedge\ load(y,\ [1,3])\wedge\ colour(y,\ [wh])\ \wedge\ follow(x,y) \tag{5.2}$$

Formula (5.2) is consistent with the data and covers 216 positive instances instead of 206. This generalization has been made possible because the learning set was not large enough to be representative of all the possible cases. Increasing the number of instances of the second class, this overgeneralisation would disappear.

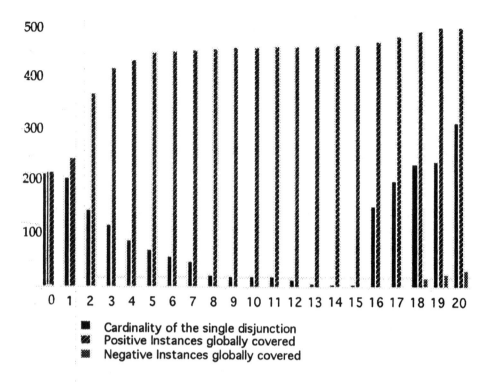

Fig. 5.1 - Results obtained using the fitness scaling method with a population of 800 individuals, using a crossover probability $p_c = 0.5$ and a generation gap of 35%.

On the other hand, we notice the lack of a unique disjunct corresponding to the 98 instances classified by Rule 1. We explain this fact as an effect of the deceptive action of the large disjuncts which interact negatively with the growth of smaller alternative concept definitions.

6. Conclusions

In this paper we presented an extension of a method described in [5] for learning concept descriptions in first order logic, using an inductive engine based on a genetic algorithm. Several substantial improvements have been introduced. First, the concept description language has been extended in order to include internal disjunction and negation. Second, we have shown how this genetic learning paradigm can be integrated with a deductive module in the very same way as in [6].

Two techniques have been introduced to learn disjunctive concepts. The first one learns one disjunct at a time, whereas the second one allows subpopulations to be formed. Even if the work in this direction is still in an early stage, we have presented a sharing mechanism which proved effective in allowing stable subpopulations, corresponding to different disjuncts, to be formed.

References

1. T. Mitchell : Generalisation as Search. Artficial Inteliegence, 18, 203-226 (1983).

2. J.H. Holland: Escaping Brittleness: The Possibilities of General Purpose Learning Algorithms Applied to Parallel Rule-Based Systems. In R. Michalski, J. Carbonell & T. Mitchell (Eds.), Machine Learning: An AI Approach, Vol. II. Morgan Kaufmann, Los Altos, CA, pp. 593-623 (1986).

3. K.A. De Jong, W.M. Spears: Learning Concept Classification Rules Using Genetic Algorithms. Proc. IJCAI-91, Sidney, Australia, pp. 651-656 (1991).

4. C.Z. Janikov: A New System for Inductive Learning in Attribute-Based Spaces. Lecture Notes in Artificial Intelligence, 542, 378-388 (1991).

5. A. Giordana, C. Sale: Genetic Algorithms for Learning Relations. Proc. 9th Int. Conf. on Machine Learning, Aberdeen, Scotland, pp. 169-178 (1992).

6. F. Bergadano, A. Giordana, L. Saitta: Machine Learning: An Integrated Approach and its Application, Ellis Horwood, Chichester, UK (1991).

7. K.A. De Jong: Analysis of the Behaviour of a Class of Genetic Adaptive Systems. Doctoral Dissertation, Department of Computer and Communication Sciences, University of Michigan, Ann Arbor, MI (1975).

8. D.E. Goldberg :Genetic Algorithms, Addison-Wesley (1989).

9. T. Mitchell, R.M. Keller, S. Kedar-Cabelli: Explanation-Based Generalization: A Unifying View. Machine Learning, 1, 47-80 (1986).

10. R. Michalski: A Theory and Methodology of Inductive Learning. In R. Michalski, J. Carbonell & T. Mitchell (Eds.), Machine Learning: An AI Approach, Vol. I. Morgan Kaufmann, Los Altos, CA, pp. 83-134, (1983).

11. K. Deb K, D. Goldberg: An Investigation of Niche and Species Formation in Genetic Function Optimization. Proc. 3rd Int. Conf. on Genetic Algorithms, Fairfax, VA, pp. 42-50 (1989).

Evolutionary Learning for Relaxation Labeling Processes

Marcello Pelillo, Fabio Abbattista and Angelo Maffione

Dipartimento di Informatica
Università di Bari
Via G. Amendola, 173 - 70126 Bari (Italy)

Abstract. Relaxation labeling processes are a class of parallel iterative procedures widely used in artificial intelligence and computer vision. Recently, a learning algorithm for relaxation labeling has been developed which involves minimizing a certain cost function with a gradient method. Despite the encouraging results obtained so far, the gradient algorithm suffers from some drawbacks that could prevent its application to practical problems. Essentially, these include the inability to escape from local minima and its computational complexity. In this paper we attempt to overcome the difficulties with the gradient procedure and propose the use of genetic algorithms for solving the learning problem of relaxation. Some results are reported which prove the effectiveness of the proposed approach.

1. Introduction

Constraint satisfaction (or consistent labeling) problems arise quite often in artificial intelligence and computer vision [1], [2]. They consist of assigning labels to objects so that existing domain-specific constraints are satisfied. Basically, there are two formulations of the consistent labeling problem depending on the way in which constraints are specified. In one formulation, referred to as the *discrete* problem, the constraint model is expressed in a logical fashion: an object-label configuration can be either completely allowed or forbidden, and no intermediate possibility is considered. In a more general formulation, instead, constraints are defined in terms of a set of real-valued *compatibility coefficients*, which quantitatively express the degree of agreement of object-label configurations. This is known as the *continuous* labeling problem and can be solved by means of relaxation labeling processes [3]-[5].

Relaxation processes were introduced by Rosenfeld *et al.* [3] for attempting to solve constraint satisfaction problems arising in the machine vision domain, and have found a variety of successful applications (see e.g. [6] for a review). They are iterative procedures that attempt to enhance an initial ambiguous labeling assignment in a manner that is "consistent" with the constraint model. Hummel and Zucker precisely defined the notion of consistency for the continuous labeling problem, and laid the foundations of relaxation processes [5]. One of the major features of relaxation labeling is that global consistency can be achieved by means of simple local computations and this makes the algorithm particularly suited for parallel implementation.

A number of authors have emphasized the importance of determining "good" compatibility coefficients [7], [8] and several statistical-based interpretations such as correlation [3], or mutual information [9] have been provided. Recently, Pelillo and Refice [10], [11] have introduced a new standpoint for deriving compatibilities that has proved to be quite effective. The key idea behind that work consists of determining compatibility coefficients in such a way that the performance of relaxation over a sample of learning data is "optimal." After defining a differentiable error function, they have developed an iterative gradient-based algorithm for attempting to minimize it. The resulting process can be thought of as a *learning* process, as the performance of relaxation (measured in terms of the error function) improves over time. Although the experimental results obtained so far are very encouraging and demonstrate that the optimization approach clearly outperforms the standard statistical one, the gradient-descent algorithm suffers from some inherent drawbacks that could prevent it from being applied to real-world problems. To begin with, the surface defined by the error function can be a very complex one and can have many poor local minima. Although this seemed not to occur in the experiments performed so far, in principle the gradient-descent algorithm can be easily trapped into one such minima. Another problem with the gradient algorithm is its computational complexity as it requires a number of operations of the order of the fourth power of the number of labels. Moreover, some relaxation schemes are not differentiable [12] and this prevents the gradient algorithm from being applied.

In the last few years, genetic algorithms (GAs) [13], [14] have gained wide popularity as optimization procedures especially for their properties of robustness and simplicity. They were pioneered by Holland, inspired from the mechanisms of natural evolution, and have found successful applications in a number of difficult optimization problems. Genetic algorithms work with a population of "individuals" which evolves according to some simple (randomized) genetic operators. As discussed by Goldberg [13], GAs present several advantages over calculus-based optimization methods. Firstly, they efficiently explore complex search spaces, and are able to find nearly globally optimal solutions, without being trapped into local optima. Also, they involve simple arithmetic operations, and do not require any auxiliary information (like derivatives) about the objective function other than the values of the function themselves. As a consequence, the GA-based learning algorithm does not depend on the relaxation scheme adopted; this is not true for the gradient algorithm as the use of different relaxation schemes involves modifying the derivative formulas. In addition, we found GAs particularly attractive for our learning problem for they are much less computationally costly than gradient methods. Finally, GAs are easily implementable on parallel hardware [13].

In this paper we discuss the use of GAs for learning the compatibility coefficients for relaxation labeling, and present some experiments over both a toy and a practical application which show the effectiveness of the proposed approach. The paper is organized as follows. Section 2 briefly discusses relaxation process and formulates the learning problem. In Section 3, instead, the use of GAs for our learning problem is addressed, and Section 4 presents some results. Finally, Section 5 concludes the paper.

2. Relaxation Labeling and the Learning Problem

Relaxation labeling involves a set of objects $B=\{b_1,\cdots,b_n\}$ and a set of labels $\Lambda=\{1,\cdots,m\}$. The purpose is to label each object of B with exactly one label of Λ. In all practical applications it is possible to construct, for each object b_i, a vector $p_i^{(0)}=(p_{i1}^{(0)},\cdots,p_{im}^{(0)})^T$, such that

and
$$0 \leq p_{i\lambda}^{(0)} \leq 1, \text{ for } i=1\ldots n, \text{ and } \lambda=1\ldots m$$

$$\sum_{\lambda=1}^{m} p_{i\lambda}^{(0)} = 1, \text{ for } i=1\ldots n \ .$$

Each $p_i^{(0)}$ can be interpreted as the *a-priori* probability distribution of labels for the object b_i. By concatenating $p_1^{(0)}$, $p_2^{(0)}$, $\cdots$, $p_n^{(0)}$ we obtain an initial weighted labeling assignment for the objects of B, denoted by $p^{(0)} \in R^{nm}$.

The compatibility model is represented by a matrix of nonnegative real-valued compatibility coefficients R; its element $r_{ij}(\lambda,\mu)$ measures the strength of compatibility between λ on object i and μ on object j: high values correspond to compatibility and low values correspond to incompatibility. We will find convenient to "linearize" the compatibility matrix R, and consider it as a column vector r.

The relaxation algorithm accepts as input the initial labeling $p^{(0)}=(p_1^{(0)T},\cdots,p_n^{(0)T})^T$ and updates it iteratively taking into account the compatibility model, in order to achieve global consistency. At the t-th step the labeling is updated according to the following formula [3]:

$$p_{i\lambda}^{(t+1)} = p_{i\lambda}^{(t)}q_{i\lambda}^{(t)} \Big/ \sum_{\mu=1}^{m} p_{i\mu}^{(t)}q_{i\mu}^{(t)} \tag{1}$$

where the denominator is simply a normalization factor, and

$$q_{i\lambda}^{(t)} = \sum_{j=1}^{n} \sum_{\mu=1}^{m} r_{ij}(\lambda,\mu)p_{j\mu}^{(t)} \tag{2}$$

represents a "contribution" function that measures the strength of support that context gives to λ for being the correct label for b_i. The process is stopped when some termination condition is satisfied and the final labeling is usually used to label the objects of B according to a maxima selection criterion [12].

Now, suppose that a set of instances of the problem we intend to solve is available. To be more specific, it is supposed that a number of learning samples exist:

$$L = \left\{ L_1, \cdots, L_N \right\}$$

where each sample L_γ ($\gamma=1...N$) is a set of labeled objects of the form

$$L_\gamma = \left\{ (b_i^\gamma, \lambda_i^\gamma) : 1 \leq i \leq n_\gamma,\ b_i^\gamma \in B,\ \lambda_i^\gamma \in \Lambda \right\}.$$

For each $\gamma=1...N$ let $p^{(L\gamma)} \in R^{n_\gamma m}$ denote the unambiguous labeling assignment for the objects of L_γ, that is:

$$p_{i\alpha}^{(L\gamma)} = \begin{cases} 0, \text{ if } \alpha \neq \lambda_i^\gamma; \\ 1, \text{ if } \alpha = \lambda_i^\gamma. \end{cases}$$

Furthermore, suppose that we have some mechanism for constructing an initial labeling $p^{(I\gamma)}$ on the basis of the objects in L_γ, and let $p^{(F\gamma)}$ denote the labeling produced by the relaxation algorithm, according to some stopping criterion, when $p^{(I\gamma)}$ is given as input.

A relaxation process is a function that, given as input a vector of compatibilities r and an initial labeling $p^{(I)}$, produces iteratively the final labeling $p^{(F)}$. Here we consider the relaxation operator as a function of the compatibility coefficients only, the initial labeling being considered as a constant. In order to emphasize this dependence we will write $p_{i\lambda}^{(F)}(r)$ to denote the $i\lambda$-component of the final labeling.

Broadly speaking, the learning problem for relaxation labeling is to determine a vector of compatibilities r so that the final labeling $p^{(F\gamma)}$ be as close as possible to the desired labeling $p^{(L\gamma)}$, for each $\gamma=1...N$. To do this, we can define a cost function measuring the loss incurred when $p^{(F\gamma)}$ is obtained instead of $p^{(L\gamma)}$, and attempt to minimize it, with respect to r. As both $p^{(F\gamma)}$ and $p^{(L\gamma)}$ are composed of n_γ probability vectors (the $p_i^{(F\gamma)}$'s and the $p_i^{(L\gamma)}$'s respectively), it seems natural to make use of some divergence measure between probability distributions. The best known of such measures is Kullback's directed divergence [15], which was actually experimented in the previous work with the gradient algorithm [11] and yielded better generalization results than the more traditional quadratic error function. However, Kullback's divergence measure requires that the two probability distributions be absolutely continuous. In our case, this means that

$$p_{i\lambda_i^\gamma}^{(F\gamma)}(r) \neq 0, \quad \text{for all } i=1...n_\gamma$$

which amounts to requiring that the relaxation algorithm assigns nonzero probability to the correct labels. Therefore, the use of Kullback's measure could cause a run-time error when, for some i, this condition is not met.

Fortunately, Lin [16] has recently proposed a more robust information-theoretic divergence measure which does not require the absolute continuity property, and is closely related to Kullback's measure. According to Lin's measure, the cost (or error) for sample γ turns out to be:

$$E_\gamma(r) = n_\gamma - \sum_{i=1}^{n_\gamma} \log_2(1 + p_{i\lambda_i}^{(F_\gamma)}(r)) . \tag{3}$$

Notice that $E_\gamma(r)=0$ if and only if $p^{(L\gamma)}=p^{(F\gamma)}$ and it attains its maximum value, n_γ, when relaxation assigns null probabilities to all the correct labels. The total error achieved over the entire learning set L can be defined as

$$E(r) = \sum_{\gamma=1}^{N} E_\gamma(r) . \tag{4}$$

In conclusion, the learning problem for relaxation labeling can be stated as the problem of minimizing the function E with respect to r. In [10], [11] this problem is solved by means of a gradient method which begins with an initial point r_0 and iteratively produces a sequence $\{r_k\}$ as follows: $r_{k+1}=r_k-\alpha_k u_k$, where u_k is a direction vector determined from the gradient of E, and α_k is a suitable step size. It is readily seen that the number of derivatives that are to be computed is of order of m^3 and for each of them about m calculations are needed. Therefore, the overall computational complexity of the algorithm turns out to be $O(m^4)$ [11], and this makes it unfeasible for problems where the number of labels is too large.

3. Learning Compatibility Coefficients with Genetic Algorithms

Genetic algorithms are parallel search procedures largely inspired from evolution in natural systems [13], [14]. In contrast with more traditional optimization techniques, GAs work with a constant-size population of points which, in the GA terminology, are called chromosomes or individuals. In our application each chromosome represents a vector of compatibility coefficients r: each coefficient $r_{ij}(\lambda, \mu)$ is mapped into a fixed-length string of bits, and the whole chromosome is obtained by simply concatenating these strings. Moreover, every chromosome is associated with a "fitness" value that determines its probability of surviving at the next generation: the higher the fitness the higher the probability of survival. Clearly, in an optimization problem, a chromosome's fitness must be closely related to the corresponding value of the objective function.

A GA begins with an initial population of s members chosen either heuristically or at random. In its simplest version, a GA uses three simple operators: reproduction, crossover, and mutation. Reproduction consists of choosing, in a probabilistic way, the individuals that are to be copied in the next "generation." The probability of chromosome i of being reproduced is proportional to its fitness, according to the following formula

$$P_i = F_i \Big/ \sum_{k=1}^{s} F_k \qquad (5)$$

where F_k represents the fitness value of the k-th chromosome of the current population. Once that the best individuals have been selected, the crossover operator is applied between pairs of individuals in order to produce new offsprings. The operator proceeds in two steps. First, two members of the mating pool are chosen at random; next, a cut point is determined (again) randomly and the corresponding right side segments are exchanged. The frequency with which crossover is applied is controlled by a parameter P_c. Recall that in our application each chromosome represents a vector of compatibility coefficients; hence, the crossover point is allowed to fall only at the boundary between two succeeding coefficients. Doing so, crossover does not create new compatibility coefficients but, instead, simply exchanges coefficients between vectors. The task of producing new compatibility coefficients is assigned to the mutation operator which consists of reversing the value of every bit within a string with fixed probability P_m.

Basically, GAs are maximization procedures as they tend to favor high-fitness individuals and, instead, we are dealing with a minimization problem. Therefore, a mapping between the objective function E defined previously, and the fitness function F is required. To do so, we used the following formula proposed by Caudell and Dolan [17] in their experiments of neural network learning:

$$F(\mathbf{r}) = \tan\Big\{ \frac{\pi}{2}(1 - E(\mathbf{r})/E_{max}) \Big\} \qquad (6)$$

where E_{max} is the maximum value of E (that is $\sum n_\gamma$). Notice that minimizing E is equivalent to maximizing F, because F is a decreasing function of E. This formula has the advantage of strongly favoring good individuals in the reproduction phase; in fact, F tends to infinity as E goes to zero: therefore, near-optimal individuals are allocated a very high probability of being reproduced into the successive generation, according to formula (5).

One problem that could arise in using GAs is a premature convergence toward mediocre individuals. This is usually caused by early domination of a few extraordinary members in a mediocre population. In addition, during the course of the optimization process, it is common to have that the population average fitness is close to the population best fitness. This is an undesirable behavior for the GA because average and best individuals will have nearly the same number of copies in next generations. In order to avoid such situations Goldberg [13] suggests scaling the fitness function as $F' = aF + b$ where a and b are appropriate parameters determined so that 1) the average scaled fitness F'_{avg} equals the raw average fitness F_{avg} and, 2) $F'_{max} = kF_{avg}$, where F'_{max} is the scaled maximum fitness value, and k is the desired expected number of copies for the best population member. Following Goldberg's suggestion in the experiments reported in this paper, a value $k = 2$ was used, which corresponds to having (on the average) two copies of the best population member in the successive generation.

In contrast with the gradient algorithm, the GA-based learning procedure is much less computationally costly as it requires, on each generation, a number of operations roughly proportional to m^2. In fact, this is the number of calculations needed to compute the fitness function, as seen in formulas (1)-(4), and to perform both the mutation and the crossover operations. Of course, the computational complexity of the GA scales linearly with the population size s, and many generations are usually needed to find an optimal solution.

4. Experimental Results

In order to assess the effectiveness of the proposed evolutionary learning algorithm, some experiments over both a toy and a practical application were carried out. The first task involved labeling the sides of a triangle and the second one consisted of labeling words with their parts-of-speech. In the preliminary phase of our work several runs of the GA were performed over the toy-triangle problem (which is less costly) aimed at finding a good set of parameters for our problem. The best results were obtained using $P_c=1$ and $P_m=0.01$. This is in accordance with the suggestion that crossover probability should be high, and mutation probability should be low. In both the applications we made a comparison between the gradient and the genetic algorithm; in the latter case we used a fixed population size $s=50$. Moreover, in the triangle example each coefficient $r_{ij}(\lambda,\mu)$ was encoded into a 9-bit string, while in the part-of-speech task 11 bits were used. In the gradient experiments the step size α_k was set to 0.1, which seemed to be near optimal.

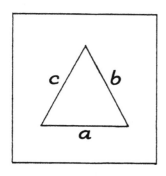

	a	b	c
1.	>	>	>
2.	<	<	<
3.	>	–	>
4.	>	>	–
5.	–	>	>
6.	<	+	<
7.	<	<	+
8.	+	<	<

Fig. 1. A triangle and its meaningful interpretations.

4.1. Labeling a Triangle

This is the standard toy application for relaxation processes, introduced by Rosenfeld *et al.* [3] for studying the behavior of the algorithm. The problem consists of labeling the sides of a triangle over a background, according to a 3-D interpretation. Each side can be interpreted as a convex edge (+), a concave edge (−), or as one of two types of occluding edges (> or <). There are $4^3=64$ possible labeling configurations, but only eight of them correspond to meaningful interpretations (see Fig. 1).

In the experiments presented here we idealized a very unfavorable as well as unrealistic situation for the learning algorithm, in that the initial labeling assignments were strongly biased toward incorrect, but meaningful interpretations. Fig. 2 shows the learning set used in the experiments: the task was to train the relaxation process to produce the desired labelings (corresponding to the eight meaningful cases), given the input labelings, in exactly three iterations. It is easily seen that standard statistical compatibility coefficients (like correlation) perform poorly on such a task.

Case	Initial labeling				Desired labeling				Case	Initial labeling				Desired labeling			
	>	<	+	−	>	<	+	−		>	<	+	−	>	<	+	−
1)	.300	.700	.000	.000	1	0	0	0	5)	.000	.000	.300	.700	0	0	1	0
	.300	.700	.000	.000	1	0	0	0		.300	.700	.000	.000	1	0	0	0
	.300	.700	.000	.000	1	0	0	0		.300	.700	.000	.000	1	0	0	0
2)	.700	.300	.000	.000	0	1	0	0	6)	.700	.300	.000	.000	0	1	0	0
	.700	.300	.000	.000	0	1	0	0		.000	.000	.700	.300	0	0	0	1
	.700	.300	.000	.000	0	1	0	0		.700	.300	.000	.000	0	1	0	0
3)	.300	.700	.000	.000	1	0	0	0	7)	.700	.300	.000	.000	0	1	0	0
	.000	.000	.300	.700	0	0	1	0		.700	.300	.000	.000	0	1	0	0
	.300	.700	.000	.000	1	0	0	0		.000	.000	.700	.300	0	0	0	1
4)	.300	.700	.000	.000	1	0	0	0	8)	.000	.000	.700	.300	0	0	0	1
	.300	.700	.000	.000	1	0	0	0		.700	.300	.000	.000	0	1	0	0
	.000	.000	.300	.700	0	0	1	0		.700	.300	.000	.000	0	1	0	0

Fig. 2. Learning set used in the toy-triangle problem.

Initially, ten independent runs were performed using the gradient algorithm, starting from randomly chosen points: the best and the average performance of the algorithm are shown in Fig. 3(a). Next, the GA was run up to the 1,000*th* generation; the results are shown in Fig. 3(b), where both the population best and the population average performance are plotted. The best objective function value found by the GA was $E=5.607$ while the best of the gradient algorithm was $E=6.258$. The corresponding compatibility coefficients were used to run the relaxation algorithm over the learning set initial labelings, and the results are shown in Fig. 4. As we can see both the points produce six labeling errors but the errors corresponding to the gradient point are much more serious.

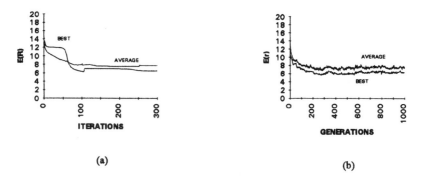

(a)   (b)

Fig. 3. Behavior of the error function during the learning process for triangle case: (a) gradient algorithm, (b) genetic algorithm.

Case	Final labeling (a)				Final labeling (b)				Case	Final labeling (a)				Final labeling (b)			
	>	<	+	−	>	<	+	−		>	<	+	−	>	<	+	−
1)	.450	.550	.000	.000	.014	.986	.000	.000	5)	.000	.000	.513	.487	.000	.000	.996	.004
	.450	.550	.000	.000	.014	.986	.000	.000		.955	.045	.000	.000	.970	.030	.000	.000
	.450	.550	.000	.000	.014	.986	.000	.000		.955	.045	.000	.000	.970	.030	.000	.000
2)	.451	.549	.000	.000	.018	.982	.000	.000	6)	.045	.955	.000	.000	.036	.964	.000	.000
	.451	.549	.000	.000	.018	.982	.000	.000		.000	.000	.587	.413	.000	.000	.996	.004
	.451	.549	.000	.000	.018	.982	.000	.000		.045	.955	.000	.000	.036	.964	.000	.000
3)	.955	.045	.000	.000	.970	.030	.000	.000	7)	.045	.955	.000	.000	.036	.964	.000	.000
	.000	.000	.513	.487	.000	.000	.996	.004		.045	.955	.000	.000	.036	.964	.000	.000
	.955	.045	.000	.000	.970	.030	.000	.000		.000	.000	.587	.413	.000	.000	.996	.004
4)	.955	.045	.000	.000	.970	.030	.000	.000	8)	.000	.000	.587	.413	.000	.000	.996	.004
	.955	.045	.000	.000	.970	.030	.000	.000		.045	.955	.000	.000	.036	.964	.000	.000
	.000	.000	.513	.487	.000	.000	.996	.004		.045	.955	.000	.000	.036	.964	.000	.000

Fig. 4. Results of three iterations of relaxation over the initial learning labelings, using (a) the best point of the GA, (b) the best point of the gradient algorithm.

4.2. Part-of-Speech Disambiguation

Labeling words according to their parts-of-speech is a fundamental problem that arises in many different contexts such as speech recognition, speech synthesis, and optical character recognition [18]. The problem is usually approached by two consecutive steps. In the first one, each word within a sentence is associated with a list of potential labels; this can be accomplished by means of word-ending rules and/or a dictionary look-up. Due to the presence of homographs in natural language (that is words belonging to more than one syntactic class) a second phase is required, wherein a *disambiguation* is carried out on the basis of context. Pelillo and Refice [19] recently used relaxation processes for accomplishing the disambiguation phase: in this application the object to be labeled are words, the labels are the parts-of-speech, and compatibility coefficients express the compatibility between neighboring syntactic classes.

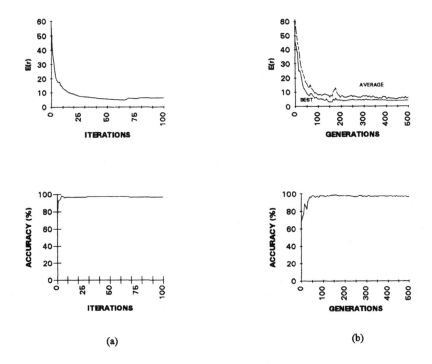

Fig. 5. Behavior of the error function and the disambiguation accuracy, using (a) the gradient algorithm, (b) the genetic algorithm.

In the experiments reported here the initial labeling assignments were constructed using a dictionary look-up which provided, for each word, the list of its possible labels: these labels were given uniform probability. Also, the "context" consisted of the right word only, and the relaxation algorithm was stopped at the first iteration. The label set Λ used contained the main parts-of-speech: verb, noun, adjective, adverb, determiner, conjunction, preposition, pronoun, and a special miscellaneous label. We used as the training set a labeled 1,000-word sample text containing 26 sentences extracted from some issues of the EEC Italian Official Journal. We started the gradient algorithm with a correlation vector estimated from a separate 1,500-word sample text (this choice produced the best results in [11]). The behavior of the error function as well as the disambiguation accuracy during the learning process for both the gradient and the genetic algorithm is shown in Fig. 5. In this case the best objective function value found by the GA was $E=3.041$ (98.65% disambiguation accuracy), and the best of the gradient algorithm was $E=4.886$ (97.30% accuracy).

5. Conclusions

In this paper the use of genetic algorithms to learn the compatibility coefficients of relaxation labeling processes has been proposed, and a comparison with gradient-based algorithms has been made. Genetic algorithms present several advantages over traditional gradient methods which make them very attractive for our learning problem: in particular, they are able to escape from local optima, do not require derivative information, and involve simple arithmetic operations.

In order to test the feasibility of the algorithm two series of experiments were carried out over both a toy and a practical application. In both the problems poor local minima were not actually encountered by the gradient method; nevertheless, the GA was able to achieve always better results within few generations. It should be pointed out that the ability of GAs to escape from local minima was just one of the motivations that led us to experiment them on our learning problem. One additional attractive feature of GAs is their computational complexity. In fact, a number of calculations proportional to m^2 is performed on each GA's generation (m being the number of labels) and this should be compared with the $O(m^4)$ calculations performed by the gradient algorithm on each step, to evaluate derivatives. Therefore, we can conclude that the GA is a reliable and effective technique for the relaxation labeling learning problem, and is particularly suited for real-word high-dimensional applications where the gradient method becomes impracticable. Currently we are experimenting the GA over different, "gradient-hard" applications and are trying to improve the performance of the algorithm. Also a comparison with the simulated annealing algorithm is in progress [20].

References

[1] R. M. Haralick and L. G. Shapiro (1979). The consistent labeling problem: Part I. *IEEE Trans. Pattern Anal. Machine Intell.* 1(2), 173-184.

[2] E. Charniak and D. McDermott (1985). *Introduction to Artificial Intelligence.* Reading, MA: Addison-Wesley.

[3]   A. Rosenfeld, R. A. Hummel and S. W. Zucker (1976). Scene labeling by relaxation operations. *IEEE Trans. Syst. Man Cybern.* **6**(6), 420-433.

[4]   L. S. Davis and A. Rosenfeld (1981). Cooperating processes for low-level vision: A survey. *Artificial Intell.* **17**, 245-263.

[5]   R. A. Hummel and S. W. Zucker (1983). On the foundations of relaxation labeling processes. *IEEE Trans. Pattern Anal. Machine Intell.* **5**(3), 267-287.

[6]   J. Kittler and J. Illingworth (1985). Relaxation labeling algorithms - A review. *Image Vision Comput.* **3**(4), 206-216.

[7]   R. M. Haralick, J. L. Mohammed and S. W. Zucker (1980). Compatibilities and the fixed points of arithmetic relaxation processes. *Comput. Graph. Image Processing* **13**, 242-256.

[8]   D. P. O'Leary and S. Peleg (1983). Analysis of relaxation processes: The two-node two-label case. *IEEE Trans. Syst. Man Cybern.* **13**(4), 618-623.

[9]   S. Peleg and A. Rosenfeld (1978). Determining compatibility coefficients for curve enhancement relaxation processes. *IEEE Trans. Syst. Man Cybern.* **8**(7), 548-555.

[10]   M. Pelillo and M. Refice (1992). An optimization algorithm for determining the compatibility coefficients of relaxation labeling processes. *Proc. 11th Int. Conf. Pattern Recognition*, The Hague, The Netherlands, 145-148.

[11]   M. Pelillo and M. Refice (submitted). Learning compatibility coefficients for relaxation labeling processes. *IEEE Trans. Pattern Anal. Machine Intell.*

[12]   S. W. Zucker, Y. G. Leclerc and J. L. Mohammed (1981). Continuous relaxation and local maxima selection: Conditions for equivalence. *IEEE Trans. Pattern Anal. Machine Intell.* **3**(3), 117-127.

[13]   D. E. Goldberg (1989). *Genetic Algorithms in Search, Optimization, and Machine Learning.* Reading, MA: Addison-Wesley.

[14]   J. H. Holland (1992). *Adaptation in Natural and Artificial Systems.* 2nd ed., Cambridge, MA: MIT Press.

[15]   S. Kullback (1959). *Information Theory and Statistics.* New York: Wiley.

[16]   J. Lin (1991). Divergence measures based on the Shannon entropy. *IEEE Trans. Inform. Theory* **37**(1), 145-151.

[17]   T. P. Caudell and C. P. Dolan (1989). Parametric connectivity: Training of constrained networks using genetic algorithms. *Proc. 3rd Int. Conf. Genetic Algorithms*, George Mason University, 370-374.

[18]   K. W. Church (1989). A stochastic parts program and noun phrase parser for unrestricted text. *Proc. IEEE Int. Conf. Acoustics Speech Signal Processing*, Glasgow, Scotland, 695-698.

[19]   M. Pelillo and M. Refice (1991). Syntactic category disambiguation through relaxation processes. *Proc. EUROSPEECH 91*, Genova, Italy, 757-760.

[20]   M. Pelillo, F. Abbattista and N. Abbattista (1993). Globally optimal learning for relaxation labeling by simulated annealing. *Proc. 7th Int. Conf. Image Anal. Processing*, Bari, Italy.

Increasing Cohesion in Automatically Generated Natural Language Texts

Elisabeth A. Maier and Elena Not*

Istituto per la Ricerca Scientifica e Tecnologica (IRST), 38050 Trento-Povo, Italy

Abstract. In this paper we show how the quality of machine-generated texts can be improved by augmenting a text planner with sophisticated components for the generation of textual phenomena. We discuss this point by introducing an example from our corpus of texts as so far generated by the schema-based planner RSE. We then describe the weaknesses of schematic approaches and show how a hybrid text planning architecture, which includes techniques to flexibly generate links between discourse units eliminates those disadvantages. Finally, we will show how the hybrid architecture adopted from [7] has been changed and extended in order to treat thematic progression and to generate referring expressions.

1 Introduction

The growing need for the quick availability of large amounts of documentation – ranging from machine manuals to weather reports – has led to an increasing importance of text generation. About 20 years ago research started in the area of sentence generation and over the years systems have been developed which cover the full repertoire of linguistic phenomena for various languages. Recently, interest moved towards issues related to the production of multiparagraph texts.

A whole family of text generators was based on a schema-oriented architecture ([15], [19], [14]). Schemata are abstract skeletons of the text to be generated that consist of sequences of predicates which are instantiated with knowledge from a data base.

Schematic text planners were soon found to be too inflexible for the generation of variant texts. Therefore, a number of researchers tried to formalize Rhetorical Structure Theory (RST, [13]) in order to use it as a tool for the planning of texts. RST builds on the assumption that the coherence of texts can be explained by means of relations which hold between segments of text. In RST about 20 such relations have been identified: among them are relations like SE-QUENCE, which connects chronologically related events, ELABORATION, which occurs when one text segment provides more detail for another text unit, MO-TIVATION, which links an action with the motivation for its execution, etc. In various implementations of the theory these relations have been operationalized

---

* We would like to thank Lee Fedder, Oliviero Stock and Carlo Strapparava for comments on a previous version of this paper.

as so-called *plan operators* (see, e.g., [16], [8]). For every plan operator, a set of application conditions and a specification of the effects of the corresponding relation exist. Both the condition and the effect parts of the plan operators address various types of knowledge: the use of a plan operator can, for instance, depend on the type of text to be generated, on the knowledge available in the knowledge base, on the preferences and the expertise of the potential reader, etc. This dependency on many different types of information may, however, introduce excessive complexity and intransparency in the plan operators, when they are extended for application in different domains. To solve this problem, a new architecture was developed ([7]) which separates out the various types of knowledge addressed in plan operators. The textual phenomena generated by this text planner were, however, restricted to the production of text structures.

We adopted this architecture as a starting point for the development of a system also capable of generating textual phenomena like thematic progression, a subclass of conjunctions and referring expressions.

2 The Problem

In this section we show how texts have been generated so far in the framework of the IRST-projects MAIA ([22]) and ALFRESCO ([21]), where the Rhetorical Schema Environment RSE has been used for text planning ([3]). We will point out why this approach is insufficient for the production of highly connected text.

Both ALFRESCO and the natural language component of MAIA, CONCIERGE, include intelligent multimedia interfaces that allow the user to access textual and visual information. In case the system chooses text as output modality the text planning component selects and organizes the content to be included in the response by "filling" one or more schemata with the relevant knowledge. Each schema is specified in a language designed for that specific purpose. It consists of two types of constructs: queries addressed to the knowledge base and operators for the construction of the text plan. The resulting text plan is specified in a format, which is an adaption of SPL, the Sentence Plan Language ([10]) which served as input specification for the PENMAN generation system ([9]).

In RSE new schemas can easily be written and executed at different levels of generality. Even though it can generate a broad variety of texts, RSE suffers from the deficiencies typical for schema-based text planners: they do not allow reasoning about the text plan produced, since they do not provide enough information about the discourse structure. In fact, schemas neither can give any motivation for their specific order nor do they have an explicit representation of the *links* between the different text units. All this hampers the introduction of textual factors that improve the quality of text. Although being perfectly coherent the texts lack linguistic cohesion. As an example, consider the following text produced by RSE, which is a description of the Natural Language Processing group of IRST [2].

---

[2] English gloss: 1. The Natural Language group is part of the Interfaces department.

Example 1.

1. Il gruppo Linguaggio Naturale appartiene all'area Interfacce.
2. I ricercatori del gruppo Linguaggio Naturale sono Lee Fedder, Enrico Franconi, Alberto Lavelli, Bernardo Magnini, Elisabeth Maier, Elena Not, Fabio Pianesi, Oliviero Stock
3. - che e' il responsabile del gruppo Linguaggio Naturale -
2. *(cont.)* e Carlo Strapparava.
4. L'elaborazione del linguaggio naturale comprende la sintassi, la semantica lessicale, la pianificazione del testo, il parsing, l'input malformato e la generazione in linguaggio naturale.
5. Fabio Pianesi si interessa di sintassi.
6. Alberto Lavelli e Bernardo Magnini si interessano di semantica lessicale.
7. Elisabeth Maier ed Elena Not si interessano di pianificazione del testo.
8. Alberto Lavelli si interessa di parsing.
9. Alberto Lavelli si interessa di input malformato.
10. Lee Fedder si interessa di generazione in linguaggio naturale.
11. Il gruppo Linguaggio Naturale contribuisce ai progetti CONCIERGE, MAIA e FIRST.

This text, even though grammatically correct and perfectly coherent, does not sound natural: there is no linguistic structure that emphasizes the textual links between the discourse units; the anaphoric references are simple repetitions of the object names (as for *gruppo Linguaggio Naturale*). This adds unnecessary verbosity to the text and artificially emphasizes the separation between the sentences. Furthermore, the text planner does not allow a dynamic elaboration of the text based on the information contained in the knowledge base. The structure of the text, therefore, is always the same.

In the following sections we present a text planning architecture that enriches the schematic structure of machine generated texts with discourse structures which can be applied flexibly. We show how the resulting text structure can be used to produce additional textual phenomena and how these principles have been implemented.

3 The Approach

The core of our architecture is based on the text planning system as reported in [7]. It is realized as a modular architecture which distinguishes two general types

---

2. The researchers of the Natural Language group are Lee Fedder, Enrico Franconi, Alberto Lavelli, Bernardo Magnini, Elisabeth Maier, Elena Not, Fabio Pianesi, Oliviero Stock - 3. who is the responsible of the Natural Language group - and Carlo Strapparava. 4. Natural language processing includes syntax, lexical semantics, text planning, parsing, ill-formed input and natural language generation. 5. Fabio Pianesi is interested in syntax. 6. Alberto Lavelli and Bernardo Magnini are interested in lexical semantics. 7. Elisabeth Maier and Elena Not are interested in text planning. 8. Alberto Lavelli is interested in parsing. 9. Alberto Lavelli is interested in ill-formed input. 10. Lee Fedder is interested in natural language generation. 11. The Natural Language group contributes to the CONCIERGE project, MAIA and FIRST.

of knowledge: declarative knowledge, which represents linguistic information, and procedural knowledge, which controls the information flow during the text planning process ([18]). Declarative knowledge has been further specialized into various subcomponents each responsible for a specific set of linguistic decisions.

The core system is able to generate both conventionalized schematic structures – like the RSE text planner – and structures existing on the lower levels of text. In text linguistics the former type of discourse structures is known as *Generic Structure Potential* (GSP, [6]). This approach describes text as a sequence of text units, each unit being specified by means of a semantic predicate. For modeling lower levels of text structures we use a *relational* approach, which is based on RST and related approaches.

The core system has been reimplemented and adapted for the generation of texts as occurring in MAIA and ALFRESCO. Some of the knowledge sources have been significantly extended, others have been merged, new modules have been added. The new architecture now includes the following components:

a network of communicative goals
In computational linguistics the intention behind a discourse unit ([4]) has often been captured by the notion of *communicative goal*. It is commonly agreed upon that communicative goals have an influence on a number of linguistic decisions. For the use of communicative goals in the text planner they have been organized into a hierarchical network. In our system sequences of communicative goals are used to represent the intentional structure of a GSP.

a network of discourse structure relations
RST relations and discourse links identified in related approaches (in the following called *discourse structure relations*) have been collected and classified ([11]). In the given architecture this classification is represented as a decision network which – while traversed – determines the most specific relation being applicable.

a module for the treatment of focus information
Focus corresponds to that discourse element that is in the reader's center of attention. It identifies both at a global and at a local level what the discourse is about. Rules motivating plausible focus shifts in the discourse are used to constrain what has to be generated next.

a module for the treatment of thematic progression
This module, described in detail in section 4, is responsible for the distribution of information across the sentence. Elements of a proposition have to be located at positions with different levels of prominence according to their role in context.

a component for the construction of referring expressions
For every object or abstract entity to be mentioned in the text, this component determines the expression that most effectively refers to it, achieving semantic correctness and linguistic cohesion issues (see section 6).

a knowledge base
The knowledge base consists of two parts: (1) a so-called Italian Upper Model which captures a linguistically motivated representation of meaning and (2) a Domain Model which includes information specific to the application. Within the text planning process the knowledge base is used for the selection of relevant

information and for drawing inferences about the information to be expressed.

None of the above components can be considered in isolation as the linguistic phenomena they are responsible for are strongly interdependent. When an item of a knowledge source is chosen it triggers *realization statements* that impose constraints on other knowledge sources.

To clarify how the core text planner works we outline how a new proposition is planned and embedded in the context. As an example, we take proposition 3 of Example 1 and show how this fragment, which has formerly been produced by the RSE text planner, can be reproduced by the new system. After the generation of proposition 2 the communicative goal DESCRIBE-GROUP-COMPOSITION is active and has to be achieved. The concept in focus is the instance representing **Gruppo Linguaggio Naturale**. The activation of the goal triggers a number of realization statements of which *highlighting* of discourse structure relations is one. Highlighting restricts the number of relations which are considered for the expansion of the text; in our example ELABORATE-FUNCTION is one of the preferred. For one of the instances in proposition 2 – **Stock** – functional information is available. This allows the application of the highlighted relation which is defined as follows:

```
(defsystem
:name elaborate-person
:input elaborate-person
:output ((elaborate-function (select-knowledge functional-attributes)
                             (grow-tree elaborate-function))
         (elaborate-interests (select-knowledge interest-attributes)
                              (grow-tree elaborate-interests))))
```

As specified in the output slot of the definition above the choice of the relation ELABORATE-FUNCTION results in the execution of the two realization statements **select-knowledge** and **grow-tree**. The first of these operations leads to the selection of those information types from the knowledge base, which are able to express the relation at hand; i.e. the function of the instance **Stock** is selected, which is one of **responsibility**. Next, a new text plan node is created (**grow tree**), textual content is filled into the node which is then added to the current text plan using the relation ELABORATE-FUNCTION. In the following we show the SPL for the two propositions 2 and 3:

```
(var1 / identity
 :sem-attributes
 domain (var2 / researcher
         :sem-attributes global-undet-state (var3 / group
                                             :sem-attributes name g-ln )
         :ling-attributes ((det def-plu)) )
 range ((var4 / researcher :sem-attributes name fedder ) ...
        (var5 / researcher :sem-attributes name stock
               elaboration-function (var6 / identity :sem-attributes
                                          domain (var7 / responsabile ..)))))
 :ling-attributes ((given var2)) )
```

In a similar fashion, the whole text as given in Example 1 can be planned. The resulting text structure is reproduced in a graphical form in figure 1[3].

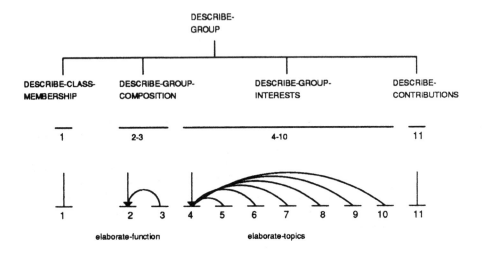

Fig. 1. Textual analysis of Example 1.

As will be shown in the following chapters the core architecture described here was augmented in order to handle a number of textual phenomena: Thematic Progression / Focus Shift, Textual Structures and Referring Expressions.

4 Thematic Progression and Focus Shift

As one of the most important cohesive devices *theme* concerns the distribution of information across the sentence. It is referred to in the literature as the position which serves as the point of departure of individual propositions. Theme is also the element which establishes the link to preceding context. For English, the theme usually occupies the sentence-initial position. The remaining constituents of a sentence are referred to as *rheme*.

Closely related, though not necessarily the same, is the notion of *focus*. We use focus for the discourse element which is in the center of attention. For the development of the focus, specific rules have been identified which have been

---

[3] The numbers in the figure refer to the sentence numbers of Example 1. The elements of the GSP are listed in capital letters; the names of the discourse structure relations are written using lowercase letters. If two text segments are linked by a relation the target of the arrow indicates the *nucleus* of a relation, which is the more important of the two text units. The less important of the two text units, which is sketched as the source of the arrow, is called the *satellite*. Both notions and the way of graphical representation are adopted from RST.

developed into a focus algorithm in [15]. This algorithm was subsequently refined in [2]. In these approaches, for each sentence a current focus (CF) and a potential focus list (PFL) can be determined. The determination of focus is dependent on the CF and the PFL of the previous sentence. Though not necessary for the example discussed here, we claim that the choice of focus (like the choice of theme) depends on the structure of text - and by structure we mean not only the segmentation of a text but also the links between the discourse segments. Therefore, the algorithm as specified by McKeown has to be extended accordingly. This extension will be subject of further research.

When considering Example 1 we find, that the continuation of proposition 4 by sentences 5 through 10 sounds slightly odd because of wrong thematic choice. According to McKeown's focus algorithm the foci of the propositions 5 to 10 of Example 1 are the topics of interest as specified in the preceding proposition 4. While the text sounds unsatisfactory when the focus is put in rhematic position, this is not the case when the focus is located within the theme. In fact, if the same propositions were phrased differently with the topics being in the thematic position instead of the persons, the text would sound better (see Example 2):

Example 2.

4. L'elaborazione del linguaggio naturale comprende la sintassi, la semantica lessicale, la pianificazione del testo, il parsing, l'input malformato e la generazione in linguaggio naturale.
5. **Di sintassi** si interessa Fabio Pianesi. (...)
10. **Di generazione in linguaggio naturale** si interessa Lee Fedder.

For many sentences linked to the surrounding discourse by means of an ELABORATION relation we find the same behaviour (see, for instance, also proposition 3 of example 1). We therefore conclude that the choice of theme and its interdependency with the current focus depend on the relation under consideration. Or in other words, the choice of theme can be made by one realization statement of the discourse structure relation that accesses focus information. Augmented by those new realization statements the new definition of the relation ELABORATE-PERSON looks as presented below. For both relations the focus is the element to be put in thematic position. Focus also contributes to the determination of the most effective referring expressions.

```
(defsystem
:name elaborate-person
:input elaborate-person
:output ((elaborate-function (select-knowledge functional-attributes)
                             (determine-theme equal-current-focus)
                             (grow-tree elaborate-function))
          (elaborate-interests (select-knowledge interest-attributes)
                               (determine-theme equal-current-focus)
                               (grow-tree elaborate-interests)))))
```

5 Explicit Textual Structure

It is commonly agreed upon that the comprehensiveness of a text increases as more markers, which indicate how the text has to be interpreted, are embedded in the text. Discourse structure relations, for example, are often signaled by means of so-called *cue phrases*. While some relations are typically realized by conjunctions (SEQUENCE, for instance, is often signaled by *then*), others do not have characteristic realizations (like most of the relations of the type ELABORATION). Those relations have to be inferred by the reader during the processing of the text.

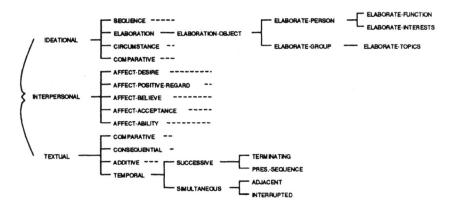

Fig. 2. Fragments of the network of discourse structure relations.

In the classification of discourse structure relations as shown in figure 2 three *meta-functional* types of relations can be distinguished: *ideational* relations, which are mostly concerned with semantics, *interpersonal* relations, which address the participants of a discourse, and *textual* relations, which point out how units of text have to be interpreted in sequence. Ideational and interpersonal relations refer to knowledge *outside* the text, while textual relations concern *text-internal* links. Textual relations, for example, are used to enumerate a sequence of arguments or indicate where a list of arguments begins and where it ends; they signal the interruption and the resumption of the discourse. While ideational and interpersonal relations have been widely acknowledged and integrated in many text planning systems, textual relations so far have not been treated. Also the text planner described in [7] did not generate textual relations, although the potential was available in the knowledge resources. Our text planner was extended in order to treat textual relations and their co-occurrences with ideational relations.

As an example of how our text planner deals with the introduction and realization of textual relations consider example 3. This new improved text has been obtained by introducing a textual relation which explicitly signals the end of the (ideational) elaboration sequence contained in the sentences 5 through 9.

250

Example 3.

4. L'elaborazione del linguaggio naturale comprende la sintassi, la semantica lessicale, la pianificazione del testo, il parsing, l'input malformato e la generazione in linguaggio naturale.
5. Di sintassi si interessa Fabio Pianesi.
6. Di semantica lessicale si interessano Bernardo Magnini e Alberto Lavelli.
7. Alberto Lavelli si interessa anche di parsing e di input malformato.
8. Di pianificazione del testo si interessano Elisabeth Maier ed Elena Not.
9. Di generazione in linguaggio naturale, infine, si interessa Lee Fedder.

On the ideational plane propositions 5 through 9 are linked to proposition 4 by means of the relation ELABORATE-TOPICS. On the second level of analysis, propositions 5 through 9 are linked to each other by means of the relation TERMINATING. The former relation cannot be indicated with cue phrases - it is signaled by means of lexical identity chains ([6]). The textual relation, instead, is responsible for the choice of the conjunction *infine*, which indicates where the chain of elaborations ends. The presence of such a marker in the text facilitates the reading especially in cases like the above, where it has to be inferred by the reader which and how many units of text are related.

6 Generation of Referring Expressions

Reference is one of the major sources of linguistic cohesion, since it guides the attention of the reader through a chain of sentences where identical objects occur. Reference employs compact linguistic forms which simplify the discourse and allow the identification of the intended referent (object, abstract entity or piece of text). Referring expressions also mirror the salience of the referent: personal pronouns are used to highlight the elements in higher focus, while various types of deictic adjectives and pronouns can be used to signal various levels of salience for elements mentioned recently. If a definite or indefinite noun phrase (NP) is used, the head noun and its most appropriate modifiers are chosen.

In some of the earlier generation systems the referring expression problem was only partially addressed. In the TEXT system ([15]), for example, only some pronominalizations are dealt with during the surface generation. [1] considered the influence of the speaker's communicative intentions on the choice of the most effective NP. Recent approaches proposed more complex algorithms that address the generation of attributive expressions and discriminant expressions (for a complete survey see [20]).

It is widely recognized that discourse structure plays a fundamental role in influencing the generation of referring expressions: both segment boundaries and focus influence the objects' degree of salience and thus constrain rules for pronominalization and for the choice of definite NPs. As the *discourse context* changes during the progress of the discourse the salience of text segments is updated.

The discourse structure consists of different and complementary layers of structure ([4]): intentional structure, linguistic structure that signals segment boundaries, attentional structure that mirrors the progression of the focus throughout the discourse and semantic structure expressed in the links between the propositions.

In our text planner every time a new sentence is added to the text plan, the discourse structure information consisting of the four layers as introduced above is used to decide whether the current text segment has to be expanded or whether a new segment has to be created. In any case, the set of text segments is updated. Also, the new *context set* is determined, which consists of all those entities, which are mentioned in the text segments with high salience values. The elements of the context set contribute to the disambiguation of anaphora.

When an **anaphoric reference** has to be generated, conditions for intersentence pronominalization are checked first[4]. Pronouns are introduced to refer to objects with the highest level of salience by using the *basic rule of centering* ([5]). This rule specifies that a pronoun has to be used when the focus element of the current utterance also serves as focus in the previous utterance; this rule does not apply to sentences belonging to different segments[5]. This simple, but rather efficient rule does not treat multiple pronouns which occur in the same sentence but refer to different objects: this is subject of future research.

If the generation of anaphoric pronouns is to be excluded and if the object to be referred to is neither in focus nor does it belong to the discourse context then it has to be reintroduced by means of a **proper noun**.

For the generation of a **definite NP** that discriminates the referent from the other elements in the context set, we have adopted an approach similar to the one presented in [20]. First a concept that describes the semantic type for the object is chosen. This is done by taking into account the information stored in the domain model and some concept preference rules based on pragmatic settings (e.g. the communicative goal and the user's level of expertise). If the semantic type of this concept cannot provide sufficient discriminatory power, more attributes have to be added, until the referent is uniquely identified ([17]).

In the following we show how referring expressions can improve the linguistic cohesion of our sample text. Using the algorithm described above Example 4 can be generated.

Example 4.

1. Il gruppo Linguaggio Naturale appartiene all'area Interfacce.
2. I ricercatori **del gruppo** sono Lee Fedder, Enrico Franconi, Alberto Lavelli, Bernardo Magnini, Elisabeth Maier, Elena Not, Fabio Pianesi, Oliviero Stock
3. - che e' il responsabile **del gruppo** -
2. (*cont.*) e Carlo Strapparava.
6. Di semantica lessicale si interessano Bernardo Magnini e Alberto Lavelli.

---

[4] Rules for intra-sentence occurrences of pronouns are encoded directly in the grammar and are dealt with by the tactical component.

[5] Using a non-pronominal anaphora signals the transition to a new segment determined by the discourse structure.

7. **Alberto Lavelli** si interessa anche di parsing e di input malformato.
10. **Il gruppo Linguaggio Naturale** contribuisce ai progetti CONCIERGE, MAIA e FIRST.

In sentence 2, the head noun *ricercatori* is modified to express that the researchers belong to the Natural Language group. Since the reference to the group crosses a segment boundary a definite NP is preferred over a pronoun. In sentence 3 segment boundaries do not contribute to the determination of the referring expression for *group*. A pronoun cannot be used because the referent is not in focus. Therefore a definite NP is used. In the second part of sentence 6, a personal pronoun cannot be chosen for *Alberto Lavelli* since it would create ambiguity with respect to *Bernardo Magnini*, the other element in focus. The name of the researcher is thus repeated. Sentence 9 initiates a new discourse segment that is independent from the others. The reintroduction of the full name for the Natural Language group is chosen to signal this fact.

7 Conclusion and Future Work

In this paper we discussed the extensions of a text planner in order to generate a number of textual phenomena: textual discourse links and their corresponding cue phrases, thematic progression and referring expressions. Other phenomena, which also increase the textuality of discourse like lexical cohesion and temporal references are currently under investigation. Further improvements concern the treatment of pronominalization in generation. New rules for the introduction of pronouns will be defined that depend on context information like discourse structure relations, segmentation, semantic and pragmatic features.

Currently the planner is embedded in a multimedia-environment. In the near future the planner will also be integrated in a multilingual setting (English, German, Italian). Special emphasis will be given to the generation of procedural texts, like e.g. instructions.

References

1. Douglas E. Appelt: Planning English Sentences. Cambridge University Press (1985)
2. Susan E. Brennan, Marilyn W. Frieman, and Carl J. Pollard: A centering approach to pronouns. In: Proceedings of the 25th Annual Meeting of the Association for Computational Linguistics, Standford, California (1987) 155–162
3. Giuseppe Carenini, Fabio Pianesi, Marco Ponzi, and Oliviero Stock: Natural language generation and hypertext access. Technical Report 9201-06, IRST, Trento-Povo, Italy (1992). to appear in Applied Artificial Intelligence, Hemisphere Publishing Company, Washington, 7(2) (1993)
4. Barbara J. Grosz and Candace L. Sidner: Attention, intentions and the structure of discourse. Journal of Computational Linguistics 12(3) (1986)
5. B.J. Grosz, A. Joshi, and S. Weinstein: Providing a unified account of definite noun phrases in discourse. In: Proceedings of the Twenty-first Annual Meeting of the Association for Computational Linguistics (1983)

6. M.A.K. Halliday and Ruqaiya Hasan: Language, context and text: Aspects of language in a social-semiotic perspective. Deakin University Press (1985)
7. Eduard Hovy, Julia Lavid, Elisabeth Maier, Vibhu Mittal, and Cécile Paris: Employing knowledge resources in a new text planner architecture. In Robert Dale, Eduard Hovy, Dietmar Rösner, and Oliviero Stock (eds.): Aspects of Automated Natural Language Generation; Proceedings of 6th International Workshop on Natural Language Processing. Springer (1992) 46–57
8. Eduard H. Hovy: Planning coherent multisentential text. In: Proceedings of ACL (1988)
9. Information Sciences Institute, Marina del Rey, California. The PENMAN User Guide (1989)
10. Robert Kasper and Richard Whitney: SPL: A sentence plan language for text generation. Technical report, USC/ISI (1989)
11. Elisabeth Maier and Eduard Hovy: Organising discourse structure relations using metafunctions. In: Helmut Horacek and Michael Zock (eds.): New Concepts in Natural Language Processing, Pinter Publishers, London (1993)
12. Elisabeth A. Maier: The extension of a text planner for the treatment of multiple links between text units. In: Proceedings of the 4th European Workshop on Natural Language Generation, 103–114, also available as Technical Report No. 9301-15, IRST, Trento-Povo, Italy (1993).
13. William C. Mann and Sandra A. Thompson: Rhetorical Structure Theory: A theory of text organization. In: Livia Polanyi (ed.): The Structure of Discourse. Ablex Publishing Corporation (1987)
14. K.F. McCoy: Contextual effects on responses to misconceptions. In: G. Kempen (ed.): Natural Language Generation. Martinus Nijhoff Publishers (1987) 43–54
15. Kathleen R. McKeown: Text generation - Using discourse strategies and focus constraints to generate natural language text, Cambridge University Press (1985)
16. Johanna D. Moore and Cécile L. Paris: Planning text for advisory dialogues. In: Proceedings of ACL, US Chapter, Vancouver (1989)
17. Elena Not: Generazione di espressioni in linguaggio naturale che descrivono le entità del dominio. Technical Report 9301-05, IRST, Trento-Povo, Italy (1993)
18. Cécile L. Paris and Elisabeth A. Maier: Knowledge resources or decisions? In: IJCAI-91 Workshop on Decision Making throughout the Generation Process (1991)
19. Cécile L. Paris: Combining discourse strategies to generate descriptions to users along a naive/expert spectrum. In: Proceedings of IJCAI, (1987) 626–632
20. Ehud Reiter and Robert Dale: A fast algorithm for the generation of referring expressions. In: Proceedings of COLING-92 (1992)
21. Oliviero Stock: Natural language and exploration of an information space. In: Proceedings of IJCAI-91, Sydney, Australia (1991)
22. Luigi Stringa: Un approccio integrato all' intelligenza artificiale: Il progetto MAIA dell' IRST. AI*IA Notizie 4(1) (1991)

Production of Cooperative Answers on the Basis of Partial Knowledge in Information-Seeking Dialogues

L. Ardissono, L. Lesmo, A. Lombardo, D. Sestero

Dipartimento di Informatica - Università di Torino
C.so Svizzera 185 - 10149 Torino - Italia
E-mail lesmo@di.unito.it

Abstract

This paper presents the component of a plan-based consultation system that selects the relevant information to be included in the answer to the user's question. The relevant information can be determined on the basis of both the recognized plan and the form of the input question. We classify the possible user requests by establishing a correspondence with the possible answers.

We show how it is possible to respond in a cooperative way also in presence of partial knowledge about the constraints of the plans. Moreover, in order to limit the clarification dialogues that the system may need to carry out in the recognition of the user's plans and goals, we characterize the notion of relevance of the ambiguity among alternative hypotheses on the user's plans and goals on the basis of the characteristics of the constraints present in the plans.

Introduction

Natural language interaction between a human user and a computer is often more fluent and natural if the machine recognizes the goals that the user has in mind [Allen, 83]. On the basis of the recognized goal(s) the automated system will be able to produce a cooperative response, perhaps correcting some erroneous assumptions the user has made. Unfortunately, the user can be more or less clear in making his/her goals explicit: often, only some detailed subgoals are expressed, or the desire to get some information, without a statement of the reason why that piece of information is required. So, the process of goal recognition consists in inferring some general goals, as well as the plan the user has adopted to achieve it, from the incomplete data provided by the input utterances.

In this paper we present an approach to the generation of cooperative and flexible answers in a plan-based consultation system on a restricted domain. We assume that the most reasonable response can be determined on the basis of both the recognized goal and the form of the input question. So, we must face the classical problem of plan recognition with the goal of identifying the actual plan at a level of detail sufficient for determining which information can be useful to the user. Moreover, we need to classify both the possible user requests and the possible answers by establishing some form of correspondence between them.

As far as plan recognition is concerned, we adopted as the basic framework the model proposed in [Carberry, 88], [Carberry, 90]. However, we believe that an important aspect in response generation is the trade-off between the use of lengthy clarification dialogues (necessary if the user's goals have to be fully understood) and the requirement of making the dialogues as short as possible to increase the acceptability and the naturalness of the system. In order to limit the size of the dialogues, we follow Van Beek and Cohen's proposal [Van Beek and Cohen 91]: they introduce the notion of relevance of the ambiguity among the hypotheses on the user's plans and goals. They state that an ambiguity is relevant only when it leads a cooperative system to produce different answers, each of them associated to a different hypothesis on the user's plan. In general, an answer consists of the basic information the user asked for and may include some extra information (as suggestions to make his/her plan better or reasons why the recognized plan cannot be executed). When supplementary information has to be provided the correct recognition of plans and goals is of paramount importance. However, it is clear that if all the plans the user is possibly pursuing are affected by the same problems, the same answer is suitable for all of them; only in the opposite case a clarification dialogue is needed. Van Beek and Cohen evaluate the relevance on the basis of the constraints that appear in the alternative possible plans: in fact are just the unsatisfied constraints that must be communicated to the user as reasons for the failure of the plan.

We extend the notion of relevance in two ways:

- First, we argue that complete information on the truth value of constraints is not always available when the system builds the answer. In particular, the truth value of some constraints could be known only to the user, whereas in other cases neither the user nor the system can (at the time of the interaction) tell whether the constraint is satisfied or not. We show that even in these cases a useful answer can be given, although less specific than the one that could be built in case all the useful information is available.

- Second, in Van Beek and Cohen's approach the only source of ambiguity is related to constraints. On the other hand, we suppose that actions may be executed in different ways (the alternative ways of performing them are represented as different specializations). This must be taken into account when the relevance of an ambiguity is evaluated.

As far as the actual production of the answer is concerned, it is known that in some approaches (e.g. [Pilkington, 92]) the generation of answers is guided by frames that define their basic structure (e.g. answers that describe a certain topic, answers comparing different topics, etc.). We consider a set of basic deep structures for questions (see [Carberry, 90]) and we analyze the structure of cooperative answers proper for each of them. Afterwards, relevant information for the answer is determined through the analysis of the contextual information (collected in previous sentences), the current situation (information extracted from the question of the user), the plan identified on the basis of this information and the knowledge about the organization and the structural components for a proper answer to that kind of deep structure.

The Consultation System

The consultation system, [Ardissono et al 93], delivers information on a restricted domain. The strategies for inferring the intentions of the user and for building the answers are domain independent, while a plan library holds the domain knowledge. The system analyzes task-oriented dialogues where the user asks questions to build a plan that he is going to perform in a future time. A user model is integrated into the system in order to evaluate the effects that it can have on the flexibility and the cooperativity of the answers returned to the user.

The domain we are considering is a CS Department; in particular, the consultation system should provide the user with useful information about the activities s/he can execute in the Department and the offered services. For example, how to access the library, when and where to talk to a professor, etc.

The knowledge about actions and plans is stored in a plan library [Ardissono et al, 93] structured on the basis of two main hierarchies: the Decomposition Hierarchy (DH) and the Generalization Hierarchy (GH) [Kautz and Allen, 86]. The first one describes the plans associated with the actions and is used for explaining how to execute a complex action. The second one expresses the relation among more general and more specific actions (the greater specificity is due to additional restrictions on parameters).

Each action is characterized by its applicability conditions (which are of three types: preconditions, constraints and restrictions on the action parameters), its effects and the associated plan. In general, actions may have more than one decomposition, that are represented as specific cases of the main action and are differentiated on the basis of the modality of execution of the action (for example, in fig.1 the actions TALK-PROF-BY-PHONE and TALK-PROF-FACE-TO-FACE represent two different ways of performing the TALK-PROF action).

We suppose that the system has complete knowledge on the plans that can be performed in the domain and that the user's world model is consistent with the system's one[1]. So, given the user's utterances, the system is always able to find some plans pertinent to them. On the other hand, even in its domain of competence, there exist conditions that the system is not completely informed about. In these cases, it may be able to suggest a plan for getting the information.

The operations of the system may be grouped in two main phases: a hypothesis construction and a response generation phase.

The hypothesis construction is carried out by means of the following steps:

1) Action identification: a set of actions is selected from the plan library, each of them possibly representing the aspect of the task on which the user's attention is currently focused.

2) Focusing: the set of Context Models (CM), representing the current hypotheses on the user's plan, produced by the analysis of the previous sentences, is filtered and updated to take into account the shift in focus signalled by the user's utterance.

3) Expansion of the CMs that are part of only one higher level plan up through the DH, in order to gain a larger view of the user's goals.

4) Downward expansion along the DH: For each CM, its actions are repeatedly decomposed into more elementary ones, until all steps of the CM are sufficiently simple for the user. In this way, the information necessary for generating an answer is collected.

5) Backward expansion through enablement links: each CM is expanded in order to include the actions needed for satisfying the preconditions which the user is supposed not to be able to plan by himself. When a precondition to be expanded is of the form " Know(IS, x)" and the system knows the value of "x" it can include such information in the response, so avoiding the expansion.

After all of these steps have been performed, the system has a clearer idea of the user's possible goals and plans. Now, it can start up the process of answer generation, which will be analyzed in details in the following paragraphs.

---

[1] For example it is not the case that the user's utterances refer to an attribute of an entity that is not defined in the system knowledge base.

On the Relevance of Ambiguities

As stated above, we avoid lengthy clarification dialogues when they are useless, i.e. when their purpose is to distinguish among candidate plans all of which fail because of the same unsatisfied constraints [Van Beek & Cohen, 91]. The first thing to do is to evaluate the plans, in order to decide whether they are correct and can be carried out without problems, or if any restriction on the parameters or constraint fails to be verified. This task is accomplished by a critiquing procedure that extracts, for each candidate, the possible failing conditions.

However, complete information on the truth value of constraints is not always available when the system should build the answer. In particular, the constraints present in the plans can be divided into three categories: some of them are known to the system (they are in its domain of competence) and are to be used in order to evaluate the relevance of ambiguity. Some involve information concerning the user (e.g. if he is a student) and they are generally not known to the system; they can be included in the answer as assumptions for its validity, in order to avoid further questions to the user. Finally, the truth value of some constraints may be unknown to both the user and the system, but the user can verify them by himself (e.g. the availability of a book in the library); these also should be included in the answer, by providing a recommendation to check them. This classification of constraints supports the construction of partial answers to the user's questions, so avoiding the necessity to collect all information required to check the validity of the candidate plans. In this way, dialogues are shorter and they do not imply too many questions to the user.

Another important aspect of the ambiguity among the hypotheses is that sometimes all the plans selected as alternative hypotheses fail due to some set of constraints definitely false. In these cases, it may happen that the set of failing constraints differ from one hypothesis to another, but they have a not empty intersection that suffices for ruling out all the alternatives. So, the ambiguity could be relevant from Van Beek and Cohen's point of view (because different negative answers could be provided), but a single negative answer specifying the common constraints could be supplied, so avoiding any clarification dialogue. For example, if somebody asks how to access the library, the different selected plans (borrowing a book, consulting a paper, etc.) are characterized by different sets of constraints. However, if we suppose that the library is closed for repair for a long period, a negative answer mentioning the failing constraint "open(library)" is enough as a motivation for the impossibility to pursue the action[2].

Such considerations bring about a further distinction on constraints. In particular, we define the permanent constraints as those that do not change their truth value for a long time. The notion of permanence is quite fuzzy and depends on the context. So, for example, the constraint "open(library)" is not permanent in case the library is regularly open every day.

On the basis of these ideas, we refine the notion of relevant ambiguity by stating that the relevance should be evaluated by taking into account only the constraints whose truth value is known to the system, while the others are considered later in the

---

2 Notice that the same considerations apply to the more general case where each alternative hypothesis is affected by a different negative permanent constraint, with the only difference that the negative answer to the user must be structured in such a way as to explain the motivation for the failure of each alternative. So, for each of the involved permanent constraints, the list of the affected plans should be given.

answer. Moreover, the clarification dialogue can be avoided when permanent false constraints affect each of the alternative hypotheses.

The above considerations reduce the number of situations where the ambiguity is relevant with respect to Van Beek and Cohen. On the other hand, by taking into account the presence of different ways of performing the actions, we introduce a further source of ambiguity. However, by analyzing the information to be included in the various types of answers, we see that sometimes the problems due to this kind of ambiguity can be disregarded in the construction of the answer. For this reason, we treat it separately from the previous one, by starting up an appropriate clarification dialogue when necessary.

The Structure of the Answers

In order to classify the answers that the system must produce, we consider a number of typical user's utterances in information seeking dialogues that are represented through immediate goals [Carberry 90][3]. Since we do not consider the problem of indirect speech acts, we suppose that the immediate goal directly corresponds to the user's intentions. The structure of the answers is derived from the plans identified for the user's goals and it is defined on the basis of the form of the immediate goal. In particular, we consider the following basic components of answers:

1. The set of instances satisfying the constraints specified in the user's utterance.
2. A description of the overall applicability conditions of a certain action or plan[4] identified from the user's utterance.
3. A description of the plans selected from the user's utterance. The answer includes two different kinds of information: a top-down hierarchical description of the actions composing the plans and a possible description of the steps that enable the actions present in the plans by making their preconditions true.
4. The truth value of a certain condition. Information on the possibility of executing a certain action in the domain is a special case, since the evaluation of the overall applicability conditions of the action is required.

In the following, we will match the general patterns for the questions with the form of the answers.

a) Information Seeker (IS) states that s/he wants a certain condition to be true, or s/he wants to perform a certain action.
Want (IS, Know (IP, Want (IS, X)))
(X is a condition or an action; IP is the Information Provider)

a.1) X is of the form *know x*
Ex a1:*I want to know the timetable of Geometry*

---

3 An immediate goal is a logical representation of the user's intentions extracted from the semantic representation of his/her utterance.

4 In general, information about the possible consequences of the action (or plan) may be part of the answer. However, a general treatment of this problem is not considered, since it would require to reason on the possible evolution of the world due to the performance of the actions.

- If the system knows the list of instances satisfying the description x, such list is returned as direct answer. The response also includes the description of the partial plan represented by the CM. In case more than one decomposition is compatible with the input, a clarification dialogue is started up, in order to solve the ambiguity.

For example, referring to Ex a1, a possible answer is[5]:

It is: Monday 16.00-18.00, Wednesday 9.00-11.00, ...; the lessons will be given in classroom number 5.

- If the system doesn't know x, still it may be able to suggest a plan for retrieving the information. In order to be cooperative, the answer is integrated with information about the action involved by X (again, in case of ambiguity between multiple decompositions, a clarification dialogue is started up).

With respect to the previous example a reasonable answer could just be:

You can find it in the show-case, near the class-rooms. The lessons will be given in classroom number 5.

If no action whose applicability conditions are verified is found, the system returns a negative answer explaining to the user the motivations of the failure.

a.2) X is a condition different from *know x*

Ex a2:*I would like to have the authorization to access the library*

This case is dealt with as in the second point of a.1), with the only difference that the condition to be satisfied does not involve the predicate Know. The response to Ex a2 is:

To access the library you have to be a computer science student or you need an authorization from a faculty of the department.

The library is open from 9.00 a.m. to 17.00 p.m. every working day.

a.3) X is an action

Ex a3:*I need to talk to Prof. Smith*

If the overall applicability conditions of the action are satisfied, a description of it is returned, otherwise a negative answer is returned. A major difference from cases a.1) and a.2) is the fact that here the action is directly mentioned by the user's utterance instead of being inferred by the system. No clarification dialogue is started up, because we suppose that the user is interested in all the possible ways to perform X; the answer includes the information present in the CMs extended with information about the actions that represent the different ways of performing X as specified in the plan library. Of course, if the active CMs already refer to a specific case, that means that the dialogue so far has established an interest of the user, so only he information relevant to that case is included. We will consider in detail the answer to Ex a3 in the next section.

b) IS states that a certain condition P is true.

---

[5] For the sake of readability here, as in the following, we write the answers in a linguistic form although no language generator currently exists; the actual output is composed of a list of logical forms, representing the components of the selected plans that have to be included into the answer (preconditions, constraints, decompositions, etc).

Want (IS, Know (IP, P))
(P is a condition).

Ex b1:*I'm studying the material for Geometry*
In this case an acknowledgement is returned and the system waits for more information.

c) IS wants to know how to satisfy a condition, or how to perform an action.
Want (IS, Know-how (IS, X, Y))[6]

This can be subdivided into three cases that correspond to and are treated as a.1-a.3.
The examples are:
Ex c1:*How can I know the timetable for Geometry?*
Ex c2:*How can I have the authorization to use the library?*
Ex c3:*How do I talk to Prof. Smith?*

d) IS wants to know if a certain condition P is true.
Want (IS, Knowif (IS, P))

Ex d1:*Is the library open today?*
•If P is true, the system answers in a positive way and complete the answer with the description of the applicability conditions of the partial plan recognized by the hypotheses construction phase.
•If P is false, the system returns the list of instances that satisfy the condition and complete the answer with the description of the applicability conditions of the recognized partial plan. It is interesting to consider which subset of the instances of the predicate is meaningful for the user in questions like " Is Prof. Smith the teacher of Geometry?". In this case, if Prof. Smith is not the right teacher, there are two kinds of alternative responses, depending on which of the two noun phrases (NP) the user's attention is fixed on: in this case, the list of the courses taught by Prof. Smith, or the list of teachers for the Geometry course. To solve this ambiguity, semantic and contextual information may be very useful. Our system chooses the response relative to the NP associated to the most relevant referent. In order to do that, it searches the CMs starting from the current focus and looking for the referent of each of the individuals mentioned in the question; the system builds the answer by selecting the subset of instances that satisfy the condition in the question and such that one of their components is the found referent.
•If the system does not know the truth value of P, the same treatment of the second case of a.1) applies.

Referring to Ex. d1, the possible kinds of answers are:
Yes. Remember that to access the library you have to be a computer science student or you need an authorization from a faculty of the department.

---

[6] For the sake of simplicity in the form of the immediate goals, we introduce a new operator Know-how, defined on the basis of Knowref as:
Know-how (IS, X, Y) ≡ Knowref (IS, Y,
  (Y = decomposition(X) OR (∃A (X = effects(A) AND Y = decomposition(A)))))

No, it will be open tomorrow from 9.00 a.m. to 5.00 p.m. Remember that to access the library you have to...
I don't know. Look for the timetable into the show-case next to the door.

e) IS wants to know if a certain action A is valid in a certain situation.
   Want (IS, Knowif (IS, Executable (A)))

   Ex e1:*May I meet Prof. Smith today?*
   This case is treated in the same way as a.3 and the two utterances have the same answer. A detailed description is in the next section. A possible negative answer is:
   No, you can not. Prof. Smith is not in the department today. He receives every Tuesday from 9.00 a.m. to 11.00 a.m. in office 42.

f) IS wants to know the referent satisfying a certain description P.
   Want (IS, Knowref (IS, x, P(x)))

   Ex f1:*Who is the teacher of Geometry?*
   This case is dealt with in a way similar to a.1, although the syntactic form of the immediate goal is not the same; the only difference is that here the direct answer consists of the referent satisfying the description, while in a.1 it contains the instances satisfying the condition mentioned in the question.

g) IS wants to know the set of instances satisfying a certain condition P occurring as applicability condition of a certain action A .
   Want (IS, Knowref (IS, x, (P(x) AND App-cond (P, A))))
   (where App-cond states that the action A has the condition P among its preconditions, constraints or restrictions on the parameters)

   Ex g1:*I would like to know the name of the teacher of Geometry, to talk to him.*
   g is a special case of f in which the user specifies the action involved by P he is interested in. It is treated in the same way as f, apart from the fact that if more than one way of performing A is selected, and none is already present in the active CM, a clarification dialogue is started up to select the decomposition interesting for the user, that will be described in the answer. For instance, if one can talk to the teacher of Geometry only by phone, then the phone-number should be included in the answer. In case more than one alternative is available (talk by phone or talk face to face) a clarification dialogue is started up.

In the classification above, we often used the tasks of describing a partial plan and generating a negative answer.
   1) The description of a partial plan contains the following information:
the action involved in the plan; the list of the constraints of the CM that involve information concerning the user and with unknown value; the list of preconditions of the action that the user can plan by himself and a trace of the planning of the preconditions that are too difficult for him (for the preconditions of the form Know(IS, x), if the system knows the value of "x", it gives directly such information); the list of constraints of the CM that involve information directly verifiable by the user. Furthermore, for each constraint in the domain of competence of the system, the

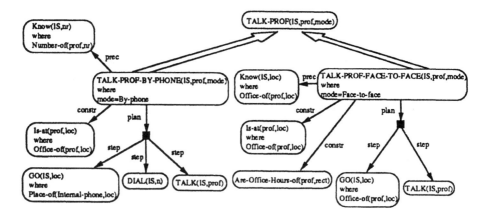

Fig. 1. A portion of the plan hierarchy. TALK-PROF is an action that can be accomplished either via the TALK-PROF-BY-PHONE action or via the TALK-PROF-FACE-TO-FACE action (that specialize the parameter "mode" representing the modality of execution of the TALK-PROF action). Each action can specify preconditions for its execution ("prec" arcs) and constraints ("constr" arcs). For instance TALK-PROF-BY-PHONE requires that the phone number is known (a precondition, since some other action can be done to make it true) and that the professor is in his/her office (a constraint, since it is beyond the control of the user of the system). It is further specified via the plan: go to a phone, then dial the number and finally talk to the professor.

system lists to the user the values of the parameters satisfying the constraint[7] (see the example in the next section).

2) The generation of a negative answer is structured in the following way:
for each failing plan: if it contains a permanent false constraint, the name of the main action of the plan is specified to the user, together with the failing constraint. Otherwise, if the plan fails because of at least one false constraint that is not permanent, the name of the main action of the plan is specified, together with the whole set of failing constraints. In this case, the latter specification is fundamental to avoid that the user believes that it is possible to execute the plan when just one of the constraints becomes true, without being aware of the others. In both cases, as in the description of the action, the system provides the list of values that verify the constraints in the domain of competence of the system.

An Example

Let us consider the example a.3, that we repeat below for convenience of the reader:
Ex a3:*I need to talk to Prof. Smith*

---

7   Although giving the list of instances satisfying the constraints could seem a redundancy when they are true, we think that this kind of information is very important in information-seeking dialogues, where the user may be interested in a plan that is going to be executed in the future.

By analyzing the immediate goal the system identifies the action TALK-PROF (see fig.1).

Let's suppose that the sentence is uttered during the office hours of Prof. Smith. Since the constraint is known to the system, it knows that its value is true. On the other hand, it does not know if the professor is in his office (constraint Is-at is unknown). In this case the response covers both the actions of talking by phone and talking face to face because the immediate goal explicitly mentions the TALK-PROF action; in particular, a precondition of talking by phone is that one has to know the phone number, so such information is included in the answer. As far as the action of talking face to face is concerned, the answer includes the office number of the professor (that is a precondition of the action) and his office hours (values of the parameters that satisfy the constraint of the action). Moreover, the answer contains a warning to the user about the need to check whether Prof. Smith is in his office, because this constraint (unknown to the system) can be directly verified by the user. The actual information currently delivered by the system is the following:

TALK-PROF-BY-PHONE:
- values of the parameters of the preconditions:
Number-of(Smith, 64)
- Actions in the plan:
GO(IS, Int-phone-loc), DIAL(IS, 64), TALK(IS, Smith)
- Constraints to be verified by the user:
Is-at(Smith, Office-42)

TALK-PROF-FACE-TO-FACE:
- values of the parameters of the preconditions:
Office-of(Smith, 42)
- Actions in the plan:
GO(IS, Office-64), TALK(IS, Smith)
- Constraints to be verified by the user:
Is-at(Smith, Office-42)
- Values of the parameters of the constraints known by the system:
Are-office-hours-of(Smith, "Tuesday 9.00 a.m. - 11.00 a.m.")

A possible linguistic description of the output above is:
You can phone Prof. Smith by going to the internal phone and dialling the number 64. Or you can talk to him face to face by going to the office 42 on Tuesday from 9.00 a.m. to 11.00 a.m. In both cases, remember to check that he is in his office.

Let's suppose to add to the plans in the figure the permanent constraint that teachers are not absent for a long time. If Prof. Smith is on vacation, this constraint invalids both actions, independently from the other ones. For this reason, they can be disregarded and a negative answer containing only this constraint is returned. The output of the system is:
TALK-PROF:
negative permanent constraint: Is-at(Smith, Office-42)
and the corresponding linguistic form is:
You can not, because Prof. Smith is not in the Department for a long period.

Notice that, in case the constraint Are-office-hours-of is false, in Van Beek and Cohen's approach the ambiguity would be relevant, because there are different failing constraints.

Conclusions

In this paper, we presented a component of a plan-based consultation system, namely the one that takes care of selecting the relevant information to be included in the answer to the user's question.

One of the main goals has been to limit the clarification dialogues that the system carries out in order to recognize more precisely the user's plans and goals. This has been achieved by adopting an approach similar to the one proposed in [Van Beek and Cohen, 91], but extending it to cover the cases of ignorance about the truth value of some constraints associated to the plans. A further extension concerns the ability of the system to manage the case where different plans are associated with the same action.

In order to focus on the main topic (response generation), the description of the system had to be simplified. One of the features that are relevant in the present context, but that could not be discussed, is the adoption of a double stereotype approach [Chin, 89] for the description of the difficulty level of the elements in the knowledge base and to characterize the knowledge typical of the users on the system domain of competence. As a first step in this direction, we introduced three competence levels for the user and three difficulty levels for the tasks in the plans of the plan library [Ardissono at al, 93]. Information about the difficulty degree of the various actions is embedded in the plan library by labelling the plans with a weight to be intended as a requested competence threshold (if the user is sufficiently expert for an action, it is taken as elementary for him, otherwise its steps must be specified). Preconditions are labelled in an analogous way, to specify which users know how to plan them by themselves and which ones need an explanation. Although some people think that the double stereotype approach is too restrictive, we think that a generalized version of it as described in [Cahour, 92], [Jameson, 92] can be a good basis for adapting the performance of a system to the different kinds of user.

Of course, many other extensions should be introduced to make the system a really "natural" consultant. Among others, it seems that the most important steps would be toward the integration of pragmatic knowledge of the domain of interest and toward the management of uncertain knowledge about plans and goals. The first extension is required if topic changes in dialogues due to the contemporary existence of different goals have to be accounted for (as suggested by [Conte et al, 89]). The ability to handle uncertain knowledge is needed if the preferences shown by humans in understanding the interlocutor have to be modelled accurately [Carberry, 90b]. In any case, we believe that the selection of the appropriate information to be communicated to the user is a fundamental step that makes the interaction simpler and more natural.

At the moment the plan recognition component of the consultation system is implemented, while the response generation module is not. The implementation language is Common Lisp. The user' utterances are now inputted to the system in their logical form. However, we are going to connect the consultation system to the natural language interpreter GULL [Ardissono et al, 91], [Terenziani, 91], in order to build their semantic representation automatically.

References

[Allen, 83] J.F.Allen. Recognizing intentions from natural language utterances. In M. Brady and R.C. Berwick editors, *Computational Models of Discourse*. 107-166. MIT Press, 1983.

[Ardissono et al, 91] L.Ardissono, L.Lesmo, P.Pogliano, P.Terenziani. Interpretation of Definite Noun Phrases. *Proc. 12th Int. Conf. on Artificial Intelligence*. Sydney, Australia, 1991.

[Ardissono et al, 93] L.Ardissono, A.Lombardo, D.Sestero. A Flexible Approach to Cooperative Response Generation in Information-Seeking Dialogues. *Proc. 31st Annual Meeting ACL*. Columbus, Ohio, 1993.

[Cahour, 92] B.Cahour. How do experts categorize the interlocutor during consultation dialogues? *Proc. 3rd Int. Workshop on User Modeling*, 84-93 Wadern, 1992.

[Carberry, 88] S.Carberry. Modeling the User's Plans and Goals. *Computational Linguistics* 14, 23-37 [1988].

[Carberry, 90] S.Carberry. *Plan Recognition in Natural Language Dialogue*. ACL-MIT Press, 1990.

[Carberry, 90b] S.Carberry. Incorporating Default Inferences into Plan Recognition. *Proc. 8th Conf. AAAI*, 471-478 Boston, 1990.

[Chin, 89] D.N.Chin. KNOME: modeling what the user knows in UC. In A.Kobsa and W.Wahlster editors, *User Models in Dialog Systems*. Springer Verlag, 1989.

[Conte et al, 89] R.Conte, C.Castelfranchi, A.Cesta. Natural Topic-Change in Plan-Recognition. *Proc. 4th Portuguese Conference on Artificial Intelligence*, Lisboa, 1989.

[Jameson, 92] A.Jameson. Generalizing the Double-Stereotype Approach: A Psychological Perspective. *Proc. 3rd Int. Workshop on User Modeling*, 69-83 Wadern, 1992.

[Kautz and Allen, 86] H.A.Kautz, J.F.Allen. Generalized Plan Recognition. *Proc. 5th Conf. AAAI*, 32-37 Philadelphia, 1986.

[Pilkington, 92] R.M.Pilkington. Question-Answering for Intelligent On-Line Help: The Process of Intelligent Responding. *Cognitive Science* 16, 455-489, 1992.

[Terenziani, 91] P. Terenziani. A Rule Based Approach to the Semantic Interpretation of Natural Language. In *Computer and Artificial Intelligence*, Vol.10, N.3, 193-214, 1991.

[Van Beek and Cohen, 91] P.Van Beek, R.Cohen. Resolving Plan Ambiguity for Cooperative Response Generation. *Proc. 12th Int. Joint Conf. on Artificial Intelligence*, 938-944, Sydney, 1991.

Coping with Modifiers in a Restricted Domain

Fabio Ciravegna   Erica Giorda[1]

CENTRO RICERCHE FIAT, strada Torino 50,
I-10043 Orbassano (To) ITALY

Abstract. The role played by the adjectival and adverbial phrases in a sentence is generally considered as a minor one. Nevertheless some of them have a strong influence in the information carried by the phrases they modify, and - in some domains or applications - they carry the main information. For example in a diagnostic domain an adjectival modifier in a NP as *funzionamento non molto corretto* (literally "working not very correct") carries the main information. Moreover this kind of modifiers may introduce vague and subjective expressions that have to be formalized in some ways. In this paper we introduce an approach to the compositional treatment of their meaning that reduces the complexity of the expressions they are involved in, and allows to formalize their vagueness. The treatment is particular to our approach to knowledge extraction from texts and to the domain we are working on, but it can be extended to other contexts or applications.

1 Introduction

Natural language diagnostic descriptions are affected by the presence of linguistic modifiers (adjectival and adverbial phrases, negations, etc.) that are used to express abnormal statuses, unexpected or lacking characteristics, and so on. The modifications introduced by those modifiers depend on both the modifier itself and the terms they are applied to. Human beings are able to deal easily with such forms using both the information coming from the context and a kind of general method. Also natural language systems must be able to cope with those modifications, without asking for a complete 'a priori' list of all the possible modifications for every term contained in the lexicon. The problem we address is - for example - to understand how it is possible to recognize that *a bad mounting* is a "fault" even if the concept "process" is associated to the word *mounting* in the lexicon. Another feature of some modifiers is that they can introduce subjective evaluations in quantity and/or quality (as in *not very good*), that must be formalized in some ways. Quantifiers are another kind of modifiers, but we won't consider this case. In the diagnostic domain, a modifier can contribute in highlighting a relation, describing an undesired object feature or even changing the semantic identity of the term it is applied to (as in the case of "bad mounting"). The goal of the modifier analysis is then to determine whether the modifier specifies:

---

[1] Grantee of Centro Ricerche Fiat

- a normal status (es. *normally worn*);
- an abnormal status (*abnormally worn*);
- a level of a normal/abnormal status (es. *heavily worn object*).

In this paper we propose to cope with modifiers through the following steps:

1. formalization of the meaning of each modifier (for ex. of "good")
2. normalization of the meaning of their composition (ex. "not very good");
3. normalization of the phrases containing the modifiers (NPs, VPs, etc.) to some kernel descriptions; for example both "a not proper mounting" and "a bad mounting" may be reduced to the same basic description.

The method is particular to our approach to knowledge extraction from texts and to the domain we are working on, but it can be extended to many other contexts or applications. In the rest of the paper we will first introduce our approach to knowledge extraction and then the treatment of the modifiers.

2 Knowledge Extraction as a Multistage Process

Even though there is not a unique approach to automatic knowledge extraction, we can define it as a multistage process in which the natural language input (NLF) is transformed into a semantic representation of the relevant information (MRF). The characteristics of that process depend on the given kind of texts and information. Systems operating on generic contexts integrate general and domain oriented knowledge sources to cope with the complexity of the language and of the domain; two kinds of approaches may be pointed out:
- semantics driven approaches integrating aspects as event expectation to fill in some script-like and/or frame based structures [1].
- syntax driven approaches with strong pragmatic/syntactic recovery strategies [2].

We use an approach similar to [1] to extract knowledge from diagnostic texts, but: the role of event expectation is reduced (as the information is expressed in our texts through the complex composition of a small number of object classes), and the role of the general knowledge sources is taken over by the domain oriented ones.

Different knowledge sources contribute to the text analysis as: an independent syntax, a case frame based semantics, a deep lexical semantics and a powerful knowledge of the world. Bottom Up and Top Down strategies are mixed for text analysis [3]. For this paper purposes, the approach may be logically split up into the following steps:

(a) paraphrasis of the expressions;
(b) translation into a knowledge based formalism;
(c) pruning of the non relevant information;
(d) normalization of the content into a pre-defined shape;
(e) translation into a set of data base commands.

The paraphrasis of the expression (a) is used to reduce many linguistic forms to some kernel descriptions: verbs are nominalized (to break => the break-up), unusual terms are substituted with synonymouses or hyperonymouses (cangureggiamento => malfunzionamento [i.e. moving as a kangaroo => bad working]), etc. The final goal of this process is to obtain a normalized expression whose content may be easily translated (b) into a knowledge based formalism. The non relevant expression is then pruned (c) and the remaining information is normalized into a pre-defined shape (for example to fit into a logical structure based on a database organization) (d). As last step a set of rules translates this output into data base commands (e). These different tasks are separated in the sense that they are supported by different processes using different knowledge sources, but they are interleaved for the sake of optimization. In this paper we focus on the paraphrasis of the expression and on the role of adjectival and adverbial phrases.

3 Paraphrasing the Linguistic Expressions

We define the first step towards the translation from NLF to MRF as the 'paraphrasis of the expression', i.e. the transformation of the natural language input into a simplified version of the text written in a natural language oriented formalism. For example forms as *not very good* may be normalized to *bad* depending on the terms they are applied to, and the domain we are working on. At the same time forms as *not adherent object* may be paraphrased into *lack of adhesion on an object*. To be able to separate the paraphrasis task from the others (both for modularity and efficiency) we operate only at the level of the basic constituents of the sentence (NPs and VPs), without trying to find out their mutual connections: paraphrasis is then limited to the 'local' reduction of forms to basic constituents. Roughly speaking, the goal of the 'paraphrasis of the expression' step is to 'normalize' (when possible) the object descriptions found in the sentences onto the descriptions contained in a phrase vocabulary listing all the known object of the domain. For example, given a user description as "not proper mounting", the goal of the 'paraphrasis of the expression' is to reduce it (if possible) to one of the faults contained in that vocabulary (the "bad mounting", in this case). The knowledge sources used at this level are essentially lexical semantics, knowledge of the world and syntax. This normalization is powerful enough to reduce the linguistic and semantic complexity of the descriptions of the objects mentioned in the text (we have to cope with object descriptions composed by as many as ten words) [4]. In the recognition of the basic constituents a main role is played by the treatment of the linguistic modifiers. We define the modifiers as phrases that:

- don't identify a referent, when alone;
- must be connected to another phrase;
- introduce elements or features of the entities referred by the parent phrases.

Adjectival (AdjP), Adverbial (AdvP) and Prepositional Phrases (PP) are typical examples of modifiers. In particular the role of the adjectival and adverbial phrases is generally considered as a minor one; we think instead that it is a main role, at least in some domains. As a matter of fact a sentence may assert that *an engine works*, while another sentence may instead assert that the same engine *doesn't work very well* or *doesn't work at all*. From a diagnostic point of view these assertions are definitely more informative than the previous one, because of the use (in the Italian translation) of two adverbial phrases. The same role is played by the adjectival phrase in sentences as *an incorrect working of the device*. In the rest of the paper we will focus on the treatment of some kinds of AdjP and AdvP.

4 Adjectival and Adverbial Phrases

We classify the Adjectival and Adverbial modifiers in two main lexical classes: *functors* and *specifiers*. These classes are divided into subclasses defining their semantic value and compositional behaviour. A set of applicable modification functions is associated to each subclass. **The specifiers** define in general object features as "colour", "shape", "consistency", "dimension", "weight", etc. and they are applicable only to Nouns or Verbs. Examples are "heavy", "early", etc. **The functors** are the only modifiers acceptable for specifiers: considering the specifiers introduced above (describing "colour", "shape", etc.), and excluding problems of stylistic "shading" of the expressions, the only relevant modifications concern the level ("grado" in Italian, es. *too heavy*) or the quantity ("quantità" in Italian). In general we define a functor as any modifier that introduces modifications in level and quantity (modifying NPs, VPs, specifiers and functors). Examples of functors are *non* (not), *molto* (very), *poco* (little), *scarso* (scarce), *insufficientemente* (insufficiently), *normalmente* (normally), etc. The functors have the following behaviour:

(1) from a syntactic point of view: they always precede the term they modify when applied to Nouns, Adjectives, or Adverbs (as in "not very" the "not" modifier precedes the "very"); they may follow or precede a Verb and even appear in the middle of compound forms (as in *non è molto ben montato*, literally "it not is very well mounted"); in this last case it is to be interpreted as "not very well" + "mounted".

(2) from a semantic perspective: their value can be displayed on a level or quantity scale and their composition still mapps on the same scales (es. *scarso* [scarce] is mapping onto a scale ranging from TROPPO [too much] to INSUFFICIENTE [insufficient]; *not scarce* is still on the same scale).

The idea of defining these elements as 'functors' comes from the fact that they seem to act as unary functions on the semantic identity of the linguistic objects they modify. This organization doesn't depend on whether the modifier is adjectival or adverbial, since we try to capture its 'deep meaning' independently from the syntactic type. As a matter of fact there exists a parallelism between the semantic system of the adjectives and that of the adverbs, so that, at least in Italian, in most cases the AdvPs modify the Verbs as the AdjPs modify the Nouns [5]. When it is possible we try to paraphrase the AdvPs into the corresponding AdjPs and the Verbs into the corresponding Nouns.

5 The Compositional Treatment of the Modifiers

Given the mentioned behaviour, it is possible to organize the treatment of modifiers to paraphrase the expressions they are involved in. This treatment has a limited cost in computation and in information to be stored in the lexicon. **For the functors** we introduce the already mentioned scales of quantity and level; each functor is defined in the lexicon as pointing to a specific value in one of them; for example "little" could be defined as pointing to a low level in the quantity scale, or to the level "scarcely" in the level scale. It implies that all the functors are normalized onto a dozen of pointers on the scales. Regions are defined on these scales: critical regions indicate changes in the semantic identity of the object they are applied to. For example *normally* points onto a region to be considered critical when that term is applied to <fault> and non critical otherwise ("a normal wear" is not a fault). For each value on a scale, all the possible combinations with the other levels on the scales are shown. Each combination consider just two levels, as the composition of two functors is interpretable as another functor: as a matter of fact, given (1) and (2), we can state that forms as *non molto* (as in "non molto regolarmente") (*not very* as in "not very regularly") may be compositionally interpreted as: "not"("very") => "little"[2]. The information to be stored in the lexicon is then reduced to the mapping onto the ranges of the scales for each functor, and the permitted combination within the various levels of the scales. **The specifiers** are defined in the lexicon as belonging to classes derived from a list similar to the one introduced above (colour, shape, etc.). The result of the composition between the different levels of the scales and the specifiers has been defined for each class. Only the normalized forms and the differences with respect to the default (if any) are defined for each entry in the lexicon. For example forms as *non molto frequentemente* (not very frequently) are interpreted as:

"not"("very") => "little";   "little"(frequently) => "rarely".

The Nouns/Verbs are defined in the lexicon as belonging to a semantic class (es. "break" and "to break" collapse into "break_fault"); the possible modifications given by functors or specifiers are defined for each class; only differences with respect to the default are specified for each entry. For example: "normal" (<fault>) => <characteristic>, i.e. *normally* + *worn* produce the *wear* characteristic. So, a form as *montaggio non molto corretto* (mounting not much correct), may be treated as:

"not"("much") => "little";   "little"("correct") => "incorrect";

"incorrect"(mounting) = "incorrect"(<process>) => <fault>

The form to be searched in the lexicon will be *"incorrect" mounting*. Modifiers can sometimes be applied directly to nouns: An example may be *non montaggio* (i.e. not mounting).

6 Conclusion

The proposed approach allows to normalize the modifiers and their compositions into equivalent forms (the level on the scales) to be used in the paraphrasis of the expression step. Each level of the scale is associated to a unary function of semantic transformation to be applied to the modified term. The argument of that function may be a level in a scale (i.e. another functor or the result of a composition of some functors), a class of specifiers, or a semantic class belonging to the taxonomy of the domain (for ex. "fault"). The normalization of similar forms into the same description is useful to allow for the 'paraphrasis of the expression' step to reduce the user descriptions to the kernel descriptions contained in the lexicon (for example: "not

---

[2] Here the different levels and the associated semantic functions are represented as words between quotes (i.e. *"little"(correct)* represents the function associated to the level "little" when applied to the term *correct*).

proper mounting", "bad mounting", "not-as-planned mounting", "not really proper mounting", are normalized on *"bad" mounting* in order to reach a DB code). Moreover the formalization of the meaning of each modifier gives a method for interpreting the vagueness of many forms (as for *montaggio non molto corretto*). The semantic transformations operated on the semantic class (i.e. "incorrect" + <process> => <fault>) avoid to memorize all the possible transformation for each entry in the vocabulary (i.e. a mounting is a process, but if it is associated to "bad", "incorrect", "not correct", etc. it becomes a fault): it is then just necessary to memorize the behaviour of each class with respect to the application of each level on the scales (and - for nouns/verbs - also with respect to the specifier classes). It allows to capture the lexical generalities and reduce the information in the lexicon. This approach to modifier analysis appears to be definitely simpler and common sense based - although not much arbitrary - than the one proposed by [6]. It is of course more "naive", but easier to manage in real systems and sufficient for our purposes. The method is reasonably transportable to other domains; what it is not transportable is the granularity of the scales and the normalization of each modifier on the scales. This method to cope with modifiers has been implemented in the SINTESI system, a tool to extract knowledge from diagnostic text. SINTESI currently operates with a vocabulary of about 9.000 terms and 8.000 object descriptions and a knowledge base consisting of about 50 classes of objects. The syntactic knowledge is based on a dependency grammar; the semantic module is based on caseframes. It has been tested on about 1.000 texts with a rate of 85% in recall and 90% in precision. It is currently under test as a natural language interface for a textual data base at FIAT Auto S.p.A.

References

1. Jacobs P., Rau L.: "Integrating Top Down and Bottom Up Strategies in a Text Processing System", 2nd Conference on Applied Natural Language Processing, Austin, February 1988.
2. Hobbs J.R., Appelt D.E., Bear J., Tyson M.: "Robust Processing of Real-World Natural-Language Texts", 3rd Conference on Applied Natural Language Processing, Trento, Italy, March 1992.
3. Ciravegna F., Campia P., Colognese A.: "Knowledge Extraction from Texts by SINTESI", COLING 92, Nantes, July 1992.
4. Ciravegna F., Campia P., Colognese A.: "The Treatment of Conjunctions in an Information Retrieval System", in F. Sorbello (ed.) "Le prospettive industriali dell'intelligenza Artificiale", Palermo, October 91.
5. Renzi R., Salvi: "Grande Grammatica di Consultazione" vol I and II, "Il Mulino" editions, Bologna, 1988.
6. Hobbs J., Croft W., Davies T., Edwards D., Laws K.: "Commonsense Metaphysics and Lexical Semantics" Computational Linguistics vol 13 n 3,4 1987.

Acknowledgment. This work would not have been possible without the effort spent by Paolo Campia and Alberto Colognese in the past years on the SINTESI system.

Explanation Strategies in a Tutoring System

Giacomo Ferrari[1], Michele Carenini[2] and Paolo Moreschini[2]

[1] Department of Linguistics University of Pisa 56100 - Pisa (ITALY)
[2] AITech Artificial Intelligence Technologies, s.n.c. 56125 - Pisa (ITALY)

Abstract. In this paper the design and implementation of an Intelligent Tutoring System will be described (ESPRIT BRA IDEAL, *Interactive Dialogues for Explanation And Learning*[3]). A special attention will be given on the explanation strategy selection mechanism, which allows the system to provide explanation about a particular domain to a user, in a most cooperative way. The advantages provided by the particular context in which the interaction takes place (namely, one of tutoring), allows the developer to use techniques and devices which showed to be particularly efficient respect to other man- machine interaction systems.

1 IDEAL

The ESPRIT Project IDEAL (*Interactive Dialogues for Explanation And Learning*) aimed at carrying theoretical, empirical and computational studies on explanation dialogues in domains which can be structured in terms of tasks. The main objective of the Pisa unit was the implementation of a demonstrative prototype. The chosen domain was that of e-mail systems: the user can ask questions about different procedures to use e- mail, as well as about generic concepts of the e-mail environment. The development of the system focussed essentially on two components, the Knowledge Representation System and the modules for the interaction between the system and the user. The Knowledge Representation is based on the distinction between knowledge of the procedures to do something inside the domain, and knowledge of the objects of the domain. The knowledge base is then divided into a TKS, Task Knowledge Structure, and a DTS, Domain Taxonomic Substructure (see [7]). Interaction with the user is managed by various modules, which form the Dialogue Manager, DM. The DM receives the result of the parsing, i.e. a structure called *logical form1*, representing a description of the input sentence. Parsing fell out of the aims of the project, and is, then, only simulated in the demonstrator. Once the DM receives the logical form, it activates the Focus Structures Managing Mechanism, which consists of a stack of the tasks currently being explained and a stack of the objects involved in the explanation. The mechanism returns the current state of the stacks, and the DM

---

[3] The ESPRIT Basic Research Action No. 3160 IDEAL consortium was composed by City University of London, Dept. of Business Computing (prime contractor); Queen Mary & Westfield College; University of Pisa - Dipartimento di Linguistica; CNR of Pisa - Istituto di Linguistica Computazionale; University of the Aegean - Dept. of Mathematics.

tries to match the result with the antecedent of an IF-THEN rule which decides the next step. Some rules allow to build an appropriate query to the Knowledge Representation System, which returns the relevant portion of knowledge, constituted by a task structure, TS, or by a frame structure, FS (for objects). The DM is then able to select the right output strategy, i.e. the appropriate explanation behaviour to be verbalized by the Response Generator. The logical form returned by the DM (*logical form2*) contains all the information necessary to the Response Generator to create the appropriate output. Other rules, instead, allow the DM to select immediately the appropriate output strategy, without queries to the Knowledge Representation System. The implemented prototype is constituted by three blocks: the Interface, the Dialogue Manager, and the Knowledge Representation System. A complete description of each module (from both a theoretical and an implementative viewpoint) can be found in [2], [3], and [6].

2 The answer generation system in an ITS

Answer generation systems, being based on the recognition and the use of the two agents intentions, have often shown to be computationally too expensive to be used in practical applications (see [1]). In IDEAL the particular nature of the interaction allowed to avoid this problem. In a tutoring situation, the roles assigned to the dialogue participants are well-defined and not exchangeable ones: the system (expert) has a certain amount of knowledge to be transmitted to the user (novice). It has been empirically derived that this kind of dialogue is strongly unbalanced towards the expert (see [7] and [9]). The main activities of the expert is to inform the user and to check the users comprehension; the dialogic functions performed by the user are to request to be taught something, to confirm or deny he has understood something, and to request alternative explanations. We call a "tutoring scenario" a situation in which the novice asks something to the expert, which provides the appropriate information and checks the users understanding. This procedure is to be repeated up to the end of the explanation. The (theoretical) task of both the agents is that, at the end of the explanation, the agents knowledge bases be equal.

3 The Knowledge Representation System

IDEAL's data structure and its management stand between a knowledge representation system and a data base: as far as the former is concerned, IDEAL has no inference rule, deduction mechanism, etc.; as far as the latter, usually, in database query systems, no conversational context based on the dialogue structure is created; in IDEAL, instead, the control on the structure which has been explained is kept constant, and interruption phenomena can be managed, as well as new explanations on already treated topics. Figure 2 shows a sample task. A task structure is a tree constituted by nodes (t1, ..., t7); the branching of the tree is labelled by an operator which can be *alt* ("alternative", symbolized

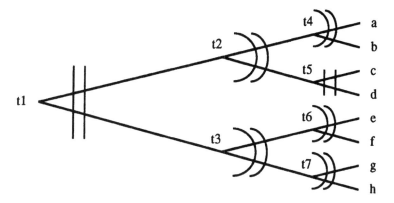

Fig. 1. A sample task structure

by two straight lines) or *seq* ("sequence", represented by two semi-circles). Two branches linked by an *alt* operator represent a possible alternative; two branches linked by a *seq* operator represent a sequence of procedures or actions to be performed in order to obtain some result[4]. Terminal nodes (labelled with a, ..., h) represent atomic actions. The strategic component tends to traverse all the task extracted from the knowledge base, taking into account its structure, and is controlled by a module which manages interruptions, repetitions, alternative strategies, etc.

4 Explanation strategies

Explanation strategies have been designed as oriented graphs. Some strategies can be called directly by rules, while others can be evoked by higher-level strategies; in other words, graphs are organized in a hierarchy to allow the adoption of the most appropriate strategy. Control actions and tests are also available.[5] Let us consider a typical explanatory situation. At the beginning of the session, the system assesses its domain (e-mail), and asks the user if he wants to know something. This is due to the strategy START, which is always activated at the beginning of a session:

(START)
<introduce> → (START1)

---

[4] There can be also another operator between two branches, namely alt-eq (standing for alternative [paths to] equivalent [goals]), which indicates two alternative paths to accomplish the same goal. For a detailed description of IDEAL's Knowledge Representation System, see [5]

[5] Graphs can be read in this way: (INITIAL STATE), (state), <action>; the arrow → can be read as an oriented arc (e.g.: "<x> → (n)" means "after the performance of action x, go to state n").

```
(START1)
    <PUSH PROMPT> → (START2)
(START2)
    <PUSH EXPLAIN_OBJECT> → (START3)
    <PUSH EXPLAIN_TASK> → (START3)
    <PUSH SOLICITATE> → (START3)
(START3)
    <confirmation> → (START4)
(START4)
    <PUSH PROMPT> → (START5)
(START5)
    <conclude> → (START6)
    <(START2)>
(START6)
    <POP>
```

The arc labelled <introduce> corresponds to the assessment of the domain and to the (fixed) question *Are you interested in something particular?*. The PUSH PROMPT arc gives the user the possibility to ask something. Suppose the user asks a question as *How can I modify a list of address names?*. The logical form corresponding to this question is the following:

((SENT-CLASS REQ) (ACTION MODIFY) (THEME LIST))

When the DM receives this logical form as input, it searches for the first rule in the antecedent of which a logical form of this kind appears[6]:

((SENT-CLASS REQ) (MAIN-VERB ISA ACTION) (THEME ISA OBJECT))

considering it together with the current state of the focus stacks. Being the explanation at the beginning, the stacks are empty; the consequent actions (listed in the THEN part of the rule) are then "query-to-tks" and "select-output-strategy". The first action is accomplished by extracting from the knowledge base the relevant portion of knowledge, i.e. the (sub)tree whose root is labelled with "modify-list"; once it has been realized that modify-list is a task, the appropriate output strategy is selected, and the arc PUSH EXPLAIN-TASK is traversed. This graph is mainly constituted by three steps: an introduction to the topic to be explained, (which causes the output *You can modify your list of address names either by adding or removing a name.*), the PUSH to another graph, namely TEACH_TASK, and the final check on the users comprehension, with the relative

---

[6] The matching with a rule does not take place necessarily on constant values, but the IF part can contain variables; the instantiation of the variables in the IF part creates the rule environment, from which the value of the variables to be used in the THEN part is determined. The first rule which matches, following the insertion order in which it appears, is selected.

selection of an alternative strategy (exemplified here by the arc PUSH EXAM-
PLE) in case of a users negation of his understanding. The graph TEACH_TASK
controls the structure of the task to be explained, which can be constituted by a
sequence of actions, possible alternatives, or a single action. In this case, modifying a list of names can be accomplished either by adding a name to the list or
removing one; the following ouput is generated: *This task can be accomplished by
one of the following steps: insert_name or remove_name*; the action on the first
ALT (for ALTERNATIVE) graph is a question to the user: *Which step do you
want me to explain?*. The user's answer, e.g. *Insert_name*, allows the system to
proceed in the explanation, getting back to the EXPLAIN_TASK graph, and the
following text is generated: *To add a name to your list, you must digit <insert>
followed by the name you want to insert*. The graphs TEACH_TASK, SEQ (for
"sequence") and NAME are traversed, and the output is produced: *This task is
constituted by a sequence of these steps: digit the string <insert> and digit the
string <name>*. For each step in the sequence (if it is a procedure; of course no
check is done for atomic actions), a check is performed, and the user must confirm (or deny) his comprehension of that step. After the explanation is finished,
and all the graphs are POPped up to the EXPLAIN_TASK one, a final check
is performed: *Did you understand how to insert a name?*. The users negative
answer makes the system start a clarification subdialogue, through which it can
provide examples[7] about the task or create analogies on particular aspects of
the task. The users confirmation on his comprehension, instead, takes the system
back to its initial state, ready for further requests[8]. The user can also ask questions about particular objects, as in *What is a file?*. In this case, the arc to be
traversed in the START graph is PUSH EXPLAIN_OBJECT, and a definition
of the object, as it has been stored in the Domain Taxonomic Substructure, is
provided. In the demonstrator, after the explanation of an object, the system
does not perform any check on the users understanding; it only asks the user
if he wants to know something else. Obviously, the system is not linked to any
particular domain: the only restriction is that it must be used with a knowledge
representation which includes some distinction between procedural information
and taxonomic structures.

5 Conclusions

The system presented in these pages has been implemented only as a demonstrator. The main efforts inside the project were the definition of a Knowledge
Representation System respectful of psychological intuitions, and the attempt
to implement a system both efficient and portable. The system has been implemented on Macintosh using Macintosh Common Lisp, and it has been easily

---

[7] The strategy EXAMPLE is structured so to point to several examples about a single
topic. At the end of the example, the system performs another check on the users
comprehension, and, in case the user answers again he hasnt understood, a new
example is chosen.

[8] For a detailed description of the strategies, see [4].

ported on a SPARCStation. If compared with the requirements set by [8], IDEAL fails to meet most of the linguistic and dialogic ones. It is unable to synthesise text from knowledge, and to tailor answers to the user. It is, instead, well performing on the side of flexibility, searching through knowledge, and extendibility. In a word, it has good qualities as to the deep functions of dialogue management, while is weak in the "low level" functions. However, another characteristic of IDEAL, its modularity, makes it easily open to improvements. In fact, although the parsing phase has only been simulated in the demonstrator, the implementation of a parsing system which returns the appropriate logical form, to be interfaced with the system, is currently under development. The answers to the user's queries (which in the demonstrator corresponds to the retrieval of canned pieces of texts) can as well be interfaced with a verbalizer to generate actual sentences.

References

1. P. R. Cohen, C. R. Perrault, "Elements of a plan-based theory of speech acts", Cognitive Science **3**, 177-212, 1979.
2. G. Ferrari, I. Prodanof, M. Carenini, P. Moreschini, "Dialogue management for tutorial dialogues", in *Discourse Structure in Natural Language Understanding and Generation*, AAAI Fall Symposium Series, November 15-17, 1991, Asilomar, Monterey, CA, 1991.
3. G. Ferrari, I. Prodanof, M. Carenini, P. Moreschini, *Interactive Dialogues in Explanation and Learning*, ESPRIT BRA #3160 IDEAL - ATR#1, Dipartimento di Linguistica, Università di Pisa - Istituto di Linguistica Computazionale, CNR, Pisa - AITech s.n.c., Pisa, 1991.
4. G. Ferrari, I. Prodanof, M. Carenini, P. Moreschini, *Plans and Strategies in Explanation Dialogues*, ESPRIT BRA #3160 IDEAL - ATR#4, Dipartimento di Linguistica, Università di Pisa - Istituto di Linguistica Computazionale, CNR, Pisa - AITech s.n.c., Pisa, 1991.
5. G. Ferrari, I. Prodanof, M. Carenini, P. Moreschini, *The Knowledge Representation System in an ITS*, ESPRIT BRA #3160 IDEAL - ATR#5, Dipartimento di Linguistica, Università di Pisa - Istituto di Linguistica Computazionale, CNR, Pisa - AITech s.n.c., Pisa, 1991.
6. G. Ferrari, I. Prodanof, M. Carenini, P. Moreschini, *General Overview of a Dialogue System's Functions in Explanation and Learning*, ESPRIT BRA #3160 IDEAL - ATR#6, Dipartimento di Linguistica, Università di Pisa - Istituto di Linguistica Computazionale, CNR, Pisa - AITech s.n.c., Pisa, 1991.
7. H. Johnson, P. Johnson, *Theoretical Knowledge Representations for supporting dialogues in Explanation and Learning*, Deliverable No 6B1, Report No 1, ESPRIT BRA 3160.
8. C. Paris, "Generation and explanation: building an explantion facility for the Explainable Expert Systems Framework", in Paris, Swartout, Mann (Eds.), *Natural Language Generation in Artificial Intellingence and Computational Linguistics*, Kluwer Academic Publishers, Norwell, MA., 1990.
9. E. Serantinos, P. Johnson, "Question Analysis and Explanation Generation", *Proceedings of the Twenty-Fourth Hawaii International Conference on System Sciences*, Hawaii, Usa, 1991.

Maintaining Consistency in Quantitative Temporal Constraint Networks for Planning and Scheduling

Roberto Cervoni[*][+], Amedeo Cesta[*], Angelo Oddi[*][‡]

[*]IP-CNR, Consiglio Nazionale delle Ricerche, Viale Marx 15, I-00137, Roma
[+]Via Tiburtina 147, I-03100, Frosinone
[‡]Via Tiburtina 171, I-03100, Frosinone

Abstract. A module for quantitative constraint propagation forms the core of any problem solving architecture devoted to planning and scheduling in realistic applications. This paper deals with temporal constraint propagation in quantitative networks. We are interested in developing a module that efficiently checks the consistency of an incrementally built temporalized solution. The paper presents a clean definition of the consistency checking problem in temporal networks and describes an algorithm that is correct and complete with respect to such a definition. A sufficient condition for inconsistency is also presented which is useful for improving the algorithm, and the computational complexity of the approach as a whole is discussed.

1 Introduction

Most knowledge-based architectures for planning and scheduling practical applications perform an incremental constraint posting on a current partial solution, removing one or more flaws at each step. To cope with realistic domains, a problem solver should be able to explicitly deal with time, in particular quantitative time. The problem of maintaining consistency among quantitative temporal constraints plays a significant role in problem solving architectures that cope with planning and scheduling problems.

Our current effort is devoted to the development of an efficient temporal module to be used in different architectures and able both to manage problems of a reasonably large dimension and to quickly check consistency of a given set of constraints. The need for efficiency arises from the fact that consistency checking is the most frequent activity in incremental constraint posting. In particular we are using the module in a Temporal Data Base *a la* HSTS [MUS92] where the solution is incrementally built and indexed by state variables that represent dynamic features of a physical domain. In this paper we present a first set of results of our investigation on quantitative temporal networks. The paper presents the general problem of consistency maintenance in quantitative networks and studies a particular implementation of such networks. For such an implementation, an algorithm is given for consistency checking, then its correspondence with formal definitions and its computational complexity are studied. Moreover we present a sufficient condition for inconsistency detection that speeds up consistency checking.

The paper is organized as follows: Section 2 presents the definition of temporal network and temporal consistency, Section 3 describes the algorithm for constraint propagation, its correctness and completeness, and a property characterizing the role of cycles in the computation; computational complexity is then discussed, while some comments conclude the paper.

2 Maintaining Consistency in Temporal Networks

The first system to explicitly deal with numeric duration of actions is Vere's [VER83], while the first comprehensive attempt to analyze the problem is Dean's Time Map Manager (TMM) [DEA87]. TMM is a general purpose tool for managing temporalized information devoted to applications in planning (see [DEA88]). The problem of managing temporal durations is also relevant for Knowledge Based Scheduling [RIT86], altough a specialized treatment of time is often used (see for example the description of the temporal modules of OPIS [LEP87]). Recently some scheduling algorithms have been seen which take explicit advantage of more flexible temporal reasoning modules [MUS93, SMI93].

The basic definition of a network of temporal constraints is the following:

Definition 1 - (*Temporal Network*) - A temporal network is a directed graph whose nodes represent time points and whose edges represent distance constraints among time points.

Nodes represent points in the time line in which some change happens (e.g. start-time or end-time of events), while edges (^{1}) uniformly represent both activities' duration (e.g. "heat water for at least 10 minutes but not more than 20") and distance constraints among distinct activities and events (e.g. "Patricia arrived 5 minutes after Roberto left").

In a temporal network both nodes and edges are labelled with a couple of variables, denoted by *[lb,ub]*. In the case of nodes, *lb* represents the earliest start time possible for the time point, given the constraints in the network, while *ub* represents the latest start time. In the case of edges, *lb* represents the minimal duration of the constraint while *ub* represents the maximal duration (that is, a user can specify the duration of a constraint ei in the form: $lb_{ei} \leq duration_{ei} \leq ub_{ei}$). A particular node in the graph, named *reference*, has the constant value *[0,0]* as a label, and represents the beginning of the considered temporal horizon.

The couple *[lb,ub]* for a node identifies an interval of possible values for the time variable *ti* representing the instant of occurrence of the event. Given a set of constraints (edges) and their durations, the couples *[lb,ub]* associated with each node of the network are calculated with respect to the reference point using a constraint propagation algorithm whose characteristics we are going to explain. Before starting the next section we just observe that the temporal problem we are dealing with is different from the qualitative temporal constraint problem addressed in [ALL83, VAN92], but it is equivalent to the *Simplest Temporal Problem* defined in [DEC91].

2.1 Defining Consistency

To formalize the problem of maintaining a temporal network consistent, we need to introduce some basic definitions (part of the terminology is taken from classical graph theory).

(^{1}) In the following we shall consider edges always directed.

Definition 2 - (*Minimal Distance on a Path*) - Let c be a path between the nodes i and j of a temporal network. The minimal distance, $dmin(i,j,c)$, between the nodes i and j on the path c is defined as the sum of the lower bound lbi of the duration of the c's edges whose direction is concordant with the direction from i to j, minus the upper bound ubi of the duration of the c's edges whose direction is discordant with the direction from i to j.

$$dmin(i, j, c) = \sum_{i concordant} lb_i - \sum_{i discordant} ub_i$$

Definition 3 - (*Maximal Distance on a Path*) - Let c be a path between the nodes i and j of a temporal network. The maximal distance, $dmax(i,j,c)$, between the nodes i and j on the path c is defined as the sum of the upper bound ubi of the duration of the c's edges whose direction is concordant with the direction from i to j, minus the lower bound lbi of the duration of the c's edges whose direction is discordant with the direction from i to j.

$$dmax(i, j, c) = \sum_{i concordant} ub_i - \sum_{i discordant} lb_i$$

Figure 1, where nodes are represented as circles, presents an example to better show the meaning of definitions. The minimal and maximal distance from node 2 to node 6, are calculated as follows:

$dmin(2,6,c)=20+50-20+30=80,$ $dmax(2,6,c)=30+70-10+60=150.$

As we said above, each node i in the graph has a time variable ti associated; from the two previous formulas we can obtain that the minimal time difference between t_6 and t_2 is 80 and the maximal time difference is 150:

$80 \leq t_6 - t_2 \leq 150.$

The definitions and the example allow us to quickly understand the similarity among time and space that suggested the name of Time Map to Dean and McDermott [DEA87]. In fact concordant edges drive towards the arrival point while discordant edges depart from it. We are seeing time "from a side" as we were observing a robot moving in space.

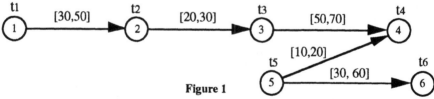

Figure 1

More generally, between two nodes a number of possible paths exist. Each path adds a constraint to the temporal distance between the extremities. For this reason the following three basic definitions are given.

Definition 4 - (*Minimal Distance*) - Let i and j be two nodes in a given temporal network. The minimal distance between i and j is the maximum among the minimal distance on every path c between i and j:

$Dmin(i,j)=max_c\{dmin(i,j,c)\}$

Definition 5 - (*Maximal Distance*) - Let i and j be two nodes in a given temporal network. The maximal distance between i and j is the minimum among the maximal distance on every path c between i and j:

$Dmax(i,j)=min_c\{dmax(i,j,c)\}$

Definition 6 - (*Distance Interval*) - Let i and j be two nodes in a temporal network. The Distance Interval between i and j is given by the couple *[Dmin(i,j),Dmax(i,j)]*.

Using the given definitions we can define the notion of temporal consistency of a network.

Definition 7 - (*Temporal Consistency*) - A connected temporal network is said to be (temporally) consistent if and only if for each couple of nodes $<i,j>$ the associated distance interval is not empty, that is, the following property holds:
$$Dmax(i,j) \geq Dmin(i,j).$$

This means that, taken any couple of nodes $<i,j>$ connected by at least one path, if the network is consistent then between the temporal variables ti and tj, associated with i and j respectively, a set of possible temporal distances exists. This implies that it is possible to choose ti and tj so that $(tj - ti) \in [Dmin(i,j),Dmax(i,j)]$.

Now the problem we are interested in is the one of determining how the bounds associated with the nodes can be updated when new bounds are posted on edges. We need to associate with the network a *propagation* functionality that, manipulating the constraints represented in the network by the edges, updates the nodes' bounds to preserve the consistency of such bounds with all the constraints in the network. Such a propagation function should have the following basic property:

For each couple of nodes $<i,j>$, the related bounds *[lbi,ubi]* and *[lbj,ubj]* should not contain values that do not satisfy the distance constraints holding on those nodes.

If after the application of the propagation function one of the nodes' intervals *[lbi,ubi]* results empty the network is inconsistent because no value for the variable t_i exists which is compatible with the current constraints. Now we introduce a new definition of temporal consistency that is equivalent to Definition 7 but better points the attention on the bound intervals associated with nodes. It is worth noting that the only way to constrain the nodes' bounds is explicitly imposing constraint on edges.

Definition 8 - (*Temporal Consistency*) - A connected temporal network is (temporally) consistent if for each couple of nodes $<i,j>$ it is possible to determine the related bound intervals *[lbi,ubi]* and *[lbj,ubj]* in a way that the following property holds:
for each value of ti chosen within *[lbi,ubi]* there exists a value of tj within *[lbj,ubj]* so that the following property holds:
$$Dmin(i,j) \leq tj-ti \leq Dmax(i,j).$$

This second definition of consistency shifts the attention on the fact that when a network is consistent, choosing a plausible value for a time variable causes the existence of a corresponding value for all the other time variables in the network. The equivalence between Definition 7 and 8 can be shown as follows:

- from 7 to 8: Definition 7 says that the relative distance associated with nodes i and j must be contained in the interval *[Dmin(i,j),Dmax(i,j)]*; as a consequence if that interval is not empty, it is possible to determine the two intervals *[lbi,ubi]* and *[lbj,ubj]* according to Definition 8.
- from 8 to 7: it is trivial.

Once defined a precise notion of temporal consistency, we approach the problem of designing an algorithm able to check that property on a given network and to update the intervals associated with nodes.

2.2 Constraint Propagation and Consistency Checking

To build a propagation function for the temporal network, we start analyzing the simple case shown in Figure 2: a network with two nodes and an edge between them. The problem to be solved is the following:

> Given an interval *[lb,ub]* associated with the edge whose modifications should be performed on intervals *[lbi,ubi]* and *[lbj,ubj]* so that for each value $ti \in [lbi,ubi]$ $(tj \in [lbj,ubj])$ there always exists a value $tj \in [lbj,ubj]$ $(ti \in [lbi,lbi])$, such that tj and ti satisfy the inequality:
> $$lb \leq tj-ti \leq ub.$$

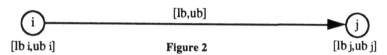

Figure 2

[lb i,ub i]   [lb j,ub j]

The following proposition plays a crucial role in the resolution of the problem:

Proposition 1 (^{2})

Given the simple temporal network in Figure 2, the following property holds:
(1) The bounds *lbi, lbj, ubi, ubj* satisfy the relations:

  a) *lbj:=max[lbj,lbi+lb];*   b) *ubj:=min[ubj,ubi+ub];*
  c) *lbi:=max[lbi,lbj-ub];*   d) *ubi:=min[ubi,ubj-lb];*
  e) *lbi≤ubi;*   f) *lbj≤ubj;*

if and only if

(2) For each $ti \in [lbi,ubi]$ $(tj \in [lbj,ubj])$ there always exists a value $tj \in [lbj,ubj]$ $(ti \in [lbi,ubi])$, such that tj and ti satisfy the inequality:
$$lb \leq tj-ti \leq ub.$$
(also written as *(tj-ti)* $\in [lb,ub]$).

Proposition 1 is important because it establishes that to update interval associated with nodes to let them satisfy the consistency relation of Definition 8, it is necessary (and sufficient) to apply the four operations *a), b), c),* and *d)* defined above, checking that conditions *e)* and *f)* are never violated. Such operations constitute the solution to the *propagation* problem for the particular case of the elementary network in Figure 2. That solution, that we call *local*, is based on two different propagation actions whose name derives from the direction of the constraint from node *i* to node *j*:

* the *forward* operations:
   a) *lbj:=max[lbj, lbi+lb];*   b) *ubj:=min[ubj, ubi+ub].*
  that update the interval associated with the destination node *j* with respect to the source node *i*;
* the *backward* operations:
   c) *lbi:=max[lbi, lbj-ub];*   d) *ubi:=min[ubi, ubj-lb].*
  that update in the opposite direction node the *i* with respect to the destination node *j*.

Once defined the local propagation operations, we can detail an algorithm that given a network is able to propagate local changes through all the nodes' intervals to establish the validity of Definition 8. In fact after each local propagation we need to check

---

(^{2}) For lack of space the proofs of the Proposition 1 and the Theorems that follow are omitted. Those interested can request the extended version of the paper [CER93].

consistency of intervals in all the nodes connected to the first two (the simplest case of Figure 2 is still valid in the general case of a complex network). Of course propagation to the rest of the network is needed just in case of modification of any starting nodes' intervals. Broadly speaking the algorithm for the propagation of the effect of a modification (e.g. the insertion of a new constraint) on a temporal network will work as follows:

> Given a consistent temporal network on which modifications have been performed by adding new edges and/or shrinking intervals associated with previous edges, the propagation algorithm will apply the local propagation operations to all new and modified edges and then to all edges connected to nodes whose related intervals have been modified by the local propagation. The propagation process generated in such a way should continue until the local propagation operations either do not produce modifications on intervals' values any more, or an inconsistent condition $lbi > ubi$ is verified at some node i.

3 Propagation Algorithms for Temporal Networks

As we said above, the problem described above is equivalent to the simplest problem described in [DEC91] where it is said the problem can be solved in polinomial time in the number of nodes N. A number of different algorithms exist which solve similar problems (e.g. the well-known Floyd-Warshall algorithm and other shortest path algorithms, see [COR90]). Our rationale in developing a different algorithm can be justified as follows:

- We were bound to develop a tool able to accept incremental constraint posting. The abovementioned algorithms generally work on the overall graph and are not particularly efficient with respect to the incremental insertion;
- We found it useful to have an algorithm working directly on a network which is isomorphic with the partial solution the problem solver is building in the Temporal Data Base;
- We were interested in developing an algorithm endowed with some localization property and in studying other optimization criteria of the whole process.

3.1 A Basic Propagation Algorithm

Let us remember the two possible ways of modifying a temporal network:
- shrinking the interval *[lb, ub]* associated with an edge;
- adding a new path between two nodes of the network.

Each modification in the temporal network creates a propagation source through the network itself. In the following we speak of *propagation sources* to refer to constraints' modifications that request the network revision.

We now state a first propagation algorithm in a Pascal-like language. The main procedure of the implemented version, named *propagate* (see Figure 3), receives the list of propagation sources as a parameter. The boolean value *fail* points out an inconsistency at any point of the computation. The propagation process behaves by continuously popping up a new constraint among the sources (being a source either a new edge or a previous edge whose duration has been further constrained): the new constraint in the network is created and a propagation process starts (the innermost while-cycle in the Pascal-like procedure of Figure 3). The propagation process resembles the structure of Waltz's algorithm for constraint propagation [WAL75]. The process uses a working stack which is initialized with the propagation source, then it mainly applies the local modification operations to the edge popped from the stack and updates the content of the stack itself. The stack is updated by inserting the edges, different from *current-edge*, linked to the nodes joined by the *current-edge*, if these nodes have been modified; on the contrary if the nodes are not modified the propagation process stops.

```
Procedure propagate (propagation-sources);
    var     source, current-edge: EdgeType;
            stack: StackType;
            fail: Boolean;
    begin
        fail ← False
        while (propagation-sources <> NIL) and (not fail) do
            begin
                source ←  pop(propagation-sources);
                <insert source in the temporal network>;
                stack ← {source};
                while (not-empty stack) and (not fail) do
                    begin
                        current-edge ← pop(stack);
                        <apply both forward and backward operations to current-edge>;
                        if  <one of the intervals associated to the nodes
                            connected by current-edge is empty>
                        then
                            fail ← True;
                        else
                            stack ← stack ∪ {all edges≠current-edge connected to the nodes
                                whose intervals have been modified by the local operations};
                    end
            end
end;
```

Figure 3

The distinction among different modification actions is based on the four basic local operations *a)*, *b)*, *c)* and *d)* of Proposition 1. The updating cycle performed by propagating modifications continues until either no more effects will be caused by the local operations or a node verifies the $lb > ub$. It is worth noting that a valuable property of this kind of algorithm stands in the fact that when a modification is completely absorbed by a node then the propagation automatically stops. This is a localization property that other approaches (e.g. Floyd-Warshall) do not have.

3.2 Correctness and Completeness of the Algorithm

The algorithm *propagate* checks consistency by analyzing the temporal interval $[lb_i, ub_i]$ associated with those nodes belonging to the sub-network interested by the modification. If one of the intervals is empty the network is inconsistent. What we want to clearly demonstrate now is that the kind of consistency detected by the *propagate* is equivalent to the property stated in Definition 8. To this purpose let us give the precise definition of *algorithmic consistency*.

Definition 9 - (*Algorithmic Consistency*.) - A temporal network is said algorithmically consistent if and only if the application of the propagation algorithm guarantees the condition $lb_i \leq ub_i$ satisfied for each node in the network.

The equivalence between the two types of consistency (the one practically checked and the one formally defined) is given by the following Theorem:

Theorem 1
A temporal network is algorithmically consistent if and only if it is also temporally consistent.

Because of Theorem 1, the algorithm we have designed is correct and complete. It recognizes as consistent only network in situations defined by Definition 8. It is worth noting that in a problem solving architecture the temporal constraint propagation module is not in charge of cutting the search space that is the heuristic-decision module's responsibility. As a consequence, both correctness and completeness of the propagator are crucial properties.

The result achieved until now consists of a careful understanding of the basic mechanisms that allow to check consistency. From now on we can address the problem of improving the algorithm's efficiency by better understanding both the structure of the problem and the algorithm itself.

3.3   Improving Propagation Efficiency
As seen before, the *propagate* algorithm works on a stack to incrementally propagate modifications across the entire network. Each time the interval of a node is modified, the algorithm inserts the set of edges entering the node and the set of edges leaving the node in the stack, but the edge causing the modification is of course excluded. It may happen that the source edge which initially caused the modification is re-entered in the stack; when such a situation happens we say the propagation algorithm has *entered a cycle*. A cycle of the propagation algorithm is not necessarily connected with an oriented cycle in the temporal graph, but can be also generated by the existence of a closed not oriented path.

If the algorithm is cycling it is inevitable that a condition $lb>ub$ eventually happens. Early recognition of cycles allows the system to promptly stop the propagation signalling inconsistency without cycling for a while. This is particularly useful in incremental constraint posting because in such a case we need to backtrack and revise some previous choice.

The following Theorem guarantees that the recognition of a cycle is a sufficient condition to declare failure.

Theorem 2
A sufficient condition for the inconsistency of a temporal network is that the propagation algorithm executes updating operation on a closed path containing the source edge.

Given such a property we can modify the previous algorithm to detect a cycle. The new algorithm is similar to *propagate*. The differences consist of marking the source edge at the beginning of the process and then, when the algorithm updates the working stack, before pushing a new edge in the stack of performing a test to check if the inserted edge is the propagation source; in such a case an inconsistency is immediately detected.

The improvement described in this paragraph could be judged small, but we consider rather important the fact of having formally demonstrated the sufficient condition. Moreover, the presence of the cycle is particularly dangerous as shown in Figure 4 and pointed out in [DAV87, page 318].

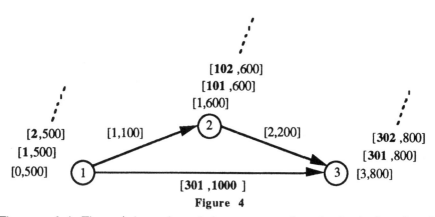

Figure 4

The example in Figure 4 shows the updating process made active by the insertion of a constraint between nodes 1 and 3 (labelled with interval [301, 1000]). Such a process involves a closed (not oriented) path and continuously modifies the lower bounds of nodes' intervals with step 1 (e.g., the lower bound of node 1 is set to 1, 2, 3 ...). A similar thing happens for the upper bounds but we do not show it in the Figure. As a consequence, an inconsistency is detected only after a number of iterations given by the length of the smallest nodes' intervals on the closed path. The inconsistency occurs because the maximal distance on the path $<(1,2), (2,3)>$ is less than the minimal distance along the path $<(1,3)>$; as a consequence the distance interval between nodes 1 and 3 results to be empty.

3.4 Complexity of the Algorithm

A characterization of the worst case in our algorithm can be computed in terms of the maximum number of edges inserted in the working stack once a source edge is added. The choice is justified because such a maximum is directly proportional to the number of updating actions performed (such operations are the crucial part of the algorithm). Calculating the number of edges is not easy, but we can estimate an upper bound in the following way:

> Let us observe that, unfortunately, a node can be modified several times without causing any inconsistency. If the graph containing N nodes is complete, each time that a node is modified *(N-2)* edges are inserted in the working stack (the maximum number of insisting edges but the node that introduced propagation). Let k be the maximum number of modifications that can be performed on a node in the case that the graph is fully connected. Because of the bound k to the number of modifications on a node, the complexity (measured as the maximal dimension of the working stack) will be:
>
> $$O(2 (N\text{-}2) + k(N\text{-}2)(N\text{-}2)) = O(kN^2)$$

We are currently investigating the possibility of determining justified criteria to rank the edges in the working stack in order to maintain the constant k sufficiently low (the best option being of course $k=1$) by appropriately selecting the next edge to propagate through ([3]).

([3]) A similar constant is also introduced in the complexity evaluation of Waltz's algorithm proposed in [MAC85].

In realistic applications, it is reasonable to assume that the number of temporal relations that an event has with respect to other events does not increase when the total number of events represented in the network increases. In such a case, the temporal network results in a sparse graph: a graph such that a number of edges bound by a constant arrive to and depart from each node. In this situation, the complexity results to be $O(kaN)$. In fact, being the number of edges $E=aN$, we may rewrite the complexity value as $O(kaN)=O(kE)$.

At any rate, the current bound is satisfactory enough. It is worth saying that the complexity evaluation just described concerns the problem of the incrementally updating of a network in a previous consistent state and on which some modifications have been done. An important remark to be done concerns the average case complexity. As we said above, the algorithm updates the temporal network in a way to bound propagation effects around the sub-network actually affected by modifications. As a consequence we are expecting an improvement of the complexity in the average case analysis. Such an expectation has been supported by a first run of tests. According to the current experimentation when a new consistent constraint is inserted the average number of updating operations is a small fraction (about 10%) of the total number of edges in the network, while when an inconsistent constraint is inserted, the use of the property stated by Theorem 2 causes a decrease of the number of updating operation of about 50÷60 % in the average case. We are currently sharpening our analysis to arrive to an experimental characterization of the average case.

3.5 Choosing a Solution

We conclude the presentation of the algorithm discussing how to select a consistent assignment for the variables ti once we have a propagated network. If the network is consistent it is possible to specify a set of values for the ti that are compatible with each of the intervals associated with the nodes. There exists at least one of this choice satisfying Definition 8. The choice cannot be casual because two generic ti and tj should have a distance included in $[Dmin(i,j),Dmax(i,j)]$. This observation does not represent a limitation because the propagation algorithm eliminates just the values of the $[lbi,ubj]$ which are *surely* incompatible with the given constraints, avoiding to cut out any legal solution.

Two possible choices are always plausible: assigning to ti either all the lbs or all the ubs. The demonstration of this statement is given by the observation that in a consistent network given two nodes x and y the following relations hold (for lack of space the proof is omitted):

$$Dmin(x,y) \leq lby - lbx \leq Dmax(x,y),$$
$$Dmin(x,y) \leq uby - ubx \leq Dmax(x,y).$$

Such relations show that choosing the lower bound or the upper bound always generates a choice consistent with the network constraints.

4 Discussion and Conclusions

The algorithm described so far have been implemented in a tool for temporal constraint maintenance. The tool is written in Common-Lisp and runs on different hardware supports. Particular attention has been devoted to design the primitives of the tool to allow creation and retraction of constraints. In the present status the tool can be easily incorporated in different applications to serve as a basic temporal reasoning support. We have used it in a Temporal Data Base *a la* HSTS [MUS92] and developed both a temporal planner and a scheduler.

What we have presented here are some steps towards the creation of an efficient temporal propagator. The current study is grounded on clean definitions and on formal demonstration of the basic properties among them (it is worth reminding the sufficient condition stated by Theorem 2). We hope to keep this style while adding new features to the system. As mentioned above, we are currently extending the formal analysis to an algorithm able to perform propagation on more that one edge in parallel, and are empirically evaluating the average case complexity.

This research can be inserted in a current trend devoted to the critical analysis of the TMM system. Other authors have concentrated their attention on revising basic definitions [MAT91], and on the analysis of the persistence clipping problem [SCH92]. In the present work we have carefully described the mechanisms regulating the consistency maintenance and presented an algorithm endowed with reasonable computational capabilities.

Acknowledgements

Many thanks to Luigia Carlucci Aiello that encouraged us to write this work and commented a previous draft of the paper. The authors are partially supported by CNR under "Progetto Finalizzato Sistemi Informatici e Calcolo Parallelo", Grant n.104385/69/9107197 to IP-CNR. Amedeo Cesta is also partially supported by CNR under Special Project on Planning.

References

[ALL83]   Allen, J.F., Maintaining Knowledge about Temporal Intervals. *Communications of the ACM*, 1983, 832-853.

[CER93]   Cervoni, R., Cesta, A., Oddi, A., Maintaining Consistency in Quantitative Temporal Constraint Networks for Planning and Scheduling. Technical Report IP-CNR, Rome, June 1993.

[COR90]   Cormen, T.H., Leierson, C.E., Rivest, R.L., *Introduction to Algorithms*, MIT Press, 1990.

[DAV87]   Davis, E., Constraint Propagation with Interval Labels, *Artificial Intelligence*, 1987.

[DEA87]   Dean, T.L., McDermott, D.V., Temporal Data Base Management. *Artificial Intelligence*, 32, 1987. 1-55.

[DEA88]   Dean, T.L., Firby, R.J., Miller, D., Hierarchical planning involving deadlines, travel time, and resources. *Computational Intelligence*, 4, 1988, 381-398.

[DEC91]   Dechter, R., Meiri, I., Pearl, J., Temporal constraint networks. *Artificial Intelligence*, 49, 1991, 61-95.

[LEP87]   Le Pape, C., Smith, S.F., Management of Temporal Constraints for Factory Scheduling. Technical Report CMU-RI-TR-87-13, Carnegie Mellon University, June 1987.

[MAC85]   Mackworth, A. K., Freuder, E. C., The Complexity of Some Polynomial Network Consistency Algorithms for Constraint Satisfaction Problems. *Artificial Intelligence*, 25, 1985, 65-74.

[MAT91]   Materne, S., Herzberg, J., MTMM - Correcting and Extending Time Map Management. In: Hertzberg, J., (ed.), *European Workshop on Planning* (EWSP-91). LNAI 522, Springer-Verlag, 1991, 88-99.

[MUS92]   Muscettola, N., Smith, S.F., Cesta, A., D'Aloisi, D., Coordinating Space Telescope Operations in an Integrated Planning and Scheduling Architecture. *IEEE Control Systems Magazine*, Vol.12, N.1, February 1992.

[MUS93]   Muscettola, N., Scheduling by Iterative Partition of Bottleneck Conflicts. *Proc. 9th IEEE Conference on AI Applications* , Orlando, FL, 1993.

[RIT86]   Rit, J.F., Propagating Temporal Constraints for Scheduling. *Proceedings of AAAI-86*, Philadelphia, PA, 1986.

[SCH92]   Schrag, R., Boddy, M., Carciofini, J., Managing Disjunction for Practical Temporal Reasoning. *Proceedings of KR'92*. Morgan Kaufmann, 1992.

[SMI93]   Smith, S.F., Cheng, C., Slack-Based Heuristics for Constraint Satisfaction Scheduling, *Proceedings of AAAI-93*, Washington, DC, 1993.

[VAN92]   vanBeek, P., Reasoning About Qualitative Temporal Information, *Artificial Intelligence*, 58, 1992, 297-326.

[VER83]   Vere, S.A., Planning in Time: Windows and Durations for Activities and Goals. *IEEE Transactions on Pattern Analysis and Machine Intelligence,* Vol.PAMI-5, No.3, May 1983, 246-276.

[WAL75]   Waltz, D., Understanding Line Drawings of Scenes with Shadows. In: Winston, P.H., (ed.), *The Psychology of Computer Vision*. McGraw-Hill, 1975.

Making an Autonomous Robot Plan Temporally Constrained Maintenance Operations

S. Badaloni[1], E. Pagello[1,2], L. Stocchiero[2] and A. Zanardi[2]

[1] Dipartimento di Elettronica e Informatica, Padova - Italy
[2] LADSEB-CNR, Padova, Italy

Abstract. We present a system that can determine temporal scheduling of actions of an autonomous mobile robot by constructing a plan taking into account temporal constraints. Both qualitative and metric temporal information are represented in a constraint based network. Planning tasks are performed on the basis of the knowledge derived by this temporal knowledge representation system. Ordering temporally qualified actions falls out from maintaining temporal consistency. We applied it to plan under temporal constraints the actions of a manipulator mounted on a mobile platform in the case of the maintenance intervention over a hydraulic circuit.

1 Introduction

We address the problem of planning temporally constrained actions of an autonomous robot by using a temporal reasoning system. In the application we are interested in this paper, we need to represent the following facts:
- events may occur besides the changes due to the agent actions,
- actions are not instantaneous,
- temporal knowledge about the world is coarse,
- there exists some strict deadline to be included in the plan construction,
- complex plans may involve complex ordering constraints.

To this aim, planner systems based on the classical STRIPS assumption [8] are not adequate: in fact, actions are instantaneous and all changes in the world result from the agent's actions; in other words, the agent has a complete knowledge of the world relevant to plan its actions. In other non-linear planning systems, the problem of planning simultaneous actions has been addressed but, in most of them, a too simple world model is adopted, where actions are supposed to be completely independent. Thus, the effect of two simultaneous actions is taken as the sum of their individual effects: this is not always the case. As a consequence, it would be impossible to plan two actions temporally overlapping. A more interesting approach has been introduced by Allen, by considering the planning system as a specialized inference process on an interval based temporal logic that can reason about simultaneous actions.

However, since in Allen's temporal logic [1, 3], only qualitative temporal information can be handled, it would be impossible to deal with plans involving deadlines and quantitative temporal constraints. In order to express explicitly temporal quantitative constraints and treat deadlines, we propose to include the metric information relative to the durations of intervals in the temporal world model making possible to construct a plan composed by actions fully constrained both qualitative and quantitative.

The main ideas are:
- planning can be viewed as reasoning on temporally qualified actions
- any type of temporal constraints can be explicitly represented (i.e. qualitative relations between temporals intervals, durations of intervals and metric information associated with the relations between two intervals).

The temporal reasoning system presented in this paper has been designed to help coordinating the actions needed to solve the problems listed below thanks to its capability to deal with the time abstraction. The paper is organized as follows: in the first section we will describe the experiment in which we have applied the temporal scheduling system; in sections 2, 3 the planner system together with the temporal knowledge representation network will be described. Finally, after having described the general structure of our system, we show in section 4 how to plan a sub task with certain temporal constraints by temporally qualifying the sequence of actions.

2 The Robotized Hydraulic Maintenance Experiment

The system described in next sections allows an autonomous robot to accomplish temporally qualified actions needed for satisfying hydraulic maintenance duties. The experiment consists in simulating a maintenance intervention on the mock-up of a hydraulic circuit by means of an anthropomorphic robot - designed by CESI [4] - placed on a mobile base and equipped both with force and 2&1/2 D vision sensors, that must move in an unstructured environment. The experiment is being accomplished for demonstrating the results of the Research Project on Planning Robot Task by Sensorized Robots (ALPI Project) - a subtask of the Special Research Project on Robotics (PFR) of the Italian National Council of Research (CNR) - which collects about ten different italian partners and is coordinated by LADSEB [16].

An hydraulic mock-up has been built at CESI, in Milan, where the robot demonstration will take place, with standard components as valves, taps, temperature and pressure indicators. The robot operating on the mock-up, is an autonomous controlled crawler mobile chart carrying a manipulator, with vision, ultrasonic, and force-torque sensors. The robot mission is to inspect and operate a valve of this hydraulic circuit used as a testbed. The main steps in the experiment are: reaching the work area, reading the data from the measurement instruments and determining the actions to be done on the several handles.

The LADSEB Institute, besides coordinating the whole project, is involved in solving the first and the third experiment steps. The first step consists in finding a collision free motion both for the mobile base and for the PUMA's gripper. To solve the collision problems we are applying a technique derived from our past study on designing fast algorithms for detecting collision among convex polyhedra [13]. Our algorithm allows some local spatial reasoning by considering restricted portion of the C-Space [14], in order to build a preplanning procedure [15]. The computed plan then can be executed on-line by using the prediction theory developed in [5].

The third step consists in finding the exact position and orientation of one handle, inserting the tool, held by the robot gripper, in this handle, and rotating it until some final condition has been achieved. We applied to this case our experience acquired within the Esprit CIM-PLATO Project where we have experimented a simulated model of Salisbury's three-fingered hand, [6]. In order to work locally in Padova on the this step, a Unimation Puma 560 was mounted at LADSEB on a fixed base and equipped with a Lord force/torque sensor FT30/100 mounted on the wrist. To manipulate the handle, we used a special tool with three rigid pins, which took the place of a three-fingered hand [7].

3 The Planner System

Planning tasks are performed on the basis of the knowledge derived by the temporal knowledge representation network. Knowledge about actions is represented by a set of temporally qualified facts and by a set of planning rules. The temporally qualified entities are those according to the Allen ontology [2]:

- property: *holds(P, I)*, the property P is true in the interval I
- event: *occur(A, E, I)*, in which E is the event occurring in the interval I and associated to the action A; the interval I is expressed as *etime(E)*
- process: *occurring (P, I)*, indicating the process P occurring in the interval I.

The planning rules are expressed in the form:
$$G \longleftarrow [A_1,...,A_n], [constr_1,...,constr_k]$$

with the following intended meaning: G is true or provable if $A_1,...,A_n$ are true such that $constr_1,...,constr_k$ are satisfied. A_i represents an action to be performed or an assumption to be made about the future while $constr_i$ represents a temporal constraint that may exist between the intervals in which actions occur. To apply a rule in backward chaining, the consequent G is unified with the goal and the set of constraints is introduced into temporal knowledge representation network; consistency is checked and then the antecedents become the new subgoals. A rule may be applied by the system also in forward chaining in order to compute the consequences of the assumptions made about persistence of properties and action attempts in order to predict which world will be like. In fact, two hypotheses have been assumed:

- a property persists until some event can change it,
- the agent can attempt to execute an action. This fact is expressed by imposing that:
$$try(A, E, I) \longrightarrow occur(A, E, I)$$

The planner is then composed by a part working in backward chaining from the goals in order to determine which actions should be performed and which assumptions should the agent make about its future behaviour and its future world; and by another part working in forward chaining to compute the consequences of its assumptions.

At the beginning, given a goal and an initial description of the world, the system works in backward chaining by instantiating actions and by making assumptions trying to find a sequence of actions that verify the initial goal. This means that the ordering of actions satisfies the temporal constraints between intervals in which actions take place.

The assumptions made during the planning process must be consistent; if they are not then the planner has to be invoked.

Furthermore, knowledge about the world is codified in:

- a set of domain constraints concerning the structure of the world which express some basic principle: e.g. two intervals in which mutually exclusive events take place are disjoint
- the temporal structure of each event associated the an action in terms of the temporal relations between the intervals in which preconditions, conditions and effects of the action hold; these intervals are named *pre(E), con(E), eff(E)*.

The planning mechanism, that is based on that proposed by Allen [3], provides the temporal scheduling of temporally qualified actions of the autonomous agent, including deadlines.

4 The Temporal Knowledge Representation Network

To represent temporal knowledge in our system we have combined two paradigms: that of the Allen interval-based temporal logic and that of the constraint programming thus making possible the integration between qualitative and metric temporal information. Indeed, the problem of maintaining a temporal data base can be viewed as a problem of constraint propagation. In fact the temporal relations between intervals represent local constraints imposed on them in an explicit way that have to be satisfied globally, while the process of extracting new knowledge is based on the fact of making explicit the implicit constraints that are then created.

All temporally qualified entities are referred to intervals. A possible evolution of the world is described in terms of events (action-event or external event) and properties associated to intervals and in terms of the temporal constraints between intervals that determine their location in the world history. In our system, the temporal qualitative and metric information is represented in a constraint network whose nodes represent intervals and the directed arcs the set of tightest constraints allowed between each pair of intervals. Such a network obtained by deductive closure on the temporal constraints is called minimal network.

In the present application, the set of possible relations between two intervals are those proposed by [1] and by [9], where Allen's thirteen mutually exclusive relations are grouped on the basis of the notion of 'conceptual neighbourhood'. Starting from the idea that we can easily discover neighbouring concepts by imagining gradual changes in the represented world, Freksa has proposed the following definition: two relations between pairs of events are (conceptual) neighbours if they can be directly transformed into one another by continuously deforming the events. As an example, the relations before (<) and meets (m) are conceptual neighbours, since they can be transformed into one another directly by lengthening one of the events while the relations before (<) and overlaps (o) are not; in the former case a relation *pr* (precedes) can be defined in order to represent the set {<, m}. This representation seems cognitively more adequate since it allows to process directly coarse temporal Knowledge. Furthermore, by compacting the knowledge base, it reduces considerably the computational effort: this is the main reason we used this approach.

The metric constraints represent the duration of intervals, that is, the temporal distances between the beginning and the ending of an interval; the uncertainty relative to such a duration can be expressed as its range of variability (e.g. I1 (1,5), that is the duration of I1 is in between 1 to 5 (referring to some time scale)). Furthermore, in our system it is possible to represent the quantitative information associated with the relation between two intervals: e.g., if I1 before I2 is true then it is possible to represent not only how long the two intervals are but also how much I1 is before I2. This allows us to avoid a problem that arises in other temporal systems: if the metric information is associated only to interval durations, it is necessary to introduce fictitious intervals between the ending of an interval and the beginning of another one.

Thus the network is completely characterised from a temporal point of view; any kind of temporal information that is available can be represented, except for absolute datation. Temporal constraints can be expressed in a unique framework based on intervals and metric constraints concerning the beginnings and endings of intervals are represented without referring to them explicitly.

The metric information associated to intervals is expressed as their duration. If the information is coarse, then more than one duration can be associated to each interval. The metric information associated to relations (distances between two intervals) is expressed as 4 ranges of variability in R of the distances $(I2_s - I1_s)$, $(I2_e - I1_s)$, $(I2_s - I1_e)$, $(I2_e - I1_e)$ between the starting Ij_s and ending Ij_e of any two intervals I1 and I2. The metric values that are unknown are not specified or can be considered as maximum range of variability.

If we know, for ex., that I1 precedes I2 of 5-10 minutes and that the maximum duration from the starting point of I1 and the ending point of I2 must not exceed one hour, we represent as:

$$I1 \{b,((-\infty,+\infty),(0,60],(5,10),(-\infty,+\infty))\} I2$$

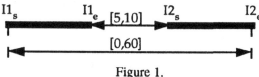

Figure 1.

There is an interaction between qualitative and quantitative knowledge: in fact, the qualitative relations impose metric constraints on the extremes of intervals that must be consistent with those imposed as input knowledge on the durations of relations and intervals. On the other hand, the metric information constrains the qualitative one: e.g., if the duration of I1 is greater than that of I2, then I1 cannot be contained into I2.

Coming back to our example, if we input the information that I1 (1,5) and I2 (10,20), then the system verifies the consistency and computes the minimal network.

$$I1 \{b,((6,15),(16,60),(5,10),(15,59))\} I2$$

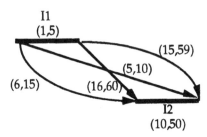

Figure 2.

The computation of the minimal network is a constraint propagation problem. Indeed, extracting new information from this temporal database can be configurable as a Constraint Satisfaction Problem (CSP). Temporal relations imposed on intervals are local constraints that have to be satisfied globally. For this reason, to solve the network, we have used the CLP(R) language [10], a logic programming language able to handle arithmetical constraints in a declarative way together with normal clauses. It incrementally tests the consistency of a set of constraints while collecting them in the goal reduction process. To guarantee homogeneity, all the temporal scheduling system has been implemented in this language.

When a new interval or a new constraint has to be included into the network the system has to calculate how this new information propagate in the network, or, in other words, to compute all the logical consequences of the input data. This is done by computing the minimal network: by definition it is the intersection of all the equivalent networks, that are the networks defining the same solutions. In the minimal network every pair of values allowed by an explicit constraint belongs at least to one solution. The computation of the minimal network for the interval algebra is NP-hard because of the presence of disjunctive constraints [18]. Polynomial algorithms can be applied to subclasses of networks obtained by considering only one relation for each constraint and only one duration for each interval. The number of these networks increases in exponential way with the number of arcs and with the number of relations associated to each arc (k^n with n number of arcs and k number of relations for arc). Thus it is evident the advantage to use the relations proposed by Freksa since it reduces the number of labellings of each arc.

The algorithm used by our system to compute the minimal network is:

1) search all the consistent networks obtained considering one constraint (qualitative and metric) for each relation and one duration for each interval.

2) for each such network

    2.1) translate it into the network whose nodes represent the interval extremes and the directed arcs are labelled with the range of variability of the distances between nodes.

    2.2) apply the All-Pair Shortest-Path algorithm ($O(n^3)$ with n number of nodes) to obtain the minimal ranges of variability for the distances.

    2.3) transform these distances into durations of intervals and into qualitative/metric relations between intervals.

3) merge these networks obtaining the minimal network relative to the original constrain.

In step 1, the search space is explored using CLP(R) capability to incrementally check the consistency of a set of metric constraints, so that the problem is solved with a simple search with backtracking. This certainly improves the efficiency of the system.

5 Results

We illustrate in the following the application of our approach to the temporal scheduling in a simplified but significant sub-task of the experiment of the ALPI project, the one where the robot has to turn the valve handle of the hydraulic circuit within a fixed time (a deadline) starting from a given instant. Furthermore, the water tap positioned in the upstream with respect to the valve has to be turned on: we consider this action accomplished by an external agent to be an external event. In this way, we have selected a scenario, characterised by simultaneous actions (including external events) and a deadline to be satisfied by the autonomous robot in accomplishing the task. In other words, the autonomous robot has to do something within a fixed time by constructing a plan which has to take into account some temporal constraints.

The initial knowledge about the world consist of the facts that, at the starting time, (1) the robot stays at the laboratory, (2) the water tap positioned in the upperside of the valve will be turned on after 15 minutes after the starting time, and (3) the goal has to be reached within 20 minutes from the reference instant.

Thus, the description of the first two properties consists of the following temporally qualified sentences:

      (1) holds (to_stay_at(lab), i_at_lab)

      (2) holds (open_tap, i_tap_o)

where, in the Allen style, holds(p, i) means that the property p is true in the interval i. In our system, knowledge about intervals is represented by using:

      int (i_name, [list_durations])

where each duration is expressed by an interval in R represented with the parameter d(extr, extr) where extr is each of the two extremes of the interval, and pinf and minf mean respectively $+\infty$ and $-\infty$.

In the considered scenario, the temporal intervals have been supposed to have the following values (fig. 3):

int (i0, [d(pinf, pinf)])	the reference interval
int (i_tap_o, [d(50, pinf)])	the tap stays open for at least 50 minutes
int (i_goal, [d(10, pinf)])	the goal has to be verified for at least 10 minutes
int (i_valv_tur, [d(0, pinf)])	the interval during which the valve handle is turned is supposed to have an indefinite duration
int (i_at_lab, [d(0, pinf)])	the robot stays at the laboratory in a time interval of indefinite duration

The knowledge about the constraints is expressed as:

constr (i1_name, i2_name, [list_relations])

including in the list_relations all the known qualitative and metric constraints. So their values in the experiment are (fig. 3):

constr (i0, i_goal, [d11(0,20)])   the goal has to be reached within 20 minutes (d11= (i_goal$_s$ - i0$_s$))

constr (i_goal, i_valv_tur, [d])   the valve handle has to be turned during i_goal (d is the qualitative relation during)

constr (i0, i_tap_o, [d11(15,15)])   the tap is turned on 15 minutes after the beginning of the reference interval

constr (i0, i_at_lab, [hh])   the robot is at laboratory since the initial instant for a certain time (being hh = head to head [9]).

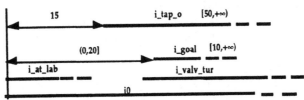

Figure 3 - The initial world description.

The actions that the robot has to plan taking into account these temporal restrictions are:
- reaching the working area
- reading the manometer, which has the precondition of being in front of the manometer and has the effect of knowing the manometer value
- turning the valve handle, which has as preconditions the fact of being in front of the valve, of knowing the manometer value and that the tap has already been opened; the effect is that the valve has been turned
- opening the water tap positioned in the upperside of the valve, which has the precondition of being in front of it and the effect that the tap has been opened.

The planning rules have been defined in correspondence with each action. We show in the following the rules for the case of turning the valve handle:

holds (valv_turned,T1) <---
    [occur (turn_valv, E, etime(E))], [constr (T1, eff1(E), [e])])

occur (turn_valv, E, etime(E) <---
    [holds (stay_at(valv_pos), pre1(E)), holds (read_val_man, pre2(E)),
    holds (tap_open, pre3(E)), try (turn_valv, E, etime(E))]

being pre1,2,3(E) and eff1(E) the name of the interval in which the preconditions and the effect of the event E (action-event) take place, and "e" the relation equal.

The temporal relations that must hold among the event associated to the action "turn_valv", its effect and its precondition is represented by the following temporal structure:

temp_struct (occur (turn_valv, E, etime(E)),

    [int (etime(E), [d(1,4)]), int (pre1(E), [d(0,pinf)]), int (pre2(E), [d(0, pinf)]),

    int (pre3(E), [d(0,pinf)]), int (eff1(E), [d(0,pinf)]),

    constr (pre1(E), etime(E), [di]), constr (pre2(E), etime(E), [oc, d21(minf, -1)]),

    constr (pre3(E), etime(E), [di]), constr (etime(E), eff1(E), [m])])

(where di, oc, m are the relations during inverse, older contemporary of and meets respectively). It states that the "turn_valv" operation has to last [1,4] minutes and the measure of the manometer has to be recorded for at least one minute since the beginning of the operation.

    The disjointness of intervals in which mutually exclusive events take place is stated by the domain axioms.

dom_constr ([holds (stay_at(X), T1) ,holds (stay_at(Y), T2),

    not(X = Y)], [constr (T1, T2, [b, bi])])

dom_constr ([occur(go_to(X), T1), holds (stay_at (Y), T2)],

    [constr (T1, T2, [b , bi])])])

dom_constr (occur (go_to(X) ,E1, etime(E1)),

    occur (go_to(Y) ,E2, etime(E2)), not(E1=E2)],

    [constr (etime(E1), etime(E2), [b, bi])])])

expressing that it is not possible to stay at different places at the same moment, it is not possible to stay in a place and to go to another one and that it is not possible to go to different places at the same moment, respectively (b and bi are the relations before and before inverse).

    Now, the temporal scheduling system has to prove the goal in the form:

        holds (valv_turned, i_valv_turn)

which, on the basis of input and derived knowledge, is satisfied by instantiating the temporally qualified actions in the plan (fig. 4):

occur (go_to(man_pos), ev(4), etime(ev(4)))

duration [1,10]: beginning (0,16) ending (1,17)

occur (read_man, ev(3), etime(ev(3)))

duration [1,2] : beginning (1,17) ending (3,18)

occur (go_to(valv_pos), ev(2), etime(ev(2)))

duration [1,10] :beginning (2,18) ending (3,19)

occur (turn_valv, ev(1), etime(ev(1)))

duration [1,4]: beginning (15,19) ending (16,20)

    In fig. 5 it has been reported part of the minimal network relative to the sub-problem we have analized.

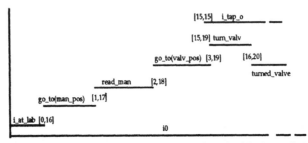

Figure 4 - The intervals in which events associated with the actions occur.

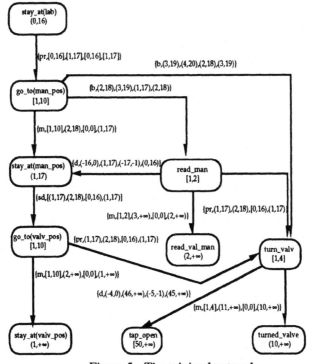

Figure 5 - The minimal network.

In the obtained plan, as a consequence of the temporal constraint propagation, the two actions of going to the manometer position ev(4) and going to the valve position ev(2) are correctly ordered so that their effects do not interfere: during the process of goal reduction the planner does not care about the fact that the action "going to the manometer" could destroy the precondition of the action "staying at the valve position" (fig. 4). The obtained sequence of actions is also well synchronised with the open_tap interval, thus taking into account that an external agent may have correctly executed this action or an external event may have caused it according to the temporal constraints. The ending point of the interval associated to the event turn_valv has a value between 16 and 20 (with respect to a time scale), thus showing that the deadline has been satisfied.

The main result we have obtained is that, starting from an incomplete temporal layout of actions and events, the ordering of actions in the final plan falls out directly from maintaining the temporal constraints consistency and by computing the minimal network. A plan is a set of temporally qualified actions.

6 Conclusions

We presented a temporal scheduling system constituted by a planner algorithm and a world model that includes the representation of qualitative and metric temporal information making possible the robot to deal with simultaneous actions and deadlines. Integrating metric information makes the system more expressive with respect the Allen planner. Another planning approach able to manage durations and windows of actions is Deviser [17] that uses a reasoning based on preconditions and effects of actions. Therefore, it substantially remains a state-based approach. In our approach, on the contrary, everything is compared on the scale of time, and preconditions and effects are handled as relations among the temporal intervals in which they are valid. Hence more correlations can be expressed within the same temporal framework.

Nevertheless, other approaches, even if they do not deal with planning problems, allow to represent explicitly metric information: they often make use of temporal points. In [11], for ex., the information is represented in two separate networks: one with qualitative information, in which nodes represent intervals, and one with metric information, in which nodes represent ending and starting points of intervals. Maintaining information in this way is quite expensive, as it is necessary to compute the constraints imposed by one network on the other one in an iterative way. Besides, it is not possible to express disjunctive metric relations and to directly associate each qualitative relation of a disjunctive set to its correspondent metric relation.

Meiri instead [12] makes use of one only network with two kinds of nodes: one kind represent intervals, the other temporal points. Constraints between intervals consist of Allen disjunctive qualitative relations, while constraints between points consist of the set $(<,=,>)$ of qualitative relations or metric relations (ranges of variability of the temporal distances). Meiri also defines the qualitative relations (before, starts, during, finishes, after) between a point and an interval. This approach allows the direct representation of qualitative and metric information, but it is necessary to consider a redundant number of nodes in the network (3 nodes for each interval) and it is still not possible to associate a qualitative relation in a disjunctive set to its correspondent metric relations.

In comparison with the above approaches concerning the integration of metric information, our system is more compact since it represents explicitly in the network only intervals, but it is still as expressive as the Meiri's one allowing the user to impose metric boundaries on the temporal distances between the ending points of intervals. Finally, the decreased number of disjunctive qualitative relations between intervals and the use of CLP language considerably reduce the computational effort.

Acknowledgements

This research has been partially granted by the Italian Special Program on Robotics of the CNR (Progetto Finalizzato Robotica), by the Italian Special Program on Automated Planning of the CNR and by the Italian Ministry of University, Science and Technology.

References

1. J.F. Allen: Maintaining knowledge about temporal intervals. CACM 26,11, pg. 832-843, 1983.

2. J.F.Allen: Toward a general theory of action and time. Artificial Intelligence vol.23, pg.123-154, 1984.

3. J.F. Allen, H.A. Kautz, R.N. Pelavin, J.D. Tenenberg : Reasoning about plans. Morgan Kaufmann, San Mateo, Calif., 1991.

4. M. Aspes, L.Bortoli, L.Orsenigo, L. & M. Maini.: Multisensory Autonomous Robotic Inspection and Manipulation in an Unstructured Environment. Robotics and Automation IEEE Newsletter, Vol. 6, No. 4, pp. 22, 32, 1992.

5. S. Badaloni, E. Pagello & C. Sossai : An Autonomous Mobile Robot in a Temporally Rich Domain: Some Considerations from the Standpoint of A.I. In T. Kanade, F.C.A. Groen and L.O. Hertzberger (Eds.), Proc. of IAS-2, Amsterdam, pp. 672-682, 1989.

6. P. Bison, C.Mirolo, E. Pagello & L. Stocchiero: Grasp Planning for a Three-fingered Hand. Chapter 16.6 of the book on "Integration of Robots into CIM", R. Bernhardt, R. Dillman, K. Hörmann, K. Tierney (Eds.), Chapman & Hall 1992, pp. 155-164

7. G. Chemello, E. Pagello, C. Sossai, L. Stocchiero: Reasoning and planning on sensor data: an application of a many-valued logic. In Proc. of the ISIR '92 Workshop, Barcellona, pp. 61-66, 1992.

8. P.E. Fikes, N.J. Nilsson: STRIPS: A new approach of theorem proving to problem solving. Artificial Intelligence 2, pg. 189-208, 1971.

9. C. Freksa: Temporal Reasoning based on Semi-Intervals. Artificial Intelligence vol.54, pg.199-227, 1992.

10. J.Jaffar, S.Michaylov: Methodology and implementation of a CLP system. Proc. of the 4th Int. Conf. on Logic Programming, Melbourne, pg.196-218, 1987.

11. H.A.Kautz, P.B.Ladkin: Integrating metric and qualitative temporal reasoning. Working Notes AAAI Spring Symposium Series, 1991.

12. I. Meiri: Combining Qualitative and Quantitative Constraints in Temporal Reasoning. Working Notes on AAAI Spring Symphosium Series, 1991.

13. C. Mirolo & E. Pagello:A Solid Modelling System for Robot Action Planning. IEEE C.G. & A., Vol.9, No.1, pp. 29-34, 1989.

14. C. Mirolo & E. Pagello: Local Geometric Issues for Spatial Reasoning in Robot Motion Planning. In Proc. of IROS '91, Osaka. pp. 569-574, 1991.

15. E. Modolo & E. Pagello: Collision Avoidance Detection in Space and Time Planning for Autonomous Robots. Proc. of the Intelligent Autonomous Systems (IAS-3), Pittsburgh Feb. 15-18, 1993, F.C.A. Groen, S. Hirose, C. C. Thorpe Eds., IOS Press, pp. 216-227, 1993.

16. E.Pagello: Planning Manipulation Task in a Unstructured Environment (in italian). Proc. of the 2nd Meeting of PFR,U. Cugini Ed. May 1991 Milano, Italy, pp. 159-175

17. S. Vere: "Planning in time: windows and durations for activities and goals", IEEE Trans. P.A.M.I. 5 (3), pg.246-267, 1983.

18. M.Vilain, H.Kautz, P.vanBeek: Constraint Propagation Algorithms for Temporal Reasoning: a revised report. in D.S.Weld, J.DeKleer : Readings in Qualitative Reasoning about Physical Systems, Morgan-Kaufmann ed., pg.373-381, 1990.

A Generative Constraint Formalism for Configuration Problems*

Markus Stumptner   Alois Haselböck

Institut für Informationssysteme, Technische Universität Wien
Paniglgasse 16, A-1040 Vienna, Austria

Abstract. Traditionally, constraint satisfaction systems have been considered an especially well-suited representation to configuration problems. However, a conventional constraint system with a predefined set of variables does not capture the flexibility inherent in composing systems out of a multitude of components of varying types. We propose an extended constraint satisfaction scheme that allows the incremental extension of a constraint network in accordance with the component-oriented view of configuration. Components can be individually represented and connected, while *resource* constraints express non-local requirements on the interaction of components. Constraints may be *generative* in that they lead to introduction of new variables, and are *generic* in that they may be defined to hold for all components of a given type.

1 Introduction

Design and configuration are traditional testbeds and application areas for AI techniques. Basically, configuration of technical systems is the task of *selecting* an appropriate set of components from a pre-defined "kit" (note that this set of available components must not be explicitly enumerated, but is usually described in a generic manner), *assembling* the selected components and thus deriving the structure of the resulting system, and possibly adjusting certain component *parameters*. Despite the success of rule-based configuration expert systems such as R1/XCON [McD82], recent years have seen a trend towards more soundly based knowledge representation schemes in various areas of AI. For configuration problems, constraint satisfaction (CS) techniques were embraced in a number of prototype systems [MA86, CGS+89] and form the foundation of the configuration approach described in [MF89], which focuses on the assembly of systems by connecting components.

Example 1. (from [MF89]) Assume a computer system has to be configured to meet an order specification of a customer. One of the required features is a printing function. The *key component* implementing such a printing function is a printer. After the selection of an appropriate printer type, additional components like interface cable or driver software must be chosen appropriately. This

---

* This work was supported by Siemens AG Austria under project grant CSS (GR 21/96106/4).

example demonstrates both function-component relationships and the idea of key components which, if chosen for configuration, result in the selection of a set of subordinate components.

However, the traditional constraint approach is limited in expressiveness and does not provide hooks for representing important features of configuration problems, namely the organization in terms of components and the dynamicity of the problem, i.e., the fact that the number of components may not be predetermined. In contrast to rule-based systems, where new components are explicitly introduced into working memory by actions specified in rule RHS's, the traditional constraint approach, while cleaner and more declarative, is effectively static. Mittal and Falkenhainer proposed *dynamic CSPs* (DCSPs) in [MF90] to avoid the latter problem, pointing out improved clarity and optimization possibilities.

Example 2. (from [MF90]) The variable *package* with the domain {*luxury, deluxe, standard*} denotes the three offered car models in a car configuration domain. The *luxury* package provides an *air_conditioner*. In the notion of DCSP, this can be specified by the following constraint:

$$package{=}luxury \stackrel{RV}{\Longrightarrow} air\_conditioner.$$

This constraint establishes the activation (i.e., inclusion of the corresponding component) of the *air_conditioner* variable in certain situations (if the *package* is *luxury*). In addition, compatibility constraints restrict the configuration space. The following example states that, if both an *air_conditioner* of type *ac1* and an automatic sunroof opener are chosen, a battery of capacity *medium* must be included in the configuration:

$$air\_conditioner{=}ac1 \ \& \ opener{=}auto \rightarrow battery{=}medium.$$

However, the DCSP approach still suffers from strong limitations, since the component structure demanded in [MF89] remains unclear, while multiple occurrences of components with equal behavior are not supported at all. E.g., in describing a twelve-cylinder engine, every constraint on cylinder behavior would have to be written down twelve times. Bowen and Bahler [BB91] use a language based on the semantics of Free Logic to address this problem.

A different trend led to the development of strongly dynamics-oriented representation schemes for configuration. These were based on the realization that a central activity during configuration is the accumulation of entities that together provide for some needed functionality. The main assumption of the so-called *resource* paradigm is that functionality-based selection from a component library should be the central operation in a configuration system [HJ91].

Example 3. Consider another example from a computer configuration domain. The customer requests a PC with 8 MB RAM. The company has memory units of 2 MB capacity a piece in stock. A motherboard is initially equipped with 2 MB, but it has vacant slots for up to 32 MB. Thus, after the selection of the motherboard alone the working-memory resource shows a deficit. In the resource-based approach, configuration is fundamentally considered a task of resource balancing.

In our example, the selection of an appropriate set of additional memory units will lead eventually to a compensation of the customer's memory requirements by the total amount of RAM provided on the motherboard.

The way in which these mechanisms interact with the constraint-based and connection-oriented view of configuration is usually not clearly defined, especially since resource schemes do not support explicit connections, and there is no real formal basis for the existing systems. For example, [HJ91] uses rules and constraints for various parts of the knowledge base, integrated by a global blackboard and agenda. Our aim is to provide a formalism that expresses resource relationships clearly in CSP terms, while still providing a component-oriented view and the possibility of dealing with systems containing a multitude of similar, but perhaps differently connected components.

We start out by describing our constraint-based framework for configuration.

2 Configuration Expressed in Constraint Satisfaction Terms

Traditionally, a constraint network consists of a finite set of variables with associated domains, and a set of constraints restricting the constellations of variable assignments. A constraint satisfaction problem (CSP) is the task of finding one or all assignments of values to variables such that all constraints on these variables are satisfied. Mittal extended this scheme by including special *activation constraints* which explicitly require variables to be active or inactive dependent upon the state of other parts of the constraint network, where "active" means that the variable will take part in the solution, while inactive variables will not need to be assigned a value. A variable in the DCSP scheme specifies some global functionality to be provided by the system, and values comprising the domain of that variable can be considered components. A qualitative request for some functionality is thus explicitly expressed by the connection to a so-called *key component* which provides that functionality. This connection is described as an assignment to a port of the requesting component. On the other hand, resource-oriented systems deal with quantitative functionality, i.e., if a certain *level* of functionality is specified, it can be provided jointly by a set of components, e.g., by adding up the *amount* which each of them provides.

Consequently, we propose a scheme which provides features that can be used as a direct representation of components, ports, and attributes, while preserving the spirit of the constraint approach. This is done by considering ports as component-valued constraint variables and quantitative functionalities as numeric-valued properties of components. We introduce extensions to allow reasoning about the relationship between properties and components, component types, and component creation. The decision to move in that direction is not unfounded; note that the activation constraints of the DCSP formalism (which allow reasoning *about* constraint variables) represent exactly such a mechanism. We merely choose a set of features that can represent the important characteristics of the domain.

Definition 1 Configuration Domain. A *configuration domain* $\mathcal{D}$ is a tuple $\langle \mathcal{C}, P, \Gamma \rangle$, where

- $\mathcal{C}$ is a possibly infinite set of component variables. The domain of each variable from $\mathcal{C}$ is a finite set $T = \{\tau_1, \ldots, \tau_t\}$ of component types.
- $P = \{p_1, \ldots, p_m\}$ is a set of property names. Furthermore, there exists a set $D = \{\mathcal{C}, D_1, \ldots, D_n\}$ of domains and a function Dom that maps elements of P to elements of D. The sets $D_1, \ldots, D_n$ are called *atomic domains* (i.e., they contain numeric or symbolic values, but are disjunct from $\mathcal{C}$).
- Γ is a finite set of generic constraints including activation and resource constraints. (Generic constraints are presented in the next section.)

In this scheme, both components and their properties are represented by constraint variables. The type of a component is specified by assigning a type symbol from T to that component variable. Depending on its type (assignment), a component will have a varying number of properties, whose existence is guaranteed by satisfying so-called *activation constraints*. The name of a property variable is composed from the name of the originating component and the property name, e.g., if property $p \in P$ is defined for component $c \in \mathcal{C}$, then the property variable is named $c.p$. The set of all possible property variables can thus be intensionally specified as $\mathcal{P} = \{c.p \mid c \in \mathcal{C}, p \in P\}$. We adapt the terminology of [MF90] and refer to the component and property variables that actually occur in a given constraint network as *active* variables.

The domain $dom(c.p)$ of a property variable $c.p$ is defined by $dom(c.p) = Dom(p)$. According to the definition of Dom, $dom(c.p)$ can be either an atomic domain D_i, in which case we call $c.p$ an *attribute* of c, or $dom(c.p) = \mathcal{C}$. In the latter case, we call $c.p$ a *port* of c. The assignment of a component c' from $\mathcal{C}$ to a port variable $c.p$ represents a connection between c and c' via the port p of c.

3 Generic Constraints

3.1 General Framework

Since the exact set of components that exist in a specific solution is not predefined, it is not possible to explicitly write down every constraint that would be involved in the solution. Even if an upper limit were known, we still would have to write down a separate set of constraints for each component constellation. Instead, we specify relationships in terms of *generic constraints*. A generic constraint is a constraint schema where meta-variables act as placeholders for component variables. We present a clausal description of generic constraints and define consistency.

A clause is a formula of the form $A_1 \wedge \ldots \wedge A_m \supset B_1 \vee \ldots \vee B_n$ where the A's are the *negative* literals and the B's are the *positive* ones. A clause with an empty right hand side represents a conflicting constellation and is denoted by $A_1 \wedge \ldots \wedge A_m \supset \perp$.

Three different forms of literals can be used:

1. $\pi(v_1, \ldots, v_k)$ where it can be decided for every assignment $v_1 = x_1, \ldots, v_k = x_k$, whether the assignment satisfies the predicate π. For now, the predicates we are interested in are equality (for all domains), and the arithmetic comparison predicates ($<$, $>$, $\leq$, and $\geq$) for variables whose domains consist of numbers. If at least one of the v_i is not active, then $\pi(v_1, \ldots, v_k)$ evaluates to false in every case.

2. $active(v)$ is true, iff the variable v is active (i.e., selected for solution).

3. $v_1 \equiv v_2$ is true, iff the active variables v_1 and v_2 are identical (note: not only identical assignments).

A clause γ is said to be *range-restricted*, iff each variable occurring in the right hand side of γ also occurs in the left hand side. We adopt this restriction to constraint schemata. A clausal constraint schema is said to be *range-restricted*, iff each meta-variable X representing a component variable on the right hand side of γ also occurs on the left hand side.

Example 4. The following statements show some examples of range-restricted clauses:

"*The first slot of a frame must be connected to modules only.*"

$F = frame \wedge F.slot_1 = M \supset M = module.$

"*Only components which actually provide some service may be connected to the first slot of a frame.*"

$F = frame \wedge F.slot_1 = M \supset active(M.service).$

The last example expresses the restriction that "*a module must not be simultaneously be mounted on $slot_1$ and $slot_2$ of a frame.*"

$F = frame \wedge F.slot_1 = M_1 \wedge F.slot_2 = M_2 \wedge M_1 \equiv M_2 \supset \perp.$

We defined constraints as range-restricted clauses because this allows a simple definition of consistency, while preserving high expressivity.

Definition 2 Consistency of Generic Constraints. Let γ be a range-restricted constraint clause with meta-variables $X_1, \ldots, X_k$. Further, let $V \subseteq \mathcal{C} \cup \mathcal{P}$ be a set of active variables, and $V^C \subseteq V$ is the set of all component variables of V. If t is an assignment tuple for the variables V, a generic constraint γ is said to be satisfied, iff

$$\forall c_1, \ldots, c_k \in V^C : \gamma[X_1 \mid_{c_1}, \ldots, X_k \mid_{c_k}] \text{ is satisfied.}$$

In other words, if γ is satisfied for all possible substitutions of the meta-variables with active component variables, then the generic constraint is said to be consistent w.r.t. the active variables and their assignments.

3.2 Activation Constraints

Property variables belong to components of specific types. Therefore, if the type of a component is derived (the variable is assigned), the appropriate set of property variables that specify the features and behavior of the component must exist. The existence requirements for the corresponding attributes and ports depending on the type of component are expressed by *activation* constraints in the terminology of standard DCSPs ([MF90]).

Let $\mathcal{D} = \langle \mathcal{C}, P, \Gamma \rangle$ be a configuration domain, τ is a type symbol from the domain T of all component variables of $\mathcal{C}$, p is a property name from P. To state the fact that all components c of type τ have (among others) the property p, the generic constraint for the activation of a property variable $c.p$ has the form

$$C{=}\tau \stackrel{\mathrm{RV}}{\Longrightarrow} C.p$$

where C is a meta-variable.[2]

Definition 3 Consistency of Generic Activation Constraints. Let γ be an activation constraint schema of the form $C{=}\tau \stackrel{\mathrm{RV}}{\Longrightarrow} C.p$. γ is said to be *satisfied*, iff for all active component variables c of type τ a property variable $c.p$ is active.

Conversely, to avoid the activation of property variables not triggered by activation constraints, we assume a *closed world* in the following sense: if in a solution a property variable $c.p$ is active, then (1) a component variable c must be active, (2) a type τ must be assigned to c, and (3) an activation constraint instance of the form $c{=}\tau \stackrel{\mathrm{RV}}{\Longrightarrow} c.p$ has to justify the existence of that property variable. Thus, the use of activation constraints restricts the derivation of property variables to an intended set and therefore facilitates a compact and clear description of the type-specific features of each component.

3.3 Resource Constraints

Many configuration tasks require reasoning on *sets* of components. For example, modules occurring in some part of a system may require a power supply unit with power output at least as high as their combined consumption. Performance requirements for a system are also usually expressed in such a manner, e.g., "install a sufficient number of printing presses such that at least 5000 sheets per hour can be printed". In standard constraint satisfaction theory this can be done by stating constraints on sets of variables, i.e., defining an n-ary constraint if there are n variables involved. Because the variables are fixed, no problem arises. In dynamic CSPs with an unlimited number of variables, where the selection of an appropriate set of variables for the solution is a problem-specific task of inference, expressing constraints on sets of variables is more difficult.

Therefore, we augment our generic constraint theory by the introduction of *resource constraints*. Resource constraints express aggregate properties of sets of components (such as the total capacity of an ensemble of printing presses). They are created by extending the definition of constraint literals to allow the use of resource functions in arithmetic constraint expressions.

---

[2] The term "RV" stands for "require-variable." This is the only kind of activation constraint introduced in [MF90] that is used in our approach. For example, "require-not" constraints can be expressed either by definition of types that do not activate these properties, or by *limiting* resource constraints (see below).

Definition 4 Resource Function. A resource function r is a triple $\langle \sigma, p, \phi \rangle$, where σ is the aggregate function (such as *card*, Σ, *min*, *max*), $p \in P$ is a property name (called *resource property*), and ϕ is a selection predicate defined on the set of components C. The function r is computed by applying σ to the set $\{c.p \mid c \in C \land active(c.p) \land \phi(c)\}$.

We require that aggregate functions are monotonic and that, if a component possesses the resource property, it will indeed contribute to solving the resource constraint, i.e., numeric resource properties are restricted to non-negative values.

Example 5. Let the set of types of printing presses be

$$T = \{Hodder\_1100, \ Sheffield\_de\_luxe, \ Smart\}.$$

The example described above can be represented by the following constraint:

$$5000 \ / \ \Sigma\{Press.output\_per\_minute \mid Press \in T\} \ \leq \ 60min$$

where Σ is the aggregate function, p is *output_per_minute*, and $\phi(c)$ is ($Press \in T$).

A resource function can, in principle, be used in constraint literals in every place where a constant numeric value can occur. A constraint that contains a literal with a resource function is called a *resource constraint*. Consistency is defined for resource constraints as for ordinary constraints. The difference lies in the fact that satisfying a resource constraint may require the creation of an appropriate set of components so that the conditions placed upon the value of the resource function will hold.

Note that resource constraint expressions do not need to explicitly specify a consumer, i.e., system requirements can be handled elegantly without references to special "environment" or "system" components.

4 Solving Configuration Problems

A configuration problem consists of a domain description (i.e., a knowledge base comprising component types and the generic constraints governing them), a set of initial variables (i.e., specific components that are required to be part of the solution), and a set of additional constraint instances (for expressing problem requirements).

Definition 5 Configuration Problem. Let $\mathcal{D}$ be a configuration domain with component variable set $\mathcal{C}$, property names P, and generic constraints Γ. A *configuration problem* in $\mathcal{D}$ is a tuple $\langle V^I, \Gamma^I, \mathcal{D} \rangle$, where $V^I \subseteq \mathcal{C} \cup \mathcal{P}^3$ is the set of initial variables and Γ^I is a set of constraint instances on V^I.

The variables in V^I define a partial constraint network, consisting of the constraints in Γ^I and the appropriate instances of generic constraints in Γ.

---

[3] Remember, $\mathcal{P} = \{c.p \mid c \in \mathcal{C}, p \in P\}$ is the set of all possible property variables.

Definition 6 Solution of a configuration problem. A *solution* $\mathcal{S}$ of a configuration problem $\langle V^I, \Gamma^I, \mathcal{D} \rangle$ is an assignment to a set of activated variables V ($V \subseteq \mathcal{C} \cup \mathcal{P}$, $V^I \subseteq V$), such that all (generic) constraints are satisfied.

Below, we describe an architecture for a constraint satisfaction problem solver able to solve configuration problems stated in the formalism described above. We sketch conditions under which termination can be guaranteed, and give a few suggestions how efficiency improvements can be achieved by (1) adapting well-known techniques like forward-checking or an intelligent choice of backtrack points in conflict situations, and (2) using problem-independent heuristics that guide the expansion of the search tree.

4.1 A Backtracking Architecture

Consistency and backtrack search techniques are standard methods for solving CSPs [HE80]. The design of our configuration procedure is motivated by keeping as close as possible to classical constraint propagation.

The task of finding a solution $\mathcal{S}$ to a configuration problem $\langle V^I, \Gamma^I, \mathcal{D} \rangle$ can be treated as a problem of deriving a constraint network R starting from an initial network $\langle V^I, \Gamma^I \rangle$ where R is dynamically constructed to meet the generic specification and the (initial) requirements on the device to assemble. At each situation during search, R represents a classical constraint network where constraint restrictions on the variables are propagated until a consistent state is reached. Constraints in that network represent instances of generic constraints, with meta-variables replaced by ordinary constraint variables. The network will grow for exactly the following reasons:

- If a type τ is assigned to a component variable c, all the property variables $c.p$ are added to R as required by activation constraints of the form $C{=}\tau \stackrel{RV}{\Longrightarrow} C.p$. Using a partial choice strategy [MF87], such an activation will not be postponed until the type of c is fixed, but will already occur at the moment when *all* types remaining in the domain of c define an activation constraint for p.
- If a port variable has been chosen for assignment and no existing component is eligible, a new component c is added to R.
- Further components are needed to satisfy a resource constraint (see below).

Figure 1 sketches a backtrack search shell where a special resource constraint handler is embedded into a classical procedure for solving discrete CSPs. At any point during search, the constraint network R embraces all the currently activated variables and constraint instances.

We first describe the main loop of the constraint solver without considering resource constraints. In this case, the algorithm consists of the following steps: First, for any pending activation constraints, new property variables are generated and added to the network R (1). Next, an as yet unassigned variable is chosen as current object of interest (2). If no unassigned variable exists, the

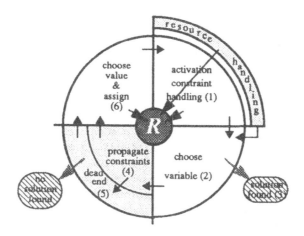

Fig. 1. A architecture for solving generative constraint problems.

procedure terminates and outputs a solution (3) . Assuming this is not the case, in the next step constraint propagation is performed on the constraint network R, i.e., inconsistent domain values are filtered out from the current domains of unassigned variables (4). The minimum condition is that all domain values of the current variable must be proved to be locally consistent with the already assigned variables. If a variable domain becomes empty, a dead-end situation is recognized and backtracking occurs (5). If this is not the case, then in the final step of the loop, a value from the (remaining) domain of the current variable is chosen and an assignment is performed (6). In those cases where a port variable $c.p$ was chosen for assignment and no eligible component exists in R, a new component c' is chosen from C, added to R, and assigned to $c.p$. This assignment may (and usually will) lead to the addition of new constraint instances to R.

For implementation purposes, we distinguish two simple categories of resource constraints: those that limit component generation and those that promote it (called respectively *limiting* and *generative*). Since all aggregate functions we use in resource constraints are monotonic, these categories correspond to the cases where the constraint expression states an upper respective lower bound for the resource function value.

The phases in the execution cycle of the algorithm where resource constraints are relevant are indicated by shading in Figure 1. In the constraint propagation phase, resource constraints act as ordinary constraints monitoring consistency of the constraint network R, i.e., they are used in an essentially *destructive* manner. This phase involves only the limiting resource constraints.

Example 6. The following *limiting* resource constraint restricts the number of modules providing *isdn* service to at most one:

$$card\{M.service \mid M{=}module \land M.service{=}isdn\} \leq 1.$$

Let the variables of the current network R and their partial assignments be

$$m_1 = module, \quad m_2 = module, \quad m_1.service = isdn,$$
$$dom(m_2.service) = \{isdn, analog, digital\}.$$

The value *isdn* will be removed from the domain of $m_2.service$ at constraint filtering time because an assignment of *isdn* to that variable would violate the above denoted resource constraint.

In the resource handling phase, the generative resource constraints are checked and may trigger the creation of new components. If R is the current constraint network and γ is a generative resource constraint such that γ cannot be satisfied by the components in R, then new components will be created and added to R. To ensure that the new components will be useful for satisfying γ, it must be guaranteed that each of them will actually possess the resource property p and satisfy the selection predicate ϕ. This is achieved for each new component c by introducing the constraint $active(c.p) \land \phi(c)$ into R.

Example 7. Similar to the example above, a *generative* resource constraint which demands at least two modules providing *isdn* service can be expressed by

$$card\{M.service \mid M = module \land M.service = isdn\} > 1.$$

If the current state of R is

$$m_1 = module, \quad m_1.service = isdn,$$

then the resource constraint is not yet satisfied by that configuration fragment. Therefore, in the resource handling phase a new component variable, say m_2, is added to R and the following constraint derived from the selection predicate of the resource constraint is associated with that new component to ensure that this activation has some effect to the resource constraint:

$$active(m_2.service) \land m_2 = module \land m_2.service = isdn.$$

The problem solving process with our formalism can be considered as a sequence of stable phases. During each phase, the constraint network remains fixed. A new phase is started by the creation of new variables with the subsequent introduction of new constraints. In each of the stable phases described above, problem solving proceeds as in a conventional CS solver. If an assigment to all variables is reached without new variables being activated, that assignment is a solution. If new components are generated, problem solving continues with the new, extended network. In general, this sequence of phases cannot be guaranteed to be finite. Finiteness can be induced, however, by resource constraints that place an upper bound on the availability of some resources (e.g., key components), combined with a fair strategy for type assignment to component variables.

4.2 Guiding Search

A wide array of optimization techniques has been developed for constraint satisfaction systems. In each of the stable phases described above, CSP optimization methods like forward checking [HE80] or backjumping [Dec90] can be used.

It is also possible to use standard CS heuristics, like variable ordering. However, since the variable set is not static, no fixed variable ordering can be defined. Instead, orderings need to be specified in generic terms depending on, e.g., variable domain or kind of variable (property or component), and will tend to be problem-specific. As an example, assume a problem where a set of components is to be connected in an aggregate hierarchy, with each component possessing a port representing the connection to a part in the next higher level, while higher-level parts possess ports that represent the slots in which lower-level components may be inserted. If the slots of the higher-level components are preferred for value assignment, assembly will proceed in a predominantly top-down manner.

Since it will be rarely feasible to generate all possible solutions to a given configuration problem (i.e., we are dealing with an *exemplification*, not an *enumeration* problem [BB91]), the route along which search proceeds will not only determine the time in finding a solution, but also the structure of the configuration. It may therefore be hard to separate search efficiency and solution quality.

The strategy for solving resource constraints strongly affects the efficiency of the search process. Implementation of resource-oriented systems has centered on some sort of balancing algorithm [HJ91]. There is one central heuristic that can be used, namely estimate the number of components that will be needed to satisfy the current requirements, both in terms of resources needed for specific connections and of resources that jointly provide some specific functionality. The first are represented in our scheme as port variables which require the connection to components of specific types, the second by resource constraints. Since both resource constraints and port variable assignments use components from the same pool ($\mathcal{C}$), no special coordination mechanisms are required.

In both these cases of component generation, the component types help in pruning the search space, since in the first case (specific connection) usually the types of components to be connected will be explicitly specified by constraints on the domains of these components, and in the second case (resource constraints) the possible types of new components will be restricted to those that actually provide the resource property.

5 Conclusion

We have presented a coherent formalism for describing and solving configuration problems that extends the traditional constraint satisfaction framework by the ability to explicitly reason about the existence of components. This representation scheme is therefore suitable for describing problems whose solution size is not known *a priori*, while basic concepts like components, connections, and properties are explicitly specified at the constraint level. We have identified specific classes of constraints that may lead to the dynamic creation of new components and discussed how these influence the operation of a constraint solver. Previous approaches have either not allowed to fully specify either the dynamic aspects of the problem, or possible connection topologies. In contrast, we provide a scheme in which these different aspects are brought together under one roof for the first time.

The formalism is used by the authors in the definition of an object-oriented constraint language intended for the configuration of large technical systems. In [HS93], we present somewhat more complex problem descriptions and also discuss how different problem architectures can be represented. A prototype system using this approach is currently being used in a test application with a real-world knowledge base. One aspect that we have not dealt with in this paper, but which is already implemented as part of our system, is the use of type hierarchies (taxonomies) as a useful abstraction mechanism in constraint problems [MF87]. However, the information contained in types in our approach was flexible enough and powerful to enable the specification of taxonomic reasoning mechanisms that further guide the specialization and selection of components. These mechanisms provide a host of additional openings for employing optimization techniques in our system. Our current research examines such approaches, resulting in the definition of a complete object-oriented knowledge representation system based on constraint semantics.

References

[BB91]   James Bowen and Dennis Bahler. Conditional existence of variables in generalized constraint networks. In *Proc. AAAI Conf.*, pages 215–220, 1991.

[CGS⁺89] R. Cunis, A. Günter, I. Syska, H. Bode, and H. Peters. Plakon – an approach to domain-independent construction. In *Proc. IEA/AIE Conf.*, Tennessee, 1989. UTSI.

[Dec90]   Rina Dechter. Enhancement schemes for constraint processing: Backjumping, learning and cutset decomposition. *Artificial Intelligence*, 41(3):273–312, 1990.

[HE80]   Robert M. Haralick and Gordon L. Elliott. Increasing tree search efficiency for constraint satisfaction problems. *Artificial Intelligence*, 14:263–313, 1980.

[HJ91]   M. Heinrich and E.W. Jüngst. A resource-based paradigm for the configuring of technical systems from modular components. In *Proc. CAIA*, pages 257–264, February 1991.

[HS93]   Alois Haselböck and Markus Stumptner. An integrated approach for modelling complex configuration domains. In *Proc. of the 13th Int. Conf. on Expert Systems, AI, and Natural Language*, Avignon, May 1993.

[MA86]   Sanjay Mittal and Agustin Araya. A knowledge-based framework for design. In *Proceedings AAAI Conference*, pages 856–865, 1986.

[McD82]   John McDermott. R1: A rule-based configurer of computer systems. *Artificial Intelligence*, 19:39–88, 1982.

[MF87]   Sanjay Mittal and Felix Frayman. Making partial choices in constraint reasoning problems. In *Proceedings AAAI Conference*, pages 631–636, July 1987.

[MF89]   Sanjay Mittal and Felix Frayman. Towards a generic model of configuration tasks. In *Proc. 11ᵗʰ IJCAI*, pages 1395–1401. Morgan Kaufmann Publishers, Inc., August 1989.

[MF90]   Sanjay Mittal and Brian Falkenhainer. Dynamic constraint satisfaction problems. In *Proceedings AAAI Conference*, pages 25–32, August 1990.

Selecting Observation Time in the Monitoring and Interpretation of Time-Varying Data*

Luigi Portinale

Dipartimento di Informatica - Universita' di Torino
C.so Svizzera 185 - 10149 Torino (Italy)

Abstract. A lot of previous approaches to monitoring involved a continuous reading of the system parameters in order to recognise when anomalies in the behavior of the system under examination can trigger the diagnostic process. This paper deals with the application of Markov chain theory to the selection of observation time in the monitoring and diagnosis of time-varying systems. The goal of the present paper is to show how, by assuming a framework where the temporal behavior of the components of the system is modeled in a stochastic way, the continuous observation of critical parameters can be avoided; indeed, this kind of approach allows us to get a useful criterion for choosing observation time in domains where getting observations can be expensive. Observations are then requested only when the necessity for a diagnostic process becomes relevant and a focusing on the components that are more likely to be faulty can also be achieved.

1 Introduction

In most important real-world diagnostic applications the behavior of the modeled system is significantly variable during time; different proposals have been developed in the attempt of either extending static (i.e. time independent) diagnostic techniques [3, 7, 11] or proposing new approaches directly addressing problems concerning time-dependent behavior [10, 16]. In fact, the diagnosis of systems with time-varying behavior involves important aspects such as observations across different time instants and explicit description of state changes of the system to be diagnosed with respect to time. The basic consequence of these aspects is the augmented complexity of both the modeling and the reasoning tasks with respect to the time invariant case [13]. In [7, 14] it is shown that, at least in some cases, it is possible to de-couple time-invariant and time-varying behavior of the components of the modeled system, in order to reduce the complexity of the problem, augmenting the modularity and still exploiting, in a relevant way, the machinery developed for static models.

In some recent papers [3, 19], we proposed a diagnostic framework for time-varying systems based on such a model decomposition. The approach concerns a component oriented model of the system to be diagnosed, where each component may

---

* This work has been partially supported by CNR under grant n. 92.00061.CT12 and MURST.

assume different behavioral modes [6]; one of these modes represents the "correct" mode and the others are different kinds of "faults". We assume that the mode of a component may vary during time. The whole model is decomposed into two different levels as in [7]: a behavioral model showing the relations between behavioral modes and their observable consequences, assuming a form of "steady state" (i.e. time independence) condition[2]; a mode transition model showing the "natural" temporal evolutions of each component. Diagnostic hypotheses can be obtained by the first level using classical machinery developed for static models and then related to each other, across different time points, using the second level. In particular, in [19] we showed that modeling temporal evolutions of the components as Markov chains is a reasonable and suitable choice in order to augment the flexibility of the approach when dealing with uncertain evolutions.

Moreover, there is another aspect which is fundamental when studying the time-varying behavior of a system, that is *monitoring*. It is well recognized that there is is a close relation between monitoring and diagnosis of time-varying systems [16]. The usual view of the concept of monitoring versus diagnosis is that the former concentrates on *fault detection* while the latter on *fault identification* or *localization*. In this view, monitoring represents the process of discovering anomalies in the behavior of the system; such anomalies can thus trigger the diagnostic process eventually explaining the abnormal behavior of the system. Some interesting approaches have been recently proposed in this context using either *qualitative reasoning techniques* [9] or *teleological models* [16] and assuming, as in the most part of approaches to monitoring, that some critical (or even all) parameters are continuously observed to guarantee fast fault detection. However, there are cases in which the continuous availability of observations necessary to diagnostic reasoning is not guaranteed. Some systems, in fact, cannot be equipped with the suitable instruments, for collecting information about their components, at the desired level of detail, but such information can be gathered by means of additional tests and/or elaboration of available data. For instance, in a computer system, observation collection may involve a certain number of tests and a deep investigation of its components that may prevent the components themselves to perform their usual work; the same problem occurs in chemical plant troubleshooting where all the electro-mechanical apparatus undergo periodical control whose frequency depends on their criticality (see [1]). The possibility of formalizing the decision process through which periodical controls are decided is very appealing; in such cases, the availability of good models of temporal prediction is of paramount importance in order to understand the temporal evolution of the system under examination.

The goal of the paper is to show that, in the case of discrete systems, the stochastic diagnostic framework described in [19] can be used to take a different view of monitoring integrated with diagnosis that allows us to avoid the continuous reading of observable parameters. This makes the approach suitable to domains where: (1) uncertainty about temporal evolutions of the components of the modeled system is present and probabilistic information about mode transitions is available; (2) observations are expensive or quite difficult to get and so should be required in a suitable way.

---

[2] An extension that allows for a form of time dependence in this model is presented in [4].

The paper is organized as follows: in section 2 we discuss some basic notions of reliability of physical system components; in section 3 we briefly introduce a stochastic diagnostic framework for the interpretation of time-varying data, based on some reliability assumptions and in section 4 we present a criterion for the selection of observation time in such a framework. Some open problems are briefly outlined at the end of section 4 and in the conclusions.

2 Reliability of Physical System Components

Reliability theory [21] deals with the application of particular probability distributions to the analysis of the life cycle of the components of a physical system. Let X be a random variable representing the lifetime of a component and $P[A]$ be the probability of a generic event A; $F_X(t) = P[X \leq t]$ is the *probability distribution function* of X (probability that the component is faulty at time t). In particular, in the case X is a discrete random variable, $F_X(t) = \sum_{i \leq t} p_X(i)$ where $p_X(i) = P[X = i]$ is the *probability mass function* of X.

In the following we will assume that time is *discrete* (we will use natural numbers to denote time points) and so we will deal with discrete probability distributions and discrete random variables[3]. It has been recognized [21] that, in the usual life phase of a component, its failure probability (in one time instant) p is constant and, in particular, if we consider the lifetime X of a component to be a discrete random variable, in such a phase X follows a *geometric distribution* with parameter p ($P[X = t] = p(1 - p)^{t-1}$).

This is the only discrete distribution satisfying the so called *memoryless property* which is defined in the following way: $P[X = t+n | X > t] = P[X = n]$; in the case X is interpreted as the lifetime of a component, this means that in a given instant t, the probability of failure in the future is independent of the previous history . It is then reasonable to assume a memoryless distribution of the lifetime of the components of a system in order to analyse its behavior.

In model-based diagnosis it is important to take into account the fact that a component can fail in a lot of different ways and that these ways of failing can be related to each others (for instance one failure mode can be possible only after a given sequence of other failure modes). Moreover, there can be some faults that are more critical than others, so in some cases, it could be acceptable to have a component in a given "slight" faulty state where the basic functionalities of the system are still guaranteed with a graceful performance degradation. This does not necessarily mean that a "slight" fault is not repaired (rather, in the majority of cases it is reasonable to think that, if that fault has been singled-out, it is repaired), but it is not so important, for system functionality, to perform a repair action when the component exhibits that fault. This simply means that we can take the risk of having that fault, rather than spending time in continuously reading system parameters in order to discover it.

The basic idea is to define, for each component of the modeled system, a set of *critical modes*, corresponding to particularly serious faults. The fact that the component evolves in one of such modes must be avoided as much as possible. In

---

[3] The generalization to the continuous case does not pose particular problems.

particular, the system must be taken under control in order to ask for observations and possibly perform a diagnosis, when the probability of a component being in a critical mode becomes relevant.

In the next section we will present a diagnostic framework where a precise criterion for selecting observation time, can be formalized by taking into account the aspects mentioned above.

3 A Stochastic Diagnostic Framework

Let us now briefly recall some notions concerning stochastic processes.

Definition 1. A stochastic process is a family of random variables $\{X(t)/t \in T\}$ defined over the same probability space, indexed by a parameter $t \in T$ and taking values in a set S called the state space of the process.

Parameter t usually represents time, so a stochastic process can be thought as the model of the evolution of a system across time.

Definition 2. A Markov chain is a discrete-state stochastic process $\{X(t)/t \in T\}$ such that for any $t_0 < t_1 < ...t_n$ we have that:

$$P[X(t_n) = x_n | X(t_{n-1}) = x_{n-1} \ldots X(t_0) = x_0] = P[X(t_n) = x_n | X(t_{n-1}) = x_{n-1}]$$

(1)

We will be concerned only with Discrete-Time Markov Chains (DTMC) and in particular with *time-homogeneous* DTMC in which the probability of transition from one state to another (equation 1) does not depend from n. In this case, the past history of the chain is completely summarized in the current state since the sojourn time in a given state follows a geometric distribution.

3.1 Representing Diagnostic Knowledge for Time-Varying Data Interpretation

As discussed in [19], we decompose the model of the system to be diagnosed into two parts: a **logical static behavioral model** (with no representation of time) and a **mode transition model** showing the possible "natural" temporal evolutions of the behavioral modes of each component of the system.

In the logical model, the fact that a component c is in behavioral mode m at time t is represented by the atom $m(c,t)$[4]; the relationships between behavioral modes and their manifestations are expressed as Horn clauses and the model is atemporal, in the sense that different instances of the temporal variable t cannot appear in a given clause.

In the mode transition model, we extend the assumption concerning the probability distribution of the lifetime of a component in the usual life phase, to the different behavioral modes of the component. This means that we assume a memoryless distribution of the time spent by a component in a given mode, so that the

---

[4] At each time point, the modes of a component are mutually exclusive.

state transition model will be a DTMC. The **Associated Markov Chain** $AMC(c)$ of a component c is a DTMC whose states represent the behavioral modes of c. If p_i is the probability of being in the current mode m_i at the next time instant, then the sojourn time S_i in m_i is geometrically distributed with parameter $(1 - p_i)$. Notice that, assuming that a component has several fault modes and modeling the transitions among such modes as a Markov chain, allows us to generalize the concept of failure probability to the concept of transition probability from one mode to another. As for any DTMC, we can define the **transition probability matrix** of the chain as $P_c = [p_{m_i m_j}(c)]$ where each $p_{m_i m_j}(c)$ is the transition probability, in one time instant, from mode m_i to mode m_j of the component c. In particular, the (nth power) matrix $P_c^n = [p_{m_i m_j}^n(c)]$ where $p_{m_i m_j}^n(c)$ is the probability of reaching mode m_j from mode m_i in n time instants of the component c.

Example. Let us consider the simple system in figure 1 consisting of a tank T,

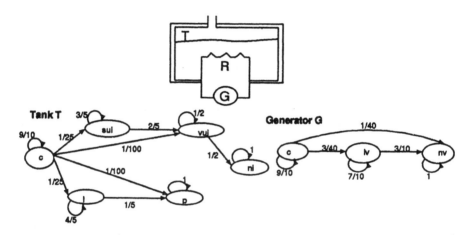

Fig. 1. System diagram with $AMCs$

covered by thermal insulation and containing some water heated by means of a resistor R connected to a generator G. We will restrict our attention to components T and G whose $AMCs$ are also showed in figure 1[5]. The corresponding transition probability matrices P_T and P_G can be easily derived from the $AMCs$. Behavioral modes are shortened as follows: *c=correct, sui=slight underinsulation, vui=severe underinsulation, ni=no insulation, l=leaking, p=punctured, lv=low voltage, nv=no voltage.*

---

[5] An important topic is actually how $AMCs$ are built; for the aims of the present paper it is sufficient to assume that they are given a-priori.

3.2 Probabilistic Characterization of Temporal Diagnostic Problems

In this section, we outline how we can probabilistically characterize a diagnostic problem at different time instants (a more detailed discussion can be found in [19]). A *temporal diagnostic problem* is a 4-tuple $TDP = < BM, COMPS, AMC, OBS >$ where: BM is the static behavioral model, $COMPS$ is the set of components of the system to be diagnosed, AMC is the set of Associated Markov Chains of the components in $COMPS$ and OBS is the set of observations to be explained and represented as a set of ground atoms in the language of BM. The suitable notion of explanation can be extracted from the spectrum of definitions defined in [5][6].

We can determine, from a temporal diagnostic problem, a set of atemporal diagnostic problems by considering sets of observations $OBS(t_k)$ at given time instants t_k. An *atemporal diagnostic problem* at the time instant t_k is a 3-tuple $ADP(t_k) = < BM, COMPS, OBS(t_k) >$ where $OBS(t_k)$ are the atoms in OBS having temporal parameter t_k. Solving $ADP(t_k)$ corresponds to determine an assignment of modes at time t_k, $W(t_k)$, to each component in $COMPS$ explaining the observations in $OBS(t_k)$. This assignment is an *atemporal diagnosis*. Obviously, the time instants which are of interest in the diagnostic process are just those for which we have some observations; we will call such instants *relevant time instants*. The basic goal of the work is to show that, in case observations can be asked by the diagnostic system, it is possible to characterize in a precise way the relevant time instants.

Let us assume, as in the most part of the previous work on diagnosis, that each component fails *independently* from each other (i.e. the behavioral mode of a component cannot influence those of the others). We indicate as $m^c_{W(t)}$ the mode that $W(t)$ assigns to c; because of the previous assumption, if $t_i < t_j$ are two consecutive relevant time instants, we have

$$P[W(t_j)|W(t_i)] = \prod_{c \in COMPS} p^n_{m^c_{W(t_i)} m^c_{W(t_j)}}(c) \quad (n = t_j - t_i)$$

Given different atemporal diagnoses at each relevant time instants, we can relate them across such instants to form **temporal diagnoses**, using the $AMCs$ (see [19] for details); the interesting aspect of this approach is the possibility of ranking the temporal diagnoses we get; indeed, it is easy to show that the probabilities of temporal diagnoses at time t can be recursively computed, given the a-priori distributions $P[W(0)]$ by the following formula[7]:

$$P[W(0), ...W(t - \Delta), W(t)] = P[W(0), ...W(t - \Delta)]P[W(t)|W(t - \Delta)] \quad (2)$$

where the first factor is the probability at the previous step and the second can be computed by means of the matrices P^Δ_c. We will discuss the problem concerning the computation of such matrices in section 4.2.

---

[6] For the sake of simplicity, we do not consider contextual information (see [5] for a discussion).

[7] Actually, some problems are related to the fact that a revision is needed on the probabilities of diagnoses when new observations supply new evidence for the atemporal diagnostic hypotheses; however, this is outside the scope of the present paper (a possible solution is discussed in [19]).

4   Selecting Observation Time

The use of Markov chains to model temporal evolutions of components allows us to exploit the underlying theory in order to integrate a notion of monitoring in the diagnostic framework presented in the previous section. In particular, we can define a criterion to select observation time, assuming a notion of incremental diagnosis in which observations are asked for when needed (i.e. when the necessity for a diagnosis becomes relevant).

Definition 3. A **transient set** of states is a set in which every state can be reached from every other state and which can be left ; each element of the set is called **transient state**; an **ergodic set** of states is a set in which every state can be reached from every other state and which cannot be left once entered; each element of the set is called **ergodic state**; if all the state of a chain are ergodic the chain itself is said to be **ergodic**; an **absorbing state** is a state which once entered is never left (i.e. the probability of remaining in this state is 1); a chain all of whose ergodic states are absorbing is called an **absorbing chain**.

Since probabilistic knowledge about possible temporal evolutions of the components is assumed to be available, we can determine, at each time instant, the probability of the component being in a given mode; this means that we could monitor the system under examination, by asking observations when the probability of a component being in a critical mode becomes "too high". However, the theory of Markov chain gives us another more interesting possibility: computing the mean passage time from one mode to another.

4.1   Reducing AMCs

As mentioned before, an absorbing chain is a chain all of whose ergodic states have probability of remaining in that state equal to 1. This is clearly the most common case when modeling the temporal behavior of a component, because if only natural changes (i.e. no repair actions) are modeled, it is quite natural to get a model in which faults degrade until a permanent one is reached. Actually, another possibility concerning natural changes is to have *AMCs* where only proper subsets of the modes of the component are ergodic, i.e. the chain is not ergodic, but there is the possibility of reaching a set of faults through which the component can move without leaving the set. We can then consider non ergodic *AMCs* but, for our aims, they can be analysed by means of the theory of absorbing chains.

   The $r \times r$ transition probability matrix of an absorbing Markov chain can be written in a canonical form [15]:

$$\begin{pmatrix} I & \emptyset \\ R & Q \end{pmatrix}$$

where, if s is the number of transient states, I is the $(r - s) \times (r - s)$ *identity matrix* (with 1 on the diagonal and 0 elsewhere), $\emptyset$ is the $(r - s) \times s$ *zero matrix* (with all entries equal to 0), Q is a $s \times s$ matrix concerning the chain as long as it stays in transient states and R is a $s \times (r - s)$ matrix concerning the passage from transient to absorbing states. For an absorbing chain, there exists the $s \times s$

matrix $N = (I - Q)^{-1}$ called the *fundamental matrix*. The generic element n_{ij} of N indicates the mean number of times that the chain is in transient state s_j starting from transient state s_i. By summing the ith row of N, we get the mean number of times that the chain is in a transient state, starting from s_i. In matrix terms, if ξ is a column vector with all entries 1, we have that $\tau = N\xi$ is a $s - component$ column vector whose ith element t_i is the *mean time to absorption* $(MTTA)$ from state s_i. Thus τ represents the mean time needed by the chain to reach an absorbing state, for each possible starting transient state.

Let us consider a component c; we define $\Gamma(c) = \{m_i \; / \; m_i$ is a critical mode of $c\}$. When dealing with the critical modes of a component we make the following assumption: if a fault mode m_i of a component c is a critical mode $(m_i \in \Gamma(c))$ then also every other fault mode m_j reachable from m_i in $AMC(c)$ is a critical one $(m_j \in \Gamma(c))$. The reason is that if m_i is critical, any other mode to which the component can degenerate should clearly be considered critical as well. In this sense, it is sufficient to specify the first critical mode on each path, starting from the "correct" one, on the $AMC(c)$. Let us call such modes *minimal critical modes*. Since minimal critical modes are the first of a "chain of modes" to avoid, we will be interested in analysing the behavior of the component c until such minimal modes are reached. The criterion to select observations can be defined by considering the mean time to absorption on "reduced" $AMCs$.

Definition 4. Given $AMC(c)$, the **reduced AMC(c)** is the Markov chain obtained by transforming the set of critical modes of $AMC(c)$ into a single absorbing state.

This means that all modes in $\Gamma(c)$ are collapsed into an absorbing state S_{ab}; every arc in $AMC(c)$ entering a mode $m \in \Gamma(c)$ will enter S_{ab} in the reduced $AMC(c)$ with the following trick: for each mode $m' \notin \Gamma(c)$ and for each arc e of $AMC(c)$ from m' to $m \in \Gamma(c)$, create a single arc, on the reduced $AMC(c)$, from m' to S_{ab} with transition probability equal to the sum of those of each arc e.

Remark *A reduced AMC is absorbing.*

Example (cont.) Let us consider again the system of figure 1; we assume that $\Gamma(T) = \{p, vui, ni\}$ (p and vui are minimal critical modes) and $\Gamma(G) = \{nv\}$. Figure 4.1 shows the reduced $AMC(T)$ $(AMC(G)$ remains the same) and the corresponding transition probability matrix in canonical form. It can be easily shown that, by using the fundamental matrices of the reduced $AMCs$, the $MTTA$ vectors for the remaining transient modes are:

$$\tau(T) = \begin{matrix} l \\ sui \\ c \end{matrix} \begin{pmatrix} 5 \\ \frac{5}{2} \\ 13 \end{pmatrix} \quad \tau(G) = \begin{matrix} lv \\ c \end{matrix} \begin{pmatrix} \frac{10}{3} \\ \frac{25}{2} \end{pmatrix}$$

This means that, for every non critical mode, we may know the mean time needed to reach a critical one. Notice that, given a relevant time instant, if there are diagnoses mentioning critical modes, we should ask for observations as soon as possible, possibly every time instant (repair actions should then be undertaken by taking into account the probability of diagnoses). Let t_i be the current relevant time instant and $W_j(t_i)$ be the generic atemporal diagnosis at time t_i. Given a mode m of a component c, we indicate as $MTTA_c(m)$ the mean time to absorption from mode

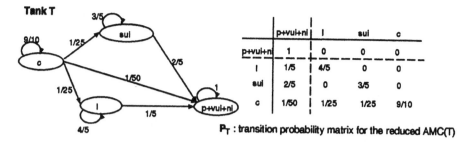

Tank T

	p+vul+ni	I	sui	c
p+vul+ni	1	0	0	0
I	1/5	4/5	0	0
sui	2/5	0	3/5	0
c	1/50	1/25	1/25	9/10

P_T : transition probability matrix for the reduced AMC(T)

Fig. 2. Reduced $AMC(T)$ and corresponding matrix

m on the reduced $AMC(c)$. Consider now $W_j(t_i) = \{m^j(c_1, t_i) \ldots m^j(c_k, t_i)\}$ where $m^j(c_h, t_i)$ is the mode assigned to component c_h by $W_j(t_i)$; we can then identify the following temporal extents

$$\Delta_j^{(i)} = min_{c_h}(\lfloor MTTA_{c_h}(m^j(c_h, t_i)) \rfloor)$$

$$\Delta^{(i)} = min_j \, \Delta_j^{(i)}$$

The next relevant time instant can be now determined as $t_{i+1} = t_i + \Delta^{(i)}$. It should be clear that equation 2 in section 3.2 allows a probabilistic ranking of temporal diagnoses, so the selection of $\Delta^{(i)}$ could be performed just for the most probable diagnoses. Obviously, in order to make the approach dealing with diagnoses concluding critical modes, we have to impose $MTTA_c(m) = 0$ if m is a critical mode of c. This means that we should try to discriminate diagnoses at the current time instant and performing the corresponding repair.

Example (cont.) Consider again the system in figure 1 and let us assume the following diagnoses at time t_0 (the name of the predicate $m(c, t)$, determining the behavioral mode of c at t, corresponds to the name of the behavioral mode): $W_1(t_0) = \{c(T, t_0), lv(G, t_0)\}$ and $W_2(t_0) = \{sui(T, t_0), c(G, t_0)\}$. Then we can compute

$$\Delta_1^{(0)} = min[\lfloor MTTA_T(c) \rfloor, \lfloor MTTA_G(lv) \rfloor] = 3$$
$$\Delta_2^{(0)} = min[\lfloor MTTA_T(sui) \rfloor, \lfloor MTTA_G(c) \rfloor] = 2$$
$$\Delta^{(0)} = min[\Delta_1^{(0)}, \Delta_2^{(0)}] = 2$$

The next relevant time instant will be $t_1 = t_0 + 2$. Suppose at time t_1 we ask for new observations and we get $W_1(t_1) = \{sui(T, t_1), lv(G, t_1)\}$ and $W_2(t_1) = \{c(T, t_1), nv(G, t_1)\}$. Looking at $AMC(T)$, we can conclude that it is not possible for T to become "correct" from the mode sui, so there are only three possible temporal diagnoses whose probabilities are:

$$P[W_1(t_0), W_1(t_1)] = P[W_1(t_0)]P[W_1(t_1)|W_1(t_0)]$$
$$P[W_1(t_0), W_2(t_1)] = P[W_1(t_0)]P[W_2(t_1)|W_1(t_0)]$$
$$P[W_2(t_0), W_1(t_1)] = P[W_2(t_0)]P[W_1(t_1)|W_2(t_0)]$$

We do not discuss here the details concerning the computation of such probabilities (see [19]), however it is worth noting that the conditional probabilities in the above formula can be computed by using the matrices P_T^2 and P_G^2. Notice that $W_2(t_1)$ contains a critical mode (nv), so if the probability of such a diagnosis is not "low", we have to take into account the possibility of G being in a critical mode, trying to discriminate the diagnoses at the current time. Obviously, the granularity of time must be suitable to allow that. It is worth noting that the proposed approach is suitable in order to get a structural focusing on components that are more likely to be faulty at a given time instant; in fact, the following abstract process can be used in order to obtain a component oriented diagnostic process (let $MTTA_{c_h}$ be a vector):

$$\text{Ask\_Observations}(MTTA_{c_1}, \ldots MTTA_{c_h});$$

1. $t := t_0$; $rt_i := MTTA_{c_i}(correct)$ $(i = 1 \ldots k)$;
2. $rt_m := min_i \, rt_i$;
3. $t := t + rt_m$;
4. check component c_m at time t and let $D_1 \ldots D_j$ be the possible diagnoses (assignments of behavioral modes to c_m);
5. $rt_j := rt_j - rt_m$ $(j \neq m)$;
6. if repair then $rt_m := MTTA_{c_m}(correct)$ else $rt_m := min_j(MTTA_{c_m}(D_j))$;
7. goto 2.

If a repair action is undertaken, than the component under examination is restored to the "correct" mode, otherwise we have to use its possible behavioral modes at the current relevant time instant (and the corresponding $MTTA$) to determine the next one.

4.2 Computing Transition Probability Matrices

As mentioned in section 3.2 in the discussion of equation 2, the computation of the probability of temporal diagnoses can be performed, knowing the temporal distance Δ between two consecutive relevant time instants, by using the matrices P_c^Δ. Concerning this aspect, two possibilities can be explored:

- computing matrices P_c^Δ while the diagnostic system is idle, i.e. while, after the computation of Δ, it is waiting for a new set of observations;
- precomputing off-line, for each transient state of each reduced AMC, the $MTTA$ and so precomputing all the possible matrices P_c^Δ of interest.

Both approaches have some drawbacks. Indeed, in the first case the computation of the matrices must be performed in at most Δ time instants. However, it is worth noting that, as pointed out in [18], the computation of the power P^n of a stochastic matrix P, can be done without great difficulty for $n \leq 1000$; in fact, computing P^n requires $O(\log_2 n)$ multiplications and a naive matrix multiplication algorithm has complexity $O(m^3)$ where m is the dimension of the matrix[8]. The second approach is

---

[8] Some other algorithms, like Stressen's algorithm that runs in $O(m^{\log_2 7})$, overperforms the naive one when m is large.

clearly not reasonable when the number of matrices to be precomputed is too high; it might also happen that many precomputed matrices are rarely or never used causing a waste of memory space. The advantage is that the computation of the matrices can be done off-line.

5 Conclusions and Future Works

In the present paper we discussed a stochastic approach, relying on the theory of absorbing Markov chain, aimed at defining a strategy for observation time selection in the interpretation of time-varying data for diagnostic purposes. The work extends the framework presented in [19] by defining a criterion, based on the notion of *mean time to absorption*, able to determine when to require the observations of the parameters of the system to be diagnosed. The framework relies on the availability of probabilistic information about the natural temporal evolutions of the system components, by extending some usual assumptions followed in reliability theory and it is particularly suitable to model the uncertainty underlying such evolutions. It also presents a lot of similarities with approaches proposed for clinical time-varying data interpretation where, however, the underlying stochastic model of time is better interpreted as a *semi-Markov process* (see [20]). The approach aims at avoiding the continuous reading of critical parameters when monitoring the system to be diagnosed and it is suitable to a structural focusing on the components which are more likely to be faulty. It take its place in the context of some recent attempts trying to show the usefulness of classical markovian analysis in important AI task like diagnosis [20], temporal reasoning [2] and qualitative reasoning [8].

As the discussion in section 4.2 suggests, some experimental work has to be done in order to test the usefulness of different strategies on different problems and domains, with particular attention to the problem of the computation of matrices P_c^Δ; however, it is worth noting that the hardest problem is certainly the computation of atemporal diagnoses and how this process can be integrated in the time-varying data interpretation framework (for instance, the granularity of time at which to require observations must be adequate to allow a reasonable atemporal diagnostic process). Finally, some future works are planned in order to overcome some of the limitations of the approach like: the assumption of independence of the temporal evolution of a component with respect to the evolutions of other components, the availability, as input data, of mode transition probability and the fact that external repair actions are not modeled. In particular, we believe that the first two aspects can be suitably dealt with the use of modeling tools like *stochastic Petri nets* [17] and of statistical learning algorithms respectively, while determining the best approach to face the last aspect is probably a more serious problem.

Acknowledgements

I am particularly indebted to P. Torasso for a lot of useful comments and advice about the paper. I am also grateful to L. Console, M. Botta and A. Giordana for some useful discussions about the topic presented in the paper and to two anonymous referees fot their useful observations.

References

1. F. Bergadano, F. Brancadori, D. De Marchi, A. Giordana, S. Radicchi, and L. Saitta. Applying machine learning to troubleshooting: a case study in a real domain. In *Proc. 10th Int. Conference on Expert Systems and Their Applications*, pages 169–180, Avignon, 1990.

2. C. Berzuini, S. Quaglini, and R. Bellazzi. Temporal reasoning via bayesian networks. In *Atti primo congresso AI*IA*, pages 248–257, Trento, 1989.

3. L. Console, L. Portinale, D. Theseider Dupré, and P. Torasso. Diagnostic reasoning across different time points. In *Proc. 10th ECAI*, pages 369–373, Vienna, 1992.

4. L. Console, L. Portinale, D. Theseider Dupré, and P. Torasso. Diagnosing time-varying misbehavior: an apporach based on model decomposition. *Annals of Mathematics and Artificial Intelligence (to appear)*, 1993.

5. L. Console and P. Torasso. A spectrum of logical definitions of model-based diagnosis. *Computational Intelligence*, 7(3):133–141, 1991. Also in [12].

6. J. de Kleer and B.C. Williams. Diagnosis with behavioral modes. In *Proc. 11th IJCAI*, pages 1324–1330, Detroit, 1989.

7. K. Downing. Consistency-based diagnosis in physiological domains. In *Proc. AAAI-92*, pages 558–563, San Jose, 1992.

8. J. Doyle and E. Sacks. Markov analysis of qualitative dynamics. *Computational Intelligence*, 7(1):1–10, 1992.

9. D. Dvorak and B. Kuipers. Model-based monitoring of dynamic systems. In *Proc. 11th IJCAI*, pages 1238–1243, Detroit, 1989.

10. G. Friedrich and F. Lackinger. Diagnosing temporal misbehaviour. In *Proc. 12th IJCAI*, pages 1116–1122, Sydney, 1991.

11. W. Hamscher. Modeling digital circuits for troubleshooting. *Artificial Intelligence*, 51(1-3):223–271, 1991.

12. W. Hamscher, L. Console, and J. de Kleer. *Readings in Model-Based Diagnosis*. Morgan Kaufmann, 1992.

13. W. Hamscher and R. Davis. Diagnosing circuit with state: an inherently underconstrained problem. In *Proc. AAAI 84*, pages 142–147, Austin, 1984.

14. L.J. Holtzblatt, M.J. Nejberg, R.L. Piazza, and M.B. Vilain. Temporal methods: multidimensional modeling of sequential circuits. In *Proc. 2nd Int. Work. on Principles of Diagnosis*, pages 111–120, Milano, 1991.

15. J.C. Kemeny and J.L. Snell. *Finite Markov Chains*. Springer Verlag, 1976.

16. F. Lackinger and W. Nejdl. Integrating model-based monitoring and diagnosis of complex dynamic systems. In *Proc. 12th IJCAI*, pages 1123–1128, Sydney, 1991.

17. M.K. Molloy. Discrete time stochastic Petri nets. *IEEE Trans. on Software Engineering*, SE-11(2):417–423, 1985.

18. M.F. Neuts. *Probability*. Allyn and Bacon, Inc., 1973.

19. L. Portinale. Modeling uncertain temporal evolutions in model-based diagnosis. In *Proc. 8th Conf. on Uncertainty in Artificial Intelligence*, pages 244–251, Stanford, 1992.

20. G.M. Provan. Modeling the dynamics of diagnosis and treatment using temporal influence diagrams. In *Working Notes 3rd International Workshop on Principles of Diagnosis*, pages 97–106, Rosario, WA, 1992.

21. K.S. Trivedi. *Probability and Statistics with Reliability, Queueing and Computer Science Applications*. Prentice-Hall, 1982.

Spatial Reasoning in a Holey World

Achille C. Varzi *

Istituto per la Ricerca Scientifica e Tecnologica (IRST)
I-38050 Povo (Trento), Italy
varzi@irst.it

Abstract. This paper outlines a basic formalism for reasoning about holes and holed things. Several domains come to interact: ontology (holes are parasitic entities), mereology (holes may bear part-whole relations to one another); topology (holes are one piece things located at the surfaces of their hosts); morphology (holes are fillable). The descriptive power of the resulting framework is illustrated with reference to some issues in the modelling, the representation, and the taxonomy of spatial inclusion.

1 Introduction

Much of our reasoning about the common-sense world involves reasoning about holes and holed objects. We put things in holes, or through holes, or around them; we jump over a hole or fall into one; we describe holes, measure them, point at or even recognize them. *What* exactly holes are, or even whether holes actually exist, these of course are questions one eventually needs to address in order to make good sense of such ways of reasoning. For instance, a non-realist attitude would require some systematic way of paraphrasing every hole-committing sentence by means of a sentence that does not refer to or quantify over holes [14]. Or, treating holes as (parts of) material objects, e.g. identifying them with hole-linings [17], would call for an account of the altered meaning of certain terms (for instance, 'inside' and 'outside' might come out ambiguous when the second argument is a hole). The general philosophical hypothesis underlying the present work is that one should resist these ways out in favor of a realist, common-sense attitude: if there is an ontology inherent in our everyday reasoning about the world, then this ontology is to comprise holes (and cognate entities such as cavities, grooves, cracks, cuts, fissures) along with stones and chunks of cheese. Of course holes are more disturbing. They are spatio-temporally localized, but they are not *made of* anything. Nor are they just regions of space; holes can move around (as happens anytime you move a piece of Swiss cheese), whereas spatial regions cannot. Yet these and other peculiarities should not deprive holes of the right to a place in the ontological inventory. This view has been largely presented in [4], where a basic formalism is also introduced to spell out some major tenets and consequences

---

* This paper stems from joint work with Roberto Casati and was written in the context of the MAIA project at IRST. A preliminary version was in part presented at the *IJCAI Workshop on Spatial and Temporal Reasoning*, Chambery, August 29, 1993.

of the theory (see also [3]). The purpose of this paper is to illustrate how that formalism can be exploited to provide a framework for more general patterns of qualitative spatial reasoning.

2 The Formal Theory

The core of the theory can be divided into four parts: (1) a preliminary *ontological* part; (2) a *mereological* part, focusing on the interplay between parts and holes; (3) a *topological* part, featuring some basic facts concerning spatial connectedness; and (4) a *morphological* part, fixing on the fact that holes are characterized by the dispositional property of being fillable. After a general outline, I shall focus upon this last part [1].

2.1 Ontology

Ontologically the theory is based on the single primitive Hxy, read "x is a hole in (or through) y": a binary relation capturing the fundamental intuition that holes are parasitic entities and cannot exist without (or be removed from) a host object. On the intended interpretation, this form of ontological dependence is a matter of generic *de re* necessity: it is to be distinguished from the sort of *de dicto* dependence that is exemplified by such sentences as "every sister has a sibling" (granted that there cannot exist sisters without siblings, it is by no means true of any sister that *she* – that person – could not have existed as an only child); and it should be distinguished from stronger forms of *de re* dependence, such as the rigid dependence of a grimace on a face (*that* grimace can only exists as an expression on *that* face, whereas one can generally change the host's matter, its shape, or even the entire host without affecting the hole in it). As a general axiom, we take the following:

AH1 $Hxy \rightarrow \neg \exists z Hyz$

It is immediately verified that H turns out to be irreflexive and asymmetrical. Moreover, AH1 suffices to certify certain fundamental facts about holes: for instance, all holes are holeless, i.e. cannot host other holes, although we take it that a hole may have other holes as proper parts (see [2] for a different view).

2.2 Mereology

The main principles governing the relevant part-whole relations can be formulated within the framework of a standard mereology (in the spirit of [15, 16]) supplemented with some specific axioms on H. We assume a single primitive Pxy, read "x is (a) part of y". Derived relations such as overlapping or being a proper part, as well as the operations of mereological sum, product, etc., are defined accordingly:

---

[1] The underlying logical machinery is deliberately left vague: a preferred option is some free logic with identity and descriptions, but a more standard alternative would also provide a suitable background.

DP1 $Oxy =_{df} \exists z(Pzx \wedge Pzy)$
DP2 $PPxy =_{df} Pxy \wedge \neg Pyx$
DP3 $x + y =_{df} \imath z \forall w(Owz \leftrightarrow Owx \vee Owy)$
DP4 $x \times y =_{df} \imath z \forall w(Owz \leftrightarrow Owx \wedge Owy)$

As axioms of the purely mereological part we assume the following:

AP1 $Pxy \wedge Pyx \rightarrow x = y$
AP2 $Pxy \leftrightarrow \forall z(Ozx \rightarrow Ozy)$
AP3 $\exists x \phi x \rightarrow \exists x \forall y(Oyx \leftrightarrow \exists z(\phi z \wedge Oyz))$

The first two axioms secure that P is a partial ordering; the addition of AP3, a supplementation principle to the effect that every satisfied condition ϕ picks out a unique entity consisting of all ϕers, yields a classical extensional mereology in the sense of [10] or [24]. We also have some auxiliary notions, such as being a (proper) hole-part:

DP5 $HPxy =_{df} Pxy \wedge \exists z Hxz$
DP6 $HPPxy =_{df} PPxy \wedge \exists z Hxz$

The specific axioms on the interplay between P and H are now as follows:

AP4 $Hxy \rightarrow \neg Oxy$
AP5 $Hxy \wedge Pyz \rightarrow Hxz$
AP6 $Hxy \wedge Hzw \wedge Oxz \rightarrow Oyw$
AP7 $Hxy \vee Hxz \rightarrow \exists w(PPw(y \times z) \wedge Hxw)$
AP8 $Hxy \vee Hzy \rightarrow \forall w(HPw(x + z) \rightarrow Hwy)$

Intuitively, these guarantee that H is mereologically a monotonic relation disjoint from O [2], with the twofold property that (i) the class of a hole's hosts forms a bottomless lattice under P (there is no way one can single out a smallest host for a given hole), and (ii) overlapping holes must have overlapping hosts (although two holes may occupy the same region, or part of the same region, without having any parts in common: imagine a holed piece of Gruyère floating inside a hole in a bigger chunk of Emmenthaler). With these axioms, we can fix several other base properties, for example that holes are not part of their hosts (*contra* [13]), that a host cannot be part of any hole, or that mereological atoms (i.e. things that have no proper parts) are bound to be holeless. Further principles can then be added to strengthen the theory: for instance, in [3, 4] we also have an axiom to the effect that no hole is atomic (though of course the parts of a hole need not necessarily be hole-parts).

---

[2] Note that AP4 does not rule out that a hole may overlap the host of *another* hole: the sum of the hole in John's pocket and the slice of Swiss cheese on Mary's plate – an entity whose existence is allowed *via* AP3 – is a scattered individual, partly material and partly immaterial, hosting every hole in that piece of cheese. On the other hand, if sums involving holes together with their own hosts are to be allowed, then the consequent of AP5 should be weakened to '$Hxz \vee Ozz$'.

2.3 Topology

We see topology as providing a natural next step after mereology [29]. It is indispensable to account for the notion of an integral or self-connected whole, which runs afoul of a purely mereological setting, and it proves useful for reasoning about spatial relations that do not involve overlapping, as with things abutting or surrounding one another. In the present context, the basic framework is given in terms of the primitive relation Cxy, signifying "x is connected with y". This follows in the footsteps of [9, 31] (see [25] or [26] for alternative foundations), though we take connection to indicate co-localization at (rather than sharing of) some point in space-time. More precisely, on the intended interpretation a thing x is connected with a thing y iff either x and the closure of y or y and the closure of x are co-localized at some point (where the closure is, as usual, the thing together with its boundary). The relevant axioms are:

AC1 Cxx
AC2 $Pxy \rightarrow \forall z(Cxz \rightarrow Czy)$

Given AP2, these axioms secure that C is symmetric, albeit not necessarily extensional. Many systems also assume the converse of AC2, with the effect of reducing mereology to topology: see e.g. [1, 18, 19, 20, 21, 22, 30], following [5, 6]. However, this would be too strong on the present interpretation of C. As noted above, an object can be wholly located inside a hole, hence totally connected with it, without actually *sharing* any parts with it: since holes are immaterial, co-localization does not imply mereological overlapping. We can nonetheless define such derivative notions as being spatially enclosed, intersecting, being externally connected, or being self-connected, as follows:

DC1 $Exy =_{df} \forall z(Czx \rightarrow Czy)$
DC2 $Ixy =_{df} \exists z(Ezx \wedge Ezy)$
DC3 $ECxy =_{df} Cxy \wedge \neg Ixy$
DC4 $SCx =_{df} \forall y \forall z(y + z = x \rightarrow Cyz)$

Thus, overlapping is included in, but does not coincide with, spatial intersection, which in turn is properly included in the relation of connection. This gives us back much of standard topology for spatial regions, for instance supporting relational lattice structures as in [20], without however forcing our ontology. As specific axioms involving H we then have the following:

AC3 $Hxy \rightarrow SCx$
AC4 $Hxy \rightarrow ECxy$
AC5 $Hxy \rightarrow \exists z(Pzy \wedge Hxz \wedge SCz)$
AC6 $Hxy \wedge HPPzx \rightarrow \exists w(ECwx \wedge \neg ECwz)$

This guarantees that holes are one piece entities located at the surfaces of their hosts, indeed of some self-connected parts thereof [3]. In particular, AC6 makes

---

[3] In view of AP7, every hole has at least denumerably many decreasing hosts, which in turn may grow indefinitely in view of AP5. By AC5 we can however associate each

sure that a hole's proper hole-parts, if any, cannot be externally connected with exactly the same things as the hole itself, thereby excluding that a single hole be identified with an infinitely descending chain of nested holes. All of these are basic properties that cannot be expressed in purely mereological terms. Among the new theorems that can be obtained, we have e.g. that a hole is connected with every host of its hole-parts, that the hole-parts of a hole are all externally connected with the hosts of that hole, or that hosting a hole is having some proper self-connected part that entirely hosts (every hole-part of) the hole. Note also that AP4 is now derivable from AC4. Moreover, topology allows us to express the intuitive distinction between holes that are wholly internal (or *cavities*) and external ones:

DC5 $\quad \mathrm{I}Hxy =_{df} Hxy \wedge \forall z(\mathrm{EC}zx \rightarrow \mathrm{I}zy)$

DC6 $\quad \mathrm{E}Hxy =_{df} Hxy \wedge \neg \mathrm{I}Hxy$

With the help of the topological notion of *genus* (maximum number of rings that can be drawn on an object's surface without separating it into two disconnected parts), we can then provide a base taxonomy of holes by further distinguishing between blind *hollows* (admit hosts of genus 0) and perforating *tunnels* (only hosts of genus >0). Other types of holes can be explained in terms of interbreeding of these basic types — for instance, an internal doughnut-shaped hole will count both as a tunnel and as a cavity [4]. We can then prove, among other things, that no hole can properly include (or be externally connected with) an internal cavity, or that a hole cannot qualify as a hollow with respect to any part of a host relative to which it qualifies as a tunnel, or, again, that no hole that qualifies as a tunnel with respect to a hollow's host can be part of that hollow.

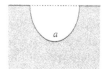 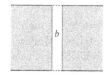 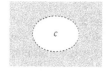 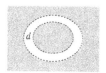

Fig. 1. A hollow (a), a tunnel (b), a cavity (c), and a cavity-tunnel (d).

2.4 Morphology

Our taxonomy of holes reflects certain peculiar topological properties of the host objects which do not, however, prevent a uniform treatment: to be a hole *is* to be a hollow, a tunnel, or a cavity. To account for this unity we rely on a very fundamental dispositional property of holes: they are fillable. Indeed much of

hole with its maximally self-connected host, regarding this as *the* (common-sense) host of the hole: every other host is either a potential part of it, or a topologically scattered mereological sum including it as a part.

[4] Knotted tunnels and such-like singularities do not pose specific taxonomic problems as long as we stick to the *intrinsic* topology of the host object: the genus is independent of the three-dimensional embedding of the surface.

our reasoning about holes depends upon our ability to reason about their potential "guests", not only about their actual hosts — a form of complementary reasoning that can be very effective. Of course you fill holes, not holed things (except in a loose way of speaking): filling is a binary relation holding between some stuff or material object and a hole or a part of a hole. We indicate this relation by 'Fxy', "x fills y". In [4] this is taken to express *perfect* filling, a notion that is meant to capture the intuitive idea that a filler perfectly "heals" the discontinuity introduced by a hole in its host object (the healing being defined by the minimal surface enclosed within the hole's rim). We can, however, assume a more general notion of filling, allowing for incomplete fillers as well as for complete but improper (protruding) fillers. Using 'F' to indicate this general notion, we can easily define complete, proper, and exact (or perfect) fillers respectively:

DF1 $CFxy =_{df} \forall z(Pzy \rightarrow Fxz)$
DF2 $PFxy =_{df} \forall z(Pzx \rightarrow Fzy)$
DF3 $EFxy =_{df} CFxy \wedge PFxy$

Thus, a hole's exact filler can be regarded as the least upper bound (relative to the partial ordering induced by P) of the hole's proper fillers, or, equivalently, as the greatest lower bound if its complete fillers. As general topo-mereological axioms we then assume the following:

AF1 $Fxy \rightarrow \neg Oxy$
AF2 $EFxy \rightarrow Exy \wedge Eyx$

while the following axiom accounts for the basic relationship between fillers and fillable entities, i.e. holes and parts thereof:

AF3 $Fxy \rightarrow \exists z \exists w(Hzw \wedge Pyz)$

Evidently this implies that filling is irreflexive, though we leave it open here whether one should also make it asymmetrical. Moreover, our axioms secure that filling be in many ways a monotonic relation with respect to parthood: for instance, a complete filler completely fills every part of a hole, while every part of a proper filler properly fills the hole. Likewise, it follows that every hole is enclosed in its complete fillers and encloses its proper fillers, which implies that a hole's perfect filler cannot intersect the hole's host (*via* AC4). One can then investigate to what extent the morphological complexity of a hole is mirrored in the topological structure of its "skin", i.e. that part of the host's surface that is potentially connected with the filler.

 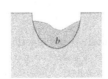 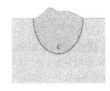 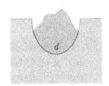

Fig. 2. Filling a hole exactly, i.e. both properly and completely (*a*); properly, but not completely (*b*); completely, but not properly (*c*); neither completely nor properly (*d*).

3   Examples and Developments

The theory sketched above illustrates the level of formalization that can be achieved, as well as the way different domains come to interact, when we set ourselves to spell out a common-sense theory of such immaterial entities as holes. Arguably, the resulting framework proves particularly effective in the ontological dispute, e.g. in connection with patterns of reasoning involving problems of the "many property" sort [27]. Here I briefly illustrate the descriptive power of the formalism with reference to some issues pertaining to the modelling, the representation, and the taxonomy of spatial inclusion.

3.1   Prepositions

An example coming from natural language processing is provided by the treatment of spatial prepositions such as 'in' (or 'inside'). Granted that a purely mereological account of 'in' as equivalent to 'part of' or 'overlapping' is inadequate, some authors have suggested a treatment in terms of mereological inclusion in the convex hull of the containing object [7, 18, 20, 21, 22]. As already indicated in [12], however, this approach fails to appreciate the essential role of containing parts as opposed to other non-convex parts (think of a fly near the stem of a wine glass: it may well fall within the convex hull of the glass, but that doesn't make it a fly *in* the glass). Restricting the scope of the convex hull to the object's containing parts (as suggested in [28]) is not entirely adequate either, for it fails to take into account the actual shape of the container. This is pointed out in [1, 30], where a multi-level account is eventually proposed emphasizing the functional dimension of containment.

Fig. 3. Inclusion in the convex hull of the object (*a*) or of the object's containing parts (*b*): in neither case is the fly *in* the glass. (From [30], pp. 207f.)

Within our framework, where common-sense holes are accepted *bona fide*, the difficulty admits of a fairly simple and rather general solution resting on the analogy between filling and being in. Roughly, to be in an object is to be in a hole of that object; and something is in a hole (wholly or partially) when it can be said to fill the hole (properly or not):

DI1 $INxy =_{df} \exists z(Hzy \wedge Fxz)$
DI2 $WINxy =_{df} \exists z(Hzy \wedge PFxz)$
DI3 $PINxy =_{df} INxy \wedge \neg WINxy$

(We take it of course that the containing part of a glass determines a true hole – a hollow, in effect – though there are other senses in which a glass can be said to be holed. At the same time, *what* exactly counts as a hole or a containing part is not at issue here: the account is effective precisely insofar as the existence of independent criteria for holehood is presupposed — e.g., insofar as the space around the stem of a glass is not taken to be a hole[5].) On this basis several additional notions can easily be introduced. In particular, we can complete the picture by defining the relations of being (wholly or barely) 'outside' in the obvious way:

> DI4 $\quad$ OUT$xy =_{df} \neg$I$xy \wedge \neg$INxy
> DI5 $\quad$ WOUT$xy =_{df} \neg$C$xy \wedge \neg$INxy
> DI6 $\quad$ BOUT$xy =_{df}$ OUT$xy \wedge \neg$WOUTxy

Note that none of the relations thus defined is fully transitive. They are not asymmetric either, except for WIN, and of course they are not reflexive. On the other hand, WIN, OUT and WOUT satisfy certain basic forms of dissectivity or monotonicity that have no analogue for IN, PIN or BOUT: for instance, it is easily established that the parts of whatever is wholly inside or (wholly) outside an object x are also so related to y, although what is (partially) in y may obviously have parts that lie outside y, and what is barely outside y may have parts that are wholly outside it.

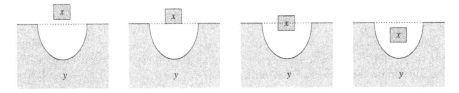

Fig. 4. Natural transition of an object x from wholly outside (left) to wholly inside (right) a hollowed object y.

3.2 Containing hulls

The above characterization can be further specialized to support richer taxonomies such as the ones presented in [7, 20, 22], which are based on the general convex-hull approach mentioned above. An alternative, more direct way of subsuming a rectified version of this taxonomy is by revisiting the original convex-hull operator (acting on regions) in terms of a "containing-hull" operator acting directly on objects. Using H, C and P, this can be introduced as a derived function $\breve{x}$ indicating the fusion of a host with its holes:

> DI7 $\quad \breve{x} =_{df} \imath z \forall y (Cyz \leftrightarrow \exists w (Cyw \wedge (Pwx \vee Hwx)))$

---

[5] Surely one can imagine to fill up that space with plasticine, but reasoning exclusively in terms of filling is deceptive here: as we introduced it, the notion of filling depends essentially on that of a hole, i.e., we have a criterion for something to be a filler of a hole, but holes exist and are what they are prior to their potential fillers.

Every defined term can then be revised under suitable replacement of convex hulls with containing hulls. In particular, we can immediately redefine the above notions as follows:

DI1' $IN'xy =_{df} Ix\breve{y} \land \neg Exy$

DI2' $WIN'xy =_{df} Ex\breve{y} \land \neg Exy$

DI3' $PIN'xy =_{df} IN'xy \land \neg WIN'xy$

DI4' $OUT'xy =_{df} \neg Ix\breve{y}$

DI5' $WOUT'xy =_{df} \neg Cx\breve{y}$

DI6' $BOUT'xy =_{df} OUT'xy \land \neg WOUT'xy$

These definitions are in effect weaker (hence more general) than DI1–DI6, and the resulting taxonomy has certain advantages. For instance it can be significantly enriched by distinguishing between the case of a filling inside (as in DI1) from that of a mere co-localized, "vacuous" inside:

DI8 $VINxy =_{df} IN'xy \land \neg INxy$

(think again of the holed piece of Gruyère inside a chunk of Emmenthaler; the small hole is inside the big one, but it surely does not *fill* it).

3.3 Modes of containment

Further refinements can be introduced, including applications to naive-physical reasoning about containment (in the spirit of [11]). For example, we can account nicely for the distinction between generic inside and topological (constraining) inside, the latter occurring only in the presence of an internal hole:

DI9 $TINxy =_{df} \exists z(IHzy \land Exz)$

Of course this implies that topological inside can never be partial, i.e. TIN implies WIN. This definition conforms to the intuitive account, according to which something is topologically inside an object if it cannot move to the outside without cutting through the object itself (think of a maggot eating its way out of a cavity in a wheel of Swiss cheese). We can in fact prove that DI9 is equivalent to the following:

DI9' $TIN'xy =_{df} WIN'xy \land \forall z(SCz \land Czx \land \exists w(OUT'wy \land Czw) \rightarrow Izy)$

Moreover, reference to the skin-topology allows us to account for such distinctions as containable vs. non-containable insides. Roughly, a containable inside is defined by a hole whose skin has at most one edge, i.e. an internal cavity or a blind hollow, whereas an external tunnel with two or more openings is typically a case of non containable inside (in this sense, skin edges play essentially the same conceptual role as "lids" in [7]). Finally, we can distinguish between various types of fillers so as to account for a corresponding variety of interaction patterns between containing and contained entity (host and guest). For instance, a plugger is typically a complete, non-exact filler some parts of which are externally connected with the host but not with the hole, so that its translational freedom [23] is constrained. From a naive-physical perspective, this is perhaps one of the most important patterns of interaction relating to holes: keeping material objects (fillers and pluggers) in place, or at least hindering their movement. Of course the shape of a hole is the shape of part of its host — a material object itself. But shapes are not the end of the story: a square-shaped complete filler will be kept in place by its square hole, but a circular-shaped filler will rotate in its circular hole. One would need here to investigate the frictional properties of the stuff of both hole-host and hole-guest.

References

1. Aurnague M., Vieu L., 'A Three-Level Approach to the Semantics of Space', in C. Z. Wibbelt (ed.), *The Semantics of Preposition: From Mental Processing to Natural Language Processing*, Berlin: Mouton de Gruyter, in press.
2. Bäckström C., 'Logical Modelling of Simplified Geometrical Objects and Mechanical Assembly Processes', in Su-shing Chen (ed.), *Advances in Spatial Reasoning, Volume 1*, Norwood: Ablex, 1990, pp. 35-61.
3. Casati R., Varzi A. C., 'An Ontology for Superficial Entities, I: Holes', in N. Guarino, R. Poli (eds.), *International Workshop on Formal Ontology in Conceptual Analysis and Knowledge Representation*, Padova: Ladseb-CNR, 1993, pp. 127-148.
4. Casati R., Varzi A. C., *Holes and Other Superficialities*, Cambridge, Mass.: MIT Press/Bradford Books, in press.
5. Clarke B. L., 'A Calculus of Individuals Based on "Connection"', *Notre Dame Journal of Formal Logic*, 22 (1981), 204-218.
6. Clarke B. L., 'Individuals and Points', *Notre Dame Journal of Formal Logic*, 26 (1985), 61-75.
7. Cohn A. G., Randell D. A., Cui Z., 'A Taxonomy of Logically Defined Qualitative Spatial Regions', in N. Guarino, R. Poli (eds.), *International Workshop on Formal Ontology in Conceptual Analysis and Knowledge Representation*, Padova: Ladseb-CNR, 1993, pp. 149-158.
8. Davis E., 'A Framework for Qualitative Reasoning About Solid Objects', in G. Rodriguez (ed.), *Proceedings of the Workshop on Space Telerobotics*, Pasadena, Ca.: NASA and JPL, 1987, pp. 369-375.
9. De Laguna T. 'Point, Line, and Surface, as Sets of Solids', *Journal of Philosophy*, 19 (1922), 449-61.
10. Eberle R. A., *Nominalistic Systems*, Dordrecht: Reidel, 1970.
11. Hayes P. J., 'Naive Physics I: Ontology for Liquids', in J. R. Hobbs, R. C. Moore (eds.), *Formal Theories of the Commonsense World*, Norwood: Ablex, 1985, pp. 71-107.
12. Herskovits A., *Language and Spatial Cognition. An Interdisciplinary Study of the Prepositions in English*, Cambridge: Cambridge University Press, 1986.
13. Hoffman D. D., Richards W. A., 'Parts of Recognition', *Cognition*, 18 (1985), 65-96.
14. Jackson F., *Perception. A Representative Theory*, Cambridge: Cambridge University Press, 1977.
15. Leonard H. S., Goodman N., 'The Calculus of Individuals and Its Uses', *Journal of Symbolic Logic*, 5 (1940), 45-55.
16. Leśniewski S., *Podstawy ogólnej teoryi mnogości. I*, Moskow: Prace Polskiego Koła Naukowego w Moskwie, Sekcya matematyczno-przyrodnicza, 1916.
17. Lewis D. K., Lewis S. R., 'Holes', *Australasian Journal of Philosophy*, 48 (1970), 206-212.

18. Randell D. A., *Analysing the Familiar: Reasoning about Space and Time in the Everyday World*, University of Warwick: PhD Thesis, 1991.
19. Randell D. A., Cohn A. G., 'Modelling Topological and Metrical Properties in Physical Processes', in R. J. Brachman, H. J. Levesque, R. Reiter (eds.), *Principles of Knowledge Representation and Reasoning. Proceedings of the First International Conference*, Los Altos: Morgan Kaufmann, 1989, pp. 357-368.
20. Randell D. A., Cohn A. G., 'Exploiting Lattices in a Theory of Space and Time', *Computers and Mathematics with Applications*, 23 (1992), 459-476.
21. Randell D. A., Cui Z., Cohn A. G., 'An Interval Logic of Space Based on "Connection"', in B. Neumann (ed.), *Proceedings of the 10th European Conference on Artificial Intelligence*, Chichester: John Wiley & Sons, 1992, pp. 394-398.
22. Randell D. A., Cui Z., Cohn A. G., 'A Spatial Logic Based on Regions and Connection', in B. Nebel, C. Rich, W. Swartout (eds.), *Principles of Knowledge Representation and Reasoning. Proceedings of the Third International Conference*, Los Altos: Morgan Kaufmann, 1992, pp. 165-176.
23. Shoham Y., 'Naive Kinematics: Two Aspects of Shape', in J. R. Hobbs (ed.), *Commonsense Summer: Final Report*, Technical Report # CSLI-85-35, Stanford: SRI International, AI Center, 1985, pp. 4:1-25.
24. Simons P., *Parts. A Study in Ontology*, Oxford: Clarendon, 1987.
25. Smith B., 'Ontology and the Logistic Analysis of Reality', in N. Guarino, R. Poli (eds.), *International Workshop on Formal Ontology in Conceptual Analysis and Knowledge Representation*, Padova: Ladseb-CNR, 1993, pp. 51-68.
26. Tiles J. E., *Things That Happen*, Aberdeen: Aberdeen University Press, 1981.
27. Tye M., 'The Adverbial Approach to Visual Experience', *Philosophical Review*, 93 (1984), 195-225.
28. Vandeloise C., *L'espace en français: sémantique des prépositions spatiales*, Paris: Seuil, 1986.
29. Varzi A., 'On the Boundary Between Mereology and Topology', in B. Smith, R. Casati (eds.), *Philosophy and the Cognitive Sciences. Proceedings of the 16th International Wittgenstein Symposium*, Vienna: Hölder-Pichler-Tempsky, to appear.
30. Vieu L., *Sémantique des relations spatiales et inférences spatio-temporelles: Une contribution á l'étude des structures formelles de l'espace en Langage Naturel*, Université Paul Sabatier de Toulouse: PhD Thesis, 1991.
31. Whitehead A. N., *Process and Reality. An Essay in Cosmology*, New York: Macmillan, 1929.

Springer-Verlag
and the Environment

We at Springer-Verlag firmly believe that an international science publisher has a special obligation to the environment, and our corporate policies consistently reflect this conviction.

We also expect our business partners – paper mills, printers, packaging manufacturers, etc. – to commit themselves to using environmentally friendly materials and production processes.

The paper in this book is made from low- or no-chlorine pulp and is acid free, in conformance with international standards for paper permanency.

Lecture Notes in Artificial Intelligence (LNAI)

Lecture Notes in Computer Science